Jesse Jackson:

the Man,
the Movement,
the Myth

Jesse Jackson:

the Man, the Movement, the Myth

Barbara A. Reynolds

nh Nelson-Hall, Chicago

Library of Congress Cataloging in Publication Data

Reynolds, Barbara A
    Jesse Jackson, the man, the movement, the myth.

    Includes index.
    1. Jackson, Jesse, 1941-   I. Title.
E185.97.J25R49   323.4'092'4 [B]   74-17813
ISBN 0-911012-80-X

Manufactured in the United States of America.

Mrs. Mae Stewart
(8-8-02 to 12-26-72)
My greatest honor is to be
Mrs. Stewart's only daughter.

Contents

Acknowledgments

God has blessed me with an abundance of friends and associates who have opened doors, given encouragement and lent strength when I had no strength. Many I can not name here, since they can not publicly be associated with this venture, but they know I am grateful.

My gratitude is extended to Vernon Jarrett, *Chicago Tribune* columnist, whose courage I attempt to emulate; Robert Smith and Scott Schmidt, both former editors of *Chicago Today*, now *Tribune* executives, who pretended they didn't know I was writing a book on company time; Noah Robinson, Jr., and Noah Robinson, Sr.; John H. Johnson, publisher of Johnson Publications Company, who paid my way to Chicago; Amos Lynch, editor of the *Columbus Call and Post,* who gave me my first newspaper job at age sixteen; Mildred Wyatt, president of Wyatt Communications; Diane Abt, producer of "Matters of Opinion" on WBBM-radio, who performed the improbable feat, and to the Reverend Jesse Jackson, whom I was fortunate enough to study under for more than five years.

Herma Ross, vice-president of Alpha Janitorial Supply, Hammond, Indiana, belongs in a special category. She transcribed tapes, researched, critiqued and has never let me down in any way.

I am also lucky enough to have two friends who tolerate me exactly the way I am. Thank you for being there: Donald Walker, president of the National Publications Sales Agency in Chicago, and Mrs. Barbara Burke, executive director of the Boston YWCA.

Also Barbara Proctor, president of Proctor and Gardner Ad Agency; Dale Perry, reporter for the *Greenville* (S.C.) *Piedmont News,* an excellent investigator; Robert Dundon, editor at Nelson-Hall Publishing Company, whose faith in me made this book possible; my many friends at the *Chicago Daily Defender* and all the beautiful people who were with me at *Chicago Today.*

Introduction

News coverage of black leadership, indeed of black anything, by large numbers of black reporters is a new phenomenon, dating from the late sixties as the civil rights movement abruptly turned from black-and-white-together to all-black. At that time, several organizations, notably militant groups, forced white daily newspapers and radio and television stations to add blacks to their reporting and technical staffs by barring any but black reporters and camera crews from covering their press conferences and other newsmaking affairs. Thus, all of a sudden, at the beginning of the seventies there existed nationwide a fairly large black press corps. And it's growing. This has meant a wider range of coverage (segments of the black community had for the first time access to the press) by a highly diverse group of reporters with different backgrounds, beliefs, experiences, and expectations. It has meant closer scrutiny of the black community, of black affairs, of black leaders by this ever-expanding and divergent group.

As these reporters took a more careful look at, and a more honest evaluation of, black problems, and at blacks elected or otherwise chosen to solve those problems, many found themselves at odds with some of the leaders. Going beyond the almost automatic adulation of leaders histor- ically held by many blacks, this new breed of black reporters began to look at the facts and report them as accurately and honestly as possible. And the facts some- times hurt. Leaders from Roy Wilkins to Roy Innis and Jesse Jackson have been made to feel most uncomfortable by this reporting that cast aside that almost automatic adulation. And that hurt. But the black community of the seventies needs accountability from its leaders—and reporters—more than it needs to be concerned about the hurt feelings of its leaders—and reporters.

Concurrent with the expanding number of black reporters has been the disappearance of the "national black leader," the single voice that represented a consensus of the community. But one leader who felt himself successor to the single national leader legacy is the Reverend Jesse Jackson. His obvious talents and his goal to succeed Dr. Martin Luther King, Jr., combine with indefatigable drive, loose style, and more than enough charisma to make Mr. Jackson difficult to cover as it is. But his fast pace, his delving into numerous and broad issues simultaneously, and his tremendous ego compound the problem. Add to this mix the desire of reporters, especially those in Chicago covering Mr. Jackson, to get beyond that adulation of black leaders, and you have trouble.

That trouble can break into the open when reporters write stories Mr. Jackson doesn't like. And Jesse Jackson has the capacity to strike back, and he does not fail to do so when he feels the need. His Saturday morning forum, the 2,000 persons who gather at PUSH headquarters every week, can at once be turned into a court room or an inquisition.

But the quest for accountability must go on. For too long black leaders have treated the black community as an infant, to be spoonfed by the omniscient, omnipresent would-be Messiah. Barbara Reynolds, a talented writer and one of the new breed of black reporters of the seventies, begins the process with this penetrating social history which gives the black community, and the world, a look at one of its most talented and complex leaders.

Paul Delaney
Reporter, *The New York Times*

Know Before Who Thy Stand —

Sign over pulpit of Operation PUSH headquarters

Chicago—the city of big shoulders and little shame—awakes from its slumber, bracing for the next affront.

Dogs are being fed and fussed over on North Lake Shore Drive, but where blacks live, children may be falling asleep at their desks because they are hungry.

The police in the ghetto are changing shifts. So are the street gangs. Before the day is over both may find someone to stick it to. The human pin cushions—the welfare mothers, the laborers—have had their fill of both. It is harder and harder to tell the good guys from the bad guys.

On Michigan Avenue, it's a special day. Streets are being confettied, horns are blaring, balloons are popping, and blacks headed south are swearing out of their bus windows: "Get that damn motorcade out of the way." It doesn't matter that the infamous King Richard of Washington is in one of the limousines en route to confer with the infamous King Richard of Chicago. Their meeting is not going to stop the hospitals from fleeing the ghetto, the poor from having to walk a mile to get a pound of almost rancid hamburger, or the cops from clubbing black drivers for minor traffic violations. Some people feel nothing would change even if Christ came to Chicago.

Chicago—a fuzzy portrait of extremes.

One side is the most "wunnerful" city in America, according to its mayor, Richard J. Daley. He is endorsed by all four major newspapers because he keeps the parts of the city they care about running well.

The other—the south and west sides—is Crisis City for some of the blacks who live there, the ones who feel its pain.

Every Saturday morning, around 10:00, about 94,000 radio dials click on to WJPC. And at least 1,000 blacks are seated at the Dr. Martin Luther King workshop— where the crises of a troubled people spin in and out through a revolving door. The Mayor could heal some of the wounds if he would; the Country Preacher would heal some of the wounds if he could.

The service at the renovated synagogue has been going on for about an hour now. The Reverend Henry Hardy, the Dean of Alliteration, is at it again identifying Thomas Na-than-iel Todd, the Towering Titan of Torts, the Black Barrister of the Bar; the Reverend Ed Riddick, the Pharaoh of Facts, the Stellar Statistician; the Reverend Willie Barrow, the Princess of Protest. On and off the stage they move, orating upon the effects of living in Crisis City—bad housing, mis-education, and victimization by the most vicious, formidable political machine in the nation.

Loretta Oliver knows exactly when to ease forward to

set the stage. Backed up by the 100-voice PUSH choir, dressed in black and white—the Dominoes of Soul—she gently opens up her heart and lets it sing. Just as the soulful gospel chords of "He Included Me" have stirred a responsive spark, an electric energy breaks loose. Two thousand eyes light up with love. Everyone is on his feet.

Jesse: I am—
Audience: *I am—*
Jesse: Somebody.
Audience: *Somebody.*
Jesse: I may be poor.
Audience: *I may be poor.*
Jesse: But I am—
Audience: *But I am—*
Jesse: Somebody.
Audience: *Somebody.*
Jesse: I may be uneducated.
Audience: *I may be uneducated.*
Jesse: But I am—
Audience: *But I am—*
Jesse: Somebody.
Audience: *Somebody.*
Jesse: I may be unskilled.
Audience: *I may be unskilled.*
Jesse: But I am—
Audience: *But I am—*
Jesse: Somebody.
Audience: *Somebody.*
Jesse: I may be on dope.
Audience: *I may be on dope.*
Jesse: I may have lost hope.
Audience: *I may have lost hope.*
Jesse: But I am—somebody.
Audience: *But I am—somebody.*
Jesse: I am—black—beautiful

> —proud—I must be respected
> —I must be protected.
> Audience: *I am—black—*
> *beautiful—proud—I must be*
> *respected—I must be protected.*
> Jesse: I am—God's child.
> Audience: *I am—God's child.*
> Jesse:What time is it?
> Audience: *What time is it?*
> Jesse: Nation time.
> Audience: *Nation time.*
> Jesse: All right—look out . . . .

Jesse Jackson, the Country Preacher, returning the adulation of the crowd, gives the command. Everybody sits and listens for the Word.

Jackson, a puzzle of personalities, is being seen through a thousand prisms. What is perceived by some may be contradicted by others. What is seen by many may be contradicted by all. Jackson, the Man for all Reasons, is a complex string of ambiguities, a string of myths and phantasms. But on one thing most can agree: he is the Politician of Hope.

His "somebody" battle cry is reinforced by similar slogans to motivate, to inspire, to reverse the once prevalent feeling of "nobodiness": "You may be in the slum, but the slum doesn't have to be in you. The new empire is in your brains. Freedom ain't free. It's not the altitude that determines how high you fly, it's your attitude."

As Jackson leans forward on the podium, it is little wonder that the audience worships this man. Sensuous in black leather vest, striped T-shirt, and tight leather pants; 220 pounds of muscle rippling through a six-foot, two-inch frame; a billowing Afro; a sculptured face; the Country Preacher projects all the manly qualities most blacks respect. Not just a flounce of physical strength, but a computerlike brain that clicks out facts, figures, and analyses in a way that the Ph.D.'s and the no D.'s can understand. His forcefulness and self-esteem trigger a similar response in his audience. They like a man who takes no crap—not from blacks, from whites, from the media—from anyone. The only person who can knock him down is his grandmother. He is in charge, unbent, unbowed, a spirited, atomic force loose in the universe of man—and his people love him for it.

Always around his neck is a gold-plated medallion of Dr. Martin Luther King, Jr.—the most sacred black martyr in America. Although Dr. King was a prophet of peace, the changing of the guard wasn't peaceful. The struggle for King's mantle began in Memphis, moments after his assassin's shot echoed around the world, and ended, perhaps, here in Chicago. The unholy war—internecine clashes—between the Reverend Ralph D. Abernathy, King's legal successor, and Jackson, whom King had appointed national director of Operation Breadbasket, was a standoff until *Playboy* proclaimed in 1969: "Jesse Jackson, King's heir apparent." Soon Abernathy toppled, SCLC in Chicago toppled, and Jackson ran off with Chicago's Breadbasket, transferring staff, followers, and resources into PUSH (People United to Save Humanity). And in 1973, *Penthouse* recorded the outcome: "He [Jackson] became the undisputed leader of Chicago's huge black population, which numbers close to 1,500,000 blacks."

The leader of 1.5 million blacks. All those folks following after one man. Incredible.

Today no matter what the movement may be called, it is the Jackson Movement. He is the leader. Jackson is their man.

As the medallion swings in syncopation with the leader's body motions, Jackson rhetorically carries on the

Dream. Some people are seeing the New King:

"If you are allowed to see Dr. King as extraordinary in his birth, as he went to and from school as a child, you can say his challenge doesn't mean much because that was him and he was extraordinary. He was an ordinary man, a man just like anybody else in town. But he had an extraordinary concern for what is right.

"Y'all hear me now."

"Right on Reverend, A-men Reverend." The crowd is in tune.

"He laid out a program to transform the despair of burn, baby, burn into the hope of learn, baby, learn, from the rhetoric of separation to the power of organization. I would be let down today if you did not see yourself as having the same possibility for being extraordinary, as great as Dr. King did."

Jackson preaches on for about an hour on the life of Dr. King—something all could benefit from.

He is winding up now: "Every great man or woman on the face of the globe who has ever moved forward in the evolution of his own soul has done it because he wanted to do so and asked God for help and God aided him. God ain't never picked nobody up out of the bed and gave 'em no jobs, but God has taken some people on their jobs and given 'em some extra strength. Am I clear this morning ya'll? You hear me today?"

"Preach Rev."

"Moses looked at a few thousand slaves in Egypt and with the help of God he saw a new nation. Dr. King looked at a few crippled black people in Alabama and with the help of God he saw a new nation. And we will have that new nation."

The Country Preacher steps back from the pulpit, well pleased with himself. And the audience is pleased: the applause booms like boisterous thunderclaps.

Everybody agrees that Jackson is a great preacher.

Better than Adam Clayton Powell ever was. Perhaps as great as Dr. King. The garbling of his speech to "down home" Southern is a put-on to relate to some in the congregation and to his radio listening audience. When he is in the board rooms of white corporations, his vernacular is scholarly.

But good preaching is not all that brings people out to brave the wind from Lake Michigan at 8:30 on a cold Saturday morning.

The PUSH platform is a national showcase for black excellence, with Jackson, the autocratic father figure, supplying the definitions of black men, black heroes, black antiheroes, black everything.

Almost always, the national and local luminaries who share the leader's platform are legitimate heroes by anyone's definition: Isaac Hayes, the Black Moses of the music world; Congresswoman Shirley Chisholm, the first black woman to run for president; actresses Ruby Dee, the late Diana Sands, Cicely Tyson; Dr. James Cheek, president of Howard University; Georgia legislator Julian Bond; actor Richard "Shaft" Roundtree; John H. Johnson, publishing czar; comedian Red Foxx, star of Sanford and Son; black mayors Kenneth Gibson of Newark and Richard Hatcher of Gary. And the PUSH tradition of honoring living black heroes is a meaningful one; Jackie Robinson received the PUSH Black Excellence Award one year before he died.

Lately, the platform has expanded to include international dignitaries, such as the heads of state from Liberia, Nigeria, and Ghana. One particular ceremony was the honoring of Ali Mirah Hanfere of Ethiopia. It was conducted in Arabic by translator Ibn Sharieff, a PUSH associate. Jackson, who can officiate over anything in keeping with the proper protocol, stood next to the official in tennis shoes and blue jeans, solemnly nodding his head in approval. By his conduct, it would have been hard to surmise that Jackson didn't know a word of what was being said. Because Chicago's Alexander the Great had involved himself in African affairs after setting foot twice on African shores, the Reverend now reverently refers to himself not only as a local and national leader but as an international leader as well.

Definitions of blackness are important here, but on occasion the codes are twisted around and Jackson, the demagogue, rewards people for what is wrong and lambasts people for what is right.

Definition: "A black man with one eye who is a doctor that heals, I have more respect for than a six-foot, two-inch muscular soldier in uniform who kills. A man is not someone who can make a baby. Anybody can do that. It can be done by artificial insemination. A man is someone who can protect and provide for the child. A black man respects black women and most of all himself. He is both ethical and excellent."

Reward: In March 1974, Sam McBride, a south side service station operator, who gained national infamy by getting closed down by federal authorities for gouging black customers, addressed the Jackson congregation. McBride had sold fifteen-cent will forms and twenty-five-cent rabbit's feet to his customers for as much as $2. The purchase entitled them to two "free" gallons of gas. McBride justified his actions with, "Will forms are something everybody should have. Rabbit's feet. They're good items. I think they are coming back." Jackson led the crowd in a standing ovation for a guy who should have been thought of as a race bandit.

Punishment: In early 1972, two widely respected black *Chicago Daily News* writers, Lu Palmer and Betty Washington, wrote a cautious piece on the future of the movement after the split between Jackson and Abernathy. This time a movement aide was used to chop the reporters' necks off from the execution block of the pulpit. The reporters later learned their homes would be picketed, and Palmer received reliable information that "friends of Jesse" were going straight to "the white folks" at Bell Telephone Company to bounce his radio program off the air. Had Jesse led the pulpit assault, the response would have been disastrous. All the emperor has to do is turn thumbs down and the church becomes a coliseum where the Christians are tossed to the lions. Although 99 percent of the PUSH audience are not fanatics, there is something about the psychology of crowds that makes one cheer— right or wrong— simply because everybody else is cheering, especially when Jackson, the instigator, is leading the charge.

Now some people are seeing Jackson as the Messiah. With arms flailing, as if he had a rod in one hand and a staff in the other, Jackson bounds across the pulpit winding up his comments on the Mayor: "Pharaoh Daley. Don't tell me you don't hear. I am telling you, not asking you, not begging you, but telling you to let my people go."

Both Dr. King and Jackson found that instead of emulating their actions, their followers elevated them into Messiahs, models impossible to emulate. But who is to blame? Nobody could be a Messiah if somebody didn't need one.

In Jackson's case, the Messianic motif is nurtured by his own comparisons of himself to Jesus, Ezekiel, or David fighting off Goliath. He often portrays himself as a Black Moses opening up the Red Sea. Jackson has ascended so far above the masses, a few at least can not relate to his going to the bathroom.

Now, you see Jackson the dollar sign, who has become a godfather to Chicago's leading black business-men through his Buy Black preachments and his muscling white corporations to do business with black corporations.

Seated in the audience is George Jones, who has a reason to be smiling. Since Jackson's foot soldiers began kicking up a storm in Chicago, Jones' profits have increased more than 50 percent. Jones, vice-president of Joe Louis Milk Company, is one of Jackson's biggest patrons.

"Say it loud, I'm black and I'm proud and I drink Joe Louis milk," Jackson used to extol.

And then there's Jackson the issue jockey, who must always be visible and vocal, either creating issues or riding issues to stay in the public mind as a national leader.

Accepted in some quarters as the one black spokesman for his race, he speaks brilliantly on every issue touching the human condition. Recently, he was the first thought leader in America to label the energy crisis a hoax, putting it in the same dirty-tricks category as Watergate and the ITT scandal. Ralph Nader and Jackson toured the country on a fact-finding expedition, and Jackson later stated his case against the big oil companies before Senator Henry (Scoop) Jackson's investigating committee. He was the first black leader to take President Ford to task for pardoning Nixon and granting amnesty to draft dodgers, while ignoring the excessive dishonorable discharges given to black soldiers. Then there are the national TV appearances: the Joey Bishop Show, the Mike Douglas Show, the Ed Nelson Show, the David Frost Show, the Today Show, the Phil Donahue Show. And there's his college lecture circuit: Fisk, Harvard, Hope, Michigan State. But there's one thing Jackson always does. He may fly 200,000 miles a year around the country, but he is always in Chicago on Saturday, along with other experts, to share his national insight with the folks back home, making the PUSH platform the best educational center in the nation.

Since Jackson's group is not an organization but a movement, he must attract and sustain a following to maintain his local base in Chicago. Thus, he is Jackson the supercop—he must serve and protect. The power of numbers has provided protection even for some of Jackson's staunchest critics, who berate him until they are in trouble and find there are few other places to run, unless they have political clout. Although Jackson has many antagonists, he will often defend his enemies, if for no other reason than to have the last word: "Told you you'd need me before I'd need you."

The power of numbers provided a sanctuary for Black Panther leader Bobby Rush. Fred Hampton and Mark Clark had been brutally murdered in a shoot-in with the state's attorney's police. Rush, the number-two man, knew he might be next. So there, before the eyes of thousands, Jackson turned Rush over to two black policemen. If Rush happened to break a leg or dislocate a shoulder on the way to the lockup, the indelible eyes of the TV cameras would have recorded that he was intact when he left. The movement has organized to save black homeowners from the trap of contract buying, saved fourteen workers from being fired from the Osteopathic Hospital, closed down markets for selling rotten meat, blown the whistle on a real estate company for victimizing more than 250 citizens. Although there is one man credited in the news for the movement's pressure group drives, there are hundreds of dedicated volunteers and staffers behind Jackson. They are grouped into twenty-two service divisions, such as commercial, political, legal, youth, and teachers. These groups are always lauded from the pulpit, but their names are hardly household words.

And then there's Jackson the politician, who must talk tough and act rough in an attempt to appear frightening to Pharaoh Daley. And Jackson did help whip Daley by unseating him at the Democratic National Convention in Miami—but Daley is Mayor of Chicago. Though Jackson claims victory for almost all independent blacks elected in Chicago, the movement has significantly boosted only one effective campaign, the one to elect Mrs. Peggy Smith Martin, who in 1972 became the second black woman ever elected to the state legislature.

Jackson's presence dominates the Saturday morning

meetings, but it is the unexpected, the little dramas, the human elements that give PUSH its spice.

In a city in constant turmoil and eternal despair, movement victories mean a lot. Jackson's success records as an all-purpose leader are grossly overrated, but when he does win, he becomes the Muhammad Ali of civil rights. When he knocks whitey down, everybody inches upward, even though he still may be standing in his own personal ditch. A well-used tactic in Jackson's psychological warfare is to armtwist whites who have been disrespectful to blacks to appear on the platform and make a public apology; an example is Potter Palmer, whose scuffed penny loafers belie the fact that he is the millionaire head of Globetrotters Communications (owner of the Harlem Globetrotters and Chicago's WVON radio station). Under Jackson's browbeating, Palmer committed himself to raising the salaries of disc jockeys, making them the highest paid in the nation. A & P, National Tea, and Seven-Up corporate representatives have all paid their dues at the confessional.

Before the eyes of thousands, a Negro turned black. Life holds few surprises for Chicagoans, but this revelation sent shock waves through the congregation. He was Congressman Ralph Metcalfe, Sr., who rose to fame in the late thirties as a U. S. Olympic sprinter. And then he sprinted into the position of the Mayor's number-one house black after the death of Congressman William (The Man) Dawson in 1970. Today, he was speaking like a man who had regained his soul: "I feel at this time like I am all black. Many are asking what happened to Ralph. Well, I say it is never too late to be black. I've had a personal meeting with myself and I am now prepared to do what my conscience and those who elected me tell me to do."

Jackson, a master of the backhanded compliment, couldn't resist this opportunity before hugging him as a prodigal father: "It took thirty-six years for your brains to catch up with your brawn."

And how do you think the black women feel when Jackson says: "Stand up, black men, we are marching this morning y'all. We are going to the picket line. We gonna close down that construction site. Black men must be able to work where they live."

And they come. Old men, too old for marching, but surefooted enough to make that first step. Young boys, who could be elsewhere shooting dope, now they're here full of hope. One by one they file to the altar of machismo. An old woman weeps. Her tired eyes know that it is not the black woman who needs liberating.

And there was the time that Walter Fauntroy, the congressman from the District of Columbia, after a scholarly discourse, suddenly erupted into song—"Dream the Impossible Dream." Most were relieved that at least the Reverend Fauntroy was a good speaker.

It's near noon. The businessmen, school teachers, postal workers, gospel singers, the loyalists are surging toward "Country." St. Clair Booker, his granite-face aide, is mopping Jackson's sweaty brow. Those looking for the "grass roots" poor among Jackson's won't find many filing out. Every leader needs two ingredients: an enemy (Boss Daley), someone to organize against, and an honorable cause (the poor), someone to organize for. What leader could admit he did neither, effectively, without someone seriously challenging his role?

And what kind of leader is Jackson. The Messiah? The Demagogue? The New King, the politician, the Godfather, the issue jockey, the Reverend Super Jess, the superstar, the local, national and international spokesman for his race? The Leader of 1,500,000 blacks in Chicago alone?

Who is this man?

2

Today, when you hear him say, "I am somebody" to motivate others, you wouldn't believe how long he was saying that to himself.

Mrs. Xanthene Norris, Jesse's high school French teacher

As a boy of eight, Jesse rushed into a corner store. With an impetuousness rare for Southern colored lads, Jesse whistled to gain attention. The white grocer was waiting on the white customers first. "Wait on me, Jack. I got to go right away and I got to have some candy." Reaching from under the counter, Jack pulled up a .45. Holding it against the young boy's face, he warned, "Goddamn you, don't you ever whistle at a white man again, you hear."

At age ten, Jesse was playing in the Happy Hearts park when a group of boys scampered up to taunt him: "Jesse ain't got no dad-die. Jesse ain't got no dad-die.

Why you always going around claiming Noah as your brother? He ain't your brother. And your daddie ain't none of your daddie. You ain't nothing but a nobody, a nobody, nothing but a nobody."

Two indelible etchings pulled from a montage of pain and humiliation in Jesse Jackson's formative years growing up in Greenville, South Carolina, frame an iconography not unlike that suffered by legions of others and, in different ways, to be suffered by legions more.

Instead of crushing him, the small town malice that tore at his birthright and the racism that denied him his human right actually fired his determination that no lie would live forever unquestioned, unchallenged, irrevocable. He would not walk through life without pausing to ask why, and if there was a crack in the answer he would assume the burden of proof to heave it open which would one day say to others, "If I can, so can you." The quiet introspection of his youth would later snowball into a fierce rejection of all stigmas attached to his illegitimacy and his race. The I-will-fix-you, I-will-show-you defense of youth would wind into a tough spirit of both defiance and revenge. No threat would go unanswered; no challenge would stand unmet. In time, he would become obsessed with the proving. Long after he had persuaded others, there would always be the critic most difficult to convince—himself—crying out for new forms of proof.

He would become the long distance runner, catching then passing up all others, continuing long after winning the race, looking for another and another competitor, becoming the eternal contestant. Never realizing or accepting the boundaries of human potential, never finding a yardstick to measure his success, never quite identifying that one singular victory by which he could proclaim himself victorious, Jesse continues. At thirty-three, he is just changing course, gradually depersonalizing himself.

Jackson must still drink from the Glory Goblet, but the vintage is shared between Jackson the man and Jackson the symbol. How bitter it would taste—in time— if it were all for himself. Is it not sweeter once he is sure of arriving at a higher plateau where he, Jackson, is the symbol of the superlative black? As the recipient of the toast, he is the stand-in for the black man as the Thinker, the Redeemer, the Atlas embodying all the attributes of manliness. To applaud him, in this sense, is to applaud his race.

As the two identities strain to fuse into one personality, today the process is lopsided, yet to be completed—if it is possible to be completed at all. Criticism is perceived as a direct tarnishing of the symbol, while praise becomes internalized, as well as an embellishment of the image.

This is why Jackson will never flash across contemporary history only to fizzle out. The contest must continue, if not for the man, at least for the symbol.

These factors attest to his invincibility as well as to his vulnerability. At what point does the applause—that affirmation of self-esteem—become an end in itself? Given a choice between a task that accomplishes much for many with no hurrahs and a shallow victory offering wide public acclaim, which would he choose? At what point does winning become so paramount that the means become irrelevant? Can a man baptized in the fire of malice and contempt emerge unburnt from the flame? Does he not become bitter, a nemesis, driven at times to make the world the very footstool he once was himself? But even more crucial, can the genius of Jackson—that rare talent to convincingly project an image better than he is—ever merge into one personality? Will the meanness that lingers behind the image fade away? The supreme question then is, can Jackson ever catch up with and walk into the greatness of his own shadow?

There are keys to unlock the enigmatic personality of

Jesse Louis Jackson. They are scattered through his past, which began as a nonevent in a neat six-room house in Greenville, South Carolina.

At 9 A.M. on October 8, 1941, at 20 Haynie Street, a midwife, Minnie Munson, slapped life into a seven-pound, four-ounce baby boy, whom she described as "the cutest youngun you ever seen in your life." She said, "It seemed the child was in a hurry to get here. By the time the doctor arrived I had just wrapped him in a blanket and laid him in bed with his mother."

The father, Noah Louis Robinson, who lived next door at 22 Haynie Street, was married, but not to Jesse's mother, Helen Burns. As Jesse himself often tells the story over the Saturday morning broadcasts: "Although my father's wife had three children by her previous marriage, he wanted a man-child of his own. His wife would not give him any children. So he went next door."

Robinson, a handsome, copper-colored Elmer Gantry type in his prime, was the kind of guy who liked the ladies, said his prayers, and would knock any cracker down if one ever mustered the nerve to call him anything other than Mr. Robinson. Nobody dared nettle Robinson about the child next door. All he would say about the matter was, "Yup, that's my boy, and he's the spitting image of me."

The naming of the infant had been carefully discussed with Matilda Burns, Helen's mother. Had the baby been born a girl, it would have been named Ella, after Robinson's mother. The name Jesse came from Robinson's father, the Reverend Jesse Robinson, who along with his twin brother Jacob, also a minister, founded the Mount Emmanuel Baptist Church. The twin preachers were first-generation descendants of the Cherokee Indians. The Reverend Jesse Robinson's wife, Ella, was a slave, whose father was Billy Cox, an Irish plantation owner and sheriff of Greenville County, around the 1850s. "With all that

Irish and Indian blood running through his veins, no wonder Jesse is hot tempered and always on the war path," the father often says.

Robinson's wholesome attitude about his son was not shared by many of the black townsfolk. In fact, the incident of Robinson's fathering a child out of wedlock and having the gall to admit it still has some of Greenville's solid citizens buzzing, some thirty-three years later. A relative said, "The whole thing is one unholy mess that should never have happened and should best be forgotten. If Jesse had any sense, he would keep his mouth shut and stop this great embarrassment. Somebody should reason with him to stop him from talking about this disgrace. I am sure the good people of South Carolina couldn't care the least about this terrible, dishonorable disgrace."

If the "mistake" is big news in some quarters of Greenville so many years after the fact, imagine how it was at the time for Helen Burns, who had to brave the barrage of spiteful, small town gossip. Jesse was conceived when Helen was a student at Sterling High School, the same school Robinson's stepdaughter was attending. For her sin of bearing life instead of destroying life, the favored option, she was excluded from the Springfield Baptist Church. But through it all, she responded to the disdain with the regal bearing of a debutante. Her composure melted the icy smirks of her accusers.

On October 2, 1943, Jesse's ᴍother married twenty-four-year-old Charles Henry Jackson. Jackson, an easy-going athlete, soon abandoned his dreams of playing professional baseball to take a $3,000-a-year job at the post office, which would provide the comforts for his family. The marriage drained the gush of petty prattle leveled at the adults, but Noah Junior and Jesse would become the new objects of insult.

Noah, who is ten months younger than Jesse, was

around seven when he discovered he had a brother. "I was playing on the playground with a group of boys and some lady called me over. She whispered to me, 'See that kid over there with the curly hair, well, he's your brother.' "

Noah did not believe the local wag, so he dashed home to get his father. "I brought him back and pointed Jesse out. I knew Jess because we often played together. The expression on my father's face told me that the lady was right. He held my hand all the way back to the house. He sank down in the telephone chair and explained what had happened, which I did not understand fully until much later. As I grew older, I used to hear my folks arguing about Jesse when they thought I was asleep. There were some problems about Pop giving Jesse money and Easter clothes. And later I was told over my father's objections not to play with Jesse. I was sent to Catholic school, so we would be separated. I'd only see him now and then until we were in high school together. But the kids used to tease me about claiming Jesse for a brother. They used to tell Jesse I didn't claim him, which wasn't true. But I think Jesse believed it."

At what age Jesse knew the circumstance of his birth is more difficult to pinpoint. His stepfather, Charles, said Jesse learned about it in elementary school. "I never told him I was not his father because I didn't want him to grow up thinking he was different." (Charles Jackson adopted Jesse on February 4, 1957.) Jesse's stepfather said, "At four and four years old, he was calling me daddy, following me around, tugging at my knee."

But one point is certain; whenever he learned, it affected him deeply. When Jesse was nine, Robinson would see him standing in the backyard, gazing into the Robinsons' window. "Sometimes I wouldn't see him right away and Noah Junior would tell me he was out there. No telling how long he could have been there. As soon as I would go to the window and wave, he would wave back and run away. Why didn't he come in? Well, my wife, who took the whole thing very deeply, would not make him welcome at first. It wasn't until he was sixteen—Jesse had caught pneumonia for the second time—that all the Robinsons and the Jacksons got together without friction. The ice started breaking, when by the time he was in college he started calling my wife 'mom' too."

Robinson also remembers how Jesse used to grieve when he would take his other sons, Noah, George, and Tony, on vacations up North. "Family pressures were such that I just couldn't take him. I didn't know until Jesse was a big boy that he used to cry when the rest of us would take off and leave him behind."

At the same time Jesse was being swirled into the vortex of personal uncertainty as the outsider looking in, the second awakening unfolded: he learned what it meant to be born under the separate and unequal dictates governing the old South.

Greenville, South Carolina—population 62,000, 15 percent black, the textile capital of the world—was never the seething lair of redneckism of a Birmingham, Memphis, or Pulaski, Tennessee. The year Jesse was born marked the last time anybody can remember the KKK promenading down Green Street in full dress regalia. In 1971, the Klan attempted a revival, but the blacks chased them off the street. During the forties, though, there was not much reason for a confrontation since blacks seldom got "out of their place." Greenville, tucked away in the red clay foothills of the Blue Ridge Mountains between Spartanburg and Atlanta, was a sleepy town of live and let live. The white supremacy codes handed down from slavery were clearly defined and adhered to. Because Jesse's father seldom stayed in his place, he was considered a rare specimen by most and he created much speculation over his odds for survival. A textile mill sampler by profession, Robinson—in his '43 Plymouth—also moonlighted as a taxi driver. Once an irate driver honked his horn too furiously at Robinson. An amateur state golden glove champion, Robinson jumped out of his cab, yanked the white man out of his car, and knocked him out. This was his second battering of whites, if local historians are correct.

On another occasion, Robinson was bent over his work at the mill when a white company executive nudged him playfully in the posterior. Robinson knocked him out too. But instead of the Ryan mill owners' firing Jesse's father as would be expected, they penalized the white guy. The wealthy Ryans took a liking to Robinson and later helped him raise the money to send Noah to Catholic school and college. Noah Junior carries Ryan as his middle name. But the cameraderie between the Robinsons and the Ryans was the exception, not the rule.

In 1948, what Jesse saw in his second-grade textbook was a reflection of how the world looked at him and how he must have guessed he looked to the world. In his geography textbook, there were two boys illustrating the different points on the equator. Facing south was Bumble, a shiny-faced befuddled-looking urchin in ragtag garb, held up by a string around his waist. But facing north was John, in starched knickers and a British-style jacket, looking clean, neat, and distinguished. Not many in his class wanted to be like Bumble.

To Jesse, Bumble and John were much more than textbook figures. He could see them on the street where he lived. Several vivid experiences especially stand out in his mind:

"All the little homes we used to live in were owned by an old man named Mr. Hellum who used to come around on Saturday afternoon in his little old truck to collect the rent. He was white, and he'd come around with his little book and those that didn't have the rent money would be running and hiding in the bushes and acting like they weren't home and he'd be chasing them to collect the rent. They were filled with fear and I always resented that," Jesse said.

The knowledge that he was expected to be subservient and inferior to whites was reinforced in many ways. Another experience Jesse recalls was the day he listened to Joe Louis flatten his white opponent but, like the others, he was afraid to cheer. "A group of us kids were gathered out in front of a cigar store listening to the radio. Although Joe Louis battered the white guy unmercifully, we stood there stoically, not daring to show any emotion over a black man beating a white one because we knew it would anger the white shopkeeper and his friends." But Jesse would not be outdone; he ran home and let out a holler for the guy he would someday be honoring at his Saturday morning meetings.

Desegregation did not come to Greenville until the early sixties, when the city's founding fathers read the signs of the time and ended segregated public accommodations after four rather tepid protest drives by local activists. But when Jesse was a boy, the white and colored signs abounded as a constant reminder of the separate places reserved for the two races. "I remember how it was when I was a kid," Jesse once recollected. "We would say we didn't want to drink water because we weren't thirsty, or we didn't want to eat because we weren't hungry, or we didn't want to go to the movie theater because we didn't want to see the picture. Actually we were lying because we were afraid."

Jesse's rejection of white supremacy was often discussed with a schoolmate, Horace Nash, as they walked past the white school to the black school, six miles away. "The one thing that stands out in my mind about Jesse was that he used to make up jokes about whites, how foolish and stupid they were. He used to have me in stitches. He used to turn things around. The white and black football teams couldn't play together. And Jesse would always say, 'That's because they're scared they'd get whupped. Because the black team is better.' He actually looked down on white people, and in those days that was unusual. Another thing I remember about Jesse was his inquisitiveness. He used to always ask why. He questioned the rules at a time when everybody else had accepted them because they had always been that way."

If the world around him often seemed disjointed, his home environment offered the sanctuary which tempered his tendency to brood over things he could not change. A strong sense of morality, tenderness laced with toughness, and a firm belief that hard work is the antidote for mischievousness launched Jesse in the direction his family hoped he would travel as a man. The church was a strong tradition in the Jacksons' lifestyle as it was in the Robinsons', who produced scores of Baptist ministers. Both Charles and Helen Jackson sang in the choir at Longbranch Baptist Church, worshipped twice on Sunday, and adorned their mantlepiece with religious bric-a-brac, a testimony to their abiding faith. (At age nine, Jesse was elected to the National Sunday School Convention in Charlotte, where he would report once a month to the full congregation—his first public speaking engagement.)

Jesse's grandmother, Aunt Tibby, as she is affectionately called, presided as the ex officio chairman of the board in the Jackson household. Odes, not mere words, describe the tenderness and wisdom of a Southern grandmother, the kind of grandmother Jesse has. She is the Rock—the one person who always believed in him and never failed him. Yet, she was hard to fool. She knew when Jesse was lying, knew what he was going to say before the words could fall from his lips, and knew what was troubling him, often when he couldn't make sense of it himself. Aunt Tibby cannot read nor write, but she can fix potatoes a dozen different ways without a recipe, concoct the proper home remedy—vinegar and alcohol baths to break a fever, onion soup and hot toddies for colds, and castor oil tinged with lemon when Jesse looked peaked—as well as quote the proper Southern adage, like some folks quote Shakespeare, which soothed, comforted, and prodded Jesse along. "If you fall, boy, you don't have to wallow. Ain't nobody going to think you somebody, unless you think so yourself. Don't listen to their talk, boy; they don't have a pot to pee in or a window to throw it out. For God's sake, Jesse, promise me you'll be somebody. Ain't no such word as *cain't, cain't* got drowned in a soda bottle. Don't let the Joneses get you down. Nothing is impossible for those who love the Lord. Come hell or high water, if you got the guts, boy, ain't nothing or nobody can turn you around." Whatever was said to him on the streets, Aunt Tibby could always negate the negative with a phrase strong enough to momentarily turn a bad situation around. Jesse was quite a phraseologist himself, even as a boy. No one remembers Jesse as much of a scrapper, although he was bigger than most youths his age. "He was the type of little guy who would stare you down and cut you down with a word. He was a great signifier, good at out-insulting those who thought they could insult him," a friend once said.

One Southern adage, a standard in the Jackson home, was a hard-and-fast rule with which Jesse and his younger brother, Charles, always had to comply: "An idle mind is the devil's workshop." This meant the Jackson boys, when not in church, in school, or playing sports, had better be working, not because the family was poverty stricken but because work would keep them out of trouble. From age six, Jesse was gainfully employed. His first job was working in a wood yard for Henry Summers, a close friend of his grandmother. Jesse would ride out to the country in an old pickup truck, help Mr. Summers pick up lumber slabs, saw them into stove wood, and deliver them around the neighborhood, "three tubs for a quarter."

At eight, he became the first black youngster to sell concessions at Greenville's whites-only football stadium. At ten, he was shining shoes in his stepfather's shoe-shine parlor, and later he worked at the Liberty Theater as a ticket collector, often letting Noah sneak in through the back door to catch a free movie. Around twelve, he caddied at the Greenville Country Club. In high school he worked at the Poinsett Hotel, across the street from a plaque enshrining the memory of segregationist John C. Calhoun, former vice-president and congressman. Jesse relished the chance to show what he thought of Calhounism the only way he could, by spitting in the food he served whites. While in high school, Jesse and friend Owen Perkins cleaned machinery at Claussen's bakery on weekends. Both protested the white-only rest rooms and drinking fountains and attempted to organize the employees in protest against segregation, low wages, and unsafe working conditions. The two, however, were just a step ahead of their times.

Despite his grandmother's moral crusade against the evils caused by an idle mind, Jesse, known as Bo-Diddley on the corner hangouts, squeezed in the time to do some tinkering around in the devil's workshop. Like many other youths, he learned to play blackjack, pittypat, and dirty hearts for money, shoot pool and craps, and hustle baseball tickets. These shenanigans worried his parents then. Today, his knowledge of street talk and his development of the "con instinct" equip him for leadership in the urban jungles much more than did the austere, aristocratic upbringing of Dr. King, who, ironically, was more a leader of the poor than Jackson is. But one thing is certain, as Jackson often says, "If it were not for the grace of God, I'd still be on the corner." Many of Jackson's boyhood friends who had hung out on the same corner are junkies, convicts, alcoholics, or otherwise social rejects. Jesse was the kind of boy who wanted to stand out, to attract attention to himself. He could have achieved this by leading the corner hustling activities. That Jesse found other avenues to express himself could have meant that somewhere in the background two women were praying.

Yet Jackson had said on an October 1973 WBBM-TV (Chicago) special, "I used to run bootleg liquor, bought hot clothes. I had to steal to survive." If Jesse, the Boy Scout, stole at all, poverty did not motivate him. Jesse's stepfather was never a janitor and his mother was never a maid, as was stated in an earlier biographical sketch.* Charles Jackson's post office job, supplemented by his wife's income as a beautician and their two sons' picking up spending change doing odd jobs, placed the family in the comfortable bracket among the Greenville poor.

Technically, almost everyone in Greenville could have been considered poor by today's standards. In the forties, the few jobs available to blacks were in the textile mills and shirt factories or as domestics. But $3,000 in those days, the net income of Charles Jackson, placed the family in a higher income bracket than most schoolteachers, allowing them to afford many of the luxuries their neighbors could not.

The house Jesse was born in was a spacious six-room cottage, trimmed with white asbestos siding, surrounded by well-kept shrubbery and a meticulously groomed lawn. While Jesse was still a toddler, the Jacksons moved off Haynie Street to University Ridge Street, near Furman University. The community was run-down, but it was still a step above the shoddy housing conditions set aside for most Greenville blacks. On Ridge, Jesse lived among a collection of unpainted, three-room shotgun houses (houses which, like in a rifle sight, you could see straight through from the front door out the back door). Each

*Phillip T. Drotning & Wesley South, *Up from the Ghetto* (New York: Cowles, 1970).

house had its coal and wood bins underneath, an open toilet on the back porch, and a wash pot in the backyard. The houses were crowded so closely together that "you could stand on the front porch and holler four blocks away." Hollering was a favored means of communication on Ridge Street, since the Jacksons were one of the few families who could afford a telephone.

The family began pushing the slums far into the background by the time Jesse was in the sixth grade at Nicholtown Elementary School; they moved into a new housing development, called Fieldcrest, and then to an eight-room house on Anderson Street, where the Jacksons live today.

Charles Jackson recalls with pride, "We were never poor. We never wanted for anything. We've never been on welfare, because I was never without a job. We never begged anybody for a dime. And my family never went hungry a day in their lives."

The townspeople remember that the Jackson boys were well mannered and well fed and that Jesse, especially, was always immaculately dressed. Their diet was the typical downhome fare: grits or oatmeal with pork chops for breakfast; cornbread, blackeyed peas, collard greens, chitterlings, and neckbone dinners, and an ample supply of chickens plucked from their backyard stock on Ridge.

Jesse's eleventh-grade French teacher, Mrs. Xanthene Norris, remembered Jesse as "A sharp dresser. He wore suits and ties when other students were wearing blue jeans." In fact, envious teenagers used to playfully tease Jesse about his penchant for dignified dress, which he wore along with what was considered a superior attitude. Once as he walked by, Jesse heard a front-porch coffee sipper quip, "There goes Noah's bastard, thinking he's better than everybody else. Look how he's dressed." Jesse wheeled around and respectfully told her, "Go ahead, call me what you will. I am Noah's bastard, if that's what you want to call me. But one day you'll be proud to know this bastard."

Although spite is a tough substance forever trapped into a memory, the chiding, the ridicule, was quite disproportionate to the special concern shown Jesse by many responsible adults—teachers, ministers, coaches—in his community who reinforced the moral tension and emphasis on excelling dominant in the Jackson home.

Southern black communities were communal in a literal sense. For the most part this is still true today. Children do not grow up through happenstance as they so often do in Northern urban areas. There is a life plan for them interwoven through the institutions of church, home, and school. Social mores were such that when Jesse was disruptive in class, he was disciplined at school, "whupped" at home, and the preacher—that autocratic figure who dictated to the community—would publicly rebuke Jesse in church. When Jesse presented a severe behavioral problem, it was not unusual for the preacher and his teachers to converge on Jesse at his home.

All three institutions, interlocking, reinforcing, and smoothing out the rough edges, were the crucible of his development as a leader. His school environs offered him the laboratory he needed to test himself, to compete and to measure his achievements. Every teacher Jesse came into contact with took note of his insecurities, masked by a stoic sense of superiority. They never perceived him as brilliant, but rather each saw him as a charmer, a spirited, fierce competitor with an almost uncanny drive to prove himself by always winning, always being number one in everything.

Mrs. Sara Shelton, his sixth-grade teacher, remembers Jesse as a big, clumsy boy who towered over her five-foot, one-inch frame although he was only twelve years old. "He was recorded in my record book as Jesse Louis Burns then and, of course, I knew the very first day about his circumstance because there was so much talk about it. But I would hear no more of it.

"He was not a serious student then. Like most boys, he thought school was a place to enjoy himself, to have loads of fun. I thought nothing of putting him in his place with a smack of the ruler. Sometimes his mother and I would counsel Jesse together about his thinking school was a playground.

"I used to tell him that the only chance he had to be somebody was to learn while it was easy, while he was young and had nothing else to do but learn. I always put the responsibility for being somebody on himself, telling him he had nobody to blame but himself if the world passed him by.

"Sometimes he would talk to me about being a football star. He would say it as a joke first the way many Southern boys would do, to keep people from teasing them about having ambition. He was very ambitious in sports, but at that age he was only excellent academically when he wanted to be. At that time, I noted he was a leader of devilment. If I could calm him down, the whole class would settle down."

By the ninth grade, his classmates were recognizing his leadership ability. He was elected president of his class and president of the honor society and the student council as well.

No other teacher gained insight into the Jackson personality as did Mrs. Norris, his confidante.

"Although he received A's and B's across the board in French, I wouldn't label him a brainy person. He was ambitious and excellent through hard work. Jesse was always the candidate. Whatever office was available, Jesse would be there signing his name. He seemed to be saying 'whether you elect me or not I'm going to run. I am the candidate.' There were plenty of people who ran against him, but usually he won. Although some kids hated his guts for always wanting to be out front, most respected him for his drive. I remember right after he won the state office of the Future Teachers of America, the kids started complaining that they were sick of Jesse winning everything, that somebody else ought to have a chance.

"In fact, I used to question Jesse myself, sometimes. His whole conversation would be full of himself. I can do this. I can do that. Sometimes, I would ask him, 'Do you have a "We" in your vocabulary?' I understood him, although it was very hard to gain entry into the inner self of Jesse. He felt he had to be a star, had to succeed because he had doubts about himself. Kids used to tease him about his circumstance, about his immaculate way of dressing. What they did not understand was that Jesse was compensating, trying to accept himself and trying to gain acceptance from others. He felt if he did not beat the drum for himself, nobody else would."

"One thing I can say for certain," she continued. "Jesse never complained, never made excuses for himself, never wallowed in self-pity. He was the only football player I ever had that asked for his assignment if he was going to miss class because of football practice. The others would make excuses. But Jesse wanted to be known not only as a good quarterback but as a good scholar too. Jesse would do all his assignments and beyond."

Mrs. Norris was also in the position to watch Noah and Jesse, since both were her students. "After you really got to know them both, you could see that Noah was much more secure than Jesse because Noah had both his natural parents. They were two different types of students. Noah was sweet little Noah. Jesse was big aggressive Jesse. Sometimes you had to pull information out of Noah, while you often had to shut Jesse up. Noah was the one sitting in the corner not quite as verbal as Jesse, but sometimes those are your better students."

It is not unusual for parents to live out their dreams

through their children. Both the Robinsons and the Jacksons had their educations interrupted. Both wanted their children to go further in life than they had. Both families prodded their eldest son to outdo the other. If the Jacksons heard that Noah got an A Jesse knew he'd better get an A. It was as if the parents could vindicate themselves through the deeds of their offspring. While the backseat prodding helped push both toward academic excellence—Noah graduated third in his class, Jesse graduated tenth—they would not grow to see each other as brothers, but as combatants, always at each other's throats.

Noah has often recognized that their relationship might have worked out better if the two had had a good slugfest when they were kids. "Maybe, if we would have knocked each other down a couple of times, we could have rid each other of what's on our chest." Another reason the two brothers respond to each other in such gladiator fashion is that it must have become tiring listening to an echo. As a reporter, I've had the occasion to hang up the phone after talking with Jesse and Noah would call. Often I'd have to catch myself, momentarily, not to think I was still talking to Jesse. Both have the same rhyming speech pattern, except Noah's is staccato, rapid fire, while Jesse's is a slower, controlled cadence. Both tend to braggadocio; both are easily insulted; both are arrogant, rebellious, and vindictive. Although both have the same faults, they see them in each other but not in themselves.

The Reverend J. D. Mathis, Jesse's coach at Sterling High, rated him at the top of all the quarterbacks he'd ever coached. "He was more versatile than any others. Jesse was the kind of kid you wanted as a quarterback, clean and an all-American type. He was big and he could take a punch and then dish out a blow. I didn't worry about seeing him get up, but I'd see the opposition laying on the ground a lot of times. He was a fierce competitor, winning letters not only in football, but baseball and basketball as well."

Mathis, who coached Jesse from age thirteen to seventeen, emphasized the connection between physical and intellectual prowess. "I used to emphasize that I expected him not only to develop his body but also his mind. I also had to warn him about the girls. The girls were falling all over themselves to get to Jesse.

"I knew Jesse all his life. His family and my family were very close friends. His personal problems affected him in an unusual way. They spurred him, urged him on to excel. It worried him, but he was the kind of youngster who kept things inside, wouldn't let you know what was troubling him. To hide his worry he took on an air of superiority, always acting like nothing was bothering him."

After graduation in 1959 from Sterling, Jackson was offered a contract with what was then the New York Giants. They had outbid the Chicago White Sox for Jackson and his white counterpart, Dickie Dietz. Jackson received his first real experience with the economic inequities of whites when the scouts offered Dietz $95,000 and Jackson $6,000 and a chance to go to college in the off season.

Jackson scoffed at the idea and accepted an athletic scholarship at the University of Illinois instead. His dream of becoming the first black quarterback at a big ten university was crudely shattered by an assistant coach, who summarily informed him that, ability notwithstanding, whites were quarterbacks and blacks played halfback or end.

The segregation that he thought had been left behind in Greenville cropped up in Illinois to convince him that was not the place to be. In college, he expected to assume the same type of leadership he had in the South, if not physically at least intellectually. However, Jackson said, "We were reduced to a subculture at Illinois. The annual interfraternity dance was the social event of the fall, but the three black fraternities [Jesse is an Omega] weren't invited. My black friends and I were down at the Veterans of Foreign Wars lodge listening to recordings, while the white folks were jumping live to Lionel Hampton in the gym."

After his freshman year, Jackson transferred to the predominantly black Agricultural and Technical College of North Carolina at Greensboro. For the first time he found himself in a milieu that gave his talents free scope, and he went on to distinguish himself as a quarterback, "big man on campus with the ladies," honor student, national vice grand Basileus of his fraternity, and president of the student body.

But more importantly, it was at A & T that Jackson became involved in civil rights and took himself a wife.

After the Montgomery boycott, the second phase of the civil rights movement erupted in Greensboro. Jackson was still in Illinois. On February 1, 1960, four black students from A & T sat down at a Woolworth lunch counter and ordered coffee. When they were refused service, they simply opened their books and began to study. Thus, the Southern sit-ins had begun when Jackson arrived, but by 1963 he was the leader. That spring, he had criticized the slow progress being made by CORE members and was promptly challenged to do better if he could. He did. Almost daily for ten months he led the continual stream of demonstrators into the segregated theaters and restaurants. On June 6, 1963, he was arrested for inciting a riot in downtown Greensboro, where he had led a column of students in a sit-down in the middle of a busy thoroughfare in front of the municipal building.

Even then, young Jackson had the aplomb that turned on and inspired others to follow him. "I know I am going to jail," Jackson told his followers. "I'm going without fear. It's a principle that I have for which I'll go to jail and I'll go to the chain gang if necessary." (He was also developing his proclivity for overstatement. At that time there were no chain gangs in North Carolina.)

As a student facing his first confrontation with white

racists, he was peppery and unafraid. Police Captain William Jackson tried to throw fear into his heart by telling him, "Now you've done it, you're really messing up now." Jackson told him, pointing to the municipal building where the mayor and city council met, "No. It's not me, captain, they're the ones that are messing up." After refusing to post bond, Jackson packed his overnight kit for his first stay in a Southern jail. "I'm going to jail because I refuse to let another man put a timetable on my freedom. We aren't asking for integration. We're asking for desegregation and there's a difference. I only want my freedom," he told the white detective, who led him away.

There have been other published accounts that claim Jesse led the demonstration in Greenville that desegregated the main library and restaurants. However, a search of police reports and interviews with the attorneys who handled the desegregation cases revealed that there is no record of Jackson ever being jailed in Greenville. Relatives have said Jackson was away in school during the Greenville protest move.

During the heat of the sit-ins, Jackson began regularly dating Jacqueline Lavinia Davis, a svelte, five-foot, one-inch beauty from Fort Pierce, Florida. She was heavily involved in the movement, becoming so intensely committed that she looked upon herself as a rebel's rebel. But actually she was a quiet rebel who thought more than she spoke. Jesse and Jackie first began to relate to each other over national issues. "He didn't appeal to me, initially," she says. "I was from a puritanical culture and I thought he was a little too quick in formulating opinions. Our involvement started on an intellectual plane while we were discussing his term paper about whether or not Red China should be admitted to the UN."

In college he was already the swashbuckling romantic figure he is today. But when he proposed he had to have some help. He was standing on the corner at the campus with a group of guys and called to her, "Hey, Jackie, you're going to marry me." Over the guffawing of his friends, who thought Jesse was kidding, Jackie initially responded to him as if he were insane. She married him in 1962 in a simple ceremony at his home on Anderson Street.

Jackson's leadership in the demonstrations, which resulted in desegregation of downtown Greensboro, made him a campus folk hero. In recognition of his efforts he was elected president of the newly formed North Carolina Intercollegiate Council on Human Rights.

Even more essential, in his senior year, he became involved with the leadership of CORE. Later he was named field director of the Southeastern operations. The CORE involvement led him deeper into the movement, where he worked under James Farmer, Floyd McKissick, and indirectly with Dr. Martin Luther King, Jr. At that time Jackson was little more than a face in the crowd to King, one of the many students participating in the nonviolent workshops he and his lieutenants directed.

The introduction to Dr. King, whom he would later look upon as a father figure, and the key roles that ministers were playing in the movement, which Jackson felt to be his niche, caused him to rethink a theme that had been hounding his consciousness since age fourteen. According to his father, Jesse began dreaming about becoming a preacher around that age.

Robinson said, "I remember the age that the dream started so well because I thought it peculiar that it was the same age when Jesse's grandfather began preaching. Jesse told me he dreamed he would lead an army across the waters like Moses did. I remember telling him I don't know if you could really lead an army, but you might be a good preacher like your granddaddy was."

At A & T, Jesse's roommate, Charles Carter, underwent a strange session with Jesse. "One night he woke up and said he had had an odd dream. He said he thought he had been called to preach. He was shaking. I never saw him look so serious before."

For about two months Jesse mulled over in his mind whether or not he should discuss the dream with anyone else. Jesse had a deep disdain for "the doom and gloom" traditional preachers. He felt that most of the preachers he had listened to had given up on this world and were concentrating on the afterlife. He felt their doctrine was a moralistic straitjacket and unresponsive to the worldly needs of the masses of black people.

Still, he decided it wouldn't hurt to discuss the call with A & T president, Dr. Sam Proctor. Jesse said, "I thought the call would be some cataclysmic religious experience like waking up some night and falling off a horse like Paul, or cutting flips in the air, shouting or something."

Dr. Proctor told Jackson that the call was a certain consciousness that you have to serve a certain role or carry out a certain mission. He advised him to go to the seminary. After the talk with Dr. Proctor, Jackson made up his mind to accept a Rockefeller grant to the Chicago Theological Seminary after he completed his bachelor's degree in sociology.

The decision to enter the ministry put an end to Jackson's intensive soul searching over his career. During his A & T stint, Jesse began the move from protest to politics.

He worked briefly for North Carolina Governor Terry Sanford, who sponsored him as one of the first black delegates to the Young Democrats National Convention in Las Vegas. His interest in politics almost led him to Duke University to pursue a law degree. Jackson said, "Caught between the ministry and Duke, I chose Chicago because I was so involved in the movement and with Sanford there, I thought I might flunk out of Duke. I really thought by going to Seminary School it would be quiet and peaceful and I could reflect."

Peace would come, but to Jackson peace does not mean quiet. Jackson's peace is a kind of internal combustion that comes with transmitting his adolescent pain into a magical phrase that inspires, that turns others on: "I Am Somebody." It does not seem like much until you see the masses say it and believe it. Jackson's peace is personal recognition, the type that comes when the headlines mention him by his first name and no one asks, "Jesse who?" It is the kind of peace that comes when the search for personal identity is giving way to public mission. It is the kind of peace that comes with knowing that there is no one in front of you and nobody even close behind. There is still some anxiety, though, because what is worse than building your kingdom, proclaiming yourself king and having someone steal your throne? But there is at least the satisfaction of knowing that even if the worst happened, history would never be complete without recording his name.

And so on October 6, 1973, after fifteen honorary degrees, after gracing the cover of *Time* at age twenty-seven, after participating in 1,515 talk shows and press conferences, after becoming the undisputed Messiah of the Chicago black business community, after being featured weekly inside or on the cover of *Jet* (which he once sold on Chicago street corners) and after being acknowledged by presidents, ambassadors, and a host of other VIPs, Jesse Jackson returned to his roots.

All of Greenville—blacks and whites alike—opened up their hearts to the most famous of native sons for a weekend-long string of festivities celebrating Jesse Jackson Day.

It was an experience of cultural shock to stand there in the eye of change, the change the King movement had so effectively fought for. Everywhere you looked there

were the startling symbols of the New South chasing away
the relics of the old that the city is trying hard to forget.

Hotels, such as the Golden Eagle Inn, flashed signs
"Welcome Home, Reverend Jesse Jackson." Less than a
decade ago, blacks were refused service there. On Main
Street, where blacks once stepped off the sidewalk when
whites approached, integrated high school bands burst into
spirited music. The business community, shaken up by
angry demonstrations in 1960, outdid itself with Jackson
paraphernalia decorating shop windows. And here and
there was a homemade welcoming sign, "Hey, Bo-
Diddley," from those who remembered Jesse from the
corner. The *Greenville-Piedmont News* donated a full-page
welcome, "Here Comes the Son." Both blacks and whites
proudly sported Jackson medallions.

Journalists from as far away as London packed the
hotels along with famous pals. Congressman John Conyers,
"Soul Train" star Don Cornelius, baseball great Hank Aaron,
FCC commissioner the Reverend Benjamin Hooks, as well
as an impressive entourage of politicians, unionists, and
followers from Chicago were there.

Everywhere Jackson went—if it were only to his
mother's house to eat—he was accompanied by rather
peculiar attendants led by a white sheriff, whose squad car
with its flashing light and bleating siren created traffic jams
in the busy thoroughfares. Behind the sheriff was a car full
of bodyguards, followed by Jackson's limousine, which was
tailed by a crew of photographers and newsmen.

Nothing was more symbolic of the changing times
and the pride of Greenvillians that their town could
produce such a man than the banquet held in Jackson's
honor at the Jack Tar Poinsett Hotel, where not so long
ago he used to work. (Jackson ate before coming to the
banquet. Perhaps he thought someone might remember
and return his gesture of spitting in the food.)

More than 1,000 of South Carolina's finest turned

out for the affair, which was billed as the largest interracial gathering in that state's history.

At the speaker's table beside Jesse were the people he felt worthy of being seated there. He was in a position to reverse the memory of the little boy standing in the backyard looking in. Now with a spotlight of his own he could pick and choose, reward and punish—something he invariably does as he did then. The only relatives honored were his grandmother, his mother, his wife, his stepfather, and one of his half brothers, Charles (Duke) Jackson, a composer and lead singer with the Independents. Noah Junior had not been invited and he had conveniently sent his father out of the city to spare him the embarrassment of being ignored on what was probably the proudest day of his life. Jesse's other brothers, George and Tony, were not included either.

Scores of speakers preceded Jackson to the podium to say the expected: "He is a voice for the voiceless, a leader of plain folk," Charles Hayes, international vice-president of the Amalgamated Meat Cutters Unions; "Jesse is a Balm in Gilead, a legend in his own time," Commissioner Ben Hooks; "When I am with him I can't help feeling I am in the presence of a giant," Coach J. D. Mathis; "Jesse Jackson is good for America," Max Heller, Greenville's Jewish mayor. Telegrams of praise poured in from around the state, including ones from Governor John C. West, Congressman J. R. Mann, and numerous other state legislators and public officials.

Then it was Jackson's turn at the podium. After praising his family seated on the left, giving special honor to his grandmother, and thanking some of the local townspeople for being "his bridge over troubled waters," Jackson made a speech, spectacular even for him.

"You gave me keys to the city, but they don't open no doors. We must move to open up the doors of a nation to the masses of poor. Don't you know babies in South

Carolina are dying from hunger? No matter how I hear about the changing South, on Sullivan Street blacks are still going to the bathroom in their backyards," he told them.

"I'm not just a football player. I'm not a boy. I am commissioned to tell the whole story. White politicians, don't you deceive. There are three whites on welfare for every one black. . . . White politicians, where is your voice? I was raised and born in the ghetto, but I am a child of the universe. War anywhere is a threat to peace everywhere."

But more importantly, he told the audience that he is past the point of needing personal praise. "My point used to be personal, now it is public. I used to preach for reputation. Now I preach for edification."

Jackson ended with, "I don't want you to worship me. To admire me, to follow me is to resist evil. I am just the imperfect tool by which an idea can be expressed."

At the end of his oration, a few noticed he was crying as he looked over the heads of people like Dr. Larry McCalla, for whom he used to caddy, and the throngs of others he had caught up with and passed. It seemed as if he was looking for that special someone. Perhaps Jack, the grocer. Or maybe it was for the local gossipmonger who had called him a bastard when he was fourteen. At that moment, Jackson, his countenance almost angelic, could well have been thinking, "There. Told you so. I told you I'd be the best damn bastard you've ever seen."

3

And what is hard to live with is that
even after we have gone through the
Martin Luther Kings, the Jim Formans,
the Al Rabys, the Stokely Carmichaels,
the Jesse Jacksons, the Fred Hamptons,
and everybody else, there may never
be an answer! *You are frustrated*
because your analysis tells you that
probably there is no solution in our
time, yet you continue to work as if
there were one. It is a real, internal
conflict.

Al Raby, Convener of the Coordinating Council of
Community Organizations (CCCO), 1966

One hundred years after the Emancipation Procla-
mation freed the "cullards" from slavery, the Civil War
again whipped northward to free the Negroes from racism.
Directing the tramp, tramp of marching feet was the
nation's first black emancipator—Dr. Martin Luther King,
Jr. After ten years of the most violent nonviolent crusade
in American history, Southerners were forced into a
second Appomattox. Begrudgingly the relics of the Old
Confederacy surrendered their cherished Southern tradi-
tions. At long last the Southern black was Americanized.
He could eat where he could afford to, move a few feet

from the back to the front of the bus, and vote without fear of being lynched. From chattel to citizen in nearly 400 years, this great event would be recorded in the annals of history as progress.

During this era of agony, indigent Southern whites deservedly caught hell. Characterized as ignorant race baiters, rednecks, and crackers, they were the scorn of the good, Christian, Northern liberal.

But in 1966, something stilled the guffaws and name-calling of the Northerners. Attention was being turned on them. Now it was Bull Connor's turn to watch the Yankees squirm. Eugene "Bull" Connor was police commissioner in Birmingham when police and civil rightists clashed in 1963. The civil rights legions, led by Martin Luther King, the biggest agitator of them all, were swinging north. First stop Chicago—the city which King had christened the capital of Northern segregation.

"What did we do? What segregation? Why us?" was the shocked response. To hear some prominent blacks and whites tell it, the city may house a few Mafia chieftains, skid row bums, and crooked cops, but a bigot was nowhere to be found among Chicago's citizens.

Congressman William Dawson, the most powerful black in the city and second, perhaps, only to Congressman Adam Clayton Powell in the nation, said: "What does he [King] mean coming in here trying to tell our citizens that we are segregated? Chicagoans know what's best for Chicagoans."

Chicago was said not to have a single segregation law on its books.

Alderman Thomas Keane, floor leader and boss of the City Council, said: "King is a disrupter of society. He is trying to destroy what we built."

Mayor Richard Daley, the statesman, intoned: "We believe that we do not have segregation in Chicago. Here we recognize every man, regardless of race, national origin, or creed, and they are entitled to their rights as provided in the United States Constitution and the constitution of Illinois."

Of all the statements of self-righteous indignation, none was more puzzling than the Mayor's. It had only been a year ago in 1965 that peaceful demonstrators were bombarded by rocks, eggs, and tomatoes when civil rightist comedian Dick Gregory led a march to the Mayor's pink bungalow in Bridgeport. Women soaked them with lawn sprinklers, the Mayor's neighbors told the marchers to "go back to the zoo," and some little girls sang:

> I'd like to be an Alabama Trooper
> That's what I'd truly like to be.
> Cause if I were an Alabama trooper
> I could kill the niggers legally.

And cheered:

> Two-Four-Six-Eight, We don't want to Integrate.

For King, Chicago would serve as a test case, "an experiment in faith." It was to be the Northern Montgomery. If he could find the key to unlock blacks from decades of economic and political exploitation in Chicago, it would prove his domino theory for toppling the other Northern citadels of deprivation.

King's style was to attack the worst first. Chicago had few equals in housing the worst slums in the nation, although in 1963 the Mayor had told an NAACP convention that there were no ghettos in Chicago. Since most of the audience lived in the very ghettos the Mayor said did not exist, he was booed from the podium. Crammed into hovels, shanties, and Victorian eyesores, the city's black poor serve as a boon to white real estate racketeers. They jam triple the number of blacks into an apartment that housed a single family when the building was white occupied—at double the rent. The real estate brokers reap an additional windfall because the city seldom pressures slum landlords to make repairs, as long as they kick back to the building inspectors.

King also lamented the fact that the national consciousness had missed the main impact of civil rights efforts, namely the realization of full equality. During the first phase of the movement there was a degree of unity among blacks and concerned whites in seeking to eliminate the more extreme forms of barbaric conduct against blacks. This unity began to erode, however, when the attention of the movement turned to the more costly goal of fulfilling the promise of equality. Whites were reluctant, by and large, to pursue the issue of equality to its fullest conclusion for black citizens. Dr. King noted that white allies who had been incensed by overt brutality failed to show the same concern for eliminating poverty, exploitation, and the more subtle forms of discrimination in employment and housing, especially in the North. In the minds of far too many, the movement had ended with the signing of the Voting Rights Act of 1965. "But the absence of brutality and unregenerable evil is not the presence of justice. To stay murder is not the same thing as to ordain brotherhood," King wrote in *Where Do We Go From Here: Chaos or Community.* *

The most persuasive factor influencing King's decision to come to Chicago was that Chicago chose him. Al Raby, then Convener of the Coordinating Council of Community Organizations (CCCO), composed of forty-three black and white groups, the strongest coalition in the North, had reached an impasse in his campaign to oust Benjamin Willis from his post as superintendent of Chicago schools. Raby, a gaunt, lanky schoolteacher, had led boycotts, during which half of the city's black student population stayed home. He had marched to City Hall,

*(New York: Harper & Row, 1967).

sprawled out in the Loop, and planned to lead a sit-down on the Dan Ryan Expressway, but he deferred because he felt indifferent motorists would just run over the protesters. Yet nothing he could think of to do produced a reaction from City Hall that indicated Willis would go.

In Chicago a summer day seldom passes without some group taking to the streets to parade, protest or plead for some gift from the mayor. Since there was nothing unusual about Raby's activities, Daley ignored him, as he does most troublemakers. Raby and his group were not big names; they were just a bunch of local yokels with noisemakers, probably financed by the Commies, was the attitude of City Hall. After three years of more than 100 protest marches, the demonstrators exhausted themselves and their vigil to shake Willis loose from the city payroll. The demonstrators, which had once numbered 25,000, according to Raby, had now dwindled down to ten marchers, including one dog.

After several urgent telegrams from Raby, King agreed to come to Chicago to give the movement a shot-in-the-arm. Black powermongers were nipping at his heels, the movement was waning in the South, and he was still an internationally respected leader with a regional base. Chicago, then, would be the experiment to prove nonviolence is a superior tactic to the burnings that had occurred in Watts and Harlem. His appearance would also provide his organization, the Southern Christian Leadership Conference (SCLC), with a national structure.

Before King could dig in his heels to help kick out Willis, the movement lost its favorite target. Superintendent Willis, the tough-talking villain who crammed black students into trailers or Willis Wagons rather than integrate the schools, retired. The civil rights groups were relieved. They had tried to equate him with the hounds in Selma to dramatize their plight, but the comparison never came off. While it was a good try and a fitting comparison,

Raby's group needed the visual effects of billy clubs crashing against black skulls, jails brimming with peaceful demonstrators, or a martyr—preferably white—flashing on the evening news.

They knew they were powerless unless they could inject some drama into the movement by involving the people of the nation and the federal government in the potpourri of social evils in Chicago. Maybe King would know what to do. The dramatics of confrontation were his forte.

For weeks King and Raby searched for the issue that would turn on the nation, producing a mass movement of inflamed citizens to Chicago. There was so much to do. Public accommodations were a problem. In Chicago the question was not where a black would sit on the bus, but where he could get the money to get on the bus. It was decided, then, that unemployment would be attacked later under the umbrella of an Operation Breadbasket program.

When the leaders discussed voting, they were hitting Chicago in its vital organs. But they backed away, lacking a strategy to cut into the Mayor's plantation, which has co-opted many of the black affluents but owns the black poor. As long as indigent blacks vote for the Democratic candidates the Mayor slates, as chairman of the Cook County Democratic Central Committee, they are entitled to their poor man's credit card. Their cooperation supposedly protects them from losing their public housing, welfare, a green card for hospital care, or a menial job. It also brings a bonus on election day. After they vote right, their prize is often a bottle of wine, a chicken, or a dozen grade-A jumbo eggs.

While the rewards may seem paltry, they are real. And the black poor were not about to trade in their food, clothing, and shelter for the kind of abstractions, like freedom and equality, that King preached. To dramatize the point, while researching voting habits of westsiders,

SCLC aide Leon Hall said, "One old lady came at me with an ice pick. This is worse than Alabama. At least there you had some fresh air."

Finally, King and his cerebral top Chicago aide, James Bevel, decided on open housing, which was and is still today the ethnics' most sensitive issue. They selected "The Campaign To End Slums" as their slogan. The decision was appropriately announced in June, the same month that seventeen-year-old Jerome Huey was bludgeoned to death on a street corner by white thugs in suburban Cicero while the young man was looking for a job. Ironically, the Mayor promptly issued a statement which indicated that he had also thought of ending slums. Daley, a master of one-upmanship, set 1967 as the year when all the slums would disappear.

King could not help but be befuddled by Daley's statement. First Daley had said there were no slums. Then he committed himself to removing them. What kind of man was he? What kind of city was this? Both the man and the city were paradoxes to King. The city the man ruled over was a kaleidoscope of magnificent skylines with squalid underpinnings. It was dynamic, static, ugly, beautiful, inviting, and hostile, depending on which side of town you were on. It had more blacks squeezed into the State Street Robert Taylor Homes than there were in the whole city of Selma, Alabama. Almost as many blacks lived in the ghetto as in the entire state of Mississippi. Back where he had come from, the black church was the mainstay of the civil rights crusade. Here the black ministers feared civil rights. Daley seemed to have taken over the pulpits, too. Still, King felt that even though Daley was a despot, he, too, would change if he could be convinced of the rightness of King's goals. "It is better to deal with one man who has the power to change things," he once said, "than with a liberal like John Lindsay, who has lost control of his city."

By the same token, King was an enigma to Daley.
What manner of man was he? Anybody who couldn't be
bought off or scared off, or who didn't need a favor, was
immediately a suspicious character to Daley. "The whole
attitude around City Hall," one political observer said,
"was that King was a little nuisance. Nobody could
understand what to do with him since he didn't have a
price."

Spectators scanning the two agreed it would be a
strange ball game. King seemed to be batting from Wrigley
Field as the third generation preacher, the intellect, the
peacemaker. Over in White Sox Park was Daley, who
needed no definition, no titles before and after his name
nor even a Nobel Peace Prize, because he had power. The
two could do nothing more than swing past each other
because they didn't speak the same language or adhere to
the same rules. Most agreed that King was out, even before
the game could begin. What could King hope to accomplish with moral force in a city which has grown
comfortable with its immorality? Hadn't King imbibed the
wisdom of Leo Durocher, whose favorite line is: "Nice
guys finish last"?

John A. Williams quipped: "I won't be surprised if
Martin doesn't disappear into Lake Michigan, with his feet
encased in concrete. He came to Chicago believing he had
power, prepared to attack the white power structure. He
did not understand he was armed with feather dusters."*

Any truth in the doomsday predictions had more
meaning for the young, low-level lieutenant at King's side
than it did for King himself. To Jesse Jackson all the
massive grief and adulation would fall as King passed on
into history, and Jesse Jackson would be haunted with the
urgency of fulfilling the martyr's dreams (or as some

The King God Didn't Save (New York: Coward, McCann, Inc.,
  1970).

would say, Jesse's dreams). Could Jesse Jackson grasp all the offenses and defenses formulating in this little war yet to begin? There would be so little time for him to learn. The tragedy of Memphis was only two years away. How could he learn to combat raw power when, like King, he was a stranger to the political councils where the important decisions are made?

At the time, however, it was doubtful that King himself was convinced of the immense value of this spunky kid, who was still a student at the Chicago Theological Seminary. Often zealously chasing his own identity, Jesse would scamper off plotting escapades and releasing embarrassing statements to the press that King, his father figure, would somehow have to erase. He thought King was humanity's ultimate offering, and imitated his speech, ideology, and style. But when he went too far, such as making policy decisions, King would have to "shame" Jesse back into place.

Jesse always seemed to be questioning things when there was no time for discussion, when there was work to do. "Doc, what do you think about this?" "If I were you, Doc, I would be doing that." He seemed to be afire with the quest for right now solutions to situations that there were no immediate answers for. His aggressiveness, lack of humility, and spasmodic foibles were not as upsetting to King as they were to others around him. Jesse Jackson was also a powerful preacher. Even then, he had unlimited energy and seemed quite sincere. King was also aware of the double standards affixed to young manhood. Had Jesse Jackson been white, his peers would have labeled him, "promising, inspired, and diligent," but a black with these same characteristics is often seen as "uppity, audacious, and arrogant."

King's more seasoned aides, like Andy Young, SCLC executive director, and Hosea Williams, voter registration director, often experienced an uneasiness around

Jesse. At times they felt he was trying to run over them. He would try to call the shots, give orders, when he was virtually a nobody. He had few status symbols tucked into his movement portfolio. Arrested only once in the student sit-ins in North Carolina, never beaten by Southern crackers, he had even been a member of the Young Democrats and a Boy Scout. Besides, he was only twenty-four. What could he know?

Young, now a Georgia congressman, remembers Jesse Jackson as a face in the crowd of thousands who poured into Selma in 1965 when King issued a call for foot soldiers. Enraged by the brutality of policemen using tear gas, whips, and electric cattle prods on women and children, which he saw beaming across the TV in his dormitory, Jesse had organized half of the student body to make the drive to Selma, where he would have his first opportunity to talk at length with King.

"I remember getting a little annoyed," Young said, "because Jesse was giving orders from the steps of Brown Chapel and nobody knew who he was. All the other marchers came up getting in line, but Jesse, assuming a staff role, automatically started directing the marchers. I also remember him telling me what a great pamphlet I wrote, *The Bible and the Ballot.* I was really flattered. It sort of took the edge off."

Although Betty Washington was a veteran civil rights reporter for the *Chicago Daily Defender,* it was at Selma that Jesse first crept into her notes. "Outside of Brown Chapel there were hundreds of people camping on the ground. In order to keep the crowd enthused, SCLC staffers were making speeches. First the Reverend Ralph Abernathy, then the Reverend C. T. Vivian, SCLC's Director of Affiliates, and up popped Jesse, wearing an odd looking porkpie hat and rugged work clothes and, of course, closely cropped hair. I thought it strange that he would be making a speech, when he was not on the SCLC staff and had not been included in any of the strategy meetings. He just seemed to have come from nowhere. Like, who *was* he? But he spoke so well, I recorded his statement anyway. I had the feeling that one day he might be important."

Mrs. Washington, now a *Chicago Daily News* reporter, also recalled Jesse's insisting that SCLC staffers find a place for him in the movement because he had heard they were planning to establish an affiliate in Chicago. "If it had been anybody else but Jesse, his persistency would have seemed pushy. But he did it in such a diplomatic way, he was concerned and just wanted in."

The Reverend Ralph D. Abernathy, the man whom Jesse would one day help blot out, brought Jesse in. "Jesse Jackson approached me asking what he could do to help keep the all-night vigil going. Later, he asked if there was anything open on the staff. He was dashing around in the downpour bringing people coffee and running errands. There was something about him that impressed me. I could see the leadership potential in him. Doc [King] did not agree with me that we ought to employ this young man on the basis of my experience with him during that short time. Reluctantly, he went along, though, because we always worked as a team."

Back in Chicago, assuming a dual staff position with CCCO and SCLC, Jesse proved he could do what had been deemed impossible—organize some of the black ministers around the Chicago Freedom Movement in preparation for King's arrival. Besides these ministers' umbilical attachment to the Mayor, Jesse and faculty members he enlisted from the university had three other basic problems to cut through. They were petty rivalries among some of the ministers, who ruled their churches like they were feudal fiefs. The jealousies escalated after they heard King was coming because he was the embodiment of everything the ministers wished to be. There was a gap between the civil

rightists demanding their rewards on earth and the
ministers teaching their flock to wait for their just due in
heaven. Also, some ministers who had become interested
in civil rights in the early 1960s had been co-opted or
intimidated by building inspectors or precinct captains.

"Most had long since made their peace with the Daley
machine," said one black politico. "Negro ministers may
think they're servants of God, but they're servants of
Daley—or maybe that's the same thing."

A typical example of the obstacles Jesse had to
overcome in daily meetings by just plain begging some of
the ministers to sacrifice materialism for the betterment of
their congregation was the dilemma of the Reverend Clay
Evans, pastor of Fellowship Baptist Church.

After Jesse enlisted Evans' support, the word leaked
back to City Hall. The Reverend Evans was building a new
church and was in the process of getting a loan to
complete construction. The screws started turning
downtown and Evans was informed that he would have to
gain the approval of his alderman before the loan would be
cleared.

A Negro alderman, who was a staunch Daley man,
reneged, but he said he might change his mind if Evans
changed his mind about King. The Reverend Evans
concluded: "Well, I might get a church, but the real
church is in the heart. Maybe I ought to back away from
the building, because it would only be a monument to me.
If I walk with King, I can build a monument to the Lord."
Evans, who was president of a top local Baptist Ministers
Conference, threw the weight of several large congregations behind King, brought Jackson into Fellowship as
associate pastor, and never left the movement even after
King's death. His church just would not get built. In 1973,
Evans' new edifice was built through a $500,000 loan from
black-owned Independence Bank, a financial institution
strengthened through conventional agreements from white
corporations at the insistence of Jackson.

When King moved into Chicago, Evans furnished the limousine to pick him up at O'Hare airport. Jesse was in the driver's seat. The success of Jackson's mission had reached King's attention and he was pleased. After bringing King into the city, Jesse told a friend that he was convinced King could whip Chicago. "You should have seen how that articulate black cat acted down in Alabama. We thought it was hell, but he was not afraid of violence and bullets and bombs. That cat can do anything."

King's first major effort came on July 11, 1966. He led a massive nonviolent demonstration to Soldier Field, proving he had broad support from the black and liberal white communities, a move which was geared to evoking a favorable response from the Mayor on the open housing issue. The police estimated the crowd turnout at 30,000; the Chicago Park District at 23,000; King's aides at 45,000; King at 65,000; and Raby at 100,000.

The *Chicago Tribune* accepted the police estimates and applauded the Negro community's "common sense for staying away from the march in large numbers. Marches and demonstrations have become tiresome and the Reverend Dr. King's rhetoric about filling up the jails of Chicago to end slums is becoming stale."

Still neither the *Tribune's* cutting remarks nor the statement of the Reverend J. H. Jackson, the black president of the estimated 6 million members of the National Baptist Convention, U.S.A., Inc., who labeled the march "undemocratic," could dim King's thunder. Later that day, he led an impressive march to the Loop, where he tacked forty demands to the door of City Hall, in emulation of his namesake Martin Luther, who nailed Ninety-Five Theses on the door of Castle church in the sixteenth century. The *Tribune* recalled, however, that the event was not "as momentous as that of Martin Luther in Wittenberg in the year 1517."

The demands called for virtually the same things as Jackson would be calling for in the '70s: a citizens' review board for grievances against police brutality, direct funding of Chicago community groups by the Office of Economic Opportunity, nondiscriminatory mortgage loans, desegregation of teachers by 1967, and at least 400 Negro and Latin American apprentices in the craft unions. "But for our primary target we have chosen open housing," King reaffirmed. "As of July 11, we shall cease to be accomplices to a housing system of discrimination, segregation, and degradation. We shall begin to act as if Chicago were an open city."

Daley's response was that the city already had a comprehensive housing plan. He released a statement boasting of killing rats and roaches and of having a tenant education program. "That's no program," King said. And he waited for something more imaginative to emanate from City Hall.

The next utterance from the city came from neither King nor Daley but from the forgotten black masses on the west side.

On July 16, 1966, the temperature had soared to 100 degrees, too hot for the kids to be jammed into their stifling sweatboxes. So a group of youngsters turned on the fire hydrants, improvising a swimming pool since none existed in the ghetto. When the firemen turned them off to save the city's water pressure, blacks reached their pressure point and fighting broke out. Snipers climbed on roofs, looting spread over several square miles, windows of white-owned stores were smashed, and the Illinois National Guard was ordered out.

Although King waded out in the midst of it all to help cool things, the morning headlines boomed "Mayor Blames King." Daley later appeared on television and polished the accusation to:

"I think you can't directly charge it to Dr. Martin Luther King, but surely some of the people who came in here and have been talking for the last year on violence—

they are on his staff. They are responsible in great measure for the instructions that have been given, for the training of these youngsters."

And Dr. J. H. Jackson, Daley's black parrot of the National Baptist Convention, mimicked: "Certain strangers are in Chicago to get youngsters to riot."

The previous summer, on August 12, 1965, a riot broke out after a black woman, Dessie Mae Williams, was killed in an accident caused by a speeding fire truck. Daley blamed the Communists and the Republicans. Fortunately for the Mayor, King served as a much better patsy.

Andy Young, King's aide, muttered angrily, "Wherever Doc goes and there's a riot they blame it on him. If he wasn't in Chicago, they'd blame it on him anyway."

Had Daley looked at the homes the blacks lived in, the schools they attended, or the fact that many were jobless, perhaps a reaction other than blaming King would have come to mind. But as the lot of the black poor improves, the less they need Daley's welfare machine, so it is not in his self-interest to improve upon an already cozy situation.

After the distraction of the west-side riots, talks once again resumed between King and Daley, but they focused on water. The rioting had forced open housing off the agenda. King was worried about staving off a blood bath, so he asked for spray nozzles to be attached to west-side fire hydrants and for the construction of swimming pools.

Now King was talking the Mayor's language. If that's all the blacks wanted, then the west side would become a playground for water sports. Water guzzled everywhere, and a downtown newspaper eagerly acclaimed that the water agreement brought Daley and King "closer together in the fast moving developments of civil rights."

King was running out of patience. His following was restless. He was beginning to feel the open housing issue would remain logjammed if he stayed at the conference

table. He had already tried moving his wife and children
into a west-side flat, at 1550 S. Hamlin Avenue, to
dramatize the squalid living conditions. Describing the
apartment, Mrs. Coretta King said, "In all my life I had
never seen anything like it. Our apartment was on the third
floor, which had no lights in the hall, only one dim bulb at
the head of the stairs. There was no lock on the front door
of this house; it always stood open. As we walked in, I
realized that the floor was not concrete, but bare dirt. The
smell of urine was overpowering. We were told that this
was because the door was always open and drunks came in
off the street to use the hallway as a toilet. For this
magnificent abode Martin had to pay $90 a month,
unfurnished."

As soon as the local newspaper published the address
of the King family, however, the building began to swarm
with carpenters, plumbers, and decorators. Not only was
King's flat repaired, but the entire building was renovated
and the heat turned on. One woman said that was the first
winter in three years that she had lived in the building that
she had not had to turn on the gas stove to keep her
children warm.

One cynic snapped: "Finally Martin has found the
solution to ending slums. All he has to do is move from
flat to flat."

King was not impressed. Once again the city had
blunted his tactics. There was nothing left to do but go to
the source of the tension. He would go where he couldn't
be ignored—into the ethnic blue-collar neighborhoods that
provide a solid wall, boxing blacks into their decaying
enclaves. He announced that the first target would be a real
estate office in Gage Park on the city's far south side. The
neighborhood was composed mostly of Lithuanian, Polish,
and Italian solid citizens.

The plan shook Daley. If anyone could predict the
reaction of blue-collar America, he could, since that was his

lineage. And all he had to do was to think back to Dick Gregory's march in Bridgeport, his neighborhood. Or the time a black college student tried to move in a few blocks away from his home and a mini-riot flared.

Raby describes what took place: "On August 5, 1966, I rode out to Gage Park with Martin. When we got there, he said 'Let's get out of the car. Nothing is going to happen. These people aren't going to do anything.' Nobody saw the stone that hit Martin as he walked to the head of the line. He fell to one knee and two United Auto Workers members stood over him to cover him, protect him, while the mob shouted, 'Kill him.' It turned out he had only been stunned and we went on with the march.

"Women were among the most vicious, screaming 'you monkeys' at the blacks and 'you white trash' at the whites. They called us all apes and told the blacks to go back to Africa. When we knelt in prayer in front of a real estate office, the whites threw rocks at us, cursed the nuns, and yelled to the priests that there wouldn't be anything in the collection box. A nineteen-year-old white with us was hit by a thrown knife. The confederate flag waved at us. So were banners boosting George Lincoln Rockwell and the Nazi Party. The police made fifty-one arrests. It must have been a difficult position for the white policemen. Their sympathies were with the white community, but they were getting stoned as well as we were."

Later that evening, King told his wife, Coretta, that the "march was worse than any of those I ever experienced in the deep South, in Mississippi and Alabama. I have never seen as much hatred and hostility on the part of so many people. To my mind they represent the most tragic expression of man's inhumanity to man. I've thought about this, remembering their faces and it—well, it reminds me of the hatred of Hitler's Germany and I had actually conceded to the inevitability of death."

The hate that erupted from this community of neat

lawns and clean bungalows, that brought whites to the streets hollering, "Wallace for God," had deep-rooted origins. Many were Polish and Italians who had fled their old south- and west-side neighborhoods when Negroes had started moving in years ago. They felt the blacks had chased them from their homes once and swore they would never retreat again. They believed that a black next door devaluated their property. And there was always a real estate panic-peddler around to incite their fears.

The King-Raby team could see the disparities from the other side. In Englewood, for example, the median educational grade level of Negroes was 10.6 years and the median income was about $4,200 a year. In Gage Park, the median educational grade level of the whites was 8.6 years but the median income was $9,600 a year. Also while King was paying $90 a month for four-and-a-half rooms without utilities, with only spasmodic janitorial services, whites in Gage Park were paying less than $80 a month for five-and-a-half rooms, with utilities and the customary services provided by management.

With the blacks vowing to continue their invasion of white areas and the whites promising to whip them back, Daley was caught in the middle. If his police cracked black heads, the west side might rebel. If he flogged the whites, they would fight back at the polls.

Daley issued a public plea for King and Raby to return to the negotiation table. Participating in the August 10, 1966, session were the Reverend James Bevel, the Reverend Jackson, Dr. Alvin Pitcher of the University of Chicago Divinity School, John McDermott, executive director of the Chicago Interracial Council, William Robinson, program consultant for the Church Federation of Greater Chicago, Chester Robinson of the West Side Organization, James Wright of the United Auto Workers, and Edwin (Bill) Berry of the Chicago Urban League.

Off the record, a city spokesman stage-whispered to

the negotiators that "the movement was making head-
way." A white high school principal, who along with
Superintendent Willis had become a hated symbol of de
facto segregation, had been removed from her post "for
health reasons." Also, the city's Urban Renewal Program
had been expanded to include twenty-two of Chicago's
worst areas, at a cost of $50 million. This was consistent
with Daley's plan to end slums by 1967.

The Urban Renewal ploy stimulated disturbing
visions of blacks being driven from their homes to a new
ghetto. Where they once lived, luxurious high rises would
spring up with rent brackets that excluded the black poor.
Urban Renewal meant black removal. The only ones to
profit from a deal like that were the big time real estate
developers, some of whom were great pals of the Mayor,
receiving fat contracts from City Hall.

The Mayor hurried on to the next point. The black
community could get 300 quick jobs as housing project
guards, a few hundred new ghetto units, and one black
journeyman glazier (he would also be the first) would be
hired by the Housing Authority. All King and Raby had to
do to receive these gifts was to curtail the marches and sign
on the dotted line of a letter which had been delivered to
King's apartment the night before. In the set of pre-
packaged quotes for release to the press was one that
began: "Today, Mayor Daley has once again demonstrated
his leadership by. . . ."

King refused to fill in the blanks and announced he
was pressing on, on into Marquette Park. There would be
different faces, but the reaction would be much the
same—one of hate not only from the professional haters,
such as the American Nazi Party, but from the just
plain folk.

On August 23, it was Jesse Jackson's turn to get his
lumps from bricks thrown by the welcoming party of
screaming, jeering whites. He did not have the stature of a

King, neither was he a top aide; so the bump did not make the headlines of the downtown papers. If it were not for the protection of the tough street gangs catching the raining bricks barehanded, there would have been more injuries, because the cops were looking the other way, according to Raby. When the gang members made a good catch, the marchers applauded. When they missed, the white protesters applauded. Raby recalled a white police sergeant being hit in the stomach by a brick. "I would call that social justice," he said.

The march into the Cragin community days later, however, was the move that pushed King closer to a victory over Daley. The police had kept the marchers on one side of the street and the hecklers on the other. When the irate whites tried to break through to the blacks, the police waded in with clubs flailing. Black cops on assignment that day, no doubt, relished their task. Whites were screaming "We live here, those fucking niggers don't. Get them the hell out of here." On TV that night whites were shocked to see hard-working, decent homeowners suffering from a malady unusual even for Chicago: police brutality against whites. The head beatings had been similar to what Daley would order in 1968 when long-hairs demonstrated at the Democratic National Convention.

Immediately, Daley felt the rumbling from the police action. Signs went up in white neighborhoods: "Don't vote for Daley." An alarmed Daley ordered his precinct captains into the field to reassure everyone that things were under control. "See," one of his ward heelers said, "look down your block. No niggers have moved in. And they won't, the Mayor'll take care of things."

While Daley was setting his legal department in motion to gain an injunction to halt the marches, the demonstrators announced their next stop. It would be Cicero—the home of Al Capone.

Although King would confirm the Cicero march,

according to Don Rose, CCCO's PR man, the announcement was first released to the press by Jesse, "who
seriously overstepped his authority. I'm not sure we ever
really meant to march into Cicero, at least not then. We
knew the move would really shake the Mayor into action,
so we were batting the threat around for leverage, never
saying anything definite about it."

Don Rose, who was on the Action Committee of the
movement's strategy group, along with Jackson, said,
"Even though things had to be cleared by the Agenda
Committee with the big muckety-mucks like King and
Berry, Jesse would often make major policy statements
without clearing them with anyone. The march announcement came one night when the cameras were on him. He
couldn't resist saying something sensational that would get
his name in the paper. What you did in those days for the
sake of unity was never to call anybody down in public, so
when newsmen asked me when we were going into Cicero,
I could only say 'it's under discussion'—which it was. But
Jesse's talking to the press brought things to a head much
quicker. It forced the issue when it was not the goal of the
Chicago movement to force it."

On August 24, a Loop daily quoted Jackson as
saying, "If we don't go to Cicero, we can't go back to
Mississippi. Some of us live in Mississippi, so by virtue of
that logic, we're going into Cicero. Negroes work there but
can't live there."

The next day, a newspaper article showed King
regaining the reins of leadership by enlarging on Jackson's
statement: 'We're not only going to walk in Cicero, we're
going to work there and live there."

Daley, whose Democratic machine was already
shaken by two racial riots, weeks of white attacks on black
rightists, and a threatened white backlash at the polls, saw
Armageddon looming. If King took 3,000 followers into
Cicero, a bleached community of 70,000, which in 1951

had violently expelled a Negro couple trying to move in, he could not guarantee that the marchers would march out again alive. The Negro couple were the parents of CBS-TV correspondent Michele Clark, killed in an airplane crash in December 1972.

In a race against time, Daley's political machinery produced an injunction limiting the number of marchers to 500. There could only be one march a day and a twenty-four hour advance notice had to be submitted to the police superintendent. In addition night marches were proscribed, as well as marches between the hours of 7:30 and 9 A.M.

King called the city's move "unjust, illegal, and unconstitutional." In a vituperative mood, he said, "We are prepared to put thousands into the streets if need be. The city hasn't seen the number of people we can put there. We're marching for something that should have been ours at birth. If the city wants a moratorium on marching then they should put a moratorium on injustice."

Two days before the marchers were to take to the streets, Daley gave in. He called a summit meeting of the city's business, civic, religious, and civil rights leaders and gave the King-Raby team the open housing pact they had been clamoring for all summer.

King was lavish in his praise of the agreement: "The total eradication of housing discrimination has been made possible. . . . Never before has such a far-reaching move been made."

The Mayor was also euphoric. "This is a great day in the history of our city."

All the voices of the white establishment chimed in with promises of good faith to work for open housing.

Archbishop John Cardinal Cody, whom the black community affectionately dubbed "Louisiana Fats," with a billion dollars worth of property, including slum housing, under his jurisdiction and a spiritual treasury of 2.5 million souls, stoutly pledged his support. Yet white mobs who had been attacking black demonstrators were predominantly Catholic and promised to hit him where it would hurt—in the collection plate. Later a black priest in the Chicago archdiocese would publicly call Cody an "unconscious racist."

The Chicago Housing Authority committed itself to lease the best housing available for welfare cases without regard to race, and public aid recipients would be encouraged to seek accommodations without regard to discriminatory practices in white communities. It also committed itself to curtail building of any more high rise apartments in the ghetto. As one Chicago style orator said, "No more will your children have to pee in the elevator."

The Chicago Real Estate Board also pledged itself to a new commitment. However, in the same breath, it announced that it would continue its legal attack on Illinois Governor Otto Kerner's state executive order banning discrimination in real estate listings. "The Real Estate Board is a prisoner of prejudice," said Len O'Connor, a stoney-faced news commentator with NBC's WMAQ-TV. "Its major source of supply and demand is prejudiced. So this compromise is spurious."

Chicago mortgage groups said it was their continuing policy to lend money without racial restriction for home purchases anywhere in the metropolitan area. This brought smiles of incredulity. The Community Relations Service (CRS) boldly vowed to inquire into support by the Federal Deposit Insurance Corporation and the Federal Savings and Loan Insurance Corporation of institutions that practiced discrimination. Unfortunately, CRS had no muscle.

But the behavior of the Chicago Human Relations Commission, which has had a record of dragging its feet for Negro house hunters, aroused the gravest suspicions. It promised to beef up its staff and begin initiating complaints against realtors guilty of discrimination. Negroes like Harvey Reynolds, who had gone to thirty-three white brokers and fruitlessly protested to the commission when he was turned away, wondered why any promise was needed to enforce an existing law.

Needless to say, the charges of sell-out by militants, who felt the black bourgeois on the negotiating team were out of step with the interests of the poor, permeated the claims of accomplishment.

Robert Lucas, the Chicago leader of CORE, now the executive director of the Kenwood-Oakland Community Organization, was fuming, and so was Chester Robinson from the West Side Organization. "This agreement is a lot of words that give us nothing specific we can understand. We want it to say: apartments should be painted once a year. Community people should have jobs in their community. There's a poverty program training people to be punch press operators and the presses are all getting automated. This situation is just pathetic. We're sick and tired of middle-class people telling us what we want."

Despite such dissatisfaction, King called a "victory rally" in a Baptist church on the west side. After numerous pep talks on the agreement, King soberly said, "Morally we ought to have what we say in the slogan, Freedom Now. But it all doesn't come now. That's a sad fact you have to live with." To whip faithful fervor back into his followers, he also said, "If these agreements aren't carried out, Chicago hasn't seen a demonstration yet."

Across the street from the church in a crowded bar, a bluesy hymn of despair wailed from the juke box—"Let's Go Get Stoned." In light of the developments going on in the church, the message made sense.

While King jetted in and out of Chicago, focusing on other national concerns, he learned that the movement had precipitated some unexpected developments. The white backlash, created by the open housing pact and the feeling that the Mayor had rewarded the rioters but ignored white rights, had jolted some bolts loose from the Daley political machine. The first fatality in the November election was U. S. Senator Paul Douglas, a kindly University of Chicago economist. As expected, Douglas received more than 75 percent of all votes in Negro precincts, proving that Daley was still the leader in the black community. However, in white areas, his losses were traumatic. In Cicero, where Douglas had produced a respectable showing in his last campaign, he received barely 25 percent of the vote. Charles H. Percy, the Republican boy wonder of Bell & Howell, emerged from the ashes of Douglas' defeat as the new U.S. Senator from Illinois. With Daley's own bid for a fourth four-year term just around the corner, it took little imagination to ascertain which group, the black civil rightists or the white home owners, would soon become expendable.

Buoyed by the Mayor's upset, King geared up to direct his efforts toward Daley's political lifeline—the vote—by calling for an intensive, massive campaign to register Negroes before the 1967 mayoral election. He also summoned a dozen SCLC aides from Atlanta to mobilize the dormant political black power.

His actions produced a frightened gasp from City Hall, but the tension waned after King weakened his move on November 9 with: "I'm not leading any campaign against Mayor Daley. I'm leading a campaign against slums. I don't engage in politics and the Chicago Freedom Movement does not endorse any candidates or engage in politics." King further stated that he would not endorse Dick Gregory for mayor. No one expected King's support to pull enough votes from Daley to throw the election to Republican John Waner. However, by leading a strong Democratic boycott at the polls, King could have shown the Mayor that blacks were no longer in his hip pocket and had to be wooed with political appointments and top level jobs like the folks in his own neighborhood.

King's tepid announcement was symptomatic of the

split in the CCCO leadership, eventually the same type of disunity over goals that culminated in the staggering defeat for King and the movement in the Albany campaign in 1962. Most of the younger, more militant blacks, according to Raby, wanted to mount an all-out attack on the Daley organization, which they considered the only way to accomplish lasting political and social change. Less numerous but better organized and more influential conservative elements stressed that Mayor Daley had made civil rights concessions when sufficient pressure was exerted, while the gains under a new white power structure would be highly uncertain. So in order to appease the conflicting black ideology, King apparently decided to "shake the Mayor but not break him."

The voter registration drive which was kicked off on December 2 soon proved to be a bust. Upon announcing the drive, King said, "Only an alert and informed electorate can eliminate injustices inherent in slum communities. The people, when they become aware of the issues, will make their feelings known to the candidate, whether it be Mayor Daley or a ward alderman." But it would not be that simple. In the South blacks and whites had fought and died before the black man became enfranchised. In the North, blacks already had the right to vote, but they felt their vote would never change the hopelessness of their lives. In 1962, an Urban League study showed only 63 percent of the blacks had registered to vote as compared with 78 percent of the whites. Of the blacks in Chicago who had registered, only 47 percent actually went to the polls—even in a presidential election.

SCLC staffers faced an insurmountable obstacle in their canvass of black areas. "A lot of folks won't even talk to us," said Lester Hankerson, who was beaten in Grenada, Mississippi, for registering blacks, the job he was trying to do in Chicago. "I would still rather be working in Mississippi. People here are not interested in first class citizenship."

"I have never seen such hopelessness," Hosea Williams said. "The Negroes of Chicago have a greater feeling of powerlessness than I ever saw. They don't participate in the governmental process because they're beaten down psychologically. We are used to working with people who want to be free."

Hankerson and Williams had run into a stone wall of welfare colonialism, which has replaced the political process as the only form of organization the ghetto knows, especially on the west side.

It is a process that makes blacks vote their fears and not their dreams. It is the kind of process that would declare Mickey Mouse a winner in the ghetto, if the Mayor slated him. Whatever candidate is elected, they feel, will not change their lives, but a tank of gas will get you to the Loop—if you can afford a car. A chicken, well, you can eat it. And a pint of wine will help you forget it all.

The machine involves the kind of process that in April, 1964, elected a dead white man to Congress and defeated his opponent, a young black woman, who was very much alive. Because of ill health, Thomas J. O'Brien, an elderly, fourteen-term congressman, had been unable to campaign for office in a predominantly black district on the west side. (Even well politicians seldom campaign on the west side.) On primary day, he died. But that did not stop black voters from giving him an overwhelming vote of support against Mrs. Brenetta Howell, a dedicated civic and civil rights leader. (In 1973, Mrs. Howell was appointed administrator of the Governor's Office of Human Resources by Governor Dan Walker.)

A former pastor of the Woodlawn Mennonite Church explained the paradox this way: "Every welfare recipient is afraid to oppose the wishes of the precinct captain. That accounts for the reluctance to register and vote for a reform candidate. Everyone living in public housing is afraid. They have been told that the machine alderman is the one who insures them living quarters, who keeps them on the welfare rolls. It is a false but a very effective threat. When you've got so little, you just aren't going to gamble."

Since King had no jobs to offer, no food to give, no shelter to share, since King had only a message of hope for those who had no hope, history repeated itself on April 4, 1967. Dick Gregory, crippled by his comedian image, by the superhuman exercise of running as a write-in candidate, and by his built-in voter resistance, received 1.9 percent of the vote.

In a perceptive column on April 5, 1967, the kind he writes about blacks every election year, Pulitzer Prize winner Mike Royko of the *Chicago Daily News* said this about the voting melodrama which has blacks screaming about abuse and exploitation on every day except election day:

> Black power was available in sizeable quantities in Chicago Tuesday. And a person didn't have to march, sing, riot, or boycott to get it.
>
> It was inside the voting machine. By pulling a lever or using a pencil, the Negro could have thrown a scare into City Hall.
>
> Instead Chicago Negroes went out and gave something like 80 to 85 percent of their vote to Mayor Richard J. Daley; about 10 percent to John Waner and just a dib and dab to Dick Gregory. And Daley didn't even campaign in the Negro areas.
>
> I'm not saying they shouldn't have voted for Mayor Daley. If he is their man—fine. But is he their man? If so, they show it in strange ways.
>
> They should remember that the city was in an uproar most of last summer because the civil rights wing of the Negro Population was marching to protest the way the Negro was being treated by the mayor's administration.

It was the mayor's house that was being picketed for the last couple of summers. It was the administration's school system that they boycotted and raged against.

It was the mayor's police department that was accused of being unkind to Negroes. The mayor's firemen were the ones shot at and stoned. And it was his fire department that was accused of being segregated.

The inconsistency mounts when you consider that the poorest Negro areas—the most riot-inclined areas—were where Daley got his best support. He didn't do much better in his own neighborhood than he did in some west side wards.

And finally, if there is a leader of Chicago's Negroes, he is Richard J. Daley, that rosy-cheeked Irishman from the Back of the Yards.

So this summer, don't sing me that old refrain of "black power." The voting machine was listening Tuesday, but he couldn't hear you even humming.

After winning his fourth term by a margin of more than half-a-million votes, polling 73 percent of the ballots cast, including a five-to-one victory in the Negro wards, Daley recognized as a foregone conclusion that his future powerhold on Chicago would not depend on his taking bold positions on civil rights.

In his inaugural address, Daley shed any trace of "enlightened bossism," which meant never again would he have to be cordial to the likes of King. "As long as I am mayor, law and order will prevail." Even before the election, Alderman Thomas Keane had tipped the Mayor's hand on just what blacks could expect from the city's far-reaching housing agreement. "There is no housing agreement," Keane said. "There were only certain suggestions put down and goals to be sought."

King continued turning his attention more toward other national concerns, and long time activist Al Raby resigned, supposedly to write a paper on black power. But privately he said, "I will no longer be a sponge for Negro frustration. And when the next riots hit, the whites had better not look to me to cool things. That was what the Chicago Freedom Movement was trying to do, but the Mayor wasn't listening. So now, I'll sit back and help bury Chicago. So what?"

And A. A. (Sammy) Rayner, a black Chicago independent alderman, added: "I wonder if any of us can accomplish what we would like. Look at Malcolm X, Dr. King, Bobby and John Kennedy. Did they do what they wanted? I have seen for myself that I can't get to the mountain top. I've got to ask if good guys ever win, except in the movies."

Perhaps it would be of value to reflect on the Chicago movement specifically in terms of what went wrong, not so much for its historical significance, but as a score card for charting the advancement of the struggle as it limps through the 1970s under the new leader, the Reverend Jesse Jackson.

First, politics as the art of compromise is a truism—true, perhaps, everywhere but Chicago. Compromise denotes reciprocity. But Chicago blacks—the largest ethnic group in the city—are bargaining from a position of powerlessness. They could have power through the ballot, but either they give away their vote to the Daley machine freely or they don't vote at all. The threat of violence is also a possibility, but blacks riot in their own neighborhoods and perpetrate fratricide, not genocide. Money talks, but too many of the black leaders—businessmen, ministers, educators—have been co-opted because they need the Mayor's blessings to survive. Thus when the Mayor makes a deal, it is from the deck of expediency, issuing out the type of concessions that provides temporary relief but never permanent cure. Structures may be overhauled at the top—a different Irish police superintendent or a different Irish school superintendent—but the bottom remains the same.

Indicative of a Mayor Daley style compromise are the Robert Taylor Homes, constructed in 1960. Congressman Metcalfe, then an alderman, had been pushing for open housing. As a concession to Metcalfe—Dawson's protege—the Mayor consented for the new projects to be built in the alderman's district. Metcalfe accepted the proposal, believing the new projects would be better than the ramshackle shanties the blacks were living in. Today more than 30,000 blacks are stacked up sixteen tiers high in the Taylor concrete reservations. And the kids still pee in the elevators. King accepted the paper open housing victory, apparently because he misjudged the resiliency of the Northern bigot. In the South, desegregation was brutally resisted. In the North, desegregation was accepted through gentlemanly compromise—the type of compromise that has resulted in Chicago's still reigning as the most segregated city in America in 1974. It was Northern hypocrisy's finest hour, raising the question: was the more than $500,000 whites raised in Chicago for the Selma campaign a subtle message for King to stay in the South?

Jesse Jackson, the new leader, would circumvent Chicago's most sensitive issue, open housing, by not dealing with it at all. But would he too fall into the trap of compromise without organizing the resources of blacks to present something of value to compromise with?

What about tactics? Strategy?

Would blacks still be marching around the Loop in the seventies or could the new leader pull blacks up to the mountain top of political power? In Gary, Newark, Detroit, Los Angeles, and the more than one hundred other cities that have elected black mayors, nonviolent civil rights campaigns are anachronisms.

There was much leeway for King's abortive thunderbolt. In the South he had never confronted a political machine. How could there even be a machine locking blacks in, when the emphasis was on locking blacks out of the electoral process vis-à-vis intimidation, the grandfather clause, and illiteracy tests, which stood until after the Civil Rights Act of 1965? The masses of blacks in the South had been enfranchised only one year when King came to Chicago. There, office seekers had to court the black community for votes. In Chicago the white or black powerbrokers who represent Daley instead of their constituency have to be courted.

According to Chuck Stone in *Black Political Power in America*,* black civil rightists have been unsuccessful in the five critical areas other special groups have used to gain political power, such as:

• Political oscillation—threatening to take their votes to another candidate.

• Retribution—punishing politicians through a "backlash vote" for opposing the group's interest.

• Educational propaganda—influencing other members of the electorate to a sympathetic adoption of the group's point of view through the use of leaflets, meetings, and public statements.

• Lobbying in Congress and state legislatures—for legislation which promotes the group's interest or against legislation which threatens the group's survival and political power.

• Proportionate control of policy-making jobs in government—placing its members in sensitive positions in order to influence public policy favorably toward their interest.

*(Indianapolis: Bobbs-Merrill, 1970).

Stone concludes: "Civil rights demonstrators make good marchers, but poor politicians. Civil rights leaders can get a good boycott, but they can never get out a good vote."

The momentum of the King coalition would alter this maxim in the South. Under the new leader, would the maxim change in the North? Or would the tactics of attempting to preach people to the polls overshadow the less glamorous work of precinct organization? Looking back over the Chicago movement, Don Rose said, "The leaders should have launched a direct frontal attack on the machine, instead of dancing on the fringes. I doubt if we could have beat the Mayor in 1967, but we could have laid the framework for 1971. Voter registration can work as it has for others. But it has to be done Chicago style, on the precinct level, neighborhood by neighborhood. And you have to offer concrete programs, as well as education, instead of tons of charisma vis-à-vis the lectern and television. With the right tactics and King's name we could have set the stage."

Could the new leader devise the correct tactics or would he just be glossed over in the annals of Chicago politics as "a very good preacher"?

The price tag on freedom runs high. But how many blacks are willing to pay the price? When King came to Chicago, it was not only the white bigots that pressured him to leave town but also the traditional Toms. It was the J. H. Jacksons, the Metcalfes, the Dawsons, the NAACP, and numerous church groups that weighed like a heavy yoke around his neck. In several marches, nine-tenths of Chicago's then nearly one million blacks stayed at home. If the leader can't change the followers, the more alike they become. What price freedom?

By mid-1967, the civil rights battleground was littered with the debris of broken dreams and broken men. In the wake of Raby's resignation, CCCO crumbled. SNCC and CORE were still agitating, but their high frequency oration did not obscure the fact that they had few listeners. With the housing agreement signed, Dr. King could leave town gracefully and SCLC could claim a victory for its first and last great confrontation in the North. After King and his aides left town, the responsibility of watchdogging the housing pact was turned over to local leaders. Unfortunately, "respectable rights groups," such as the Urban League and the NAACP, could provide little monitoring. Both were hamstrung into low profile roles because of their conciliatory approach.

When the dust cleared from the tramp, tramp of marching feet, the only bright ray of hope left was Operation Breadbasket, a program King had assigned to Jackson, believing that the private sector could be shaken up more readily than the Mayor's unyielding political machine. Quietly, SCLC's Operation Breadbasket had been gaining momentum since the latter part of 1966 but receiving little attention from the media, except from the *Chicago Daily Defender.*

By January 1967, the *New York Times* had discovered Breadbasket, reporting that the program had produced 900 jobs for blacks at five dairies, three soft drink companies, and three retail grocery chains in the Chicago ghetto. Through economic boycotts, mostly by ministers whom Jackson had recruited earlier, Breadbasket had also forced the white stores to stock and display the wares of black-owned businesses, as well as to use black banks.

That Jackson would one day represent virtually all that was left of the SCLC movement was unthinkable at the time. Jackson was given the Breadbasket assignment because he was the only King organizer based in Chicago. He didn't have a church base and could be cut down if necessary, it was thought. (Jackson did not graduate from the seminary, but he was ordained on

June 30, 1968, by the Reverends C. L. Franklin and Clay Evans.)

"Appointing a pastor to the post would have spelled trouble because the preachers were in very competitive roles. If a minister from a large congregation had been chosen, other ministers would have been irked because they didn't receive the post. To neutralize the friction is one reason why the Breadbasket meetings were always held on Saturdays in order not to compete with the churches," Don Rose said.

"Let's face it," Andy Young added, "Jesse always was a brilliant guy. And none of us wanted to spend another day in Chicago. We wanted to go home to the South, to familiar terrain. But Jesse's attitude was different. He didn't see any difference between a Southern and a Northern racist. He just had the zeal to fight both types, wherever he found them."

Besides Jackson's maturing into an impressive organizer, his gift of rhetoric was creating waves of enthusiasm at the Saturday morning forums, which started at the Seminary. As former *Chicago Today's* woman's editor, Dorothy Collins, told her coworkers after hearing Jackson, "King gave a hell of a speech, but you should have heard that kid, Jesse." Attorney Anna Langford, who in 1971 became Chicago's first woman alderman, came away with a similar impression: "After I heard that kid speak, I felt that all the rest of the Breadbasket speakers could go home—including King."

Time was running out for Jesse to remain a kid. Great responsibility loomed ahead. The Chicago movement was falling into his lap. All the issues that plagued King in the sixties would become Jackson's burden in the seventies. Blacks and whites alike were drooling to the cadence of his rhetoric. He was being labeled a rising star, a soaring meteorite. But in the downtown newspapers he was still being called an aide to King, a protégé. Just around the corner in Memphis, an assassin's bullet awaited the leader. And then in Chicago, and perhaps someday in the nation, the new black leader would be Jesse Jackson.

*Truth crushed to earth shall
rise again.*

Dr. Martin Luther King, Jr.

April 4, 1968, was a day of shock, of guilt, of sorrow—
of white fear. If they slew the apostle of nonviolence
and love, what would the alternative be?

April 4, 1968, was the day black America lost hope.
If they slew the Dreamer, what would happen to the black
man's Dream?

Martin Luther King, Jr., was shot down while
organizing a protest for the rights of garbage men. As
swiftly as that chapter closed on the balcony of the
Lorraine Motel in Memphis, another was being written.

April 4, 1968, was Jesse Jackson's date with an image
that was never meant to be. Aided by the media, the

tragedy of Memphis would force him into the public mind not only as undisputed leader of the civil rights movement in Chicago, but also as heir to King's legacy in the nation. It was never meant to be. King named the Reverend Ralph Abernathy as his successor shortly after the assassination of John F. Kennedy. It was never meant to be—at least not yet. Age, experience, and service disqualified Jackson. But events rooted in despair and J. J.'s own ingenuity, obscured by that tragic day in Memphis, would eventually make it so.

It would take only one year for the image making to swing full circle.

The November 1969 issue of *Playboy*, after an exhaustive, in-depth interview with Jackson, labeled him the "fiery heir apparent to Martin Luther King." It also said: "The Reverend Jackson's first national exposure came as a result of his closeness to Dr. King. He was talking to King on the porch of the Lorraine Motel in Memphis when the fatal shot was fired and cradled the dying man in his arms."

On the second anniversary of the martyr's death, Jesse appeared on the cover of the April 6, 1970, issue of *Time*. The inside story once again pointed out: "Jackson was the last man King spoke to before he was shot in Memphis. Jesse ran to the balcony, held King's head, but it was too late." On April 8, 1968, the *Chicago Defender* reported: "Jackson, whose face appeared drawn, talked briefly with newsmen about the moments just before and after the shooting occurred. He said he rushed to Dr. King's side immediately, but got no response when he asked, 'Doc, can you hear me?' "

Before and after the *Playboy* and *Time* accounts at least 100 other articles claimed that Jackson cradled King, that he was the last man King spoke to before he died, or that Jackson later attended a Chicago City Council meeting with the blood of King on his shirt.

These accounts, of course, were accepted as fact by

everyone—except King's staff, who had been eyewitnesses to the assassination.

Here are their reactions:

Hosea Williams, then voter-registration project director for SCLC: "The only person who cradled Dr. King was Abernathy. The last man King spoke to was Solomon Jones. It's a helluva thing to capitalize on a man's death, especially one you professed to love." Williams is now a Georgia state legislator.

Chauncey Eskridge, attorney for Dr. King: "If anyone could have gotten blood on their clothes, other than Abernathy, it must have come from the balcony after King's body was removed. Jackson's appearance at Chicago's City Council with that blood on his shirt was not only deception but sacrilege. The City Council meeting offered him a public forum to be seen and heard, and that was what prompted him to appear."

Andy Young, SCLC executive director, now a Georgia congressman: "The blood, the cradling, were all things I read in the newspaper and they are all mysteries to me."

The Reverend Ralph D. Abernathy, then vice-president and treasurer of SCLC: "I am sure Reverend Jackson would not say to *me* that he cradled Dr. King. I am sure that Reverend Jackson would realize that *I* was the person who was on the balcony with Dr. King and did not leave his side until he was pronounced dead at St. Joseph's Hospital in Memphis. I am sure that he would not say to *me* that he even came near Dr. King after Doc was shot."

Ben Branch, leader of Operation Breadbasket's band: "My guess is Jesse smeared the blood on his shirt after getting it off the balcony. But who knows where he got it from. All I can say is that Jesse didn't touch him. I think that should answer it all."

The following is a partial reconstruction of the King assassination, which focuses primarily on events after the murder, especially on Jackson's moves and how they were perceived by his coworkers. This is the first time, according to King's aides whom I interviewed, that the view from their side has been sought or reported.

It was 5:55 P.M. that April evening and Dr. King would be late again. Dinner was at five and he'd be lucky if he made it by seven—he could never keep up with his busy schedule. After rushing through a shave, he walked out of Room 306 onto the balcony of the Lorraine Motel in Memphis stuffing in his shirttail, and he began bantering with his aides who were standing in the courtyard below.

Among those in the courtyard was Solomon Jones, an aide, leaning outside a white Cadillac limousine, which was lent to King by the local undertaker for use during his stay in Memphis. Near the right rear wheel was King's chief lieutenant Andy Young; at the left rear wheel was King's attorney Chauncey Eskridge. Behind them were the Reverend James Bevel, an aide, and Bernard Lee, King's personal secretary. They were all waiting to go to dinner with King, at the home of the Reverend Samuel (Billy) Kyles, pastor of Monumental Baptist Church in Memphis.

Dr. King emerged from Room 306 to discuss briefly a pending federal court action which might put an injunction against the upcoming march on behalf of striking garbage men. Signaling to Jones, he told him to start the car. "I'll be down in a minute." He then returned to his room to hurry Abernathy along. Abernathy was sprinkling on some of Martin's fragrant after shave lotion. Seeing that he wasn't ready, King said, "I'll wait for you on the balcony."

Jackson, clad in brown trousers and a matching turtleneck, dashed down the angular metal staircase. He was stopped halfway by Chauncey Eskridge who chided him for not being properly dressed. Since King had said Jesse could go to dinner along with the other staff members, Eskridge said, "Where's your tie? You better finish dressing."

"I am dressed," Jackson insisted.

"Well, I'm going to tell Doc about you as soon as he comes out of his room," Chauncey warned, but Jesse could tell by the tone of his voice he was only kidding. He continued down the steps and into the courtyard, walking toward Eskridge.

At 5:59 P.M. Dr. King returned to the balcony, spotted Jesse, and said, "I want you to come to dinner with me." Those in the courtyard knew that the personal invitation was Dr. King's way of making up with Jesse. Jesse's behavior had been irritating to King at the last staff meeting. In fact, Eskridge had never seen his boss speak so harshly to an aide before.

In the last staff meeting the Saturday before on March 30 in his study at Atlanta's Ebenezer Baptist Church, Dr. King abandoned his usual habit of shaming his aides or "wooing them with love." He jumped on everybody. His staff had not been around when he needed them most. Dr. King had summoned everyone to Memphis to aid him in the city's first march. Nobody responded except Abernathy and Lee. "We were trying to organize the Poor People's March," Young explained. "We felt he didn't have any business going to Memphis. We were kind of mad that in the midst of our big thing Doc would let himself get distracted by some little march in Memphis. Since the Reverends James Lawson and H. Ralph Jackson were in charge, we figured his staff could handle things."

But on March 28, the worst happened. A riot flared, sparked by a black gang called the Invaders. A seventeen-year-old youth was killed by police, sixty others were injured, and 400 were arrested. King had to be spirited away for his own personal safety. This had prompted a cartoon in the *Memphis Commercial-Appeal* with the caption "Chicken à-la-King." It had been embarrassing for Dr. King, and he felt the scene might not have happened if his aides had been there to organize the crowds.

Attention turned to the Poor People's campaign and

there was more friction. Although it had already been voted on a month earlier in Miami, Jesse and the Reverend Bevel kept pressing with negative questions: "Does it make sense? Can we organize all the poor across the nation? Can we control them once we get there? What happens if Washington doesn't respond?" King became so disgusted that he walked out of the room. Jesse ran behind him to continue the discussion. King wheeled around and snapped, "If you are so interested in doing your own thing that you can't do what the organization is structured to do, go ahead. If you want to carve out your own niche in society, go ahead, but for God's sake don't bother me."

Thus the staff had to return from Atlanta to Memphis to schedule a new march and to pray this time it would be nonviolent. At this critical hour the slogans of black power were threatening to drown out the hymn, "We Shall Overcome."

Until now, King had not taken the opportunity to talk over things with Jesse. The day before, Jesse had joined Abernathy and King to accommodate photographers, almost in the same spot where King was standing now. But it would be at dinner that King expected to settle any differences lingering from the disorderly staff meeting.

Jesse took the opening from Dr. King, on the metal balcony, to introduce Ben Branch, an aspiring saxophonist whose band had been well received at the Saturday morning Operation Breadbasket meetings in Chicago.

After a quick exchange of greetings, King leaned forward, putting both hands on the green iron railing of the balcony, and asked Branch to play a special request at a rally later that evening. "I want you to play my song tonight, play 'Precious Lord.' Play it real pretty."

"I sure will," Branch answered, pleased that he had been asked. Solomon Jones, feeling a chill in the air, called up to King, "You'd better get your coat. It's getting cold."

"Okay," King said, "I'll get it." He straightened up to listen to the Reverend Samuel Kyles, who was also on the balcony near the stairs. "Doc, I'm going to get my car, they all can't go with Jones. I'll take some of the load." Taking six steps down the stairs, Kyles chatted on. Words that Dr. King never heard.

At 6:01 P.M. the sound of something like a car backfiring jolted Kyles back around. What he saw stiffened him momentarily so his legs couldn't move in the direction his brain told him to go. He rushed over to King, then ran back to his room, fell on the bed, and started screaming.

In Room 306, Abernathy heard a firecracker. He jumped, looked over his shoulder, and saw the top of Martin's shoes. He said, "Oh, my God, Martin's been shot." Kneeling over him, he could see the fright in his eyes. He patted him on his left cheek to calm him and get his attention. " 'Martin can you hear me? This is Ralph.' His lips pursed to answer me, but he couldn't speak. He looked me dead in the eye and it seemed as if he was saying, 'For God's sake don't let me down. You're the only person in the world I can depend on.' "

Abernathy then looked down in the courtyard. Everybody had hit the ground. He called out to Kyles, "Cut that crying out and call an ambulance." Kyles could not get a line. The lady who owned the black motel had suffered a heart attack at the switchboard.

Andy Young and an unidentified white man reached King's side about the same time. The stranger fitted a towel over King's wound. Young felt his pulse. He thought he felt something. "King was only wounded, he's alive." Abernathy cradled King in his lap.

Hosea Williams had just stuck his key in the door. His room was directly below King's. "I looked up and saw Dr. King's legs. I recognized his socks. They were black, ribbed support hose. I ran upstairs and saw that the bullet had torn the right side of his face away. I broke down."

From Room 215, Earl Caldwell, a black reporter from the *New York Times,* raced out thinking the motel had been bombed. He looked up and saw the trousers legs on the edge of the balcony. Rushing up the stairs, he looked down into King's eyes. The color was fading from them. He knew King was dead. He had to remember he was still a reporter. He rushed to a pay phone down in the courtyard and saw Jesse Jackson and James Bevel in a daze. He heard Jesse moan: "We were all standing below him and he was standing up there and. . . ."*

A photographer for the Public Broadcasting Library, documenting the Poor People's campaign, caught forever in his camera lens all those who were on the balcony seconds after the gun blast. They were pointing in the direction from where the shots were fired, a two-story brick rooming house about 200 feet across the street. Jesse was not identified in photos as being among them.

Hosea Williams said: "Jesse crawled up the staircase sometime after the photographer arrived. Some of those in the courtyard thought they were being fired upon too, so they took cover. I can't remember him crying. He just stood there. Then, I think he ran for a phone to call Coretta."

Hordes of police swarmed into the courtyard minutes after the shot. One had called an ambulance from his police car radio. At 6:06 P.M., two policemen, along with Young and Eskridge, helped lift Dr. King onto the stretcher. "As I grabbed hold of the cot, a white cloth someone had covered the wound with had fallen off. I saw this large hole in his jaw. I could see some of his teeth. We helped Abernathy into the ambulance. Solomon Jones, Lee, Andy, and I jumped into the Cadillac to follow Doc to the hospital," Eskridge said.

*Gerold Frank, *An American Death* (New York: Doubleday, 1972).

In Atlanta, Mrs. King had just returned from shopping for her daughter, Yolanda. The phone rang. It was Jesse. "Coretta, Doc just got shot. I would advise you to take the next thing smoking." Mrs. King wanted more details. To calm her, Jesse said, "He was shot in the shoulder. Why don't you come to the motel, and we'll get you to the hospital."

From the hospital, minutes later, Andy Young called Coretta King. "He's all right. He was shot in the neck, but still, maybe you should bring someone with you."

Back in the courtyard, Ben Branch busied himself cursing at the police officers. It was the only thing to do that made sense to him at the time. "Because I thought the police shot King, they had been watching our every move all day."

The camera crews started arriving about 6:25 P.M., NBC first, then ABC and CBS. "Jesse called to me from across the lot and said, 'Don't talk to them!' I agreed because I thought he meant none of us were supposed to talk until Abernathy got back from the hospital. So I walked away," Branch said.

Hosea Williams: "I was in my room. I looked out and saw Jesse talking to these TV people. I came out to hear what was being said. I heard Jesse say, 'Yes, I was the last man in the world King spoke to.' I knew Jesse was lying because Solomon Jones was the one and I had a feeling about what Jesse was trying to pull. I climbed over the railing and was going to stomp him into the ground but a cop grabbed me. I called Jesse a dirty, stinking, lying so-and-so, or something like that. I don't remember the exact words. What I did was wrong, I guess, but I am a very high tempered man. I had no hangups about Jesse talking to the press. That was okay, but why lie? Why capitalize on another man's name and image—a dead man, who can't speak up for himself?"

Later that evening, NBC newsman David Burrington,

reporting from Memphis, said, "The Reverend Jesse Jackson of Chicago, one of King's closest aides, was beside him when he was shot while standing on a veranda outside his motel room."

By 1 A.M. everything had been taken care of. Young, Lee, Abernathy, and Eskridge had waited at St. Joseph's Hospital and listened painfully to the chief neurosurgeon tell them he had done all he could do. At 7:30 A.M. a police escort directed them to the airport to pick up Mrs. King only to find she had cancelled her flight. The mayor of Atlanta, Ivan Allen, had met her at the airport and officially confirmed what she already knew. Mrs. King had returned home to console her four children. After King's body had been identified at the morgue, the staff all returned to the motel, emotionally drained, trying to pull themselves together to think out their next moves.

An executive emergency meeting formed as staff members drifted into Room 306. They still had to go on with the Dream. Their leader was gone, but blacks still needed leadership. Martin Luther King, Jr., had asked only two things of those around him: that SCLC be the instrument to carry out his work and that Abernathy take charge if anything ever happened. "Ralph, we're with you," James Bevel said. "Just tell us what to do." Bringing Ralph Abernathy to the forefront was a mere formality. Dr. King had ordered it entered into the SCLC bylaws after the assassination of John F. Kennedy that Ralph would be his successor. Ralph stepped forward and slid into the chair King had relaxed in earlier that day and began officiating as best he could over the staff meeting. But only one thought tugged at his brain. Days before, Martin had told him, "I'll never live to be forty. I'll never make it."

Someone missed Jesse Jackson. Funeral arrangements and the honor guard details were being discussed, and Jesse should have been there. Ralph explained that he had given

Jesse permission to go back to Chicago. "Jesse said he was going there to organize planeloads of people to come to the funeral."

"That's strange," Hosea Williams remembered saying to himself. "As he was packing, he told me he was ill and had to return to Chicago to see his doctor for medication."

Around 6 o'clock the following morning, the staff members saw Jackson again—on the NBC "Today Show." "Somebody called me, come quick, look who's on TV. I was shocked," Hosea Williams said. "The man had just told me he was sick and there he was looking as healthy as I was. I just don't see how he could have left, 'cause Memphis just wasn't the place to leave. I could not leave. I stayed with Martin until they put him in the ground."

"I thought it was ironic," Chauncey Eskridge said, "here we were prepared to go get King's body from the funeral home—the whole staff—except Jesse. While we're getting the body, he was making news."

Jackson had returned to a Chicago in flames. No sooner had the word crept from black to black, from ghetto to ghetto on the west side than the residents declared war. Their targets were buildings, street lights, firemen, windows of white- and black-owned businesses, store merchandise, everything within a three-mile reach of their frenzied rage. When the smoke cleared, nine people lay dead—all black. One thousand were homeless—all black—and the $10-million property damage in the ghetto would drive many storekeepers away.

Mayor Daley, who surveyed this pit of Acheron from a helicopter, damned the plunder of his city and immediately found a solution:

"I have conferred with the superintendent of police this morning and I gave the following instructions, '*Shoot to kill* any arsonist or anyone with a Molotov cocktail in his hand because they're potential murderers, and to issue a police order to shoot to maim or cripple anyone looting any stores in our city.' Above all the crimes, arson is to me the most hideous and worst crime of any and should be dealt with in this fashion."

Former police superintendent James Conlisk questioned the order: "Some of the looters are only seven and eight years old; many others are fourteen, fifteen, and sixteen. Do you mean we should shoot them down too?" Mayor Daley clarified his position, saying, "Mace can detain youngsters."

City officials were both angered and puzzled by the violence. Mayor Daley could not understand it at all: "I never believed it could happen here." Conlisk said: "In my opinion, these were people prone to thievery and they seized upon the opportunity like jackals."

There was, of course, another explanation for the fiery cataclysm.

Some of the blacks, no doubt, were urban pirates bent on sacking the city. Others were dramatizing a love-hate relationship—hating themselves for not loving King enough to follow him when he walked among them. Others would swear that never had they met such a man.

It was King's nonviolent tactics that many of the militant westsiders were opposed to. Not the man. Some felt like Fred Hampton, who was eighteen when he marched with King. (Hampton later became leader of the Illinois Black Panther Party and was killed in his bed by police in 1969.) "I believe there was no such thing as a nonviolent Negro until King and some others invented them. We don't need nonviolence with a violent people. You don't need to practice religion with people who don't practice it themselves. When I marched with King, I would protect myself; I was always a revolutionary, I was never nonviolent," said Fred Hampton. "I saw the things that were happening to the other people and after I took an objective look, I knew a different type weapon would have to be used. Still I had a lot of respect for King," the Panther leader admitted.

Even the tough street gangs tried nonviolence when King came to town. They were also instrumental in keeping the riots from heavily damaging the south side.

King had *lived* with the westsiders; he had come to their pool halls and churches. He was a neighbor; this was novel in itself, since most black leaders settle around the middle-class blacks on the south side. To Chicago blacks—especially those on the west side, who had never been visited by presidents, statesmen, or even their own senators and aldermen—King was a Messiah, more so in death than in life. Hadn't he been crucified?

During the disaster, Jackson pleaded for calm. His message came from the City Council, where a special memorial session had been called by Mayor Daley for honoring Dr. King. "I am calling for nonviolence in the homes, on the streets, in the classrooms, and in our relationships one to another. I'm challenging the youth today to be nonviolent as the greatest expression of faith they can make in Dr. King—to put your rocks down, put your bottles down," Jackson said.

Only twice before had Mayor Daley called special sessions of the City Council to memorialize the dead. One had been called on April 10, 1961, for Dan Ryan, president of the Cook County Board, and the other on November 23, 1963, for the assassinated President John F. Kennedy.

Today's ceremonies were dominated by a three-by-five-foot photo of Dr. King, bordered with black and purple bunting, that had been placed on the rostrum. At each end of the stage were three dozen red roses. The Children's Choir, an integrated group sponsored by the First Unitarian Church of Chicago, sang "Dona Nobis Pacem" by Cherubini and "Lonesome Valley."

Mayor Daley offered a resolution on behalf of himself and the council which pledged to choose a suitable, permanent, and lasting memorial in honor of the Reverend

King. This later turned out to be a boulevard of approximately 100 blocks running through predominantly black neighborhoods. Formerly South Parkway, the boulevard was renamed Dr. Martin Luther King, Jr., Drive. The reaction of J. H. Jackson, King's old nemesis, was to change his church mailing address to Thirty-first Street.

The resolution, adopted unanimously, read: "Whereas Dr. King possessed a deep and abiding conviction that when Americans were confronted with the contradiction between their cherished ideals of brotherhood in the religious sphere and the existence of hatred and racism, they would choose their ideal. And when confronted with the contradiction between their ideals of freedom and justice for all in the political sphere and the existence of poverty and prejudice, they would be faithful to their ideal. . . .

"That the life of Dr. King and his ultimate total sacrifice provide us with the inspiration to deepen our dedication and commitment to the goals for which he gave so much—that the relationships of all men, especially here in our city, be characterized by love and understanding. . . .

"That the advancement of the poor and least endowed be the object of our greatest concern and that we seek a world order in which peace and justice and brotherhood reign supreme . . . ."

If some dissenter had interrupted the pious expressions of the Mayor by shouting, "Bull shit," it would have made more sense than standing knee-deep in the hypocrisy in the City Hall chambers. How easy it is to praise the dead after you have cursed the living. King had brought these same ideals to Chicago during the Freedom Movement and Daley, along with some of the black aldermen sitting there, had murdered the Dream, long before the death of the Dreamer.

The contradiction was elegantly exposed by Jackson. He rose and addressed the council with: "A fitting memorial to King would not be to sit here looking sad and pious but to behave differently." Still wearing the brown turtleneck sweater said to be smeared with the blood of King, he cried, "This blood is on the chest and hands of those who would not have welcomed him here yesterday."

The speech infuriated Chauncey Eskridge and other SCLC staffers. They seriously questioned the source of the blood on Jackson's shirt and felt that wherever it came from, it was being used as a prop to focus media attention on Jackson in an effort to promote him to local and national leadership.

Others, especially the media, thought the move meritorious. For example, *Playboy* (November 1969) said, "That gesture demonstrated both the militant indignation and the dramatic flair that mark Jackson's charismatic style."

Whether dramatic flair or stage prop, the blood-on-the-shirt motif, Jackson's purported position on the Memphis balcony, and the indictments he made to the national TV viewing audience after King's assassination outlined the image he was projecting as a national public figure. The immediate effects of his emerging eminence, however, were more obvious closer to home.

The Saturday after King's murder more than 4,000 people attended Operation Breadbasket's memorial services. The Saturday before, attendance at Breadbasket was less than 400.

At the same time black intellectuals were pleading, "Lord, please don't send us any more Saviors," a new Messiah was born—or at least he would be perceived as such by many of his followers.

The conditions were ripe for a charismatic response to a charismatic leader. The bottom had fallen out of the black community with the death of King. Many blacks needed reassuring that the battle against poverty and discrimination would go on. They needed to hear that the

Dreamer was gone, but not the Dream. They needed someone to kindle in their souls a burning desire to fight on, someone to tell them they could win. All of this Jackson did so well.

Most people who attended the ceremony felt confident that Jackson was the logical choice to carry on King's work in Chicago. He knew just the right words to say. He made everyone, somehow, feel included. Whites left feeling there was still a place for them and their work. They could still be in the thick of things and not be put down by militants calling them "whitey" or "honkey." An observer, a white physician, recalled Jackson exchanging greetings with his followers after the service: "As welfare mothers, policemen, gang leaders, politicians, NAACP officials filed by, he had a personal word for everybody, he knew just when to give a black power handshake or a regular one. No one in Chicago, or perhaps the nation, could have functioned as well in a similar situation. I really believe that he is the one that can pull all sections of Chicago together."

Jackson now had the digital army he needed to expand his economic boycotts from just ministers marching to include consumer foot soldiers—the ordinary people. From hundreds to thousands, Jackson also filled his political church. He could exert influence by endorsing aldermen, senators, congressmen, and even presidents. King had shied away from partisan politics, but they would become a Jackson staple.

There was only one discrediting note. It was more of a gut feeling than a direct accusation. Reporter Betty Washington watched the crowd instead of Jackson. "His voice, his intonation, his speech patterns—everything. I felt like he was imitating Dr. King. Their voices don't sound alike, but somehow the way he emphasized his words, the way he used some of King's favorite expressions. . . . Well, I remember it had some of the people in the audience in hysterics. The way they acted it was as if King was being reincarnated in that man. It affected me immensely," she said. "It was like he was trying to *be* King, like something staged."

According to a *New York Times Magazine* article (July 9, 1972): "Don Rose, the public relations man [for CCCO in Chicago] recalled meeting with Jackson after King's death; he claims it was decided that Jackson could be sold to the press as the new King."

That meeting took place on Saturday after the Operation Breadbasket service, two days before King's funeral. Rose had placed Jesse on the "Kup" talk show, and he, Jackson, and Breadbasket aides were en route to NBC studios in Chicago. According to an aide, the gist of the conversation was, "There was very conscious effort to project Jackson as the figure most closely associated with King, a little like the myth making that evolved from Memphis. Jesse very seriously and very calculatingly discussed the ingredients and objectives necessary to assume the position of the new leader. The psychological impact of the projection and the reaction of the press to Jesse were discussed. The move was based on the very conscious conclusion that Jesse was probably the only one of the already established black personae still connected with the movement who could attract the urban young and still work on the program of nonviolence. It was an effort to update the spirit of Dr. King in the Northern urban context, an effort to get the kids who seemed to be going off in another direction. The conversation was cut and dried. He would be packaged like any other product."

Subsequently, observers pinpointed several of the subtle propaganda trappings used at Operation Breadbasket to fill in the image, to continue the linkage of Jackson to King and to obscure Jackson's boss, Ralph Abernathy.

In the early days of Operation Breadbasket, before

Jackson sauntered on stage, there was an emotional crescendo of freedom songs, gospel renditions, and organ riffs. Then either a staff member, a board member, or a political buddy exalted him by way of introduction. Usually the prefatory remarks, often through Biblical imagery, either compared Jackson to Dr. King or to deity or implied that he was King reincarnated.

At Breadbasket, Calvin Morris, who until 1971 was Jackson's number two man, said: "To those few people there is given the responsibility in life to articulate the moanings and groanings of us all. There are prophets of the old and there are prophets of the new. And in the days of the new birth when some men revile other men and in a day when some have said the Dreamer [King] is gone, God never leaves us comfortless. He always sends *His* man. His name is Jesse Louis Jackson." Jackie Robinson: "In Jesse Jackson, we have another Dr. Martin Luther King, Jr. Jesse's goals are those of all of black America." Harold Sims, former acting director of the National Urban League: "Not only is Jesse Jackson the Buck Rogers of the superindustrial age, but also the economic Messiah of the twentieth century." Carl Stokes, former mayor of Cleveland: "Jesse is now the foremost civil rights spokesman in the country. Jesse has the youth, the vitality, the public appeal. . . . He's a natural to assume the national prominence of the greatest of civil rights leaders. There is no man of whom Dr. King was more proud than our own Jesse Louis Jackson."

"No man of whom Dr. King was more proud"; besides the irony, it is a classic example of how the name of the Reverend Ralph Abernathy, King's appointed successor and Jackson's boss, was blotted out of the public mind in Chicago and the name of Jackson substituted in its place. This blackout of Abernathy was again seen at the Black Expo trade fair in 1971. Speakers lauded black leaders, past and present, from Booker T. Washington to Marcus Garvey, from Dr. King to the Black Panthers.

There was no mention of Abernathy vocally or pictorially at this massive gathering. In the background hung mobile portraits of the late Whitney Young, Dr. King, and others, including Jesse Jackson. Abernathy's portrait was noticeably missing.

According to a *Chicago Sun-Times* article (March 22, 1971) a woman staffer who was also a member of the Live Wires, a Breadbasket women's auxiliary, was fired for inviting Abernathy to speak in Chicago. "I thought it was the correct thing to do since Abernathy was my boss as well as Jesse's, but I was fired for only one reason. I was working on a program to honor Reverend Abernathy and not Reverend Jackson," she said.

Not only was Abernathy's position—the number one black leader in America respected by other blacks, according to a 1972 national Louis Harris poll—scuttled, but also SCLC, the parent organization. On Saturdays, it was often emphasized that Operation Breadbasket was the most viable civil rights group in the country, but the name SCLC was played down. Soon the downtown papers dropped SCLC from Jackson's title. Operation Breadbasket, instead of functioning as merely one of the numerous programs of SCLC, became an entity in itself, with its own board of directors and its own corporations. Eventually both Abernathy and SCLC would be of little significance in the public mind as the man and the organization empowered to lead the movement founded by Dr. King.

Although the coup de théâtre could not have been orchestrated without Jackson's angels—the white czars of the multi-media—Jackson was not an invention of the media, as it is often charged. He invented himself, his own opportunity, his own moment of glory, and these were later patented by the media. In other words, a partnership based on mutual need developed with Jackson taking the lead.

To the establishment press he served a functional purpose. After the 1968 rioting, there were people dying, and even more impressive, $10-million worth of white property had been destroyed. Momentum was also building for black acceptance of the black power theoreticians, such as Stokely Carmichael and H. Rap Brown. The white establishment needed a neutralizer for the ardent rhetoric of burn, baby, burn. What they really needed was a Booker T. Washington in bell-bottoms: someone who could capture the imagination of the young and who could out rap H. Rap Brown, but someone with more orderly oratory who would lead the militants away from the onslaught of property to another front. If Jackson wanted to boycott forty A & P stores in the ghetto, so what? There were 400 of them in and around the Chicago area. If blacks wanted jobs, so what? They'd give them a few. That's what they were supposed to do anyway. Nonviolent boycotting and demonstrating were palatable alternatives to burning and looting of white businesses—especially if rioting expanded to the white commercial store strips. Jackson offered an alternative that whites could live with. As the *New York Times* (July 9, 1972) pointed out: "Jackson is militant but nonviolent, good copy but safe copy; radical in style, not in action. The Jesse Jackson of today is not a threat to established institutions."

Thus, if all it took to boost Jackson's image was publicity, he could have it by the pageful. He could have the cover and perhaps, next, the centerfold. There would only have to be some minor theatrical touch ups. Off with the slacks and suits and on with the leather vests, medallions, and dashikis. Off with the clean-shaven head, for a bushy Afro with long, curly sideburns. From now on Jackson would talk and look blacker than black.

In contrast, Abernathy was lackluster. He was getting old. He lacked the charisma, the glamor, or the savoir faire of a King or a Jackson. And he did not turn on the young. So why wait for him to fall on his face when Jackson was available now? Jackson is somewhat like a Teddy Ken-

nedy, who can upstage a keynote speaker, even if the
speaker happens to be a presidential candidate, simply by
sitting onstage and radiating.

There is no question that the establishment press
appreciated Jackson, so much so that Calvin Morris, his
top lieutenant, used to question the rationale for Jackson's
honeymoon with the press. Press treatment of Dr. King had
been often times scandalous. Especially after he left
the South, there were waves of criticism for his suggesting
that Red China be admitted to the United Nations and for
his linking peace in Viet Nam with peace at home. Morris
feels coverage of Jesse, in contrast, has been superficial.

"Except for an article written by Richard Levine, in
Harper's Magazine (March, 1969) most coverage focuses on
him as a personality—his rhetoric, his celebrity image, his
bell-bottoms. They make him appear as a saint. If there
was any scrutiny of the organization or of Jackson's
programs, it would be impossible for the articles to be all
good. What is damaging is that the press gives him credit
for economic and political programs, without ever analyz-
ing their workability. And if you get credit before
something is perfected, one has the feeling of accomplishment not by real action, but by counting laudatory
news stories."

Another explanation for this affectionate treatment
of Jackson is that after King was murdered, editors found
that there was a vacuum of leadership in the black
community. As any black reporter on any metropolitan
daily newspaper anywhere in the country knows, the
media establishment has an insatiable need to pinpoint
that *one* black person whose words ipso facto speak for
the other 25 million blacks. Since the days of America's
first leading Negro spokesman, Booker T. Washington, this
farce has been propagated and accepted by the black leaders who accommodatingly accept the dubious distinction
of being the mouthpiece of millions.

White publishers want to know what the blacks are

thinking, what they are planning, they want to know if there are riots on the horizon—as if anyone could predict them. How many times have you read stories about someone who speaks for the blacks, but have you ever read a story about anyone who speaks for the whites? You probably haven't and you probably never will. Whites are not addressed as one amorphous glob with a single mentality, necessitating a single spokesman.

But Jackson would serve as that black spokesman. So Jackson was given carte blanche. He stands as one of the few blacks in the country who can call a major press conference and know important print and electronic media representatives will be there. And when he calls for their bosses, the editors and the publishers, they come too. Media acceptance is one track event in which Jackson outdistanced King.

While King was alive, Jackson was developing his long-standing desire to be the leader, those around him observed. Chauncey Eskridge said, "I remember one particular incident. It was one of Jesse's tasks to act as an advance man for King when he was coming into a new town. Jesse had some leaflets printed up. We thought it odd that Jesse had put himself on one of them. In fact Jesse was towering a whole head higher than King. When Martin saw it, he asked me, 'Have you ever seen anything like that to save your life?' I said, jokingly, 'Well, that is characteristic of him 'cause he is your leader.' Jesse was also very adept at moving close to Doc when the cameramen were around. He was very PR-minded when it came to having himself identified with Martin. You see, Martin was very aware of Jackson's desire to upstage him. But Martin used to laugh it off. *He* was Martin Luther King, Jr., and that was that."

An aide to Dr. King in the Chicago Freedom Movement observed: "I remember Jesse's first big speech during the open housing marches. Well, actually it hadn't been planned that way. Jesse was supposed to introduce

Dr. King, but he took the opportunity when the cameras were on him to deliver a lengthy, lengthy speech himself. You couldn't say he got carried away in his preaching because his remarks were all written down. When it was Dr. King's time to speak, he delivered only perfunctory remarks, 'cause he saw it had all been said for him.

"I also remember one of those picture deals, with Jackson being pictorially highlighted over King. The way you saw it, it was a flat picture in steps, Dr. King was at the bottom, then Jesse, then the crucifix. Dr. King looked at it and smiled and said, 'At least he put the good Lord over him.' "

A reporter at King's funeral in Atlanta: "When I arrived the preachers in the movement were in a blue funk. They had heard how Jesse had lied about what took place after King's assassination and they knew what he was up to. The Reverend Charles Billups was furious. What in the hell is Jesse trying to do? These preachers, especially Ralph, have gone through hell in the South. They've been jailed, horsewhipped, and nearly killed and now Jesse, who wasn't even out of grammar school when the real work was being done and who was not even a top aide, wants to take over SCLC and the movement."

"Later that evening," the reporter said, "Jesse came into my room. It was just before the funeral. He seemed to want a quiet place to think. So he fell across one of the twin beds and I continued working on a story I was filing for an overseas paper. I got the feeling he wasn't talking so much to me as he was to himself; he was using me as a sounding board. So I continued typing, only half-listening. From what I can remember he was projecting a role of leadership for himself. 'Now when you do this, the next step is . . . what about timing . . . reaction. . . .' I can only remember snatches of his conversation, but what I do remember, and I'm sure I'm not mistaken, was that he was trying to plan a way to get to where King had been."

Reaching the plateau where King had been is a fine

ambition not only for Jesse Jackson but for every young American, especially if black.

If it is Jesse's dream to be a world symbol of morality, courage, and human decency, then what is a nobler goal?

If it is Jesse's dream to bend institutions so they become monuments to the living instead of graveyards for tradition, to serve the black poor instead of being served by the black poor, then there is no nobler a goal.

But in studying the life of Dr. King, one finds that there was an intersection between noble goals and noble means. Should this not also be a consideration of anyone attempting to emulate or transcend the life of Dr. Martin Luther King, Jr.?

And equally as important, can a man like Dr. King be created from press releases and through the courtesy of the mass media?

*Dr. King named the program
Operation Breadbasket because
its goal was to bring bread,
money, and income into the
baskets of black and poor people.*

Rev. Ralph D. Abernathy

By 1967, the Chicago scenario had spun about. Food stamps had replaced the Depression's ration books as the poor man's currency. The WPA's fifty-cent-an-hour wage scale had faded away, with men in Lawndale wanting it back since 40 percent couldn't find work at any wage. The slogan had changed from the Double Duty Dollar to Buy Black. Dope had replaced policy as king and two black banks had replaced the two colored banks knocked out by the Depression. Things had indeed changed. Events swirled around on a merry-go-round. But when the music stopped everybody landed back at virtually the same spot because all motion is not progress. Two other factors have also remained constant since 1929: blacks may not get all they fight for but they must fight for all they get, and the boycott, until something better is invented, remains the sharpest cutting edge to stave off the Depression, which in parts of black metropolis has somehow never ended.

The art of teaming consumers against a single industry instead of the scatter-shot approach used in the old boycott method was developed by the Reverend Leon Sullivan of Philadelphia, who introduced the selective patronage program (later known as Operation Bread-basket) to Dr. Martin Luther King, Jr., in 1962. (Sullivan is presently the only black on the Board of General Motors).

In 1959, using the umbrella of the church—the oldest and strongest institution in the black community—Sullivan organized 400 Philadelphia ministers. Their collective church memberships of more than 250,000 people were called upon to redirect the buying habits of the black community. In other words, blacks were encouraged to become as discriminating in their tastes as the companies who were discriminating.

The conditions that sparked the drive in Philly were a carbon copy of the complexion of Chicago: no Negroes were manning soft drink, ice cream, bread, or oil trucks, there were no Negro driver-salesmen, and Negro white-collar workers and secretaries were missing from the crowds that poured out of the banks and insurance companies.

In the three-year drive on industry in Philadelphia, some thirty companies which had committed the "corporate sin" of discrimination became targets for withdrawal campaigns. Some of the more notable were: Pepsi-Cola, Gulf, Sun Oil, and Tasty Baking Company, which reportedly lost 40 percent in sales over a seven-week period.

According to the Reverend Leon Sullivan, the Philadelphia selective patronage program resulted in more than 5,000 jobs, directly or indirectly, channeling more than

$15 million in new income for Negro families. It was a simple tool in relationship to the net gains, he said. "For the majority of the congregations and pastors there were no meetings to attend, no protest signs to carry, no fear of reprisal for switching from brand A to brand B. The easiest thing in the world is to switch brands in the comfort of a supermarket in the Negro community and to tell everyone why you did it. A certain pride exists with those participating since the reason for the campaign is considered just."

Concept

Once called selective patronage or economic withdrawal, boycotts have grown more lethal with age. Today the correct common denominators necessary to hack at corporate vital organs are more abundantly present than in the 1920s and 1930s: enough people with enough cash concentrated in the ghetto spell the difference between black and red. In 1930, Chicago's Negro population peaked at 235,000 with a buying power of $180,000. By the late 1960s, blacks had soared past the 1.3 million mark in Chicago with a purchasing power of about $4.2 billion.

Although the concept of organized consumer withdrawal was not new to SCLC in light of the historic 381-day Montgomery bus boycott in 1955, the Reverend Leon Sullivan was called to Atlanta by Dr. King and the Reverend Ralph Abernathy to help set up a pilot project based on his experience in Philadelphia.

As a result of the meeting, Operation Breadbasket was established as an official economic arm of SCLC in September 1962, under the direction of the Reverend Fred C. Bennett, Jr.

"We named the program Operation Breadbasket because we would be operating in order to bring bread, money, and income into the baskets of black and poor people," Abernathy said.

Following the encouraging results of gaining reportedly more than 5,000 new jobs in Atlanta, which included their first target, the Colonial Bread Company, SCLC established Breadbasket affiliates in eight Southern cities.

Jacksonville (Florida) Breadbasket joined forces with a local labor union in organizing the employees of a laundry firm and significantly improved wages and benefits. Also in Georgia and Kentucky, Breadbasket was instrumental in breaking down employment barriers against Negroes in several governmental agencies.

On February 1, 1966, King addressed more than 300 ministers at Jubilee CME Temple in Chicago, where he outlined the Operation Breadbasket program as "a simple one, in which Negro ministers put pressure on employers to hire and upgrade more Negroes, especially members of their own congregations." The ministers' affirmative response to investigate employment opportunities for Chicago blacks and to form committees to work for a solution is considered the birth of SCLC's Operation Breadbasket in Chicago. Your Ministers Fight For Jobs and Rights was adopted as the SCLC Operation Breadbasket slogan.

Technique

In principle, the negotiation process carried out in consumer withdrawal campaigns in Chicago was patterned after the selective patronage program that had worked successfully in Philadelphia and Atlanta and is still used today by various action groups across the country. The process consisted of five stages: information, education, negotiation, demonstration, and reconciliation.

Information: Letters were sent to political targets requesting a listing of all job classifications, the total number of employees versus the number of blacks in each category, and salary range. Government forms that companies submitted to the Equal Employment Opportunity Commission (EEOC) were also requested. Often blacks inside the company supplied the movement with more accurate statistics than either the firm's executives or the government reports.

Virtually before the information was in the ministers' hands, they could visualize the familiar and contemptuous employment patterns: blacks, if employed at all, were in the lowest paying jobs which required little or no responsibility.

Demands for hiring and upgrading centered on the often disputed logic that if blacks made up 20 percent of the population they should have 20 percent of the jobs. For companies which served a predominantly black population, the demands were often increased to 30 percent. However, it was also taken into consideration that some companies were so far behind in black employment that a 20 to 30 percent increase would force them into bankruptcy.

Ministers were careful to couch their demands in terms of minimum increases instead of quotas, which have always had a negative connotation when they meant black addition to the work force. But when quota meant subtraction—last hired, first fired—or zero population in terms of blacks in upper echelon positions, the term was acceptable, if not as a figure of speech, certainly as an expression of intent.

Education: What the ministers meant by education was nothing that had ever been taught in an urban or suburban classroom. The ministers would switch from the subject of lack of truck drivers to Shadrach, Meshach, and Abednego without ever losing the beat of their colorful Baptist cadence, which hopelessly confused some of the white officials. In their preaching-teaching sessions, the ministers also impressed upon the executives that by denying the black man the right to work they were the main contributors to his daily diet of social injustices, shoddy housing, and poverty.

Another tactic that frustrated some white company officials was the ministers' insistence on holding educational meetings in the ghetto, the scene of their corporate crimes. This technique could be compared to house-breaking a puppy by rubbing his nose in his own waste.

Negotiation: In the spirit of their social gospel, these sessions always opened with prayer before the ministers changed into the posture of hatchet men. Prior to the meeting at least two hatchet men were selected whose job it was never to be satisfied with anything. They were always radical, pushing at the need to get more from the company than was being offered. The negotiations were a masterful stratagem to watch: the executives were not allowed to stray from the issue of jobs. Some executives often preferred to lapse into soul-soothing diatribes on how they were "sorry about the problem" or how they went to a college with a Negro who was captain of the football team and "was as good as any white boy," or "I had a colored neighbor once . . . ." But the ministers made them stay on the point of offering corporate solutions to the problem. And if the ministers had to argue among themselves, they were careful to show no disunity until the executives hit the sidewalk.

The ministers were also careful not to waste their time with company underlings who couldn't make decisions.

Demonstration: It was the hope of the ministers that negotiations would prevent the necessity of consumer withdrawal, that companies would submit to a program of economic justice without additional pressure. The basic tool used here was communications to the black community on the issues and an appeal not to cooperate with "evil" as it is found in the target company. Direct action usually consists of the following: (1) the ministerial call from the pulpit for selective withdrawal, (2) announcement over the ministers' radio broadcasts, (3) letters to Breadbasket supporters, (4) letters to stores requesting the removal of target products from their shelves, (5) winning support of other community groups, (6) picketing of large volume stores that do not remove the products, and (7) statements, primarily to the black press, explaining the rationale for the withdrawal.

Reconciliation: The conclusion of the direct action phase was to establish new relations of cooperation and assist in sensitizing company officials to their new black workers. This was a time of jubilation—often unwarranted—for the black community. Officials were encouraged to pose for press photographers to punctuate the victory. Some officials also appeared at Operation Breadbasket to emphasize their new corporate image in hopes the ghetto dollar would return. There is only one thing more difficult than calling for a boycott and that is calling it off in the minds of consumers who have found other places to shop. Targets in the ghetto were not picked at random, although the majority were deserving. Ministers sized up targets in terms of a sliding vulnerability scale. The more vulnerable marks were companies with low-profit margins so that boycotts would have quick, spiraling results. Ministers selected companies with strong competitors eager to absorb their markets, stores with few retail outlets, and businesses not conducted by phone or mail order. Ministers also took into account the image of the company. The more a company had worked to effect good race relations, the more sensitive it would be to adverse publicity.

The techniques remained unchanged except for one major adjustment—Jackson emerged as the leader over the ministerial body, a fact which was out of focus with the group's original intent. In Philadelphia, it was emphasized that there would be no peer leadership or formal structure. Without an incorporated organization, bylaws, officers, treasurers, dues, or staff, corporate attorneys find it difficult to initiate suits for restraint of trade or unfair practices because technically and legally no group exists. In Atlanta, this lack of formation prevented singling out the ringleader for jailing, bombing, and overall harassment. In Chicago, this absence of structure was intended to keep the movement honest, according to the Reverend Hiram Crawford, a negotiations team member. "As soon as the word was passed that a new powerful group had formed, people were approached with offers of Cadillacs and money, which some actually accepted as the program developed. But just as important, the lack of structure was to keep any one person from acquiring too much power. It was also intended to avert factionalism that could lead to a division in the group, but, of course, it didn't quite work out that way."

In Philadelphia, the program used rotating teams of ministers, called priority committees, with Sullivan staying pretty much in the background. In Atlanta, the rotation team was named the "call men." In Chicago, late in April of 1966, the call-men format was stressed by the Reverend Fred C. Bennett, Jr., the national Breadbasket director. "An SCLC Operation Breadbasket program is intentionally organized just as loosely as a particular situation will permit. The call-men positions are rotated frequently and there are no other officers. No more formal organization is necessary," Bennett explained.

Nevertheless, Jackson emerged as the convener of the steering committee of ministers and was formally acknowledged as the leader. Although the move violated principle, it brought to the movement the esprit, the flair, and the intellectual inspiration necessary to explode on the Chicago scene as a force incapable of being ignored.

Dairy Industry

When civil rights groups visited corporations on job head counting expeditions, many white officials found it expedient to look concerned and play the "we're trying but just can't find any qualified" role of the enlightened liberal. But on March 16, 1966, Country Delight Dairy officials acted natural when Breadbasket came to call—crass, insensitive, and patronizing.

Country Delight was selected because it employed no Negro milk drivers or driver-salesmen in jobs that paid more than $12,000 a year in overtime and commissions. This is the way the dialogue went between the Reverend Hiram Crawford, a folksy traditional Baptist preacher, and a hard-nosed top official at Certified Grocers of Illinois, of which Country Delight Dairy was a subsidiary.

Official: "Who do you people think you are? I don't let union officials tell me how to run my company and I am not about to let a bunch of Negro preachers tell me what to do. What do you think this is? . . . This is a business not a playground."

Crawford: "We are not here to argue but to find out the sins of your corporations so we might work together to solve some of the evils of this society."

Official: "You must be kidding."

Crawford: "We are very serious. When we walked in here we did not see any black secretaries, key punch or computer operators, or clerk-typists."

Official: "We got 'em, they're in the back."

Crawford: "You mean sweeping floors?"

Official: "Yeah, but they are earning a decent living. I know all about you people. You don't want to work. My brother-in-law, who was a contractor, hired some colored people once to get them off welfare. You know what they did? They worked for two weeks and quit because they said they could earn more on welfare. That experience taught me a lesson. You people are lazy. You don't want to work. You want welfare."

End of Conversation. Start of Boycott.

On Good Friday, picket lines formed in front of about forty of the ninety Certified Grocery stores that carried Country Delight products. By chance, one of the first stores picketed was owned by a black grocer, who, incidentally, happened to be a contributor to Operation Breadbasket. "Oh, the things he said when he saw that picket line. Most of the participants were college students just out to picket. Since the grocer acted so bad, they just sent for more pickets," Breadbasket negotiator Hiram Crawford said.

"In a way it was a compliment," said George Jones, vice-president of Joe Louis Milk Company and one of the Jackson businessmen. "The Certified store was so well stocked and so attractive, we just assumed it was not black owned. From that point on, we selected our targets with more precision. That mistake was never repeated," Jones pointed out.

Goons heightened the drama of Breadbasket's first encounter. In Breadbasket negotiator Crawford's words, goons are hired big guys, mostly Italian. Some weigh over 300 pounds and look like apes, they are so big and powerful. Even though the goons threatened Jackson's life, the boycott persisted until Country Delight officials called the ministers back to the conference table.

Since the boycott had sliced away more than $500,000 of the four-day weekend's gross sales, the second meeting was with the full board of directors. And all were friendly. "We pinpointed how some of the janitors had been there fifteen years and had never been promoted. That blacks wanted good jobs so they could have decent educations for their kids, decent homes, and a hard-working father for their children to look up to. We also told them how they were guilty of the sin of creating criminals in the black community," Crawford said.

After the speech-sermon, a white board member stood up and told the ministers that since he had always lived in an all-white community, he had never understood that things were so bad for Negroes. "I only have one vote," he said, "but I will use it to change the policy of this company." With the ice broken, the other nineteen board members followed suit.

Thus, what had started as a hopeless confrontation between two different species resulted in blacks and whites being able to talk to each other as men. As Dick Gregory once said, "A Negro with a gun is always mister," and the ministers had found a weapon that worked just as well. The meeting adjourned with the ministers' arms interlocked in a circle, offering up prayers for the salvation of the soul of the company's president.

Around its six-month anniversary, Chicago Breadbasket claimed its first victory. On August 8, 1966, the victors could see the offspring of their labor driving down crowded Forty-seventh Street—a Negro behind the wheel of a Country Delight milk truck.

Following the victory with Country Delight, from June 9 to July 21, 1966, Breadbasket swept through the dairy industry. Firms not hit fell in line when they heard footsteps coming. According to information turned over to Breadbasket, not one of the companies could be called equal opportunity employers. One company had only twenty-three black workers out of a total work force of 435, a percentage of about 5.3. Nearly all of the twenty-three workers were in low level positions. Another company had no black managers out of a total of fifteen, no black auto mechanics out of twenty-one, no black dairy production workers out of fifty-eight, and no black retail delivery salesmen out of 142. Overall the average of black workers for all companies was about 5 percent.

June 9, 1966—The Borden Milk Company surrendered on the spot, promising twenty new jobs.

June 21, 1966—After four days of Breadbasket's picketing several National Tea and Del Farm stores that carried Hawthorn-Mellody products, the milk company agreed to hire fifty-five more black workers and to integrate every category of the company's operations in all four plants. Both National Tea and Del Farm had removed the milk products from their stores.

July 5, 1966—Wanzer Dairies agreed to hire an additional forty-four black employees.

July 21, 1966—Bowman Dairy, which had merged with Dean Foods, agreed to hire an additional forty-five black employees in a wide variety of classifications. Jack Linton, Dean Foods' personnel director, admitted: "You can't beat them. They got that weapon and you have to respect it. If you don't, you can go broke."

With negotiated commitments from executives of the five largest dairy industries in Chicago, Breadbasket swung through the soft drink market, boycotting Pepsi-Cola, with three other large bottling companies capitulating without the need for direct action. Agreements reached were: August 22—thirty-two jobs from Pepsi; August 25—thirty jobs from Coca-Cola; September 23—fifty-seven jobs from Seven-Up; and on October 6, twelve jobs from Canfield.

Black community support was considerably unified behind the campaigns, although some civic groups, such as the Cosmopolitan Chamber of Commerce, urged that the boycott against Hawthorn-Mellody be called off. "Pastors of some churches have been urging to refrain from buying these products, which shows again how unfair some direct action groups can be," A. L. Foster, then the chamber's executive director, wrote in a black newspaper column appropriately entitled Other People's Business.

On the whole, however, Breadbasket's early success was welcomed news to Chicago's black community, which suffered a 9 percent unemployment rate—far higher than the city average of 3.3 percent for whites. This figure does not account for parts of Kenwood-Oakland, East Garfield, or Lawndale, where the unemployment rate soared to over 40 percent. And this statistical breakdown did not, of course, count the scores of jobless men who had long since quit seeking work and were not included in any federal unemployment data. Assuming all 295 jobs were actually awarded, Breadbasket's early efforts channeled an estimated $4 million dollars in wages to the black Chicago economy.

Late in 1966, Breadbasket tightened its belt before it prepared to move on to the next front. The ministers felt that job commitments were coming too painlessly, that the executives were making quick responses to get the pressure off their companies. A follow-up committee was formed to close the gap between promises and actual placement. It was agreed that the companies' commitments should be put in writing. Most often there had not been even letters from all the soft drink and dairy companies confirming the negotiated agreements. The clergymen tended to count on the good will of the company executives. Covenants would be drawn for all subsequent agreements. They are not legally binding, but they do document what each party has agreed upon. Up to this point, Operation Breadbasket had a two-man staff, Jackson and David Wallace, a white Texas schoolmate of Jackson's at the Chicago Theological Seminary. Two more ministers—both white—from the school were added, Gary Massoni and Dr. Alvin Pitcher, Jackson's professor at the Chicago Seminary. They had also been involved in the Chicago Freedom Movement before Breadbasket's founding.

The movement was gaining respect from the Chicago business world, but Jackson considered the wins easy victories: "We started with the milk industry because it was particularly vulnerable. That stuff can't stand around;

it has to be sold or the man loses. And he can't ship it back to the cows. With blacks consuming 9 percent more soda pop than whites and with temperatures in the eighties during the soft drink campaign, we had to win."

The next front—the national supermarket industry— would not necessarily be Jackson's big score. Breadbasket would win some and lose most, but it would always claim to have won them all.

Supermarket Industry

If the trend of black employment had remained constant, blacks would not be represented in the national supermarket industry in proportion to their percentage of the work force until the year 3000.

The following statistics are from F. Marion Fletcher, *The Negro in the Supermarket Industry* (Philadelphia: University of Pennsylvania Press, 1972).

Since 1940 when black workers made up 3.6 percent of the industrywide total, progress could best be measured on a slide rule. By 1950 Negro employment had risen 0.7 percent, to 4.3 percentage points, and by 1960 it had loomed at 4.6 percent, an increase of 0.3 percentage points. In 1966, two years after the Civil Rights Act of 1964 prohibiting discrimination in public and private employment, job statistics for blacks responded with a 0.2 percentage point hike to 4.8 percent. In other words, it had taken blacks twenty-six years to gain 1.4 percentage points in employment, mostly on the bottom rungs.

Fletcher predicted, "From the vantage point of 1960, the outlook for Negro employment in the decade ahead did not seem promising. Furthermore, looking ahead into the future, there did not seem to be any industry developments which would cause black employment to grow more rapidly than in the past. Even in the meat department where gains had been made, their positions seemed precarious. Industry plans to centralize meat

Displayed at Operation PUSH headquarters, these portraits reinforce
the transfer of leadership from
King to Jackson.

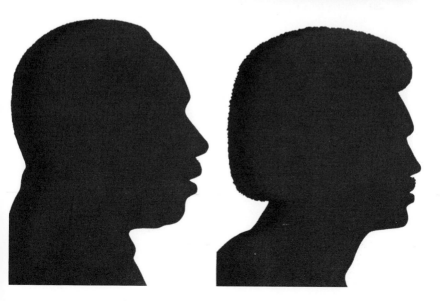

Jesse Jackson's birthplace, 20 Haynie Street, Greenville, S.C.

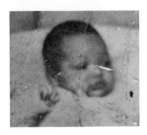

Jesse at two months . . .
and at two and a half years.

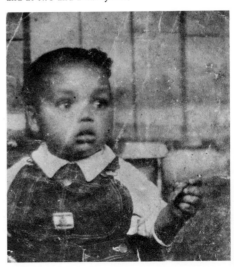

Jesse lived in this house on Anderson Street in Greenville, S.C., during his teen years. His mother and stepfather still live here.

Jesse at ten . . .　　fourteen . . .　　and seventeen.

Jackson's Chicago residence, 6845 S. Constance.

The Reverend Jesse Jackson,
August 1968.

Noah Ryan Robinson, Jesse's
half-brother (left) and Jesse's father,
Noah Louis Robinson (right).

Helen and Charles Jackson, Jesse's mother and stepfather.

Jesse Jackson and his oldest son, Jesse, Jr.

Jacqueline L. Jackson, Jesse's wife.

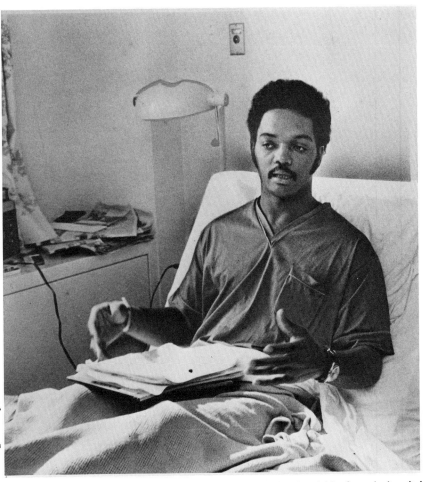

Jesse keeps tabs on organizational activities from the hospital during one of his frequent visits for treatment of sickle cell anemia.

Jesse at age thirty, 1972.

cutting in warehouses seemed to pose a threat of reducing overall employment, which would limit opportunities for Negro employment and advancement in this phase of supermarket operations. In the mid-1960s, black men and women barely had a foothold in the industry, although the minimum educational skills and high pay ideally suited the black condition. Without pressure for a change of industry policy from government officials, or civil rights groups, the plight of the black worker would continue to be progress from behind the decimal point."

Under law, blacks were protected against discrimination by the Fair Labor Standards Act, Title VI of the Civil Rights Act of 1964, and Section 1981 of the Civil Rights Act of 1875. But somehow the grocery industry had been able to evade them all, either because of the lack of enforcement powers of the governmental agencies, such as the Civil Rights Commission, or because the clout the agencies did have did not apply to supermarkets.

In 1965, President Johnson signed Executive Order 11246 requiring contractors or subcontractors with fifty or more employees and a contract of $50,000 or more with the federal government to develop written affirmative action compliance programs for each of their establishments. However, few supermarkets sell to the government. As one supermarket executive pointed out, "Government contracts are so minor in relation to other revenue-producing areas of the business that it would be simple to withdraw from the government contract business and thus eliminate the need for undertaking such a major program with respect to minority employment."

The Equal Employment Opportunity Commission (EEOC), arising from the Civil Rights Act of 1964, was given powers to review and conciliate issues of fair employment. In its lifetime the tepid EEOC became involved in only one suit against the supermarket industry in the 1960s; Mrs. Annie Brinkly charged that she was being denied a job in an A & P store in North Carolina because of her race. The case was satisfactorily settled out of court.

When all the rationales, excuses, and loopholes are juxtaposed it seems that in the 1960s, and in some cases it is still true today, fair employment practices are nobody's official business—except the various civil rights groups, which are limited by resources, money, authority, and manpower to fight for the basic human right to work.

Since the supermarket industry operates on a penny-or-less profit margin, boycotts affect not only the chain but the 9,000 or so items on the shelves; and because all the uproar has a way of making stockholders jittery, Breadbasket believed it could bring the mulish industry to its knees.

In looking at SCLC's Breadbasket campaign against the retail food industry, one finds no record of any reporter doubling back to see if the supermarkets were living up to the letter of Jackson's law, an act which would seem a natural in light of the industry's past good-will performance.

In a few instances, however, the Chicago supermarket industry has responded more notably to the pressure of Breadbasket than to the good-faith pact with the federal agencies. In other cases, supermarkets are still lurking behind the decimal point. Some worthy considerations behind the news are white resistance vs. black pressure; the courageous but not always effective efforts of Breadbasket; the unraveling of the threads of integrity by some within the movement, and the many other human conflicts that raise the question: Who is fighting whom for what?

High-Low

In keeping with its style of gradually working its way up the retail industry's vulnerability scale, SCLC's Breadbasket first approached High-Low Foods, whose fifty-four

stores were Chicago-based, with fifteen in black neighborhoods. Unlike its stronger competitors, whose operations
branched into numerous states, High-Low could be considered a captive market for civil rights-consumer warfare.
The major attraction of High-Low to community pressure
was its bottom-heavy employment picture. Although 12
percent of High-Low's employees were black, 88 percent
were cashiers, stock clerks, or security guards. High-Low
had only one Negro store manager in their fifty-four stores
(1.8 percent) and only ten Negro journeymen butchers out
of 383 (2.6 percent). Breadbasket ministers also charged
that the chain had a higher markup price for black
products. For example, Parker House sausage, which sold
for $.70 a pound in Mom and Pop stores, sold for $.98 a
pound. "Since they did not want to handle black products,
but because they were in demand, they marked them up to
ensure a greater profit," Hiram Crawford said.

On November 19, 1966, High-Low quickly responded
to Breadbasket demands for hiring or upgrading 183 Negro
employees. The agreement was hailed by Negro leaders.
Dr. Martin Luther King, Jr., said, "The development
portends new strides toward economic freedom for
America's black people." Jackson called it "green power
for Negroes in their own communities." In that same
week, Dr. King appointed Jackson director of Projects and
Economic Development for SCLC, which gave him the
responsibility of traveling around the country to produce
similar agreements—hopefully with more teeth—and to
sponsor fund raising projects.

In the six-month time period allotted by Breadbasket,
little progress was made. The Reverend Gary Massoni
reported in his master's dissertation (submitted to the
Chicago Theological Seminary faculty for the degree of
Master of Divinity, June 1971): of the 183 jobs promised
by the company only fifty-six had been filled by May of
1967, with the largest shortages in the demand for

journeymen butchers, managers, and grocery clerks. Of the
seven products the company agreed to distribute, they
balked at selling three: Baldwin ice cream, Joe Louis
milk, and Diamond Sparkle wax. The ice cream conflicted
with their own brand, for which whey wanted to restrict
the market. They claimed that the shelves were too
crowded to introduce another brand of wax, and that the
addition of another brand of milk would cut too much
into their profits. When High-Low, a family-owned business, refused to consider the black firms' demands and the
revised employment demands, Breadbasket announced a
"withdrawal of patronage" from High-Low stores in the
black community.

According to Gary Massoni, picket lines and leaflets
were dispatched to several stores on June 8, 1967. The
campaign continued until June 20, when High-Low attempted to obtain a court injunction against the boycott.
The ministers agreed to suspend picketing if they could
continue passing out "informational leaflets and if High-
Low would bargain in good faith." Circuit Court Judge
Walker Butler was to decide on the merits of High-Low's
allegations that Breadbasket was forcing the company to
violate fair employment practices laws by discriminating in
favor of Negroes. High-Low agreed to a new covenant on
July 7, 1967, just before the final hearing on the motion
for a permanent injunction.

On May 30, 1970, I found that although Breadbasket
had moved on to other fronts, High-Low had delivered on
only forty-four of the 183 jobs promised in both covenants.

However, the High-Low noncompliance was a pattern
consistently repeated in most future negotiations, where
companies resisted outside pressure and the Jackson
movement lacked the muscle to force full cooperation.

Despite the debatability of the employment results of
the High-Low covenant, it marked a crucial turning point
in the history of Operation Breadbasket.

For the first time, steps were included for black business development through gaining access to shelf space which in the past had been either nonexistent or severely limited. As George Jones, Vice-President of the Joe Louis Milk Company, observed, "We weren't sitting on our hands. But we were out picketing the little Mom and Pop stores. Our vision hadn't expanded to the large chains because we had almost no success with the little stores. It was Jackson who replaced us on the picket lines with the ministers so we could get back to our desks and take care of business."

Equally as crucial, Jackson began to direct the flow of white corporate profits earned in the ghetto into black banks as a means of strengthening the black communities' meager economic foundation.

Jackson's economic conceptualization evolves not only from Dr. King and Reinhold Niebuhr's *Moral Man and Immoral Society,* but also from watching the activities on city streets. How many times had he watched the white merchants at quitting time steal away to segregated suburbs and their help scurry off to restricted blue collar bungalows, such as Gage Park? It's not the white flight that was so irritating to Jackson, but the fat sums earned by black hands that go with it. To Jackson, the white merchants' actions in the ghetto are akin to rape—all pleasure and no responsibility. How different it would be if the money could be redirected, invested in black banks, awarded to black contractors, or shared among black businesses.

In the "Kingdom Theory" (see Appendix) Jackson outlines his economic approach to inner-city control. "We are stating that black people must understand themselves as having the authority of kings and that their dominions are their communities. An informed people is a well armed people in this struggle. Taking inventory means becoming informed of the people who benefit economically from our community but have no real investment in that community. It means seeing our money remain within our community instead of entering and leaving at an acute angle (i.e., within six hours).

"Moving from such *units* as a store, the Kingdom Theory seeks to explain basic control of each marketable product, and in fact, the store itself. Control of the store means determining who will be clerks and bookkeepers and who will have such monetary awarding jobs as butchers and meat manager roles within the store. By that same token, it is also to determine the amount of shelf space which that community feels should go to the products of black producers; who is to do the exterminator, janitorial, and scavenger services in the store; when the store chooses to expand, who will secure the construction and remodeling contracts; which banks will the store transact its financial operations in; who conducts the collection services for the store; with whom does the store have transportation business for its vegetable supplies."

The Kingdom Theory, first applied to black banks and to gain shelf space for black business, provides the main premise of Jacksonian economics.

Banking

On Thursday, May 4, 1967, at 11 A.M. , Chicago's Continental Bank had a total of $8,857,000 in federal and state non-interest-bearing accounts; Harris Trust had $8,247,000; First National, $7,625,000; American National, $2,138,000; and the city's two black banks had none. In fact, the white banks had twenty-three times as much money in non-interest-bearing governmental accounts, a small phase of the entire banking operations, than the black banks had in total capital. That there are any black banks in the urban ghetto at all is a marvel when one considers the dearth of skilled professionals, the general pathology of the economy, the pervasive social isolation, and the established white competitors whom blacks are used to patronizing.

In 1967, Chicago's two black-owned banks were Seaway and Independence, with collective assets of $10 million. Both were organized in 1964, with each capitalizing at less than $1 million. They began as correspondent banks of Continental National and Harris Trust Banks, which provided trained personnel and still provide computer services and general counsel.

In 1967, Seaway and Independence, plus the other eighteen black banks in the nation, had total assets of just over $207 million and deposits of about $185 million. If all the black banks were to merge, the resulting conglomerate would have ranked 140 among the nation's 14,000 banks.

The depressing state of black banking affairs, that would greatly improve by 1974, prompted one of the most controversial assessors of black financial institutions in America to label them as "ornamental." A. F. Brimmer, former governor of the Federal Reserve Board, said, "Black banks might be compared to small, high-cost specialty shops—catering to a limited segment of the market. But they are far from being analogous to the large scale department stores offering a full range of services to the community at large. Most black banks might be viewed primarily as ornaments—that is, as a mark of distinction or a badge of honor that provides a visible symbol of accomplishments." And as *Forbes* (September 15, 1972) pointed out, "Most money managers reluctantly agree."

Answering the candid but pessimistic projections charting the course of black financial institutions, Jackson said, "They may be piggy banks but they are our banks and we must understand that." Jackson's assertions supported the sentiments of most black Chicagoans, who until 1964 did not have the opportunity to trade at a black bank. The Depression knocked off the only two colored banks of the century. One was Chicago's famed Jesse Binga bank, which held over one-third of all the Negro deposits in the United States. "Black banks are to the economic system what blood is to the human system," Jackson said.

"If we are going to build a community with enough leverage to deal with the bad housing and the poor schools, the unemployment and the hazardous health conditions, we've got to move our black banks into position to take the offensive. If our banks carried the bonds on public housing projects, we wouldn't need to worry about financing another Robert Taylor Homes project or Stateway Gardens or another Cabrini Green. Black banks must be able to finance construction projects, home loans, scholarships, and black businesses." (Perhaps Jackson had heard the story passed around the black community about one of the city's top bankers, who said, "I have never met a Negro I'd trust for more than a $300 loan.")

"All our black banks," Jackson vowed, "are going to get their fair share." And his first thrust was a white bank-in program aimed at governmental institutions, to be followed by a drive through private industry.

On January 20, 1967, Jackson sent telegrams to several governmental officials asking that public funds be deposited in black banks. Although Mayor Richard J. Daley and Cook County Treasurer Edmund Kucharski ignored the request, then State Treasurer Adlai Stevenson III responded.

In the telegram, Jackson said, "The ministers of Operation Breadbasket have launched a campaign to help the Negro community help itself economically. We hope to relieve our city of much of the blight that pours over into the unrest of the long and bitter hot summers. We believe that the development of a strong economic program will instill in the disinherited and deprived a sense of dignity and worth.

"The Negro community has too long carried the weight of disenchantment and hopelessness in its belief that the politicians were concerned about its destiny only until election time. The Negro community wants to determine its destiny in positive and creative ways which will be the most effective rebuttal to intemperate charges by some of irresponsibility and a desire to subsist on handouts.

"It has been shown that Negro institutions can develop when given access to markets and to capital. But the despairing truth is that Negro businesses are systematically excluded from entering the mainstream of the economy by the absence of funds to launch creative ventures. Many financial institutions either refuse to lend money to Negroes or stipulate almost totally nonnegotiable terms.

"It is clear that all of these denials of opportunity interact to put the Negroes 100 years behind in their economic development. Therefore special efforts must be made to nullify the injustice and to extend economic opportunity. It is felt that the crushing pressure could be relieved if funds were provided in the Negro financial institutions which are fully accredited to handle fiscal matters.

"Encouraged by us, several corporations have already investigated and transferred funds. We know that you have a deep concern to achieve the objectives of dignity and self-achievement for all individuals. We are confident that you will extend your best consideration in this matter of crucial importance. . . ."

Stevenson immediately transferred sizeable deposits into Independence and Seaway Banks, as well as to Service Federal and Illinois Federal, two black savings and loan associations. The state treasurer also instituted a controversial antidiscriminatory policy on state lending institutions.

Stevenson threatened to cut off state funds from any financial institution that discriminated in employment or services, including the granting of loans. He also promised to channel additional funds into banks that served their communities nondiscriminatorily and backed up his policy by using the enforcement resources of state government. Illinois thus became the first state to adopt this type of policy.

With that accomplished, Jackson committed himself to "encouraging" National Tea, High-Low, and the rest of the supermarkets that banked white to reverse their trend of taking their profits earned from blacks out to the suburbs. "Cut us in or cut it out," he warned.

Shelf Space

Before 1967, the black producer without a sound marketing plan and the proper contacts was generally excluded from the grocery shelves. Often well-established products, such as Parker House sausage, which had gained a spot before Jackson moved in, were provided limited displays or were marked up too high, as in the High-Low situation.

Product, promotion, price, and place, the textbooks would have us believe, make the proper marketing mix. But unless prejudice is added from blacks and whites alike, the tested marketing theory doesn't speak to the problem of the black producer.

If the product is identifiably black, its chances for being distributed outside of the black community are still pretty slim. In fact, the segregation of black products is not even an issue. It is taken for granted by seller and producer alike.

When Gardner Stern, Jr., the president of Hillman's Foods, was asked point-blank if his chain of twenty stores in metropolitan Chicago would place Joe Louis milk (which has a picture of the Brown Bomber on its label) on his supermarket shelves, for example, in Cicero, he said, "My opinion is no."

Stern said, "Joe Louis milk in Cicero would be

unfamiliar to the average housewife. She wouldn't stop using the brand that she was accustomed to buying for brand X. And if you're talking specifically about Joe Louis milk, for example, which is identifiably black, being purchased in Cicero, let's face it, we are living in a racist society."

If a product can manage to look all-American, exhibiting no racial overtones, does that alter the plight of the black producer? Most would say, "No." For example, Grove Fresh orange juice is distributed in a wholesome-looking orange, green, and white carton. There is nothing racial about it at all, except that the salesmen and drivers are all black, and everyone in the retail trade knows that the company president is black. Thus Cecil Troy of Grove Fresh orange juice is pushed into the same bag with George Jones of Joe Louis milk.

"In 1967, I was in ten ghetto stores in the National Tea, Del Farm, and A & P chains, although they had more than one hundred stores in the black community," Cecil Troy said. "It was pure tokenism. On one occasion I approached a buyer and made him an offer far below the price he was paying for the orange juice he was using. If he had taken my offer, I think I might have cried. It would have broken me. I couldn't have serviced him at such a ridiculously low price. I just offered it to him to test my suspicions," Troy explained.

The case of Bill Aikens, president of Bonnie's Bakers, was also enough to make a grown man cry. Aikens baked a sumptuous pound cake—the same kind Sara Lee made famous. When Sara Lee branched out into the frozen food business, Bonnie's cakes began making strides because they were ready-to-eat. Following his tremendous sales leap, Aikens doubled his staff. He hired white drivers, white supervisors, and assumed a mainstream business posture until his competitors spread the word that Bonnie's Bakers was a black-owned company. Subsequently, his drivers were told in no uncertain terms to "get that nigger mess off our shelves." Aikens said, "As a result of being extended to do business as a normal businessman not boxed into a limited market, I was forced into bankruptcy. I tried again with another unidentifiably black product called Silvercup bread. The same experience was repeated." Today Aikens, reportedly, owns the Ridgeland Club, which caters primarily to blacks. He has finally arrived in the place most often reserved for black businessmen.

Examples of this insoluble marketing mix, working to restrict blacks from gaining a larger slice of the total market, abound. When people start to laud the extent of progress blacks have made, it is significant to note that Jackson's fight for shelf space, for the most part, did not center on equal treatment, which would have meant blacks gaining free access in the same manner as whites.

While whites have 100 percent access to shelf space—in and out of the black colony—blacks were fighting for about 8 percent in the confines of the ghetto.

A & P

"A & P was a very human company when my uncles were alive," lamented the debonair Huntington Hartford, nephew of the past president, John H. Hartford. "Today it is a closed shop." (*Business Week,* February 6, 1971.)

Operation Breadbasket, pitting its numbers against the nation's oldest and largest supermarket chain, would pry open the door of A & P, whose corporate soul had been buried under the weight of its landslide profits. In sentiment and on paper, the Great Atlantic and Pacific Tea Company seemed invincible. It is the blue blood of the retail industry. Food retailing systems, as they are known today, had no history when A & P invented them in 1859 by ushering in the first cash-and-carry economy store. It is small wonder that on May 26, 1967, Chicago's A & P sized

up Operation Breadbasket as little more than a worrisome
gnat in its fertile corporate valley, one that could be easily
shooed away.

The covenant with A & P applied primarily to forty
of 260 stores. The agreement included:

• The addition of 770 permanent jobs, which
included increasing the number of black managers from
fourteen to forty-one.

• Installation of sixteen black-made products,
with special advertising and sales promotions. The door
was left open for future products to be developed by
Negro entrepreneurs.

• The use of black scavengers, insect exterminators, and janitorial supply companies in a minimum of
forty stores. Advertising in Negro newspapers and the use
of Negro advertising and design firms (such as Vince
Cullers' advertising agency and Poly-Graphics Associates)
to encourage positive images of black people.

• The awarding of building and remodeling contracts to black contractors who would be financed by
black banks.

After A & P signed the covenants and posed for
pictures with Jackson to celebrate the agreement, it did
little. After the smiles for the press came off and nobody
was looking, A & P went back to its old habits. Inside the
company, Hyman Johnson, a black A & P official,
observed, "The covenant was treated like it was just
another nigger mess. The top men thought it was just a
case of some niggers being loud and vocal but were not
prepared to do very much, so they treated it as such. The
covenant was also very unrealistic. Where are you going to
find 770 blacks in six months with the kind of training
needed to move into the managerial positions and other
spots mentioned in the covenants?"

Twelve months after the agreement, A & P had hired
only eighty-three additional black employees, most of

whom were not in the more sensitive positions called for by Breadbasket. In three of the most crucial categories—checkers, meat apprentices, clerks—A & P had lost some of the blacks they had previously because of store operational declines in the ghetto.

In other categories, such as grocery warehouse supervisors, the number had remained steady at zero. To make matters worse, A & P officials told Breadbasket they had done all they intended to do.

Picketing began on July 6, 1968. "This store is off-limits," announced Jackson. "We don't use the word 'boycott,' we just are not going to cooperate with evil, which is theologically sound. In Chicago in some areas the weekly gross is $20,000, but in our black stores it is as high as $60,000 a week and black folks hold their margin of profit."

A Breadbasket chapter formed in the white north shore community cooperated with the boycotts. After sixteen weeks of steady boycotting, some stores didn't have enough money to cash a check, according to Hyman Johnson. "During that period A & P thought the picketers would just go away, that they could outlast them. But when losses started hitting roughly $10 million, they woke up."

On October 5, 1968, after the most intensive and exhaustive boycott of a major food chain in recent history, A & P signed the most comprehensive covenant SCLC's Operation Breadbasket had ever designed. Although it called for only 268 additional blacks, it included provisions for two black executives to be hired by A & P. The executives were to be selected by Breadbasket to work within the company to ensure that the letter and spirit of the covenant became official company policy.

Pleased with his organization's efforts, Jackson said of the impressive document, "That's what I call grass roots. What could be more grass-rootish than garbage removal and exterminating? Until now, we didn't even control our own rats and roaches." (*Time*, March 1, 1968.)

In 1972, statistics showed that A & P had admirably improved its employment record, often going beyond the minimum requirements that the Breadbasket ministers had negotiated. The A & P campaign was the only clearcut victory the Jackson forces ever won in their war on the supermarket industry.

The main reason the A & P covenant was implemented and others were not was largely that a black man on the inside provided the necessary watchdogging that the movement could or would not provide to ensure compliance. Hyman Johnson, who today is an assistant to the vice-president of the Chicago Division, raced around A & P like a fireman, handling all the hot spots troublesome to both his employer and the black producer as well.

For example, Archie's Mumbo sauce, a black-manufactured barbecue product, could not compete against General Foods' Open Pit, for which the company could spend over $5 million on advertising alone. "When a customer comes into a store, she impulsively picks up Open Pit. So what I may do is give Mumbo a competitive advantage by putting Open Pit on a lower shelf, where the customer has to stoop to pick it up. It's a small thing, but sometimes it gives Mumbo sauce a fighting chance," Johnson said.

Fighting off the Chicago Board of Health was another problem for Johnson. "Some of the Board of Health officials hated Jesse's guts. So they would take Parker House or Metropolitan sausages, both black products, and weigh them. Maybe they were a few grams off because all sausages shrink. But the health officials would write us up with a $200 fine, even though we had no control over prepackaged items. They often told us, 'This is what you get for letting Jesse Jackson run A & P.' I had to deal with them as well as some of Breadbasket's people who thought they were going to run things," he said.

Johnson also extends a helping hand to the black

businessman who may lack the know-how of doing business. Johnson said, "A guy came in here once and asked me to place his product. I told him that I would have to run a Dun and Bradstreet report on him first. The guy asked, 'What's that?' I told him it was a business report firm that checked financial stability. The guy told me that was unnecessary. 'You're just giving me the run-around because I'm black and you're one of those Uncle Toms.'" That exchange led to a long rap session on the art of selling, which the guy ultimately appreciated.

"There is a total lack of business sense on the part of many small businessmen," Johnson admitted. "Unfortunately, many of them have never had the opportunity to learn what business is. It's the same on the inside. Breadbasket said we must have X number of black managers before we could open our stores. So what happened was that A & P found some guys that had been good at doing what they were told and kicked them upstairs into a position of telling others what to do. They were put into a position to fail, which is exactly what they are doing, since they did not have the opportunity to move through the ranks or receive training. As a result, the black stores that were doing $40,000 to $60,000 a week are now [1972] doing about $20,000 or less—all of them. I call it masquerading as managers. They are trying like hell but they have never had the proper training."

"Integration of the job market without preparation only leads to frustration," says the Reverend Leon Sullivan of Philadelphia. "Black people have been denied an opportunity to acquire the necessary experience and haven't had adequate access to training in fields where there was the greatest demand."

In the supermarkets, as well as all other industries, it is wrong to say that blacks should not have their chance at the top. It is also wrong to deny them the basic essentials for making it, then blame them when they fail. So whose responsibility is it to change this?

Jackson's characteristic response is: "If the Army can teach a Negro to build bridges in Vietnam after a six-month training program, a company doesn't need two years to teach him how to sell soda pop successfully." (*Business Week,* April 26, 1969.) While Jackson is placing the onus on the right place, his reply does not address the problem.

Hyman Johnson of A & P said, "I was surprised to find that A & P didn't have a training program for blacks. Well, I guess in a way there is no need. They bring each other in, like the Irish do on the police force. That's the way our chairman of the board William Kane got his start. He began as a stock boy."

Capitalizing on blacks' ignorance of how the game is played, some whites who resent a black boss, especially when they have more seniority, set snares to help the black manager topple—a situation which could occur in any industry. According to a National Tea official, "After Breadbasket signed a covenant with us, some blacks who were not trained were just grabbed and promoted. They had no way of balancing themselves once they were up there because they had no one to lean on. All their district managers were white and were not happy that they were there in the first place. Our black managers began to have sizeable shrinks or unexplainable losses in inventory. In some cases, I found the delivery boys short-changed them to make them look bad. These delivery boys were representatives of white society. They knew the new manager wouldn't know if he were being short-changed. On other occasions, people would bill us for goods they hadn't delivered and infer the merchandise had been stolen. I guess the whites were playing their role in keeping blacks in their place. And too often the black manager was not trained enough to defend himself from such trickery."

In Philadelphia, rather than vacillate about the problem of whose responsibility it is to train blacks, the Reverend Leon Sullivan put down his picket signs and initiated a training program, which today has trained more than 75,000 persons for jobs with more than 1,000 companies. His training program, Opportunities Industrialization Centers (OIC), is currently operating in more than one hundred cities and six foreign countries.

On the assumption that jobs are available if blacks are equipped with the right skills, the first OIC manpower training program began in an abandoned jailhouse in 1964. The second center, along with $25,000, was donated by a local multimillionaire.

Later the federal government's Office of Economic Opportunity provided some funds for five more centers in Philadelphia. Funding from the U.S. Department of Health, Education, and Welfare, and the Ford Foundation soon followed. Private industry, some plants which Sullivan had boycotted, also pitched in with teletype equipment, canceled check machines, and mobile grocery check-out equipment. OIC trained workers not only for grocery employment, but also in occupations ranging from bookkeeper to computer programmer. The general attitude toward OIC trainees nationwide is, "If you have more good men like the others you've trained, we'll hire them." This sentiment was expressed by a spokesman for Budd Manufacturing in Philadelphia.

Sullivan offers a way of stopping the buck-passing which crushes the untrained black worker in the middle. Once trained by OIC, blacks are qualified not only to compete in industry but also to initiate their own ventures, thus multiplying opportunities for others. This effort, however, does not take the onus off industries such as A & P, which could well afford the challenge.

National Muscle

In December 1970, SCLC's Operation Breadbasket renewed the A & P fight with an announcement of a twenty-city boycott in a large-scale effort to increase

Negro hiring and the use of black products. In effect, the struggle would be a test case of the power of the economic arm of SCLC to repeat in one sweep the spectacular success it had gained with A & P in Chicago. The drive would also serve as a laboratory to measure the weight of Jackson's often-quoted theory: "We have the power, nonviolently, just by controlling our appetites, to determine the direction of the American economy. If black people in thirty cities said simultaneously, 'General Motors, you will not sell cars in the black community unless you guarantee us a franchise here next year and help us finance it,' GM would have no choice but to comply. We can affect their margin of profit by withdrawing our patronage and resisting the system instead of enduring it." (*Playboy*, November 1969.)

In answer to *Playboy's* question, "Why has all this not been done yet?" Jackson said, "Because we hadn't been sophisticated enough to see it. This is a step that we haven't been ready to take. But it will certainly be done now, because we are organizing to do it."

The shift from Chicago to the nation had been developing since July of 1967 when Dr. King proposed a national conference of clergymen as a means of launching a nationwide Breadbasket program. The conference was to be composed of 100 ministers from twenty major cities. When the conference was held on July 10 at the Chicago Theological Seminary, more ministers than had been invited responded—155 from forty-two cities—thus underscoring the strong support for the potentially history-making campaign. After the meeting was concluded, two more targets were added to the list—General Motors and the P. Lorillard Tobacco Company. One month later on August 14, during SCLC's annual convention in Atlanta, Jackson replaced Fred C. Bennett as national director of Operation Breadbasket, accepting the primary responsibility of organizing the national drive.

Eventually the A & P fight focused on the supermarket chain's national headquarters in New York City, led by the SCLC Breadbasket chapter's director there, the Reverend William Jones. This tall Kentuckian had a booming baritone voice that fouled up the acoustics in the negotiations.

Since 1969, the Reverend Jones had successfully gained concessions for jobs and business development from such companies as Wonder Bread, Sealtest Foods, May's Department Stores, and Canada Dry, but the national A & P office proved more stubborn than any of Jones' or Jackson's previous encounters.

For six months, Jones and his flock had tried to meet with A & P board chairman William Kane. Each time, Breadbasket officials were told to meet instead with regional or divisional officers. Even the complaints of young Huntington Hartford didn't bring a response. Hartford, who had supported Jackson, said, "A & P does not treat the black community as it should. Kane is high-handed in refusing to meet with Breadbasket leaders." A & P directors feared the drive would turn into a national publicity campaign. This would upset its already nervous stockholders, who were more than a little concerned that the company was sliding from its lofty position in several key cities. "We're not going to make a big to-do of this in public, because all it does is give Operation Breadbasket a boost. Frankly, we don't want to make a hero out of either Jones or Jackson," said one A & P spokesman. "The minute Kane involves himself, he implies this is an area of his jurisdiction." Thus Kane stayed away from his offices, ostensibly for a tour of stores in other cities.

In February of 1971, Jackson arrived in New York to take charge of the SCLC drive. "I'm in town and I plan to stick around until I see Kane. National confrontation has replaced regional confrontation," Jackson announced. The day after his arrival, following a sit-in and a sing-in at the posh offices of A & P's executive suite, Jackson and his followers were hauled off to jail, where they were charged with trespassing and disorderly conduct. Resolutely, A & P stuck to its guns in refusing to meet with or submit to Breadbasket's demands. Thus Breadbasket's first attempt to nationalize its Chicago efforts failed.

Reflecting on the national strength of Operation Breadbasket, many of Jackson's coworkers, as well as his boss, Ralph Abernathy, attributed its impotence to Chicago's becoming the world for Jackson, the national director, who could never break away to fulfill his national obligations.

Andy Young, former SCLC executive director: "When we put Jesse in charge of the boycott apparatus, it was to develop a nationwide structure, so we could hit thirty or forty cities simultaneously. That $30- or $40-billion market he often speaks about was his to organize. But Jesse could never get out of Chicago to do it. That's one of the reasons I got out of there after the End the Slums campaign. Chicago has so many problems it can soak up a leader and destroy him," the Georgia congressman said.

Ralph Abernathy: "A national structure was the purpose for having a national director, so we could repeat the successes of Chicago and Atlanta over and over again. Jesse's getting bogged down in Chicago is understandable. A lot of you people think that Chicago is the end. A lot of people have never left Chicago since they landed there from Mississippi. I guess what happened was that instead of Breadbasket becoming a division of SCLC, he made the one in Chicago a department in itself. That's why he never got to Buffalo, to Dallas, to Philadelphia, and to all the other cities that wanted to participate in a national boycott, which was and still is one of our most effective weapons in the nonviolent struggle."

Calvin Morris said it was basically his responsibility to

set up national Breadbasket chapters: "Dr. King challenged Jesse to divorce himself from his baby [Chicago] because he saw he was getting too engrossed in building his own personal kingdom. All the newspapers gave us credit for about thirty Breadbasket chapters across the country, but most of them were SCLC chapters. About the only strong chapters Breadbasket had outside of Chicago were in New York and Cleveland."

Gary Massoni: "By the end of 1969, Breadbasket was claiming active chapters in New York, Los Angeles, Cleveland, Atlanta, Houston, Cincinnati, Milwaukee, and Indianapolis. However, these local operations were functioning only sporadically, primarily due to the lack of assistance from the national office of Breadbasket and the lack of coordination."

Placing the responsibility on both SCLC and Breadbasket, Massoni concluded, "Neither one took seriously enough the need to organize systematically this unprecedented potential for economic power for the black community. Although a budget and eight staff members were pulled together for the national effort, significant commitment simply was not evident except in the rhetoric."

Jackson was not unaware of the need for such a drive on a national level. In a 1971 interview in *Black Enterprise*, he said, "Operation Breadbasket should have chapters in thirty or forty cities. You just can't whip a chain from Chicago alone. When we move against a company, we should do it nationally."

An organized black consumer movement is still a great idea. Although it was never orchestrated under Operation Breadbasket, it no doubt will materialize from Operation PUSH. As the leader of his own organization, it is in Jackson's self-interest to organize black consumers if for no other reason than as a support group for black businesses. The boycotting of General Motors is still part of Jackson's vocal repertoire, but the A & P campaign summed up the national muscle of Breadbasket.

Red Rooster

Breadbasket's confrontation with the Red Rooster chain was a clear illustration of how legitimate protest can be used as a cover for blackmail and how the legacy of ghetto residents is the worst of everything, not only schools, jobs, and housing but also the food they eat. It is oftentimes of inferior quality but still disdainfully overpriced. The Red Rooster story not only illustrates the power of black community groups to drive out proven ghetto gougers, but it also shows how these groups lack the resources to build satisfactory enterprises to replace them.

The Red Rooster chain, which included seven stores in the poorest areas of Chicago, came under attack from Breadbasket, one of the leading groups in the Coalition for United Community Action (CUCA), in March of 1969.

The documented negligence of the Red Rooster chains was so extreme that most of their 300 black employees purchased their food elsewhere. Reports included: an entire family of fourteen contracted food poisoning after eating hamburgers they had purchased there; check-out girls were fired for refusing to overring; a butcher was axed for complaining that meat preservatives had reached the toxic level; packages of bad meat were saved to be ground into hamburger; chickens were alleged to have been frozen for several years and chemically treated to obscure their taint; rat holes were discovered in the stores; and dogs had been observed wandering around where the meat was being packaged. The list of atrocities ran on ad nauseam. The chain's customers, many of whom were public housing residents, could ill afford to shop elsewhere, and many of the reputable chains had already begun their phase-out of the crime-ridden poverty areas of Chicago.

Charges of impropriety were hurled at Jackson by the Red Rooster employees, who, regardless of how unsanitary the conditions were, feared losing their jobs because of the threatened boycott. Black workers carried counterprotest signs: "Operation Breadbasket is wrong." "Jesse Jackson is hurting black people." Ron Johnson, Red Rooster's black personnel manager, called Jackson "an opportunist and a liar." "He's using the boycott to further enhance his own image and doesn't care one bit about the black community." In answering the charges, Jackson said, "Yes, I am an opportunist—for justice—because I seize every opportunity to try to right a wrong, whether it's in schools, stores, or anywhere black people are being disrespected. For Ron Johnson to slander my name would be detrimental to me, Breadbasket, and the entire black movement of Chicago." After the negotiations got under way, Red Rooster appointed a black straw boss to keep the fifty action groups off the main issue of scandalous consumer fraud. The black "official" did not take the pressure off Red Rooster, however. The company was boycotted by 400 protesters for eight days until Red Rooster agreed to meet the black leaders' demands for raising store standards and hiring security guards that Breadbasket had approved.

The concessions won from Red Rooster turned into a hollow victory. By September, the owners were hauled off to federal court on tax delinquency charges and soon afterward filed bankruptcy.

Besides the inability of Red Rooster to turn a profit fairly, another factor contributed to the firm's demise. This was the padding of salaries for twenty-two members of the Black P Stone Rangers street gang, who had forced their way into the company under the auspices of the CUCA and Breadbasket.

The gang members, including fifteen of the Main 21, the ruling henchmen of Chicago's largest and most vicious street gang, were employed with such incongruous titles as "outside store inspector" and "inside store inspector." Management trainee positions went to youths awaiting trial for robbery, and security guard jobs went to gang members out on bond on murder and theft charges.

"There is no question that the stores were engaging in such unethical and illegal practices," said Captain Edward F. Buckney, former director of the gang intelligence unit of the Chicago Police Department. Buckney noted that over the last several years Red Rooster had been fined thirty-two times for violations such as short weight. "Unfortunately," he said, "the Rangers used this boycott and resulting turmoil to their own advantages. The result was that when the Red Rooster managers agreed to employ twenty-two more blacks, they wound up with twenty-two Rangers."

A letter from the manager of Red Rooster to the Reverend C. T. Vivian, director of CUCA, indicated that the twenty-two men had been hired on the recommendations of Operation Breadbasket and CUCA. The inclusion of the street gangs in the movement was indicative of the times. In the late 1960s, it was in vogue to attribute the gang bloodletting to the fact that gang members were culturally deprived. Gang leaders often addressed audiences from the Breadbasket pulpit. The Rangers were held in such high esteem, police records notwithstanding, that former President Nixon invited two top members to his first term inaugural ball. There they were, resplendent in black tie and tails, while many more "deserving" blacks did not receive an invitation. Among these was the Reverend Jackson. In appreciation of the recognition, the Rangers invited Nixon to the opening of their new car wash. He declined.

National Tea

It all started routinely enough with the wrongs piled heavily on the side of National Tea, but before the drive ended, one could only wonder how two wrongs could ever bring about a civil right. In November 1966, black employment hovered around 14.6 percent with the bulk of it clustered around the categories of checker, clerk, and lugger. On December 8, 1966, the National Tea Company, which included Del Farm stores, inked a covenant with Operation Breadbasket in which it agreed to add 377 black workers within ninety days. The Breadbasket staples of banking black and distributing black products were included.

Caught up in other negotiations and interests, Breadbasket did not discover until four years later that National Tea had not followed through to its satisfaction. In an April 1970 progress statement to Breadbasket, National Tea reported that in its thirty-three stores (twenty-one National and twelve Del Farm) having 50 percent or more black trade, the following improvements had been made:

Black products: The 1970 average monthly purchase of black-manufactured products had risen over 1969. For example, in 1969 Joe Louis milk was averaging $14,581 in monthly sales. Others, however, had increased (or even decreased) slightly. Mumbo sauce went from $1,057 in 1969 to $1,200 in 1970. Johnson beauty products went down from $1,749 to $1,700.

Scavenger, exterminating, and janitorial services: Ten black scavengers were servicing nineteen stores; three exterminators covered twenty-four stores; and three janitorial firms kept up twenty-five stores, some of which were in white neighborhoods. Lillard Detective and Investigation Agency, which also provides protection for Jackson, was receiving $9,500 a month for its services.

But the ministers' main concern was that National Tea did not hire 117 black employees, depriving the black community of $4 million in salaries. National also initially did not report 238 supervisory jobs because 221 were filled by whites; did not deal with black liquor salesmen; and did not transfer accounts from twenty stores to Seaway and Independence Banks. However, National Tea did transfer monies from ten of its stores to the two black banks.

The ministers were in the dark concerning National Tea's extensive corporate holdings, and National Tea was not about to tell them. National Tea, headquartered in Chicago, with $1 billion-plus in annual sales, is the thirteenth largest supermarket chain in America. Its 955 stores in other cities are under such trade names as Elm Farm, Save Way, and Loblaw's. But more importantly, under the National Tea structure in Chicago are: Kare Drugs, O'Bee Foods, So-Fresh, and National Labs, all of which could have been the source of additional jobs for blacks had Breadbasket known of their interrelationship.

After an unusually lengthy period of negotiations, a selective buying campaign was announced against National Tea on November 6, 1970. This dragged on into June of 1971, finally fizzling out when Jackson began to focus more heavily on Chicago's political scene.

The National Tea effort revealed the first trace of the unraveling of the movement's integrity. This trend would grow more ominous as the questions of unethical conduct carried over into PUSH. Charges of impropriety, extortion, mishandling of funds—accusations virtually unheard of under King's leadership—would be raised not only by PUSH board members anonymously but also by black journalists. Perhaps it was inevitable that questions about personal integrity would have to be raised in light of the course the movement is traveling. King's movement demanded civil rights; Jackson's movement is about money—the rechanneling of jobs and public and private funds into the black community. What segment of the black community? Who should be the conduit for the funds? And what besides good faith ensures the integrity of the leader who is commissioned to direct the money flow? All are legitimate questions; answers began to surface in The People vs. National Tea consumer campaign.

What follows is a list of the circumstances which pushed the movement further away from its goal of being the moral conscience of the city for doing business the Chicago way.

- A movement minister was listed on the first National Tea covenant as an official of a company attempting to gain distribution from National Tea. This gave National Tea an excuse to accuse the entire group of attempting to line their own pockets.

- Two members of another black minister's church were surprised to witness a $5,000 personal donation coming from a high ranking National Tea official. The official who appeared at the church donated the money for the "fine work it had done in the community." The recipient was one of the top men on the National Tea negotiations team.

- A Breadbasket staffer was listed as program director of the National Tea drive in the June 10, 1971, issue of the *Chicago Tribune.* A check of National Tea's employment records also showed that he was on their payroll as a management trainee. Noah Robinson, Jesse Jackson's brother, who joined the Breadbasket staff in 1969, explained this arrangement. "Until it came to light, I don't think anyone would have made me believe that Jesse started a relationship with National Tea where this guy got paid from them, while he worked for Breadbasket. National Tea paid him and another aide $9,500 a year while they both flew around the country protecting Jesse. That went on for about a year and a half, until the president, Norm Stapelton, died. When the new National Tea president, F. Bruce Krysiak, took over he asked to see Jesse about the arrangement. Jesse sent representatives to him during the boycott but never showed up himself. Finally the word went out: "Since you have not dealt in good faith, you can picket us until the cows come home and we will not budge one inch. I'll close every damn store on the south and west side rather than create any more patronage jobs in National Tea for you."

National Tea officials also complained that the scavengers and janitors were doing a lackluster job, although in some cases they were being paid five times as much as the white companies they had replaced. Similar complaints were echoed by Walgreen's, Jewel, and A & P.

Hyman Johnson of A & P explained: "One black company we paid as high as $175 a day to mop a store, when we had paid the white company before him $35. We felt this was a good thing to do because they said they didn't have the materials. But as it turned out, A & P was supplying the mops, the buckets, the wax. All the blacks had to do was supply the manpower and it still didn't work."

The situation at National Tea reached outrageous proportions, according to a black company representative.

"We paid more to black scavengers because they had to pay a black tax on their merchandise and trucks, often they were not allowed to use the dump yards except at certain hours and they had personnel problems. But if I would tell the real truth, I'd have to say some of them just didn't give a damn. Sometimes three days would pass without their calling to tell us that maybe a truck had broken down.

"Depending on your sense of humor, we had a comical situation over here for a while. Our neighbors were complaining about the garbage outside creating rats and flies. The Board of Health was fining us $200 a crack. So the store managers got scared and started hiding the garbage inside the stores in the coolers or behind this or that. It was a holy mess. So when the health inspectors came by they saw the garbage inside the store and closed us down a day or so. Sometimes because I was black I would call some of the scavengers and plead with them to straighten up, but many took the attitude that since Breadbasket put them in, there wasn't a damn thing we could do about their falling down on the job. One scavenger presented us a bill for $375 for one store. For eighteen years the company before him was paid only $65 a month. When I corrected him, he told me he was going to sic Breadbasket on us. It was very disgusting. I felt like a man without a country. You try to help blacks and at the same time you owe some loyalty to your company. I was really in a bind."

Early in 1971, food chain negotiators and Breadbasket officials gathered at the Marion Business School in Chicago to settle the matter. Chain representatives brought along pictures that illustrated how the floors had not been scrubbed, how people had mopped around boxes, and a host of other complaints. The store representatives had come there with one thing on their minds—to stop what they agreed was the nonsense of paying blacks five times as much to do one-fifth as much work. Some, however, decided to continue with the scavengers, reportedly because of the problems they were having with the crime syndicate.

When black scavenger firms took over at A & P's forty stores in Chicago's ghetto on October 19, 1966, two trucks were set afire. Jackson, whose life was threatened repeatedly during the scavenger flare-up, said, "Other scavengers have experienced violent acts like finding their containers destroyed, alleys blocked by white-owned scavenger trucks, and threats from persons in unmarked cars. In the face of white men of power and of black men of fear burning our trucks, we will not sit idly by with our arms locked singing and bodies bent in prayer. Who deals with the question? Should a black man have the privilege to have priority on removing his own garbage and that of his neighbors? This question must be answered, for we demand respect. We will be recognized." (*Chicago Defender*, November 1, 1967.) According to Noah Robinson, the dumps also were controlled by the syndicate. "Since they owned all the dumps, they called the shots, so they kept the blacks out. Sometimes the blacks were dumping in people's backyards and the alleys. It wasn't until a black bought the Calumet City dump that things started to change."

• The boycott itself was a joke, according to Jesse Jackson's brother Noah. "Every Saturday my brother would be announcing on the radio how bad we were whipping National Tea, and their sales were actually going up. Jesse was not doing any of the picketing, so what would often happen was that the demonstrators would picket awhile on Saturday, and then go into National Tea and shop before they went home. I don't think it was a negative reaction against people who just wanted to violate Operation Breadbasket. It was just that the thing was totally ineffective. That's why Jesse saved face when he took a leave of absence during the National Tea thing. They weren't ever going to win it. You can't wallow in bed with the enemy and then expect him to respect you."

Although Jackson often attempts to, no one can pinpoint how many jobs Breadbasket gained for the black worker. Robinson pointed out, "We used to throw out figures like we got 400 jobs worth $4 million or something like that, but it's a safe bet nobody could vouch for more than 100 jobs because we were moving too fast to go back and check." However, there was no question that contracts for business had been watchdogged and followed through on—especially as businessmen began to replace the ministers as the financial cushion of the movement. This tension between priorities of jobs for the masses and contracts for the Jackson businessmen would eventually work itself out, with the group that could best serve the self-interest of Jackson becoming clearly predominant.

In National Tea's 1972 annual report to its shareholders, Krysiak stated that business for the past year had never been better. "Sales were the highest in your company's history at $1,613,853,162." Perhaps that statement best wraps up the results of The People vs. National Tea Company consumer campaign.

A bright spot in the overall dismal picture was the historic breakthrough for blacks in the construction field. On May 11, 1967, ground was broken for the first chain store in the nation ever built by black contractors. The $300,000 contract awarded to the Bush and Smith Construction firm to build a Del Farm store at 4759 S. Calumet Avenue was followed by others. Robert Martin Construction Company later was awarded contracts for stores at 3425 W. Roosevelt Road and 9001 S. Halsted Street.

The National Tea fight was the last major confrontation Operation Breadbasket had with supermarket corporations before Jackson launched his new group (PUSH) in December of 1971. Other significant covenants were signed with Jewel and Walgreen's, which resulted in only moderate concrete results, largely because of the movement's inability to follow through.

Two other observations should footnote the boycott stage of Operation Breadbasket.

From talks with white corporate leaders, Jonathan Laing, a white reporter on the *Wall Street Journal*, correctly identified Jackson's Achilles tendon—the consistent inclination to confuse news headlines or paper victories with concrete change. Jackson always was, and still is, a patsy for the Quick Score—which can be easily won by those who know how to use the media. Most all of Jackson's maneuvers are packaged for media consumption and, unfortunately for the public, the media dutifully assist by not providing close scrutiny.

Laing said: "In my talks with white corporate leaders, I find that they usually harbor these impressions: Jackson is a superb negotiator, knowing exactly when to get tough, when to pull back, and when to bring God into the discussion with the moral dimension. Some white businessmen call Jackson and his men the moral Mafia because they are so good at putting the pressure on. Others quickly identified his weakness of being publicity-hungry. So they would quickly sign the covenants and hold a press conference with Jesse. Corporate officials often felt that Jesse could get good press from the covenants and so could they, since it would emphasize their social consciousness. But from the publicity stages was about as far as some of the corporate leaders intended to go because they knew that was Jackson's first concern and he wouldn't double back on them to check on their progress."

The movement's greatest achievement in Chicago was the tremendous social momentum created which shook up all segments of the corporate community. Faux pas notwithstanding, the mere fact that a catalytic force existed with the potential to militantly push for economic redress caused many white corporations to make policy changes in favor of blacks. Not only did the Jackson movement bring to the surface white fear of retaliation, but all the commotion tugged at the corporate conscience, causing many firms to drop discriminatory barriers, simply because Jackson had so eloquently convinced them that to do so was right.

There are scores of stories about whites reacting indirectly to Jackson as the Great Sensitizer. But perhaps the best is told by Gardner Stern, Jr., the young, liberal president of Hillman's, a $60-million corporation, which has twenty stores in the Chicago metropolitan area.

Stern said the Woodlawn Organization (TWO) became a partner with Hillman's primarily because of the Jackson influence. "I used to listen to him on the radio. And then I started going to the meetings. It took a while but eventually I began to understand what he meant by 'nation time' and 'cut us in or cut it out.' I began thinking about how do you structure a business where the community has ownership and shares the profits and there still is a viable economic enterprise. About the same time I was becoming conceptually sensitized, the [former] head of the Woodlawn Organization, attorney E. Duke McNeil, approached me to be strictly tenants in a new complex they were building. I asked them how would you like to structure something where your organization could share in the ownership and the profits. And, of course, they were interested because it fit into their own objectives and we began embarking on a formula."

Today, in 1974, TWO Hillman's is the magnate store in the community group's twelve-store operation. It grossed more than $3.2 million in 1973, employs fifty-four people from the community, and expects to buy the one-third interest owned by Hillman's in less than ten years.

Stern's effort was a significant gesture because it was not a reaction to negative prodding, "My mind would never have been together for the sharing of profits with TWO if it were not for listening to Jackson. Those of us whites who have some concern have different ways of expressing that concern. When Dr. King was alive I was like a lot of other people who sat on my ass and said that he was a great man. But when he started talking about the Vietnam War I said what business is this of his. So the first step in doing something is to agree and the next is to get mobilized in some way. You get active in the organization and then maybe you write a few checks, which also can be a cop out.

"The real effort is what you can do to attack the problem and particularly when you can do something that makes economic sense as well as solving the social problem. I say to some white guys who have been turned on by Jesse that you don't have to come south of your plant in Skokie to do something meaningful. Don't think that coming to Breadbasket is all that you can do. If you really want to do something, go to your office and think: are all the suppliers you are buying from merit employees? And how many black executives do you have? Are you planning any joint ventures? This, of course, is where it gets tough."

How many other Sterns are there? No one knows.

6

*They call themselves nationalists
and exploit the legitimate
nationalist feelings of black
people in order to advance their
own interests as a class . . . .
bourgeois nationalism may line
the pockets and boost the social
status of the black middle class
and black intelligentsia, but it
will not ease the oppression of the
ordinary ghetto dweller.*

Robert L. Allen, *Black Awakening
in Capitalist America*

By 1974 Jesse Jackson had created his own economic patronage machine. It is only eight years old. And today, it can muster just enough energy to keep both the leader and the movement chugging along. Yet, Jackson's tiny contraption is nothing to scoff at. In time it could become a bulldozer—if not something to climb aboard, at least something to get out of the way of.

To black entrepreneurs, especially the big ones, Jesse Jackson is a benevolent godfather. Who could they contact to get a favor? Who looked out for them before Jackson came to town? Chicago now has six black-owned banks.

The black fat cats are getting fatter, and opportunities to make a buck are opening up for the little businessman.

Since Jackson has blessed them abundantly, the black businessmen know there is only one way to treat the godfather: good. So whatever Jesse wants, Jesse gets.

On tree-lined Constance Avenue, the leader of poor folks occupies a fifteen-room Romanesque residence. The fifty-five-year-old home purchased on August 25, 1970, for $49,500 is in secret land trust, apparently in order to shield the names of his pals who hold the note.

Automobiles like his maroon 1974 Lincoln Continental and his wife's red Toyota are often leased or loaned gratis from black automobile dealers, such as Al Johnson Cadillac. Jackson is chauffeured, not just because of his eminence but by popular demand. Speeding tickets and a couple of crashes have labeled the Reverend a bit of a public nuisance.

Other amenities include free landscaping and dinners and banquets catered to his home, as well as many of his image clothes. In his closet among the Brooks Brothers pin stripes are denim suits from Los Angeles' Fred Segals and several shades of browns from Wilson's House of Suede, many of them gifts from fans in the entertainment world.

Personal gratuities, such as these, should be expected for someone so important, but keeping the movement afloat is what counts. Jackson will never be poor, but somehow the movement always is. And here again the Jackson businessmen deliver. When the movement bought new headquarters, black businessmen put up the collateral. Black businessmen provided the seed money for special events, such as Black Expo, Black Christmas, and Black Easter. And they have been subsidizing his junior executive salary since 1966. Some businessmen are, of course, more generous than others. Al Bell, executive vice-president of Stax Records, pledged $37,000 in 1972, and made a

$100,000 loan. Jesse records his speeches on the Stax label, and also promotes the company's top-name stars.

In 1971, Jackson's boss, the Reverend Ralph Abernathy, ordered Jackson to move to Atlanta. Jesse was getting too powerful and Abernathy was getting worried. But dragging Jackson out of Chicago was about as easy as dumping Lake Michigan into a thimble. In 1971 and also in 1973 movement finances in their usual disarray made front-page news. Here again, the businessmen put their arms of protection around Jackson. Jackson didn't have to show up for either press conference. The big boys just told the journalists that Jesse didn't know about such complicated affairs as expenditures. And that was the end of that. And in 1971 when Jackson broke from Breadbasket, the businessmen told him, "We don't care what you call the movement as long as you stay the same." Thus they helped finance his split. The movement changed its name, but the game remained the same.

Besides those directly attached to Jackson in this quid pro quo relationship, there are the Black Who's Who of America sitting on his 53-member national PUSH board (see Appendix). People like Percy Sutton, president of the Manhattan borough; Mayor Richard Hatcher of Gary; Quincy Jones, composer; Dr. James Cheek, president of Howard University; Attorney John Bustamante; Wesley South, Chicago WVON-radio executive; Berry Gordy, president of Motown Records; Chicago alderman Anna Langford; Barbara Proctor, president of Proctor & Gardner Advertising Company; and Dempsey Travis, president of Sivart Mortgage Company. They add status. And, the black luminaries can get things done. This means that if Jackson's coattails were unfolded they would reach halfway across the nation.

Thus Jackson has a masterful grasp of the smooth interlocking power arrangements of services, favors, rewards—informal principles upon which Chicago and the nation are run. Blacks were always shut out from this exclusive club until Jackson improvised an economic patronage system of his own—all of which appears to be within the framework of the law.

Perhaps George Jones, vice-president of the Joe Louis Milk Company and core Jackson businessman, adequately sums up the sentiments of the black corporate giants: "If anybody buys Jackson, it must be blacks. Hypothetically, if Jackson needed a home, if his children need special medical attention or a trust fund is required to support his family in the event of death, if his radio broadcast needs sponsors, if he needs automobiles, clothes, anything at all, why not? I don't believe he should suffer just because he is leading the poor. I feel he should live in a decent manner and most of us will try to make that possible."

What about the white corporate world? They certainly must dislike Jackson the agitator, who used to create such a ruckus that the big companies couldn't discriminate against the black worker in peace. Money talks, and money tells more about how they feel about Jackson than any interview could tell. A partial list of white corporations picking up the tab for the 1973 Family Affair Banquet, obtained by Chicago's NBC reporter Russ Ewing, includes: Carson Pirie Scott department store, $30,000; Hugh Hefner, $52,000; Illinois Bell, $25,000; Goldblatt's department store, $8,000; and Ford Motor, $2,000. The same spirit of cooperation applies to PUSH Expo, billed as a black trade fair. Booths for white firms cost $3,500, while booths for black businessmen cost about $500. According to a November 10, 1973, *Chicago Tribune* article, white corporations through booth sales spent nearly $120,000 at Expo '73. The large corporations are happy to cooperate in this disproportionate relationship with Jackson because many feel their good will is a down payment against economic boycotts.

Sometimes it appears their assessment is correct. For example, on July 29, 1972, Jackson announced that he would move against the major movie studios that produce black films. Mentioning Columbia Pictures by name, Jackson said in the *Chicago Sun-Times:* "PUSH will address itself to protest the production of films that major in vulgarity, that project into the minds of our children the images of killers rather than healers. We should pass judgment on which black movies are decent and which are indecent." Although Jackson did dialogue with major Hollywood movie moguls, the chats produced surprising results. In 1973, Jackson appeared in the film *Wattstax*, distributed by Columbia Pictures (exhorting his famed "I Am Somebody" litany), as well as in the production *Save the Children*, filmed at Expo '72, distributed by Paramount. Then at Expo 1973, representatives from the Columbia-Warner Brothers Burbank complex exhibited a booth replete with Bugs Bunny wearing an Afro wig. For some reason, the fiery rhetoric of Jackson, the movie star, no longer heats up the "vulgar" film industry.

Jackson's turnabout on the film industry does not define him, because a few examples can be found of his biting the hand that feeds him. He may also accept a white corporate gift and then turn around and kick his benevolent benefactors right in the teeth. Among the amenities Gulf Oil Company provided for the movement was a company representative to handle public relations for Expo '72. The official also served on the '72 Family Affair dinner committee—a polite term for ticket salesmen. Both gestures amounted to about $40,000, but not enough to ward off a major attack on the monopolistic oil industry in 1974. However, Gulf was not mentioned by name. Ironically enough, Ralph Abernathy was brutally chastised in 1974 by the black press for taking a $50,000 Gulf cash contribution. Nothing was said about the relationship between Jackson and Gulf.

Stated simply, this is the Jackson formula for

movement development and Jackson development: Use rhetorical inspiration to fire up the ordinary people into Buy Black consumers, as well as economic foot soldiers. Use the threat of marching feet to extract business covenants from the large corporations to deliver to the black corporations, who are also being aided because more black consumers are buying black.

The second part of the Jackson equation is that the same foot soldiers represent a force that can cause corporate havoc or corporate peace. The big white corporations can have either one, depending on how they treat the godfather.

How do whites feel about the Jackson Robin Hood approach? Well, it could be worse. Perhaps Harry Reasoner best summed up the white corporate attitude on his ABC television broadcast of October 21, 1973. Reasoner said that Jackson was a reasonable alternative to the Stokely Carmichaels. "Jackson makes sure the temperature never gets out of control and he is not a racist. Jackson wants a share of power without destroying its base, which is good news for blacks, as well as for whites."

Since 1968, there had been much conflict over who would be the movement's prime beneficiaries. Should Breadbasket become more business oriented than job oriented or could there be a proper blend of both? The question was never fully resolved. However, a pattern did begin to evolve shortly after the death of Dr. King: the city's top black businessmen began taking the places of the ministers in the movement. Corporate leaders like George Johnson, president of Johnson Products; Darryl Grisham, president of Parker House Sausage; Celious Henderson, president of the Marion Business College; Alvin Boutte, president of Independence Bank; George Jones, vice-president of Joe Louis Milk; and Cecil Troy, president of Grove Fresh Orange Juice, were becoming major participants.

Some ministers left because they felt there was too

much emphasis on contracts for businessmen rather than jobs for the black poor. Others became disillusioned with the movement's inability to follow through on covenants that had been gained by painstaking negotiations. Others left to take care of the business of running a church. Another reason for the exodus was that ministers tend to think of themselves as leaders, but in the Jackson Movement there is only one leader. For whatever reasons then, the changing of the guard defused much of the tension. Whether a businessman is white or black, his primary interest is profit. Thus, Ministers Fight for Jobs and Rights, the slogan that had steered the movement through the pre-King years, was abandoned. And, it would be argued, so was the cause.

In Phase I, Jackson had expanded opportunities for black businessmen by forcing whites who wanted to continue doing business in the colony to pay a tax in the form of jobs, bank deposits, fair prices, construction contracts, the distribution of black products, and the diverting of advertising revenue into the black media.

Phase II brought his efforts closer to home as he brought the old Buy Black tactics and the black trade expositions of the thirties out of mothballs and used them in the reshaping of negative attitudes blacks held about buying from black businessmen.

Black Consciousness

Not since the Harlem Renaissance's impressionistic art forms of protest and pain had there been so much emphasis on black culture. The mid-1960s were a canvas of soulful expression and deep introspection. The Negro National Anthem of the 1920s, written by James Weldon Johnson in 1900, became the Black National Anthem of the 1960s. Poets Don Lee, Carolyn Rodgers, and Gwendolyn Brooks told it like it was and echoed the black dreams of how it soon must be. In the performing arts people were wild about James Baldwin's smashing production of *Blues for Mr. Charlie.* There was an explosion of black literature authored by blacks or by whites offering themselves as experts on blacks. Africa was discovered anew. Not only African apparel, hair styles, and dialects, but also African surnames were in vogue. Writer Leroi Jones, for example, became Imamu Amiri Baraka.

The trends of cultural nationalism were spinning off at a breathtaking rate in all different directions, like pollen escaping into the autumn air. To some blacks the so-called cultural revolution amounted to naught. The concept never crept past the superficial trappings of dashiki-wearing, nappy hair, or reciting a poem or two. Too often, for some, the cultural nationalism cult dispersed into varying stages of ambiguity. For others, it was a step off into a deeper involvement in politics, the arts, economic determination, or community control of public education. The important point, however, was that, in some cases, black leaders were recapturing the minds of blacks from their white brain trusts. The next stage was to generate a course of action through which the new feelings of black pride and dignity could find expression.

Jackson, as well as many other leaders, attempted to corral the stirrings of black consciousness erupting in the souls of black folks before they could disintegrate into a cult of capriciousness. It was often amazing to discover what was going on in the minds of some blacks beneath those billowing Afros. Black was affording the price of African art objects from Marshall Field's, a leading Chicago department store. Black was talking black and marrying white. Black was being one of the few black faces in the crowd of theatergoers at a superhip black play. Black was saying what "the police did to them" instead of "what the police did to us." This was and is not always the case. It was and is just too often the case.

Jackson's self-appointed mission was to shape and

redirect the growing sensations of black pride he himself had been extolling by his "I Am Somebody" litany toward the Chicago black businessmen. They had somehow been overlooked in all the exhortations about Black Is Beautiful. Some of the militants par excellence had not yet discovered the link between black power and buying a carton of Joe Louis milk—or perhaps they had.

Just two examples should point up the work to be done in harnessing this upsurge of black energy and turning it into a gusher of dollars for Chicago's black businessmen.

When A & P was forced to take on additional black products, Hyman Johnson, a black A & P official, thought he was being helpful by putting shelf talkers on them to identify the products as black-manufactured or distributed. "I put little markers on them saying this is a black product and the sales damn near ceased. Grove Fresh orange juice for example, which I guess some people didn't know was distributed by a black, fell 35 percent in sales, before I could snatch the tag off. And this was in an all-black store," Johnson said.

Johnson also relates the story of the failure of a black-distributed Scotch and bourbon. "The Scotch came out of a Cutty Sark bottle and the bourbon came out of an Old Fitzgerald bottle. But the black man put a black chick on each of his labels, and his stuff never moved off the shelves although Cutty Sark is one of the black customer's most popular items."

The rationale behind this negativism is as understandable as it is self-defeating. How can blacks appreciate and patronize their own businessmen when many are burdened with lingering doubts about themselves? The perpetual symbolism of white America influences black as well as white values. For example, Miss America is the incarnation of all things beautiful and feminine. But Miss America has always been white. What sinister comment does this imagery impress upon the black queens in the ghetto? How does a race defend itself against police brutality if it questions whether or not brutalization is the natural consequence of being born black? If black is inferior, then anything made by blacks must also be inferior. So the logical pattern was to Buy White—a sign of quality. The spin-offs of the cultural revolution were doing much to wash away these feelings of self-hatred, but not fast enough for Jackson, the supersalesman of black pride and black products.

Since there was nothing Jackson could do to "improve" black products, his target became the black consumers. He cajoled, teased, and whipped the negativeness out of their psyches through his scathing rhetoric. Jackson is one man who can almost cut your throat with the razor's edge of a word.

During the early Operation Breadbasket meetings, on any given Saturday morning Jackson would say: "You will show your blackness by buying Grove Fresh orange juice. Say it loud I'm black and I'm proud and I buy Grove Fresh orange juice. Say it loud.

"Now Joe Louis milk does not come from a Negro cow. That milk is just like any other milk. It's written right here on the carton. Only difference is that your husband can make $12,000 a year driving a truck for this company.

"Rather than looking through the yellow pages, you got to start looking at the black pages. Trouble is that Negroes have been programmed by white folks to believe their products are inferior. We've developed into a generation of Oreos, black on the outside, white on the inside.

"But I got news for you: a new hair style does not constitute black power, a new lifestyle does. About the only thing that can save us is waking up one morning with self-respect and willingness to do some serious work. 'Cause the Lord don't make orange juice. He may make the ground fertile but Grove Fresh makes the orange juice and you got to buy it. That's what the Lord does to keep from being called a puppeteer."

Jackson packaged his Buy Black inducements into two creative programs, Black Christmas and Black Easter. He later phased them all into a massive extravaganza called Black Expo. All had heavy cultural overtones, but underneath was a well conceived scheme to hoist black businessmen onto a new pedestal of respect in the black community —their main source of revenue.

Black Christmas: The first annual Black Christmas in Chicago was held in 1968. It was sparked by a parade which was led by a horse-drawn wagon, symbolizing the poverty of the nation's masses. More than 80,000 spectators viewed the procession as it weaved down Dr. Martin Luther King, Jr., Drive. More than ninety colorful floats representing black businesses and services and several black high school bands and marching units participated. But the star of it all was the jovial Black Soul Saint, who Jackson said came from the South Pole by the way of the Equator. This fact accounted for his complexion as well as for his unique attire: a black velvet dashiki trimmed with the colors of the Ghanian flag—red, green, and yellow. The purpose of Soul Saint was to conjure up new images. Instead of the usual material goods, Saint's gifts were love, justice, peace, and power.

However, materialism, of course, did underscore the Black Christmas festivities. The idea came from Bob Lucas, former head of Chicago's CORE, who had called for a boycott by blacks of downtown stores during the Christmas season. Jackson first supported this idea, but realizing that blacks were going to buy in the Loop anyway—"those Christmas lights are just too bright"—he later called for exclusive patronage of black-owned stores instead of a boycott. Dozens of Negro businesses set up sales counters inside the Operation Breadbasket Black Christmas Center in the old S. B. Fuller's South Center department store. Parents were encouraged to open up savings accounts for their children in black banks.

It is also interesting to note how Jackson pulls his events off. At three o'clock in the morning, he may be hit by a new idea. When that happens he spends the rest of the morning waking up everybody else in town who can help him pull off his brainchild. When the notion of Black Christmas hit him, he was in the hospital. Doctors had just informed him that he had a special blood disease—sickle cell anemia trait, predominantly peculiar to blacks of West African descent. Jackson was undaunted by the diagnosis. An African disease was worth a press release in itself.

From his hospital bed, he called Doug Andrews, director of the west-side Garfield Organization, to serve as cochairman of the event. The move would keep the poorer blacks over there from scowling about their never being included in the goings-on of the south-side blacks. Next was a call to an aide of the late Congressman William Dawson, Lawrence Woods, to publicize the parade. With Woods on his side, he'd have no trouble gaining a city permit. George Johnson, president of the largest black cosmetics firm in the country (Johnson Products), was cajoled into buying two floats: "Y'all got a big company over there, certainly y'all can afford two," Jackson said. A call to his friend Aretha Franklin assured him of the entertainment, and his staff was ordered to get busy hammering together floats.

Jackson's mind never stops churning out ideas, his ill health notwithstanding. It was already the first week in December, but Jackson pulled off an event that pleased everybody. The businessmen were happy because they were making money; the ministers were happy because the spiritual value of Christmas would be emphasized. The class antagonisms in the ghetto might be eased, since Jackson encouraged middle-class blacks to invite the poorer families into their homes for Christmas. Everybody was happy. How could anybody be against Christmas?

Black Easter: Early in 1969, shortly after the black dimension had been once again introduced into the Christmas season, Jackson announced a similar Black Easter program. Soul Saint was replaced symbolically by a black sheep as the star of the parade. The floats were all decorated in a fashion to commemorate such black heroes as Dr. Daniel Hale Williams, Paul Lawrence Dunbar, W. E. B. Du Bois, Medger Evers, Malcolm X, and Dr. Martin Luther King. Black Easter also included the presentation of Chicago's Passion Play, a moving Biblical experience, written and directed by Mrs. Willa Saunders Jones. Black Easter was also designed as a resurrection of black businesses, all of which Jackson said were being crucified. "If we are proud to be black we can spend our money where we are," was Jackson's Easter message.

Black Expo: Once a year the call goes out. The response is similar to the Jewish gathering to celebrate Yom Kippur, the Irish on St. Patrick's Day, and the Italians on Columbus Day. Black Expo is the acting out of *Harambee* (Swahili for "coming home together").

The gathering of the black clan flows into Chicago's International Amphitheater from the archipelagos of the Caribbean, from the dark passageways of Ghana where slaves were stolen from African shores, and from the Harlems in the U.S.A. Among the teeming crowds are Flip Wilson, janitors, Joe Louis, Richard Roundtree, Jacqui Verdell, welfare mothers, prostitutes, porters, painters, poets, pedagogues, Bill Cosby, Carl Stokes, Richard Hatcher, and even some of the blacks from the Daley camp. For Black Expo is home.

Initiated in 1967, the Black Minority Business and Cultural Exposition is the cornucopia of all things good about black America—something seldom heard, seldom seen. Flipping the coin on the black experience, Black Expo is the boldest, blackest, strongest imagery of success ever to be housed under one roof in America. (The first trade fair was called the Operation Breadbasket Business Seminar and Exposition held at the Chicago Theological Seminary in 1967.)

Black Expo is Sesame Street and rainbow ice cream cones for thousands of youngsters. It is art, covering every phase of the black and human experience from splashy abstracts and larger-than-life portraits of famous black Americans, past and present, to heavy symbolism of war and peace and love. It is also the concerts of Roberta Flack, Aretha Franklin, and Sammy Davis, Jr. Black Expo is black history, pictures, and biographies of Paul Cuffee, Benjamin Banneker, and Madame C. J. Walker.

The themes vary from year to year—1969: From Chains to Change; 1970: Rhythm Ain't All We Got; 1971: See the Dream Coming True (in reference to Dr. King's 1963 Washington address); 1972: Save the Children; 1973: Save the Black Colleges; 1974: Save the Worker. And each year Black Expo shines through a thousand prisms. If one could carve out the essence of this massive spectacular, it would be the imagery that speaks to the young. Black Expo expands their vision, their dreams, their hopes. They see their future roles not as laborers, public aid recipients, or hustlers but as inventors, movie producers, and thinkers. If Black Expo did nothing more than say "you've got a chance" to one ten-year-old, it has more than justified its existence.

Although the focus is on black, it would be a hard task to keep all the white vote-seeking politicians away, even if that were the intention. Mayor Daley, U. S. Senators Charles Percy and Adlai Stevenson III, and former Governor Richard Ogilvie have come. *Playboy's* great gun Hugh Hefner has participated too. And there are about as many white exhibitors as there are black.

All in all, Black Expo is testimony to the role Jackson

plays best—the magnate, the organizer, the man who knows where everybody fits on the American shuffleboard. There was a time when he called on black stars to draw a crowd. Today he is the star and everybody is eager to crowd into his spotlight. He usually shares this for a price—time, loyalty, commitment, or money to keep the movement rolling. All it takes today is a personal phone call to get the black and white luminaries gravitating his way, because he can draw the crowds. And the people are voters, consumers, and show-goers. Who could ask for anything more?

But more important, Black Expo provides the opportunity for more than 500 black companies to exhibit their products and services not only to throngs of spectators but to white firms that come to buy.

There are other opportunity fairs in Chicago designed to cut the minority businessmen in on a piece of the action, but none have the punch behind them of Jackson's. I have observed several trade fairs to which white company lackeys are sent without the authority to purchase even a rubber band. Their role is to refer. But when the minority businessman shows up for the company to deliver, all too often he gets the run-around. Too often the white companies are going through the motions of being an equal opportunity purchaser without purchasing anything. Their being on hand at the fair looks good in the financial sections of the newspapers or in their own house organs, but after seeking the publicity some white firms will budge no further. Jackson tells the white purchasing agents at the annual purchasers' breakfast preceding Expo: "We're not asking you to give us a break. Just open your minds. We're not beggars, we're producers. And a strong black economy is the best alternative to the welfare state." Since he is addressing their self-interest, what he is saying makes sense to them. And they listen and follow through because Jackson is the only force in the city of Chicago armed with the foot soldiers to "start trouble" if their good will should ever steal away.

Business Development

Behind the hoopla of programs geared to expose the black businessmen to the larger corporate world was a serious, intense effort to develop that silent partner of exposure—expertise in the art of doing business. It is somehow taken for granted that after the doors of discrimination are pried open, those who have been locked out are instantly and miraculously prepared to take advantage of the new opportunities. As was seen in the somewhat similar predicament of some black managers spinning around on lead feet at the top of A & P, this is not necessarily the case. How do you master the rules if the lack of contacts, cash and credit on the one hand and rampant racism on the other have always forbidden you from learning the trial and error art of business?

The Breadbasket Commercial Association (BCA), started in March of 1970, would be the conduit whereby the black businessmen, making inroads into the marketplace with events like Black Expo and the covenants, could build on their expertise in marketing, production, financing, and other areas essential for growth. A recent report by Dun and Bradstreet on business failures implied that the often heard expression, "If I only had more money I could make it," is an understandable but often inaccurate assessment. "More than one-half of all business failures—both white and black—were due to a combination of inexperience and incompetence," the analysis pointed out.

In BCA's short existence as a quasi-autonomous arm of Operation Breadbasket, it was headed by Noah Robinson, the O. J. Simpson of the Wharton School of Finance and Commerce. Robinson had turned down thirty-two job offers with major industry to work with his half-brother, Jesse. Before graduating with an M.B.A. in 1969 (from the

University of Pennsylvania), Noah founded a management consulting firm in Philadelphia hailed by *Fortune* as "one of the most successfully and enthusiastically supported programs of its kind in the nation." The *Philadelphia News* had said of him, "When it comes to green power, he means business. Few have traveled so fast." An Outstanding Young Man of America recipient, an honor also bestowed on Richard Nixon and Nelson Rockefeller, Noah has also received praise for his work as a chemist. A proprietary urethane sealant that he developed at Pecora Chemical Corporation in Philadelphia is now used by the Connecticut State Highway Department. The chemical was named in his honor, NR-100.

On face value, it would appear that Noah—the conservative, technical-oriented whiz kid—would be the perfect complement to Jesse, the upbeat, social-oriented, charismatic, all-purpose leader, whose genius is spread out over many areas. Who would have thought that in one year Noah would walk away from his post as executive director of BCA in disgust, publicly calling his brother "a paper tiger, who thinks power is made of press releases"? And Jesse would more discreetly say of Noah: "He reminds me of a snake an old woman took in from the cold. The snake had been all battered up and was on its last leg. And after the old woman nursed the snake and it got strong, it bit her. When the woman asked why, the snake said, 'Well, after all, I'm still a snake.' "

In any event, before the two brothers' sibling warfare caused a split, BCA, under Noah, brought in a prestigious crew of black M.B.A.'s and Ph.D.'s to provide specialized management consulting to member firms. These were divided into categories, such as production, extermination, construction, and transportation.

As in the late sixties, economic covenants hammered out with white corporations are still the main avenue by which dollars and cents are redirected into the black business community. However, today the mere threat of economic withdrawal elicits action. There is rarely ever the need to call out the troops. And today Jackson no longer threatens major corporations on a local level. The updated strategy is to aim for the top—the *Fortune* 500—so the fallout hits all urban localities where blacks and other minorities make up the bulk of the population.

Jackson explains his strategy as one which will ultimately have all the major corporations giving a pro-rata share of their business to black institutions.

"If we account for 20 percent of a firm's sales, then that firm must give us 20 percent of its business, 20 percent of its advertising dollar, 20 percent of its banking business, and 20 percent of its jobs. If our offensive aimed at a selected list of 100 of the top 500 major corporations succeeds, we will bring $5 billion into the black community. We are entitled to the business. After all, we consume some of the products these companies make. I conceive of our negotiations tactics as something of a domestic Marshall Plan for the black communities, which I hope someday will be matched in program dollars by the federal government," Jackson said.

Denying the often heard reports that he is a sophisticated shake-down artist, Jackson said, "I do not get a nickel from any contracts that are negotiated with blacks." He also admitted he could not enforce a total boycott because he doesn't control the entire black community, but he did say that the movement "influences enough people to influence the major corporations' profit margin and that's what the game is all about."

By early 1974, Jackson had "muscled" commitments from General Foods, Avon Products, the Joseph Schlitz Brewing Company, Quaker Oats and the Miller Brewing Company. If the covenants for jobs and business contracts are enforced, the agreements will redirect more than $325 million into black communities across the nation. 1975 targets are: Zenith Radio Corporation, Marcor Inc., and the Jewel companies of Chicago. (The Jewel covenant will be geared toward publicity. Jewel is already a staunch Jackson supporter.)

Though couched in moralistic terms, the covenants, in most cases, are a calculated arrangement in which corporate "peace" is opted for in exchange for providing Jackson with a base to build a national economic patronage system. By 1974, according to Jackson, PUSH satellites had developed in Memphis, Cincinnati, Columbus, Los Angeles, and Pittsburgh, with more cities interested in forming chapters than Jackson has the manpower to implement. The system, in its embryonic stage, is merely a national replica of Jackson's operation in Chicago. The working poor provide the troops which act as a weapon against white corporations which do not provide contracts to Jackson's cadre of businessmen, who in turn help finance the movement and events such as Expo.

All covenants follow the general form of the "nation time agreement" signed with General Foods. The nineteenth largest corporation in America, on September 21, 1972, agreed:

- To provide 360 jobs for blacks and other minorities, across the board.
- To initially authorize an additional $20 million of its insurance volume to black insurance companies.
- To retain black law firms, to retain at least five black physicians, and their paramedical personnel, to utilize black-owned medical supply houses for a share of its medical supplies.
- To exert every effort to find black authorized automobile dealers and to place a share of its auto fleet business with those companies.
- To increase its advertising schedule in black print media as agreed to in consultation with black publishers. The corporation will strengthen its relationship

with black-owned advertising agencies and utilize them to a greater degree on advertising projects.

• To continue that share of annual corporate contribution devoted to minority assistance.

• To continue its present business relationship involving black banks by increasing its present deposits to $500,000. The corporation will establish accounts and place tax deposits in banks authorized by the government to handle them.

• To creatively use black contractors to provide an opportunity for them to participate in corporate expansion, demolition, refurbishing, or remodeling of plant facilities.

If all the General Foods stipulations were acted upon, the agreement would be worth $65 million to black communities, according to Jackson.

I checked with General Foods and found the corporation is admirably sticking to its agreement—"with black businesses." Although General Foods could not provide dollar amounts without the consent of the businesses with whom the contracts were issued, a fairly clear overview was given by Lee A. Archer, Jr., director of equal opportunity affairs:

• Ten new contracts written with minority scavenger and maintenance companies. Five others in negotiations.

• Service and supplier contracts were let with nine additional companies. These companies represented paste-and-glue, plastics, pens/pencils, transportation, pallet repair, and manufacturing.

• $20 million in reinsurance was placed with black insurance firms. This was in addition to insurance already in effect through a black agency. The companies involved were in North Carolina and Chicago.

• Purchase of automobiles for General Foods' fleet included four minority dealers out of five which bid.

The four selected accounted for over 10 percent of the vehicles purchased. The firms were located in New York, Philadelphia, Portland, and Newark.

•   Under the banking category, General Foods increased their corporate deposits in black banks and included black banks in their tax deposit program to the amount of $10 million.

After talking with black companies across the country, easily identifiable through descriptions provided by General Foods, I verified all the business contracts.

As expected, General Foods offered no information on jobs except to say, "Our organization was able to complete each goal except those with open ends—that is, employment. We did everything in the covenants except the personnel section, which obviously takes a long time to complete," Archer said.

Archer also said, "I would like to make a special comment regarding your question on promotions. Much of all the above would have happened with or without the covenants. The PUSH agreement did heighten our corporate perception of the need and doubtlessly spurred our managers 'to do more.' However, promotions were not made as a reaction to PUSH. The number and quality of promotions have consistently increased each year as our base of eligible black managers has increased. All promotions were the result of merit—nothing else. No minority employees of General Foods have ever been promoted for reasons other than their ability and experience."

Either as an oversight or intentionally, jobs for the black worker are being deemphasized, a pattern traceable in pacts from 1968 to the present. Dollar value for jobs in the General Foods pact is about 1/100th in comparison to benefits to black firms.

Although the push for employment decreased as the self-interest of the Jackson businessmen became paramount, there is also another explanation. When the covenants are announced, they receive wide dissemination in the press. Immediately there is a foot race to the corporate door. Businessmen do not always wait for Jackson to contact them. Often they are lining up appointments with the purchasing agents minutes after the news hits the press. (They are more likely to get their foot in the door if a businessman has the Jackson stamp of approval.) But for the jobless, there is no movement official whose top priority is to deliver the jobs, and the working poor are not as aggressive in beating a path to the corporate door. So without representation from outside the company, jobs remain a low priority concern.

Although jobs are a staple of Mayor Daley's patronage system, it is a fact of life that the principle does not work successfully for Jackson's economic patronage system. Any black who has gained employment through the Daley machine readily knows whom to thank for his good fortune: "My ward committeeman got me the job" is the usual response. Blacks who have gained jobs in white firms through the agitation of the King-Jackson forces generally do not associate their employment with anything other than their own intelligence or capabilities. This notion of self-mobility is furthered by white firms to guard against their black employees becoming beholden to outside forces.

While the blacks employed may not reward the movement with donations, black businesses, which have no misgivings about who is responsible for their advancement, readily understand and support—at least marginally—the relationship of quid pro quo. Thus, I would have to give credence to the continual charges that Jackson's bartering in white corridors makes the "black affluent more affluent" but does little to enhance the economic conditions of the unemployed or underemployed.

Archer also added: "There was no fight with PUSH.

When PUSH contacted us we said since we are already marching to the same drummer why not sign a covenant. If you observe correctly, there is nothing in the covenant that says begin anything. For our part it was just a reaffirmation that we were both working in the same direction." Why split hairs over whether or not the recent issuing of contracts to black businesses was a reaffirmation of company policy or a result of movement pressure? It is perhaps enough to state that today covenant agreements have tremendous impact on the development of the national black business community, creating opportunities which may someday trickle down to the black masses through jobs in black firms.

Perhaps someday.

What about results for the Chicago black business community? By 1974, Chicago was beating its own drum as the Black Business Mecca of the World. In numbers, versatility of businesses, volume produced, Chicago is number one through the efforts of the Chicago Economic Development Corporation, the Chicago Cosmopolitan Chamber of Commerce, the Woodlawn Organization and many other groups and individuals, including Jackson. "It's Nation Time," a slogan Jackson articulates from the pulpit, has been shaped from rhetoric into reality by the honorable Elijah Muhammad, leader of the Nation of Islam, whose estimated $100 million empire has its base in Chicago.

Unlike Muhammad or the Reverend Leon Sullivan, who have built horizontal and vertical enterprises from scratch, Jackson is not a builder. He is an expansionist, placing himself in the Nader-like role of a "tree-shaker."

For those already established and for those others seeking entry onto the so-called "black capitalism" route, the covenants, the creative buy-black inducements and Jackson's climate setting have set the stage for spiraling growth.

The year 1966 opened with black producers locked

out of their own markets and often the minds of the black consumer. The ghetto was a place to make the money and in eight hours it was gone—back to the suburbs. The two black banks—Independence and Seaway National—were struggling institutions, with $10 million in collective assets. They were unable to snare the large corporate accounts because the bankers banked where they lived. If everything whites had built were removed in 1967, there would have been a large gaping hole, because black contractors couldn't even build in the ghetto.

But by 1974, Chicago had the largest and strongest financial base of any black community in the nation. Since 1910, Durham, North Carolina, had been the financial capital of black America. Durham's aggregate black wealth of about $180.8 million in financial institutions has now been outdistanced by the money men of Chicago. Eleven black-owned financial institutions in Chicago (six banks, three savings and loans, and two insurance firms) now boast some $200 million in assets, according to the June, 1974, issue of *Black Enterprise.*

Today, the black banking scenario looks like this: By 1973 Independence had swelled to $55.5 million, making it number one out of thirty-eight black banks in America. Right behind it is Seaway with $45.2 million in total assets. Highland Park was organized in 1970. At the end of 1973 it had $14.3 million in total assets.

By mid-1972, two more black-owned banks were ushered in. Gateway in spite of its infancy has $16 million in total assets. Guaranty, purchased by the Black Muslims, has $6.7 million. (Data are for January, 1974.)

In 1973, Chicago gained number six, the South Side Bank, organized by Thomas P. Lewis, former vice-president of the Independence Bank. South Side, by June, 1974, had more than $17 million in assets. It is a subsidiary of Interbank Corporation, the nation's first minority-owned holding company in the country.

Alvin Boutte, president of Independence, puts Jackson's role in proper focus: "The black consumer has gained a new respect for black financial institutions. Chicago's minority community has accepted its black banks and I think that attitude was started by Jesse Jackson. He taught us to help each other by buying black and whether you like him or not, you have to admit we are beginning to behave that way." Proof of Boutte's assertion is that Independent's black depositors have increased from 8,000 in 1969 to 30,000 in 1973. However, one downtown bank, First National, has 135,000 black accounts. So although the black consumer is growing in loyalty to black banks, the battle has not yet been won.

Boutte added: "Our leap forward began with the National Tea, A & P, and other supermarket chain deposits. Then came the fruit from the national covenants with companies such as General Foods. The transfer of deposits gave us credibility, and other white institutions, who were not pressured, followed the precedents. One example is Illinois Blue Cross which opened a medicare account providing an average daily balance of more than $2 million. The deposit made in June, 1972, constituted the largest single corporate account in any minority-owned commercial bank in the country at that time." In June, 1974, the city, county, and state treasurers had $1,426,000,000 of public funds in interest-bearing time deposits. Chicago's six black banks had $12,363,000 or less than nine-tenths of one percent, according to the *Chicago Reporter*.

Today, black bankers can take issue with those who would refer to them as ornamental. "In Illinois, there are 1,100 banks. We rank about 150. In the nation we are number 1,623 out of 14,000 banks. If we are ornaments, then the 950 banks in the state and the 13,377 banks behind us are also of no consequence," Boutte said.

"What counts," said Boutte, "is that we know the needs of the black community and we are committed to relieving them because we live there. In 1972, we had at least $6 million flowing into projects that develop the black community. And I would bet that a $9 billion institution like Chicago's First National does not have that kind of money pouring into black economic growth, and it is number two in the state where we are number 150."

Tom Lewis gave perspective to the word "climate-setting," a term often used by Jackson in making a case for his effectiveness. The term is confusing because its results are immeasurable.

Lewis said, "Jackson has an economic force that has the ability to do harm to any major corporate structure in America. And when you have that kind of force present in a city, it encourages people to be more honest than they would normally be. Jackson's force can damage the corporate image, reducing the stockholders' faith in the company, thus reducing the earnings. If Jackson did not go after a General Foods, for example, do you think they would have come to us? Jackson can deliver. He doesn't mind working and he produces, he gets things done. Make no mistake about it, Jesse Jackson is the most powerful black man in this nation. And if you doubt me, name one who is more powerful."

In the 1974 *Black Enterprise* report of the 100 black-owned firms whose sales volume for 1973 was in excess of 1 million dollars, Chicago took second place to New York City with eighteen: Joe Louis Milk, Travis Realty Company, TWO Hillman's, Inc., Roberts Motel, Inc., Lowery Distributing Company, Horace Noble Lincoln-Mercury, Inc., Sengstacke Publishing Company, Competition Motors, Ltd., Grove Fresh Distributors, Inc., the Lawndale Packaging Corporation, Johnson Publishing Company, Al Johnson Cadillac, Johnson Products, Tuesday Publications, Sivart Mortgage Corporation, Parker House Sausage, Robert Martin Construction, and Summit Laboratories.

All eighteen have one element in common—Jackson,

either indirectly or directly. More than half of Chicago's millionaire corporations have representatives on the PUSH National Board. Most have been aided through the covenants or Jackson's contacts. Roberts Motel chain is not included in any covenant, for example, but Jackson holds many of his social affairs at the popular entertainment spa, which gains repeat business through habit. Since Jackson pulls in the crowds, of course, Herman Roberts, the owner of the chain, often provides the facilities gratis.

The TWO Hillman's supermarket, which in 1973 grossed $3.8 million in sales, as was pointed out earlier, came into fruition through Hillman's president Gardner Stern, Jr., responding positively to Jackson's preachments on corporate responsibility.

Others, such as the Travis Realty Company, Horace Noble Lincoln-Mercury, Inc., and Al Johnson Cadillac, have been assisted by Jackson's personal contact. Jackson is the man who knows what artery to touch to start whatever he needs flowing his way. He is the man to know because he knows the people—both black and white—who can deliver. Although the point may seem to be belabored, the ability to piece together a string of clout-heavy connections is crucial, because blacks have always been on the outside. Or the connections blacks have had were isolated in a vacuum.

Jackson's key role is stringing the contacts and connections together in the same you-scratch-my-back, I'll-scratch-yours relationship that all systems depend upon to survive. For example, Jackson has sent business to Horace Noble. So if Jackson needs a private plane and none is available from his Sears, Roebuck pal, Noble taxis the movement people. Since Al Johnson's Cadillac business has skyrocketed because of his connections with Jackson, he is Jackson's financial troubleshooter. He chairs fund raising events and also keeps some of the movement's records without charge.

Men like Al Johnson; George Jones, vice-president of

Joe Louis Milk; Manney Lowery, president of Lowery
Distributing; and Cecil Troy, president of Grove Fresh
Orange Juice, all credit Jackson for their climb to the
black enterprise millionaires' club. (Companies whose gross
sales are in the millions may net as little as 3 percent of
gross sales, a sum which does not necessarily make the
owners millionaires, as it is commonly reported.)

Cecil Troy said, "Before Jackson came I was turning
over $265,000 in total sales. Now that my sales are over 1
million, it would be unnatural if I wasn't grateful and
didn't do what I could to keep the movement running."
Grove Fresh was incorporated in 1961.

George Jones also has a reason to be grateful. Records
show that with the 1970 National Tea covenant alone,
Jones' milk products were averaging $36,000 monthly in
the chain's twenty-five stores in the inner city. Before
Jackson turned the pressure on in 1969, Joe Louis dairy
products were averaging $174,973—and that was in yearly
purchases made by National Tea. Jones said, "My
company now has $4.2 million in gross sales. When
Jackson started his program in 1966 my gross sales were
$1.5 million, and yes, I can trace a good portion of my
increase to Jesse. Now I believe in Jesse. I believe that he
represents an honorable cause. I'd be a fool if I didn't
support him."

Are the black fat cats the kind of affluent types who
have no concern for the poor? It would be a serious
distortion to project them all in that negative image.
Although Jackson's priorities are at the top, he does
encourage philanthropic acts among his inner core of
businessmen, but most would contribute to black causes
with or without Jackson's encouragement.

The kinds of services Jackson encourages among his
inner circle are not highly publicized, but these men do
much more than lounge around their summer homes in the
Caribbean when they are not raking in the dough. For

example, in August 1972, the Jackson businessmen adopted a displaced, eleven-member black family from Mississippi, agreeing to provide food, clothing, and shelter for as long as needed. Five black youths from the Robert Taylor Homes are in college, compliments of the Joe Louis Milk Company. Jones also contributes more than $30,000 a year to black self-help projects. His company as well as Troy's have profit-sharing programs for their employees. In November 1972, George Johnson set up a $1 million grant for scholarships to students planning to major in business administration. And all are active in community leadership functions.

It could be argued that they could do more. The higher one climbs the further one gets from the actual plight of the poor—a criticism often made by those tired of the movement's endless cocktail parties and $50- to $100-a-head social affairs that none but the affluent can afford. Tight-fisted Scrooges the Jackson businessmen are not, but neither are they social welfare agencies.

As the big businessmen climb, the social momentum is pulling up a fresh crop of younger entrepreneurs. Once the doors are pushed open, anybody can enter. This Jackson has done, and through the imagery of Black Expo that triggers the imagination, young blacks are beginning to identify themselves in roles other than those of the traditional Mom and Pop grocers, beauticians, and morticians.

Miss Herma Ross, twenty-seven, is vice-president of Alpha Janitorial Supply Company, Inc., which operates a Johnson Wax distributorship. "I never would have thought of going into that type of business if I hadn't seen somebody black doing it successfully. And I saw that example at Black Expo. Once I began to seek entry I found it was not difficult to get a bank loan. Even the downtown banks were more responsive since there are now six black banks. More than 50 percent of my corporate accounts are white. And there was a time they wouldn't let you in the front door if you were black. Jesse has just created a climate for doing business in and out of the Chicago area." Alpha, which grossed $275,000 in sales in 1974, is located in Hammond, Indiana. It opened with a $500 loan in 1972.

Edgar Webb, president of Ebony Industrial Supply Company in Evanston, was prompted into expanding a small venture into the major distribution of nuts, bolts, screws, and small electrical supplies to retail outlets after visiting the 1969 exposition. "Since that first Expo, I have come from two employees to nine, from no profit to more than $200,000 in sales. I have grown because the right people can see me. It is not what you know sometimes, but who you know, and Expo brings the Who's Who of the business world to the minority community." Today, Webb is also a distributor of plastic, steel, and aluminum parts for heavy industry.

Eugene W. Blackmon, thirty-four, an inner city land developer, said contacts he made at Black Expo in 1970 brought him $17 million in business. His largest contract was for 609 apartments for low and moderate income families at Sixty-sixth and State Streets, at an estimated cost of $14 million. In 1970 Blackmon had been in business only a year and a half.

And there's Charles Petty, forty-one, president of Petty's Exterminators, who said his sales have increased by $122,000 since the first Black Expo. Petty, who has been in business fourteen years, said he has landed a major customer at Black Expo each year.

Thus, Chicago revisited in 1974 is not the same as Jackson found it in 1966, especially for those businessmen attached to Jackson's coattails.

7

*A man who wishes to make a
profession of goodness . . . must
necessarily come to grief among
so many who are not good.*

Machiavelli

For Chicago blacks, 1972 was a very good year. Playing retributive politics to the hilt, black voters retired from public office State's Attorney Edward V. Hanrahan, the man who ordered the raid against the Black Panther Party. Two Panthers were killed, one in his bed. Encouraged by the warm glow of a countermovement, former Olympic star Congressman Ralph Metcalfe sprinted from the Democratic machine as the Mayor's number one house black. Although they have given nominal support to many anti-Daley candidates, the Jackson people could claim sole credit for providing the organizational work to elect Mrs. Peggy Smith Martin as the only black woman in the state legislature. And to ice the victory cake, Jackson and a Jewish alderman, Bill Singer, joined forces to eject Mayor Daley from his coveted seat as kingmaker at the Democratic National Convention in Miami in 1972.

In other cities, Chicago's very good year would not warrant a victory bash. Replacing one Irish state's attorney, Hanrahan, with another Irish state's attorney, Bernard Carey, would hardly be considered a manifestation of black power. A politician like Ralph Metcalfe would not have been given twenty years to decide whether or not he should represent his constituency. And kicking Daley out of a convention seat in Miami is not the same as kicking him out of the mayoral seat in Chicago. The election of black mayors is, however, a phenomenon that has spread to more than 100 cities across the nation.

But Chicago is Mayor Daley's Chicago. Progress made by blacks, Republicans, or anybody else without clout or the propensity to crawl inside the bowels of the system should be measured in millimeters. To expect much more is pure puffery when you are comparing black progress against the roughest, toughest, meanest, most effective Irish-dominated machine in the nation. Blacks in Chicago are just learning the game of black power or ethnic politics. By the late 1960s, when blacks invented the wheel, the Irish had long ago rolled off with it. As sad as it is true, a bloc means little more to masses of Chicago blacks and other minorities than the stretch of street they live on.

Black political impotence in Chicago requires more than a broad definitive statement; but for openers, it should be described as threefold: When blacks elect a black politician in Chicago, chances are they are not electing a brother or a sister, but a "mother." Stated more civilly, black machine candidates can seldom represent the best interests of the black community because Mayor Daley holds the key to their survival. The Daley machine slates them, protects them, provides the money and campaign organization, and its precinct captains snare the voters. It is a political reality that without this apparatus few blacks—or white Democrats—have made it to the City Council, the State Legislature, or to Congress. Of the few independents (in Chicago, a black independent is most likely an antimachine Democrat) who did, the majority sold out to the other side. Once in office, they owed their political lives to the Daley machine and it is the Mayor they first serve. On little issues like lambasting the Republicans, Daley's men can play the role of heroes to their black constituency. But on the big issues, such as schools or housing desegregation, slum housing, gerry-mandering, not a word can be spoken. In fact, Chicago black city councilmen used to be known as the silent six. In 1974, there are fourteen. There are glowing exceptions, but the definition of a black Chicago politician as a "house Negro on the Mayor's plantation" is the rule. As in slavery, life for the house Negro is sweeter than for the Negroes toiling in the field. And who do you blame, the system or the slave?

The black electorate is sluggish and above all consistent. It tends to accommodate the status quo either by voting for the Democratic machine candidates or by not voting at all. Blacks in Chicago are continually in an uproar—and there is reason enough for their alarm. The Black Panther "shoot-in" was the most celebrated case of police brutality in Chicago, but it was not an isolated case. The Chicago Law Enforcement Study Group issued a 1974 report documenting that 79 percent of the people who are killed by police in Chicago are black, while only 15 percent are white. "During 1969 and 1970 in Chicago a black person was more than six times as likely to die at the hands of the police as a white person," the report revealed. The police have their own investigative unit and almost always the verdict is "justifiable homicide." A John

Hopkins University Report issued in February 1973 called the Chicago school system the most segregated of eighty-one northern cities studied and attributed the lack of integration to inaction by the board of education, which is headed by an Irishman, although the public school system is more than 70 percent black. There is garbage in the streets. Only 800 units of housing have been built in riot-torn Lawndale on Chicago's west side since 1943, and Lawndale is one of the most Democratic wards in the city. Dissatisfaction with the system, however, is not shown at the polls but through demonstrating, rioting, marching, or the self-mutilation of dope or alcohol—sometimes. And rhetoric—all the time. (The west side of Chicago houses some of the most militant blacks in the universe, but militant about what? Some of their neighborhood political leaders are white.)

Come election day, the sound and the fury subside. For example, preceding the 1963 mayoral election, police were caught moonlighting as burglars in what came to be called the Summerdale scandal, and more than 10,000 Italians were driven out of their homes to make way for the University of Illinois' new complex, and taxes were going up because somebody had to pay for what the politicians were ripping off. Whites became incensed and showed it where it counts—at the polls. Daley lost 51 percent of the white vote. But blacks? The four south-side wards controlled by the powerful late Congressman William Dawson and the west-side black wards gave Daley his victory margin—a resounding 85 percent of their vote. Almost the same story could be repeated for most elections involving lesser machine candidates. The anti-Daley candidate can stand for civil rights, police reform, and the machine candidate can stand for no noble cause other than getting himself elected. Indubitably blacks will vote for whomever the Mayor serves up or they do not vote at all.

There are many reasons for black loyalty to the machine. I recorded some of them as I walked and talked with the people in the streets of Chicago.

• Billie Travis, thirty-nine, has a rare talent. He can steal more votes than any other precinct judge. His talents were appreciated and rewarded by the ward committeeman, who got him a good job with the state's attorney's office. When Billie got caught with his hand in the ballot box and was indicted on vote fraud, his boss handed him a $16,000-a-year job as a ward superintendent. And Billie still gets to carry his gun. Where else could a guy with an eighth-grade education do so well?

• A twenty-five-year-old welfare mother with four children was approached in a dimly lit flat. The cooking stove was the only source of heat. One cockroach appeared and signaled the others, who advanced in battalions toward the kitchen. Why does she vote for Daley's candidates? "I have been poor all my life. My mama was poor. Her mama was poor. That's the way it was. That's the way it is gonna be. But every Christmas Congressman George Collins has a party. [Collins was killed in a plane crash in December 1972. His wife, Cardiss, was elected as his replacement.] My children and I go. They always get gifts and I get something for their Christmas dinner. Mr. Collins is a great man. You wouldn't think he would have time for people like me. But he does. He cares. Think what Christmas would be like without Mr. Collins."

• "Why do you vote for Daley's people?" a fifty-year-old file clerk in a Model Cities office in a south-side ward was asked. Her response was quite a surprise. "The Mayor is a good Christian. He goes to church every day. He is good to his family. And you never hear about him running around on his wife."

• In a bar, a young man in dirty work clothes said, "When I first came to Chicago, me and my family had nothing but the rags on our back. My precinct captain got us into public housing and some welfare, until I could find a job. The precinct captain still comes around to check on things. So when I vote Democratic I'm voting for him—my precinct captain."

• Two bar stools down, another man who had obviously been putting in some heavy drinking time said, "Who cares? Politicians are all a bunch of crooks. If somebody gives me something—some wine—anything, I'll vote. If they don't, I won't. If I get a buck, that's more than what the politicians are worth. I got a better answer to this whole mess." He pulled out a match stick and threw it at my feet. "Burn it down," he shouted.

• A Democratic precinct captain, who was promised anonymity, explained how, with little or no effort, he could commit the voters in his district. "I won't say my job is easy," he admitted. "I spend 365 days a year talking to the people. I usually stay away from controversy. I create small issues that I can solve. For example, I may call a building inspector to come out and look at a building. But just as he shows up to slap the owner with a violation, I arrive and tell the inspector to beat it. That makes me a hero forever. Sometimes, a welfare check is late. So I'll call the public aid department and raise hell. When the check arrives, I get the credit, but the recipient could have done the same thing herself."

For better or for worse, this is the marital arrangement between blacks and the machine—vote fraud, bribery, a perennial gratuity, habit, apathy—much of it abetted by Daley's army of patronage workers, who keep their jobs by ensuring the nuptial vows are never broken.

Because the system works as it is intended to work, Mayor Daley treats the black vote like some men treat their wives: they do not bother to woo them, knowing they will always be there to perform the expected. Thus the third element comes into play. The political process often ends for blacks on election day without their participation in the distribution of the spoils. Votes do more than elect politicians. Votes are IOUs guaranteeing a favorable dispensation of political appointments in significant policy-making jobs in government. Although the black vote is often the balance of power in Chicago elections, it is not rewarded in proportion to its percentage of the population or its percentage of the total vote cast during a major election. Blacks are close to 40 percent of the population, yet the Irish, who are no more than 7 percent, hold more than 75 percent of the elective and appointive positions. The fire commissioner, the police commissioner, the school superintendent, the Chicago Housing Authority director, are all white. To make a long story short, all the city's and county's significant policy-making, appointed jobs belong to whites except one, which is race-related, having little to do with operations of the city as a whole.

This is a glimpse of the black political scene in Chicago, in most ways the same as Jackson found it when he eased into its turbulent waters.

The stench of politics and its relationship to economics were realities that Jackson said he couldn't ignore. "Chicago has a one party system where there is an extreme concentration of decision making in the office of the Mayor. In terms of power there is not much left for anybody else. In the early days in order to get a bank loan you had to go through Daley. In order to build any place you had to pass some money to his committeemen. For example, if a Parker House Sausage Company gets out of line, it could be punished by slapping it with costly unfair building violations. Whether the Johnson cosmetics firm can expand depends on the mood of the zoning board. Whether or not a school gets its proper educational appropriation, that's a political decision. To me politics and economics are Siamese twins. The whole purpose of politics is to develop, expand, and protect the economic order."

Wise men dealing from a position of powerlessness do

not charge the powerful head-on. The loyal black vote is by no means the only contributor to the Mayor's strength. Labor, tons of money, patronage workers, the support of the business community, including all four major downtown newspapers as well as most of the black ones, all work together to make Jackson's mission an overwhelming struggle against the odds. In 1969 Jackson was only twenty-seven. He had not had the opportunity to learn the political system as Daley had learned it, from the ground floor up. Many of those who could advise him wouldn't because they were part of the system. Many of the blacks Jackson wanted to organize were dependent on the system and didn't want to be organized into a countermovement which would "bite the hand that was feeding them."

Thus Jackson moved circuitously, winning converts on safe, moral issues, seemingly swinging a wide arc away from Daley's power base until he could marshal enough supporters and anti-Daley political allies to snap back. This is one way to begin in Chicago politics. And then if the leader is lucky and stays alive, and neither he nor his troops have been coopted by the Mayor, he moves on to bigger things—maybe even to talking about running for mayor himself someday.

The year opened with Jackson leading a hunger drive in Republican-controlled downstate Illinois. It was Phase II of SCLC's Poor People's Campaign, begun a year earlier in Resurrection City in Washington, D.C. The issue was clearly a moral one—a civil rights drive to realize economic gains for the poor. But like everything else, hunger is political. And its solution is political.

On May 14, 1969, the Jackson Movement organized about 2,000 people to converge on the state capitol in Springfield. Jackson preached to the lawmakers, seeking legislation to stop all hunger and malnutrition in the state and "to remove the scourge of poverty and destitution from all its people, both black and white."

His position paper on human subsidy called for:

1.   The state of Illinois to declare hunger a disaster area that destroys human lives.

2.   Slums to be declared illegal.

3.   The state and federal governments to raise the subsidy for all people.

4.   The Means test to be removed since it compels people to make embarrassing public disclosures of their possessions in order to receive money for food and shelter.

5.   The Food Stamp Program to be abolished as it stigmatizes persons when their real need is for money to purchase the necessities of life.

6.   State and federal governments to establish emergency job-training programs for unemployed and hungry people, in much the same way that job-training programs were developed to meet the emergencies of war.

The first three points, according to Gary Massoni, an aide to Jackson, were the creative challenges to the legislators and to the governor's administration. Under certain agricultural legislation, an area of widespread hunger could, indeed, be declared a disaster area and thus be entitled to federal aid. Through legislation to protect the rights of tenants and through vigorous enforcement of building codes, many aspects of slum conditions could be eliminated by becoming both illegal and unprofitable to unscrupulous landlords. Raising the "subsidy" of all people in the state to a decent standard of living would be a key step in eliminating poverty in Illinois and in the rest of the country.

All six proposals were later turned down by the Illinois General Assembly. The basic reason was the Chicago clout, pointed out James Carson, an official of the Chicago Catholic Archdiocesan Committee on Poverty and a movement researcher. "We did not significantly understand the political composition of the state lawmaking body. The Democratic delegation of senators and representatives is slated by the same small group of people who slate the aldermen and judges in Chicago. These people all vote as a massive, unthinking, machinelike bloc. Unless Daley gives them the green light, they wouldn't even vote themselves a pay raise. The downstate Democrats are also slated and okayed by the Cook County chairman, Mayor Daley, and they, too, know which side their bread is buttered on. And the Republican Party was no help. They were in disarray as per usual," Carson concluded.

While the legislators were rejecting human subsidies to some 600,000 persons in Illinois, who, according to Jackson's researchers, were hungry and undernourished, the lawmakers were increasing subsidies to farmers for nonproduction. In fourteen Illinois counties, where there was less than 1 percent participation in food stamp programs, nonproduction payments ranged from $39,336 in Putnam to $911,187 in McLean. Also farm payments in Illinois were rising from $10 million in 1967 to $34.8 million in 1968. Overall in 1968 the state received $97 million for farmers not to plant food compared with only $6 million for children to eat. On the federal level, the farm subsidy program allowed 9,000 farmers to receive more than $20,000 each for doing nothing, while 40 million Americans were suffering from malnutrition.

These large sums, however, are paltry compared to what Mississippi Senator James O. Eastland alone received in 1968—$13,000 monthly for not planting cotton on 2,000 acres of his 5,000-acre plantation. But poor people are not in the same league with crops, railroads, aircraft, and oil companies, which receive lucrative amounts of welfare. These groups also have lobbyists, provide substantial campaign contributions and are represented in a sophisticated self-interest electorate, not much of which is synonymous with the poor.

Although the Jackson forces lost on all six counts, they scored handsomely on another. On the same day that

Jackson presented his human subsidy position paper, a bill was introduced by Republican Speaker of the House, the late Ralph T. Smith. If it had passed it would have cut Illinois welfare payments by 30 percent, which represented $125 million a year. Smith explained that it was one way of attempting to reduce the $4.4 billion budget which Republican Governor Richard Ogilvie had recommended. Somehow it had never occurred to Smith to reduce the budget by taking from the highway or landscaping appropriations. The point was not lost on the movement supporters, who marched around the state capitol carrying signs "Feed the Hungry."

After the august lawmakers took their seats, Jackson made an uncompromising speech attacking the cutback as a commitment to genocide. Rather than give the usually dry testimony, Jackson preached an acrimonious sermon. The red and black beret-wearing street gang members, welfare mothers, as well as some of the legislators, roared in approval. When Smith rose to table his bill, he was drowned out by the movement people, whom Jackson had packed in the gallery. It was a masterful show, with Jackson exerting full control. But the takeover of the House incensed the more venerable Republicans. Representative James C. Kirie of River Grove called the takeover "an affront to every red-blooded American." Another backlash Republican became so enraged that he kicked the wall, muttering obscenities, until two fellow legislators calmed him. In the face of the calamity, Smith withdrew his bill.

Not many knew that all the brouhaha had been staged. The move was calculated to allow Jackson to be lauded as the giant killer among his followers as payback for his support of Governor Richard Ogilvie in 1968. It had all gone according to script. Jackson had convinced his pal Ogilvie to persuade Smith to rescind the bill a day earlier. But a deal made in the confines of an office does not make the spectacular headlines of a legislative back-down by "force." And the deal was not much of a price for the governor to pay, since he hadn't moved forward on the welfare issue. He just didn't move backward. From then on, when Jackson was ribbed about forsaking the poorer blacks to cast his lot with the middle class, he could always point to the victory at the state capitol.

In a second drive on the capitol, there would be no deals. The movement would score some points, but their main thrust would be turned aside by the state lawmakers. Along with his top lieutenants, Peggy Smith Martin, the Reverend Mrs. Willie Barrow, and the Reverend Calvin Morris, Jackson geared up for a return trip to the capitol. Beginning in Rockford, Jackson pulled together a hunger trek which swept through fifteen cities from Peoria to Decatur to Carbondale to Cairo. His staff researched the communities, determining the severity of the human needs; organized local leaders in support of the campaign; and, through the press, illuminated incidents of rampant mal-nutrition and poverty to the public, while emphasizing that Illinois is the third richest state in the nation. Jackson also organized the eighteen blacks in the Illinois General Assembly into a new Coalition of Black Legislators, in order to support his return to Springfield. Few people could have accomplished such a feat. Most of the black legislators are selected and elected by Daley's machine. They were, for the most part, not used to responding to or cooperating with the wishes of black people, unless the Mayor had thought of it first.

On June 26, 1969, the Hunger Trek group returned to the capitol to gain more meaningful legislation to end hunger. Representative Robert Mann, a white liberal Democrat who had also supported Dr. King, had proposed a bill to increase the state's lunch programs. Due partly to the demonstration of statewide community support for the bill and cohesion of the black coalition, the legislation was passed. Under the bill, the state for the first time would contribute to school lunch programs, which added $5.4 million to the federal subsidy program, enough to guarantee a free school lunch for all Illinois children who were hungry. There were 204,000 children in Illinois—100,000 in Chicago—who benefited from the state supplement.

Two other Mann bills were also approved. One ended the practice of deducting any social security increase from elderly public aid recipients. The second eliminated the mandatory $90-a-month rent ceiling for public aid recipients. However, the real meat the movement had sought—a 25 percent increase in aid to dependent children at a cost of $75.6 million—was voted down, 72 to 57.

While Jackson advanced into the more conservative, Republican-controlled areas of the state, the movement began to create the climate that would close in on its primary target—the Democrats in Chicago. Jackson would not have a friendly Ogilvie to lean on. In 1968, the black electorate had helped the election of Ogilvie—not that they did anything spectacular by registering a split-ticket vote. Many voters stayed at home. Blacks were miffed over Daley's shoot-to-kill order during the King riots. Also money had been passed to some groups in the black and Spanish-speaking communities to keep the Democratic vote low in an effort to boost President Nixon's plurality. On the south side in Black-P-Stone-Nation territory the "don't vote" message was transmitted by graffiti on abandoned buildings. Other spokesmen spread the word for blacks to sit out the election as a protest against the lack of choice in the 1968 election—that there was no difference between Hubert Humphrey and Richard Nixon. Consequently, the black vote dropped more than 98,000 from what was cast in the 1964 presidential election—helping not only Ogilvie to squeak through but also Illinois Attorney General William Scott, who would also show his appreciation to the black community. But in his last election, in 1967, Daley received a whopping 5 to 1 mandate to proceed as usual from the majority of black wards. So Daley would extend almost the same courtesy to Jackson as he had to King—almost, because Jackson wasn't King.

In fact, the hunger trek rang like a replay of King's Campaign to End Slums. The leaders had changed, but Daley was the same. In 1967 Daley had said there were no slums in Chicago. In 1969 the script was handed to Dr. Morgan J. O'Connell, who was the acting commissioner of the Board of Health: "As I go through Chicago, I don't see anyone who has to go without food. I don't think a state of hunger as such exists."

From King and through his work with the Kenwood-Oakland Community Organization, Jackson had learned how to organize local communities, how to use the press to give visibility to an issue, and how to force confrontation through national attention. All three would have to be used to get Daley to admit that hunger did, indeed, exist in Chicago and to use his resources to relieve it.

Former *Chicago Sun-Times* reporter Linda Rockey, on April 14, 1969, made the issue visible with her sensitive treatment of the effects of this so-called nonexistent condition:

• At an age when well-fed babies are bouncy and giggling, an infant sits listlessly for hours, not uttering a sound.

• His brothers and sisters so crave food that they eat lead paint chips off the walls of rotting slum tenements. Their pregnant mother staves off hunger pangs with laundry starch.

• By mid-morning the heads of children in a ghetto school flop down wearily on their desks.

• A Puerto Rican mother of nine, whose husband cannot find work, cooks potato peelings on a hot plate for supper.

• A social worker describes the plight of the

elderly poor in this city as a "slow death from mal-
nutrition that goes on daily."

• Physicians, nurses, dieticians, welfare workers,
and researchers report that hunger is a daily fact of life
among Chicago's poor. But *officially* hunger does not
exist.

The *Sun-Times* followed up on Linda Rockey's
report with a hard-hitting editorial: "Mayor Daley should
commit the city to a war on hunger. He has the power to
see that action is begun; he has the skill to cut away red
tape. And we are certain he has the desire to feed the
hungry. Chicago is one of the wealthiest cities in the
wealthiest nation in the world. It cannot afford the
shame of one hungry child's tears."

One week after the *Sun-Times* editorial, the *American*
(later *Chicago Today,* now defunct) on April 26, 1969,
headlined: "Daley Declares War on Hunger."

Daley seemed astonished: "God forbid that anyone
should be hungry in Chicago. If we can only find out who
they are, I will do anything and everything to put food on
their tables."

Republican Senator Charles Percy, whom Jackson
enlisted in the campaign, documented that there were an
estimated 300,000 hungry or undernourished persons in
Daley's Chicago; yet the Mayor, the Board of Health, and
Daley's army of more than 30,000 patronage workers
could find not *one.*

For eleven months, the movement used every ploy in
the civil rights manual to force Mayor Daley to acknow-
ledge the presence of the poor.

Jackson and his lieutenants, the Reverend Morris and
the Reverend Barrow, walked the city ward by ward. The
appalling conditions they pointed to, which still exist
today, bordered on genocide—not from the barrel of a gun
but from systematic, institutional neglect.

In the Fourth Ward (the power base of the late

Claude Holman, a black alderman and ward committee-man, who once told me, "Wild horses couldn't drag me away from the Mayor's side"), more than forty-five out of every 1,000 babies died before the second week of life. The neighborhood called Kenwood-Oakland has only four doctors—all over seventy—to administer to the health needs of 100,000 people. Yet Claude Holman was chairman of the City Council's health committee.

In the Third Ward, Grand Boulevard, where at the time Ralph Metcalfe was alderman and today is ward committeeman, the infant mortality rate was 37.5 out of every 1,000 live births. Doctors serving the Robert Taylor Home projects reported that most pregnant women were undernourished.

In the First Ward, controlled by reputed Mafia underlord John D'Arco, which includes part of the wealthy Loop, as well as the deserts of despair inhabited by blacks on the near west side, the tuberculosis rate was 220 per 100,000 people, one of the highest for a community in the nation. In 1974, health statistics have not appreciably improved.

In thirty out of fifty Chicago wards, the movement, through the media, gathered this patchwork of human misery—poor blacks, whites, Indians, Puerto Ricans, and Mexicans—and laid it on the doorsteps of City Hall. Because of their political irrelevance and his insensitivity, Mayor Daley could step over them.

The movement touched on voter registration lightly by opening up free breakfast-feeding cells. The scheme was to activate the brain by way of the stomach—a ploy the machine has perfected. A typical election day tactic is for politicians, who haven't been seen since the last election, to drive up near polling places handing out chickens, hams, or turkeys. The recipient looks upon the provider as kind, sincere, and sympathetic and therefore worthy of his vote. To those who have nothing, a little bit of anything is often

everything. If the movement could succeed in transferring
this loyalty, associating the poor people's dilemma with
the machine politicians and raising the issue that survival
with dignity was a right and not a privilege, it was thought
the poor could be influenced to register and vote the
culprits out of office. The movement also attempted to
embarrass the black political leadership by opening up one
cell on the same block where William Harvey, the Second
Ward committeeman, lived, and another three doors away
from Congressman Dawson.

The movement's influence on the voters would soon
be measured in the March 1970 Democratic primary
race—the same as a general election since no Republican
candidates ever win in heavily populated black districts.
Two black anti-Daley candidates, Alderman A. A.
(Sammy) Rayner and Augustus Savage, a newspaper
publisher, both of whom were advocates of the poor,
would be running against Alderman Ralph Metcalfe, one of
the original Silent Six, and Morgan Murphy, Jr., whose
father was a board member of Commonwealth Edison. If
the poor were tired of suffering, the March election would
communicate their dissatisfaction in the only language the
Mayor understands—the vote.

On March 12, 1970, Jackson moved the hunger fight
into the city's amusement park, better known as the City
Council, where an ordinance was presented calling for $35
million—5 percent of the city budget—to establish a city
department to abolish hunger.

Before the Jackson supporters could settle themselves
in the gallery, the city clerk had mumbled through the
seven-page ordinance, Alderman Thomas Keane, Daley's
floor leader, had announced it would go to the finance
committee and Daley had declared the meeting adjourned.

Alderman Sammy Rayner, one of the three independent Democratic aldermen, screamed, "Hey you can't
do this. This is important. We must discuss this thing." On

cue from Keane, Rayner was shouted down by thirty-six other voices, a surprising number in attendance, considering it was vacation time in Florida.

The key issue was what the finance committee would do with the ordinance. Once in Keane's hand it could go to the "whatnot" committee or it could be buried in Keane's committee—the graveyard reserved for dead issues, which most often included any ordinances sponsored by a nonmachine alderman. Or it could go another route. A usual Daley trick is to weaken it, reintroduce it as his own, and let his administration take the credit for it. Claude Holman had been known to snatch an ordinance out of an independent's hand, put his name on it, and introduce it as his brainchild all in the same session.

In a surprise move, Keane announced that the finance committee would hold public hearings on March 26—nine days after the election. And this is where the ordinance became bogged down, because this was reportedly a deal between Jackson and Daley. Perhaps Jackson should have remembered from the Chicago Freedom Movement that in compromises with the Mayor, blacks always lose.

Movement researcher James Carson tells the story this way: "Before the council meeting Jackson, Calvin Morris, and Clay Evans had a meeting with the Mayor, Keane, and Holman. The Mayor was concerned about not losing the First Congressional District race between Rayner and Metcalfe. Daley thought Jackson's movement was creating too much of a stir about hungry people, which might swing votes to Rayner. Rayner was getting too much good press, making statements about the afflictions of the poor, and it was making Metcalfe look bad. So a deal was made. All Jackson's witnesses could speak if Jackson would just shut up until after the election. After Jackson accepted Daley's compromise it was all downhill for us. The Mayor didn't care how hungry the people said they were as long as they didn't do anything at the polls to hurt Metcalfe."

Rayner said, "I don't think there is any doubt in anybody's mind that Jackson plays footsie with City Hall. This was only the beginning. Jackson and Keane sat down in some smoke-filled room and agreed that the ordinance would be read but not acted upon. And mine was one of the few elections in which Jackson didn't endorse anyone. But not endorsing me was the same as endorsing Ralph, in those circles where politics are understood. Since Metcalfe thought being Negro was a disease, voting in the City Council like he was afraid the Massa Richard Daley would kick him off the team, Jackson's choice could have only been me. But Jackson hoped that by sacrificing me, he would get his $35 million appropriation for the poor but, of course, he never did."

On primary day, March 17, both congressional independent candidates lost. But more important, blacks' chances for some modicum of independence through forthright representation lost. Ralph Metcalfe breezed off to Congress, capturing Dawson's seat, with 71 percent of the vote. Murphy beat Savage with 72 percent of the vote in a more than 65 percent black district. Why? "The whites voted, the blacks didn't," said Don Rose, Savage's campaign manager. Thus an all too familiar scene had repeated itself. Year long there is a steady stream of complaints. Then on election day, there is a big yawn. After the election, the complaints start up all over again.

Consequently, when the hunger hearings began on March 26 the tales of woe didn't faze the Mayor. He had received his message from the poor at the voting booths eight days before. In fact, Daley treated the poor with more contempt than usual.

Before the hunger hearings could get underway, the Mayor called a 9 A.M. press conference, which drew all the reporters to his fifth-floor office. He kept them there until 11:30 A.M. When the press returned to the hearings, Keane masterminded the show by calling all pro-Daley witnesses to testify for the benefit of the TV cameras. C. Virgil Martin, president of Carson Pirie Scott & Co., criticized the movement's ordinance and blamed the president. "I don't think on a long-term basis the city should take on this kind of commitment," he said. By the time the poor, who knew more about their condition than the president of one of the largest Chicago department stores, got their turn, the press had gone home. And nobody listened to them.

But if the finance committee members had been predisposed to listen they would have heard:

• A frail-looking seventeen-year-old girl say, "I had two eggs for dinner last night, but I had to throw one out because it was spoiled and I'm still hungry. My mother's welfare check runs out about two weeks before we get the next one, so we often go without food."

• The Reverend Charles Garrity, head of the Uptown People's Planning Coalition where Puerto Ricans, Mexicans and Indians live, says: "We're discussing more than wall-to-wall cockroaches, we're talking about the stomachs of babies."

Jackson warned, "There are 11,000 hungry families in Chicago, including some in Mayor Daley's and Alderman Keane's home wards. Either we leave here after these hearings celebrating that Chicago took the lead in the war against poverty, or we'll bring the hungry people here to City Hall. And believe me, they'll come."

The second day of the hearings opened with Jackson proclaiming, "There is not only a generation gap in the City Council, there is a moral gap. While you fiddle, Rome burns."

Civil rights leaders and politicians rarely talk the same language. Chicago politics has nothing to do with morality. The only thing sacred to most Chicago politicians is getting elected. Once that is done there are zoning deals to be made and kickbacks and bribes to settle. Since Jackson proved he could not alter that comfortable arrangement, he could shut up now and let the aldermen get on with the business of ruining the city.

After Jackson had his say, the finance committee moved into action. A black machine-alderman, Wilson Frost, introduced a weak substitute for the movement's ordinance, placing most of the burden to relieve hunger on the state and federal governments. Frost was rewarded for his consistent loyalty to the machine in 1973 by being made president pro tem of the council. The resolution passed by a thirty-seven to two vote. Only Rayner, William Cousins, a black independent, and Leon M. Despres, a white Hyde Park liberal, voted to save it.

Then the City Council moved quickly on to more important matters. It approved 39 to 1 the Mayor's appointment of his cousin, Richard L. Curry, as Chicago corporation counsel. The Council believes in pleasing the Mayor, and nothing pleases Daley more than to have his family served by the public. And of course, the Mayor's sons are extremely blessed. John Patrick secured a windfall of public insurance policies for the Heil and Heil Insurance Agency of Evanston shortly after he joined the firm in 1972. It writes insurance policies for the city, Public Building Commission, Park District, and McCormick Place, with premiums totaling nearly $2.5 million annually. Richard M., a state senator, and his brother Michael receive lucrative work assignments from Circuit Court judges, many of whom rose to the bench by virtue of their dad's political backing. In 1973, when Daley was asked about the special privileges awarded to his offspring, he told reporters: "What kind of a world are we living in if a man can't put his arms around his sons? If I can't help my sons, they [critics] can kiss my ass." (The same statement could well be used to sum up Daley's feelings about the city's poor.)

After the council's business of nepotism was settled, Keane scurried on to conflict of interest. At Keane's urging, the sale of $52 million in revenue bonds was approved for use in the building of a $38-million parking garage at O'Hare International Airport. This was an urgent matter for Chicago's future and especially for Keane, the finance committee chairman. In 1973, *Chicago Today* would reveal that Keane was part owner of three private lots leased to the Airport Parking Corporation of America, which was given an exclusive contract by the city to run the O'Hare parking garage.

In Chicago's City Council, the greedy have no time for the needy. Thus on April 9, 1970, it executed the crowning blow, slashing the $35 million asked for by the poor to a pittance. Without telling anybody, Daley put an annual $500,000 price tag on the Frost ordinance and announced the money would come from an emergency tax levy that would be reflected in 1971 property taxes—a move which created more hatred of the poor from the city's property owners.

Mayor Daley subsequently declared hunger an emergency, which opened the way for the city's department of human resources to feed the indigent at the thirty-four antipoverty centers (all the feeding centers would be closed by 1972). The Reverend David Wallace, Jackson's communications aide, immediately called the appropriation insufficient, amounting to little more than one dollar for each of the estimated 300,000 hungry Chicagoans. But Jackson saw it as a victory: "It was a victory for us to maneuver the hunger issue out of the streets to the level of the legislative chambers both locally and nationally." On May 23, 1969 (in *Chicago Today*), Jackson predicted that hunger could well become the national issue that public accommodations were in Alabama under Martin Luther King. Jackson's agitation was successful in pushing the hunger issue onto the national agenda for a time only.

On this point of giving the issue national attention,

one would have to agree. Senator George McGovern, chairman of the Senate Committee on Nutrition and Human Needs, held hearings on hunger in Chicago, as well as in the nation's capital. On the hill, congressmen dramatized the issue themselves by trying to live on a welfare budget. The program of living on a daily food allowance averaging eighteen cents prompted Representative Abner J. Mikva from Illinois to say, "I'm hungry. You start thinking about eating too much of the time. You're concerned constantly that you're not getting enough to eat." Finally, the issue succeeded in trickling up to the president. On December 2, 1969, President Nixon pledged to banish hunger in America. He said that there were measures now in Congress that should virtually eliminate the problem of poverty as a cause of malnutrition. And on July 2, 1971, Nixon signed into law a bill to make available $17 million for child nutritional programs. However, the funds were later impounded.

Although the local newspapers reported that in Jackson's first tryout in the big leagues of Chicago politics, he barely made it to second base, a few credited him with at least adding a deft touch to the game. If Jackson had retired to the political bleachers after the hunger fiasco, nobody would have blamed him. The way the deck is stacked, it took him eleven months to get $500,000 from the city for the poor and less than five minutes for Keane to set the stage for alleged personal profiteering from a $38-million parking garage. But the experience energized, intrigued Jackson, who wants power just as badly as the Mayor who hoards it all.

On August 25, 1970, Jackson stubbornly announced at a staff retreat that in the future the movement's major focal point would be political. Economic concerns, such as negotiations for jobs, the hunger campaigns, and business development, would become secondary goals. (This position would gradually be reversed.)

By knocking off some aldermanic plums, the plan was a direct assault on the Mayor's machine. More sober-minded staffers cautioned Jackson against embarking on such grand-scale plans. The move would require back-breaking precinct organization, fund raising, and voter registration efforts. And the aldermanic election was less than six months away. To complicate matters, Jackson also indicated he might run for mayor. Despite the caveats that the movement was ill prepared for such a giant leap on such short notice, the announcement was generally welcomed by the struggling black independent movement.

Since the midthirties, when blacks began migrating from the party of Lincoln to nestle in the Democratic column, there had been an independent political movement valiantly attempting to elect "unbossed" candidates. But independents consistently lost against the vicious Daley-Dawson machine and its predecessor, the Kelly-Nash machine. Bill (The Man) Dawson, who switched from the Republican party to organize the black vote for Democratic Mayor Edward Kelly, built an impregnable black submachine on Chicago's south side, which successfully clobbered all opposition.

Dawson, shrewd and close-mouthed, redefined patronage as an instrument for containing the black poor. In white wards, committeemen passed out $10,000 jobs, for example. But Dawson would request three $3,333-a-year jobs, which spread the "wealth" and multiplied his power. Dawson's control of black votes, his compatibility with the crime syndicate, and fervid protection of white interests resulted not only in Dawson's unprecedented reign as Chicago's Black Boss but also in his serving thirteen terms in Congress—the longest political career of any elected black official in America. No man since Dawson has held such power. After his death in 1970, Daley succeeded in spreading control among several black loyalists so no one black man would ever again be in a position to single-handedly defeat him. Dawson could have, but, of course, he never did.

It was not until the midsixties that the independent struggle seemed anything but fruitless. Gains up to that point had consisted of electing, in the early forties, two "independent-minded" politicians, one a Democrat, the other a Republican. By 1964, a new militant civil rights mood aided this long history of creeping independence and resistance against party labels. Equally as important, a growing middle-income group of professional blacks began escaping the mental ghettos of Dawsonism and the physical ghettos north of Sixty-third Street on Chicago's south side. Through the efforts of enlightened community organizations, the black professional classes became identified more as split-ticket voters than going the straight party line. The Sixth, Eighth, and Twenty-first south-side wards went through a softening up process, which would be ripe for the defeat of a Hanrahan in 1972. In 1964, Rayner ran against Congressman Dawson and, for the first time in history, these three wards were carried by an independent, although Rayner lost the race. In 1968, Dawson, then in his eighties, defeated Rayner in the primary by a ratio of only 3 to 2, which was earthshaking news for a movement which could only measure success by close losses. There was no hope of close wins. By 1967, the independent struggle reaped its first clear-cut rewards in City Council. There had been others, such as the late Claude Holman, who had been elected to the council in 1955 as an "alternative" to the Daley-Dawson alliance. But before long, Holman had become coopted by Daley and was loyal almost to the point of lunacy. But the 1967 wins were for real. Harvard-trained attorney William Cousins won the Eighth aldermanic seat and Rayner captured the Sixth Ward seat, making them the only two independent black aldermen in City Council. Rayner thus was the first black to be elected in a black ward over an incumbent black machine-endorsed candidate. Both men were to become rarities in Chicago black politics. They would serve the needs of their constituencies.

Jackson's game plan was to build on and increase the already established voting patterns on the south side. This is the same modus operandi he used with the black businessmen. His maxim is to Build on Success or Develop the Developing. Unlike Dr. King, who settled in among the more depressed blacks on the west side, Jackson stuck with the more middle-class southsiders, whom he perceived as a less difficult organizing challenge. On this side of town, despite the new militant mood, Jackson would produce only minimal results, somewhat similar to those black leaders who preceded him. On the west side of town—a political gold mine for the Mayor—Jackson would provide no leadership. There in the poorest section of town, Daley is unquestionably the leader of blacks—in 1974, too, just like he was when Jackson moved into independent politics in 1970.

In preparation for the 1971 key local elections, Jackson set in motion the political education division to reinforce the climate setting he was building through his Saturday morning forums. They attract nearly 2,000 supporters and are broadcast to a listening audience of close to 100,000 (formerly on WVON, now on black-owned WJPC).

Jackson appointed Leon Davis as dean of the political education department. Davis began his political career as a local organizer in Lyndon Johnson's campaign and at the time was an administrative aide to Democratic Congressman Abner Mikva. Under the direction of Davis, the movement as a political force showed promise. He steered it away from much of the high-level rhetoric down to the nitty-gritty of precinct organization. By 1972, 700 students would have graduated from a ten-week course in fund raising, research, public relations, organizing voter registration drives, canvassing, precinct coordination, and implementation of election day activities—a euphemism for calling the state police on votenapers.

More novel functions of the political education division are to tie the politicians to their constituency and to explain the duties of public officials. If you don't know what a politician is supposed to do, you find it somewhat difficult to criticize him for not doing it. Both of these functions were carried out at the political division's first political convention on December 19, 1970. For the first time, blacks, Spanish-Americans, the young, the old, and women were allowed to participate in the selection of their candidates. The education department also drafted the issues on which the independent politicians would run for alderman. No such citizen participation is allowed by the Democrats. Their slate-making team is composed of the eighty ward and township committeemen, who form the Cook County Democratic Central Committee. Mayor Daley is chairman. These men have power which often far outweighs their intelligence. For example, Alderman Vito Marzullo, who has a sizeable black constituency, never made it past grade school. Yet it is people like Marzullo who can slate judges, state senators, and congressmen—with Daley's approval. Whatever the ward bosses come up with in secret caucuses becomes the people's choice, since blacks or anybody else in Chicago seldom ever vote Republican.

Although people involvement in the democratic process was the overriding purpose of the convention, it was also construed to force some accountability from the white and black independents. They are tricky fellows too. The saga of Alderman Fred Hubbard is a case in point.

Meekly, on August 23, 1972, after eluding a fifteen-month search by the FBI, Fred Hubbard surrendered to federal agents while he was sitting at a poker table in Gardenia, California. "You got me. It's all gone."

Hubbard's blowing more than $100,000 of Chicago Plan monies for jobs in the building trades in a series of poker and crap games was a crime for which a politician of his stature paid an unusually high penalty—two years in a federal penitentiary. But the real crime occurred in 1969, when he bamboozled thousands of poor and disadvantaged blacks into believing he was their political liberator.

Hubbard had excellent credentials compared to his machine aldermanic opponent, Lawrence Woods, a shady professional gambler, who had committed the cardinal sin in Chicago politics: he got caught while shaking down a small businessman while he was employed with the county assessor's office. A young social worker, a past president of NAACP at the University of Chicago (where he received his sociology degree), Hubbard had even engaged in a blazing gun battle, supposedly for the cause. In 1966, when he was challenging crusty, powerhouse Bill Dawson for his congressional seat, a gunman invaded Hubbard's campaign office. In an exchange of bullets, Hubbard received a severe shoulder wound, but he also fired enough shots to rout his assailant.

This clear choice between a tough in-fighter with integrity, "a real black man," and Lawrence Woods, a gangster-type ward hack in the heart of Daley's black submachine, became a rallying point for big names like Adlai Stevenson and Mayor Richard Hatcher of Gary, and for the North Shore liberals. This was it. If Hubbard could beat Woods, he would open the door to both white and black independents who could become an invincible coalition that could create havoc against the machine.

At the election night victory party, blacks and whites from across the state converged on Hubbard's campaign office to share in one of the greatest upsets in history. Hubbard had beat Woods, Congressman Dawson's secretary, by 6,924 to 4,600 votes. Alderman Leon Despres declared: "This is the biggest possible defeat the Democratic machine could have suffered. The Second Ward always has been the most secure position of the machine."

A preacher prayed, the young were dancing in the streets, and a welfare mother cried with tears of joy. Anna Langford, who would soon become Chicago's first black woman alderman, also cried. She had just received a reliable tip that the machine had secretly dumped Woods for Hubbard after the press had exposed Woods' improprieties.

Hubbard was rewarded with a $30,000-a-year job as director of the Chicago Plan, which was a federally funded program to train minorities for trade union jobs. The training funds, the hopes and aspirations of thousands of working black poor, were all frittered away on some crap and poker tables in Hubbard's fifteen-month trek between Vegas and California.

Charlie Chew had also sold out as soon as he was elected to the state legislature after being one of the best independent aldermen in the city. The only difference between Chew and Hubbard was that the politically wise blacks always expected Chew to do what was best for Chew. But Hubbard had been perceived as a liberator.

At the People's Convention, Jackson cautioned the more than 3,000 spectators to be just as enthusiastic in firing the aldermen they hoped to elect as they were in hiring them. "All too often in the past so-called independents have been elected and not long after the election strayed into the arms of some political sponsor. These political turncoats remind me of the men in Biblical days who wore tons of clothing to hide the fact they they had been castrated. Even in the summer, they would be sweating under all those robes, but the people always knew, as we do today, that they were eunuchs. Those political whores who jump into the bed of the highest bidder, will one day find themselves isolated, run over, outcasts in the movement of black political independence."

Jackson endorsed twelve aldermanic candidates, six of them black, slated from the People's Convention. In 1970, a Jackson endorsement had a bit more substance behind it than when he first implemented this pressure tactic in 1968. Then the Jackson stamp of approval meant little more than oratory, which does not win elections in Chicago. Whereas in the past Jackson would endorse but not work for a candidate, his commitment could now be backed up with troops professionally trained by his political education division. In a fashion, his organizing efforts were beginning to resemble the professional style of the Independent Voters of Illinois (IVI) and the Independent Precinct Organization (IPO) that operates in the affluent North Shore and lakefront areas. Phil Smith, a social worker whom Jackson endorsed for alderman in the Twenty-first Ward, said of a movement endorsement, "Unless you are talking about fringe areas or transitional communities that are changing from white to black, an IVI or an IPO endorsement has no real impact in black communities. In a black, south-side ward, telling a person that IVI has endorsed you raises the question of, 'Who is IVI?' " But, although blacks know what a Jackson endorsement means, it does not necessarily follow that his endorsements significantly influence the voters.

Jackson explained his motive for endorsements: "When I first came to Chicago no black groups that I knew of were doing this. If they were, they were not effective because the machine had absorbed most of the civil rights groups. I first got the idea in 1968 when I was coming out of my office on Forty-seventh Street. A guy who was half-drunk in painter's clothes stumbled up to me and said, 'Reverend, I haven't heard you say nothing about this governor's race but if Shapiro gets back in, we are in big trouble.' I didn't know anything about Governor Samuel Shapiro, but I did know something about the separation of power. I endorsed Richard Ogilvie, a Republican, for the purpose of having a balance of power, a check, and watch system on Daley. Since Ogilvie saw he needed the blacks to counteract the big Democratic vote from Chicago, we didn't have much trouble getting our welfare cuts during the hunger drive. Also as an overture to the black community, Ogilvie started opening up business contracts for blacks in African countries, as well as in the state of Illinois. Stevenson also saw the need for us. That's why he started funneling monies into black banks after we endorsed him. When so many politicians began running to us to get our support, the political education division set up a screening division to make them accountable to us in exchange for our vote."

The month prior to the February election Jackson called on two friends, Georgia State Legislator Julian Bond and the late baseball great, Jackie Robinson, to energize his Saturday morning audience into working for the candidates. Robinson told them, "If Newark can elect a black mayor and Gary and Cleveland can, then why can't Chicago elect some men and women to be aldermen—not alderboys?" The celebrities also accompanied Jackson on walking tours through the candidates' wards to drum up support. According to Leon Davis, eight instructors and 200 students headed by Alice Tregay, a political dynamo, were sent into Alderman Cousins' campaign. Two hundred students and seven instructors went to Anna Langford's ward, about a hundred to Gus Savage's, the perennial candidate, and a few instructors were assigned to the west-side candidates. Upon Jackson's urging, Illinois Attorney General Scott dispatched fifty members of his staff to monitor the elections. Jackson's original request was for Ogilvie to mobilize the National Guard to guarantee an honest election. A National Guard formation in every polling place is not as stultifying as it may sound in light of the Democrats' motto: "If you can't win it, steal it."

On election night, February 23, only two of the six Jackson-backed black candidates won. But although there was one new face, there were no new black independent aldermanic gains. Attorney Anna Langford's victory was nullified by Rayner's not running, which meant there was nothing more than a seat exchange. The other victory was incumbent William Cousins. Thus, the seat swap from one independent to another and the retention of Cousins did not sway the balance of power in City Council. The Mayor's two-thirds majority rubber stamp was still intact— as always. The dismal result was the usual vote fraud, coupled with a low black anti-Daley turnout. Daley's patronage workers always vote—their jobs depend on it. Even during the 1967 snowstorm that immobilized all modes of transportation, the Daleyites were seen dressed up like Eskimos with snowshoes on trekking to the polling places. They would have used sleds pulled by Huskies if they had had to.

Jackson shrugged off the losses saying, "Don't blame me, I wasn't running for anything." But of the wins, he said, "You could say we certainly were responsible for the election of Aldermen Bill Cousins and Anna Langford. These victories attest to the results of our hardcore organizing."

I asked four black independents (two who won, one who lost, and one who quit), as well as one politician who was a machine candidate at the time of his win to assess Jackson's influence in their elections, as well as to give their opinion of Jackson's political role.

1.   Alderman William Cousins, forty-five, a wiry, low-keyed loner, is one of the few black politicians in Chicago with an organization of his own. (In 1973, his ward was gerrymandered.) Although he is short on charisma, he is long on the old-fashioned virtues of heavy door-to-door canvassing. His ward includes the middle-income Chatham area called the mink-lined ghetto by those contemptuous of the more middle-class blacks.

"The first time I ran, I had no involvement with Jesse and I won. In the second campaign, I would have been elected if the movement had not endorsed candidates. My situation is one of grass-roots organization in my ward. I won by 7,000 votes. If the movement had been against me, it might have been a different situation. The people that were involved in my election like Alice Tregay would have been involved even if there had been no Jackson movement because I have always been involved in civil rights. Jesse's movement like any organization would not be able to elect a candidate. It could contribute. If there is a real close race, they can say the support of their group is crucial. But that would apply to all other groups that contribute, like labor. Jesse might say he elects people but you get the wrong impression if you believe it."

Cousins continued: "Jesse and the movement are pushing on a lot of fronts. But politics is the lone area in which it has the least expertise. Jesse is more adept in other areas outside of politics. This is a game he understands less than any other. Politics just doesn't follow the same rules as civil rights."

2.   Anna Langford, the first black woman to be elected to City Council, started out her political career with the regular Democratic organization, in which she was a precinct worker for almost twelve years. Finally, she got fed up, quit her patronage job, earned a law degree, and became one of the city's most respected civil rights attorneys as well as a devout Jackson supporter.

"The first time I ran in 1967 there was no political arm of Breadbasket," she said. "And I would have won that election had we not been cheated out of it. I only lost by thirty-seven votes.

"I became interested in running after Sammy Rayner got elected. I used to watch Claude Holman degrading Rayner on TV. I began seeing what a vicious little group of people the Keanes, the Daleys, and the Holmans were. And

I said that if the City Council is being run by people like that, I am going to jump in and help change it. Now in my second race, I can truthfully say that Jesse's people, along with a lot of other people, helped me in my campaign."

    3.   Phil Smith, a veteran social worker, was a former campaign manager for Sammy Rayner. He is the executive director of a small group called the Voters Organized to Educate. A man with an amazing memory, he can recite at one sitting everyone who has won or lost in Chicago politics in the last forty years, as well as cite the reasons why.

    "I would give Jesse credit for being more of a national figure than having any effect in local politics. The black independent movement in the city does not revolve around Jesse. He is a part of it, but it won't sink or swim based on any actions from Jesse. Nobody would miss Jesse if he stayed out of politics. In fact, a lot of people would rather he got out. He talks too much and turns off people who really want to work because they don't have time to listen to all that rapping. Jesse must get to the point where he develops situations instead of developing personalities. In my particular situation, the election was stolen from me. I won it but they stole it on the tally sheets. At 7:30 on election night, the City News Bureau was already announcing me the winner. I had 5,032 votes then, but when they got through stealing I didn't have but 4,748 votes.

    "I filed a suit against this illegal practice which is still sitting in appellate court and that was three years ago. Jesse only appeared in my campaign once. But movement people like Willie Barrow and people like Lola Smith, who is now Reverend Ed Riddick's wife, and Calvin Morris helped. Let's not call Jesse a politician. It's best to say he is politically oriented. The point that I am trying to make is that there are hundreds of unsung people in this city whom you tap when there is an election. They will do X

number of things and go on back where they came from
until there is another election. But they are not hung up
on press and publicity. So Jesse takes credit for their
efforts."

Smith added: "Jesse's most important contribution
to Chicago politics is the Saturday morning forum. He
brought to Chicago a consistent, articulate voice which we
lacked, a consistent voice hammering away at the chica-
nery going on in this town. He educates the people. Every
week Jesse is pounding on issues. Even the most dull
person would find some of it sinking in."

4.   Despite the urging of political independents, in
1967 Sammy Rayner quit politics and returned to his
mortuary business. His move was a serious blow to the
independent movement because his Sixth Ward was recap-
tured by the machine Democrats.

"I had to quit because I was going bankrupt," Rayner
said. "The first time I ran for alderman it cost me $10,000,
90 percent of which was mine and my father's. Both runs
for Congress cost me nearly $30,000.

"Jesse asked me to run in 1971. I told him that I still
owed $7,000 from the last campaign. Jesse promised to
raise the money. I said when I see it, that's when I will
make the decision. 'Put the money on the wood makes the
voting good.' I told him to call me when he raised it. He
never did."

An open letter to the public showed that Jackson
tried to make good on his promise to the man he himself
did not support in 1970. The tone of the letter pointed to
the mental anguish a leader suffers when his followers
won't pay the price for freedom.

Brother Rayner:
    Your recent announcement of retirement
from politics has troubled me in many ways. It

pointed out the fact that people want and need good government, but will not give the type of support that is necessary to obtain and retain it.

Sammy, I have received numerous letters and calls requesting me to urge you to run again for Alderman of the Sixth Ward. In each case, I have informed them of the type of financial situation you are in. I have tried to tell them that it is through them that God will help you and that we must understand that freedom ain't free. We must all help you help the many as you have done.

This is an open letter because I want everybody to know that I support you and will support you both financially and in any other way, so we can send back to the City Council a free man with a free voice.

Let this letter serve as a draft to you, Sammy. Don't leave us now. I know you are tired, but don't leave us now—Moses must have been tired, Malcolm X was tired, and I am tired. But let God tell us when we must rest.

> Your Brother in Peace and Freedom,
> Jesse L. Jackson

Rayner's opinion of Jackson? "He has no impact. Politics is troops, politics is organization. Politics is knocking on doors. For example, in 1968, his people promised to work like hound puppies for me in my congressional race. But they got as far as the first restaurant and ate hot dogs and drank coffee and that was it. They were supposed to be in the precincts knocking on doors but only about ten ever worked.

"Jesse does a lot of talking. With all that talking and twenty-nine cents you can't even buy a loaf of bread. I am not impressed by his political moxie because he doesn't have any," Rayner said.

Congressman Ralph Metcalfe used to be called "Rabbit" because he ran so fast. At twenty-two he was acclaimed "the world's fastest human," because in a single day he tied the world's record for the 100-yard dash and went on to set three new records in the longer sprints, capturing the silver and bronze medals in the 1932 Olympics. In 1936, he shredded Adolph Hitler's claim of Nordic superiority in Berlin by winning both a silver and a gold medal. On Mayor Daley's political plantation, Metcalfe ran just as hard, moving from precinct captain to alderman, where he became chairman of the powerful Building and Zoning Committee and was the first black ever to serve as President Pro Tem of City Council. In 1970, he replaced the late Congressman Dawson as U.S. Representative of the First Congressional District.

In 1972, the politician-athlete, now an avid golfer, had everything to lose and not much to gain by breaking away from the machine. No black man in Daley's camp—except Dawson—had more real clout or power than Metcalfe. But he apparently traded it all in for the opportunity to stand erect and independent as a man. He said he could no longer stomach police brutality toward blacks. "I used to watch police shaking down blacks on my block and here I was a Congressman and I felt powerless to stand up and fight it." Thus Metcalfe abandoned—at least temporarily—his coveted status to push for police reform.

Metcalfe, who has never been beaten by the independent opposition, gave a fresh viewpoint from the other side: "I think Jesse has played a major role in the development of the independent movement, but I don't think he has been the controlling force because he doesn't have the people who are willing to go from door-to-door and do the precinct work. They may pack his Saturday meetings, but the people don't go out and ring doorbells. I think that Jesse has played a very important role in the movement of black people toward independence and has stimulated them into having pride in themselves. But being very candid, I would say that Jackson is an individualist, having visions of being *the* black leader. But I contend we will never have *the* black leader in the civil rights movement. We must have shades of leadership. I think Jesse has relegated to himself a lot of successes that he is not entitled to. I know that he does not have the forces to move votes. He has not been able to cultivate teams of people who are dedicated enough to do this. When I ran against Sammy Rayner for Congress, I found that his volunteers are basically interested in a lot of rhetoric, attending meetings, and social affairs, but they have to operate as a team. They have to be able to go into a precinct like a hardened precinct captain and sit down and talk with the people. But they do the most talking in a friendly climate to receptive audiences that are already espousing their viewpoints."

Two months later, on April 6, 1971, the Mayor won his fifth term for office, carrying 78 percent of the vote. By this time, the political analysts had written off Jackson's role in Chicago politics as inconsequential, based on the premise that Jackson had received only thirty-five write-in votes in his bid for mayor. "The last minute endorsement Jackson gave Daley's opponent Richard Friedman had virtually no impact. Jackson's recent forays into the political arena have lessened his stature locally," concluded Joel Weisman, former political editor of *Chicago Today*.

Jackson's bid for mayor was one of the most misunderstood and miscalculated maneuvers of his early political career. In 1974, political analysts are still chortling over how Jackson lost the 1971 mayoral race, without ever considering the finer point that he never ran for mayor. Jackson's political pronouncements, animations, and theatrics were all calculated to create the illusion of running in order to reverse a state statute that makes it highly improbable for anyone to get on the mayoral ballot as an independent. In addition, the move was designed to pave the way for a new alternative or third party—the Bread 'N Butter party—for the more than 500,000 Chicagoans—both black and white—who do not vote for either party. However, no matter what he was attempting to do, Jackson's mayoral escapade was a classic example of pursuing the best ends by the worst possible set of means.

New York City has the Liberal, the American Labor, the Conservative, the Democratic, and the Republican parties. All kinds of imaginative combinations or fusions are possible under this structure. But in Chicago, the imagination of the state legislature long ago erased the possibility of a third party's ever getting on the mayoral ballot—"to deter crackpots and nuisance candidates"— Senator Cecil Partee, the black minority leader of the State Senate, explained. In 1971, the law required an independent candidate for mayor to obtain more than 60,000 signatures on his nominating petitions as compared to 4,200 for the Democrats and 2,034 for the Republicans. But the independents' signatures can't be just anybody's signatures. They have to be "virgins." In Chicago's political parlance "virgins" are voters who have not been tainted by voting for either party in the last partisan election. Now if anybody had an organization efficient enough to corral the signatures of 60,000 virgins, they would probably have to have twice that number to pass unchallenged by the Chicago Board of Election Commissioners. Although for the Mayor voters even rise from the dead to sign his nominating petitions, independents have no such luck. A misspelled name, a suspicious scrawl, an "i" left undotted are all justifications for the signatures to be challenged and the prospective candidate disqualified.

This kind of lopsided system brings to mind a Dickensian phrase: "If the law supposed that . . . the law is an ass, an idiot." Thus, when Jackson expressed a desire to run for mayor as an independent, he envisioned himself playing the role of a "sacrificial lamb" for political change. If he could force the legal sectors into changing the law, the door would be open not only for him but for any member of the independent coalition—white or black—to gain a spot on the ballot, he said. While he worked through the legal machinery, Jackson felt the only logical stratagem was for him to convince the powers that be that he was a serious candidate. Jackson's performance was bought by the crusty political barons, who should know a put-on when they see one since similar ruses are part of their election repertory. The politicians who thought Jackson, the candidate, just might wake up the black, the Spanish, the Puerto Rican, the Indian, the youth, and even some of the white folks were in a tizzy. There was much churning about and gnashing of teeth.

His announcement was immediately considered a threat by Daley. John Blair, a Chicago policeman assigned to Jackson as a bodyguard, said he was told by his boss to keep a daily log on all Jackson's activities. "I was told to report every move he made because Daley wanted to know. I was also told if I didn't make these reports, I would be replaced with someone else who would. But I managed to get around reporting anything important."

George Tagge, former political columnist for the *Tribune*, wrote: "Mayor Daley's petition, filed, December 23, 1971 (primary), needed only 4,200 signatures, but had an unprecedented 975,000. The major emphasis in gathering the signatures was made in black communities. All who signed are ineligible to sign petitions for the Reverend Mr. Jackson and if they did, their pro-Jackson signatures could be thrown out by the Chicago Election Board." As an overture to the black community, for the first time in Chicago history a black was slated for the citywide office of city treasurer.

At the same time as Jackson was going through the motions of a serious candidate, he also had to leave himself an exit, in case he received a favorable court decision, so he could select an appropriate replacement.

Backed into a precarious position, Jackson often sounded like he was talking out of three sides of his mouth. "I may run for mayor," he told some reporters. "I am certainly serious about the mayoral race," he told others. "I am more concerned with running the mayor than I am running for mayor," was another frequent phrase—one which was closer to the truth. As unpredictable as he is, Jackson is not likely to run for any political office. Jackson considers himself more of a national leader than a Chicago leader. But more importantly, he is interested in being a kingmaker: running others, and controlling their activities. This stance would leave him free to play his multiplicity of roles. Nevertheless his contradictory statements irked members of the press accustomed to his previously telegraphic announcements. One of Jackson's biggest weaknesses is that whenever he prepares to move against Daley, he usually blabs it on radio and TV and holds a press conference. Thus when he does move, the Mayor is always prepared. On the other hand, the Mayor's public posture and his private political strategies are rarely the same. Blacks never know what Daley has in store for them until the ax falls.

But this time Jackson kept the pros guessing. While Jackson's attorneys, Robert Tucker and Thomas Todd, battled in court, Jackson went on with the theatrics. On February 11, 1971, he took a leave of absence to run for mayor, with his boss Ralph Abernathy's blessing. "Jackson is a brilliant, young, nonviolent revolutionary whose candidacy offers a creative alternative to the Republican and Democratic parties. Chicago's black and poor people are in a no-man's land. The Republican party's posture in regard to black people is benign neglect and the Democratic party in the midst of turmoil takes us for granted.

Of course, more than a half-million black people in Chicago not registered to vote doesn't help any, either," Abernathy said.

In the Mayor's stacked deck, Daley controls all the aces, the kings, the jacks, all the way down to the smallest deuce. The legal battle shaped up like this:

December 10, 1970—Jackson's attorneys filed a suit in federal district court requesting a temporary injunction to invalidate the city and state codes that discriminate against independents. The suit stated that Jackson lacked the money and organization to collect the more than 60,000 signatures. Jackson said, "We need cheaper and quicker campaigns, but the present restrictions make qualifying too costly. The two regular parties do not have the constitutional right to control the whole process."

December 22, 1970—The Mayor's former law partner and confidante, Judge William J. Lynch, denied Jackson's request. Upon pressure from the press exposing the political connection, Lynch ordered a three-judge panel to convene to hear constitutional arguments. Republican Illinois Attorney General William Scott, Governor Ogilvie, and the GOP state chairman filed briefs in Jackson's behalf as friends of the court. "My pleading is that the state law is in violation of the First and Fourteenth Amendments of the U. S. Constitution," said Scott.

January 29, 1971—The three-judge panel heard all the constitutional arguments and promptly dismissed the suit in a 2 to 1 decision. Lynch and another Democrat, Joseph Sam Perry, made Republican Judge Wilbur Pell a mere ornament on the panel.

February 1, 1971—Attorneys for Jackson filed a brief with the U. S. Supreme Court calling for emergency action to place Jackson's name on the Chicago ballot. The precedent Jackson's attorneys used was the case of George Wallace, who, through an emergency ruling, was placed on the Ohio presidential ballot in 1968.

February 2, 1971—Jackson, in a symbolic gesture,

filed 7,175 signatures from black and white and the Spanish-speaking communities with the Chicago Board of Election Commissioners to gain a spot on the ballot. Stanley Kusper, board chairman, conceded that Jackson's name could be placed on the ballot without the required number of signatures "as long as there was no challenge to his candidacy."

February 8, 1971—The challenge. Jack Muller, a Chicago police detective, who became a local phenomenon for ticketing the Mayor's and other city officials' limousines illegally parked around City Hall, protested that Jackson's nominating petitions did not conform to law.

February 12, 1971—Responding to Muller's challenge, Kusper showed rare insight. "You can look at the petitions and look at Jesse Jackson and you know he does not have valid signatures." Either the way Jackson parts his Afro or too many curlicues among the signatures convinced Kusper to rule Jackson off the April 6 ballot. The board found something quirky about 3,866 of Jackson's 7,175 signatures filed. Calling Kusper's decision a farce, Jackson had left only the shred-thin hope of a speedy Supreme Court decision.

February 22, 1971—The Supreme Court unanimously denied Jackson's request that he be placed on the ballot for the general election. Supreme Court Justice William O. Douglas pointed out that the Chicago election board's decision not to print the Reverend Mr. Jackson's name on the ballot came after a three-judge federal court had upheld the Illinois election code. "What applicants ask us in substance to do is sit in direct review of the election board. The reason, of course, is that the primary election will be held February 23, 1971, and the state will begin distributing the ballots which contain the names of the winners of the independent candidates on March 8. Federal courts cannot act responsibly in those situations."

Jackson lost, but the political scenario for blacks wouldn't have changed much had he won. Only if blacks are in no great rush to elect a black nonmachine mayor would Jackson's scheme for a third party seem prudent, although he was on sound moral ground. Who could argue that an unjust law should not be changed? But it can be argued that a legal challenge—which if successful would have benefited white liberals more than blacks—should not have dominated and emerged as the only black strategy for the 1971 mayoral race.

First, Jackson's eleventh hour maneuvering, which would characterize his future political strategizing, would have been unremunerative in 1971 even if the legal machinery had cleared a spot on the ballot for an independent. The candidate—whoever the poor Joe might have been—would have been sitting on a ballot blankly wondering how he had got himself into such an incredible predicament. Not even the most rudimentary supportive campaign resources were readied—in case there had been a favorable court ruling. There were some 500,000 unorganized, unregistered voters, many of whom were totally confused over whether they would have a chance to vote for or against a black mayor. There was no war chest, no citywide organization for fund raising or getting out the vote. And there was utter bewilderment over the nonexistent mechanism for a third party. Even if Jackson's scheme had been more purposeful, anything launched four months before a major election against a machine with nearly twenty years of experience in votenaping, day-to-day precinct work, and intimidation, would prove ludicrous.

Although the ball game was over when Jackson started to play, 1971 could have been historic if he had begun creating and building an organization—precinct by precinct—for a serious challenge in 1975. Never had there been a serious citywide exercise aimed at electing a nonmachine black mayor. (Dick Gregory ran in 1967 as a write-in candidate.)

In both Newark and Cleveland trial runs, warm-up

exercises of taking precinct workers through the motions of running a mayoral race paid off the second go-around, as blacks learned from their mistakes and believed that electing a black mayor was not a Mission Impossible. In both cases, politics was not a seasonal sport. There was no break; there was no other objective than electing a black mayor from the day Kenneth Gibson and Carl Stokes lost to the next election when both men won. Understandably, there is only one boss and only one Chicago—the roughest, toughest machine in the country. And on the first couple of attempts blacks might still lose. But overdefining the problem, rapping about the problem, and grandstanding acts are self-defeating. Power is first known by its sting, not by its sound effects. But the Jackson Movement emphasizes high visibility and high rhetoric, both of which are appropriate for civil rights but not for politics.

Jackson's preemptive move also blocked any serious candidate from pursuing the normal route of running as a Democrat against Daley—that is the real tragedy. In one-leader situations a nonmachine politician would either be courageous or foolhardy to preempt Jackson, who can ruin a reputation in the black community through acerbic condemnations from his Saturday morning pulpit. Thus, State Senator Richard Newhouse, an appealing legislator in both black and white circles, abandoned his plans for a serious mayoral challenge. Newhouse said that if Jackson's legal fight had been fruitful and the movement had run a black on a third party, his bid would have been interpreted as splitting the black vote. "I think the strategy set blacks back four years. I would have been berated for jumping out there against Jackson or whomever he was going to run. People would have said I was creating disunity. By the time I was convinced Jackson was not a serious candidate, it was too late to be serious about 1971."

Although it seemed premature after Jackson's mayoral stunt, some Chicago columnists dismissed Jackson altogether. One wrote: "From the Mayor's office Jackson is nothing more than an impressive, attractive demigod who can cause much thunder but no lightning." It would not be until 1974 that the most optimistic political observers would have to agree. Jackson would keep making headlines, but those that realize the distinction between rhetoric and results would no longer be impressed.

Swinging his support behind Richard Friedman (former first assistant Illinois Attorney General and executive director of the Better Government Association, a watchdog agency for political reform), Jackson said one day before the election: "I don't want people to waste their write-in votes on me. I don't want people to stay at home and not vote. I urge everyone to vote and to vote for Richard E. Friedman."

Looking ahead to 1975—the next mayoral race—there are some severe warning signals:

In 1973, State Senator Richard Newhouse jumped out front early to avoid colliding with Jackson. But it seems no matter what Newhouse does he cannot pre-empt Jackson. On April 27, 1974, Jackson issued a call for all those interested in running for mayor to report to PUSH. "Maybe we will have two or three blacks running," he said. A letter, documenting the call for candidates, was sent out over the signatures of some black independents, who did not support the move, primarily because it ignored Newhouse's earlier bid. Days later, apparently at Jackson's urging, Attorney E. Duke McNeil announced his resignation as president of The Woodlawn Organization and on August 20, 1974, declared himself a candidate. Then on September 4 Newhouse declared. And on September 13, thirty-six-year-old Edward Allen, Jr., became the third black to declare. Allen, a political unknown, is a developer who has built more than 1,000 low-income housing units on Chicago's west side. And the list of blacks may become a foursome. Also in the race is a Jewish alderman, William Singer, who in 1973 became the first official candidate.

As the book goes to press, Chicago politics is

helter-skelter because of strong undercurrents that Mayor Daley may not run for a sixth term. In May he was hospitalized and did not return to City Hall until September. If Daley steps aside because of ill health, the mayoral post would turn into a political grab bag. Several young Irish Turks would fight it out. So might Roman Pucinski, a Polish alderman, who feels the Irish have ruled long enough. And Singer shows strong potential for capturing most of the Jewish and liberal vote. With the ethnics fighting among themselves, the field would be wide open for an attractive black to possibly squeak through the crowd of contenders, on into the Mayor's seat. However, three blacks crowded upon the mayoral ballot would hopelessly split the black vote, making it impossible for blacks to capitalize on the expected upheaval. If the Mayor does run, a unifying black candidate would oil the track for a hard run in '79.

But the saga to elect a black mayor gets stranger as it lumbers on. Jackson, who nudged his pal McNeil out front, has not given him his personal anointment. Black businessmen, some of whom support both Daley and Jackson, are saying privately that they won't give financial support to any of the three announced blacks. Meanwhile, Jackson has gone off in another direction. On August 25, 1974, WBBM-TV commentator Walter Jacobson reported that Daley and Jackson had recently huddled in the Mayor's office. "Reverend Jackson told the Mayor that if he decided not to run, State Senator Cecil Partee would be an acceptable candidate to the black community." Partee, Senate minority leader who replaced Metcalfe as Daley's number one Negro, is one of those obedient fellows whom Jackson used to refer to as eunuchs. In two later speeches, Jackson also gave Partee a big plug. Whatever happened to Jackson, the champion of political independence? If all this is confusing to the reader, imagine how all Jackson's fancy machinations must look to the black voter. If confusion is Jackson's game he is batting 500. All in all, '75 looks like '71 re-runs. The forecast for a black independent mayor looks gloomy. There still is no war chest, no organization, and an estimated 250,000 blacks remain unregistered. The first black mayor may well be a machine black in 1983—providing the machine endures that long—if today's shenanigans are any indication of the future.

Jackson's muddying of the waters in 1971—for the sake of argument—could have been a simple miscalculation. But in 1974, his maneuvers appear obstructionist. Ineffectiveness in Chicago politics is normal. Obstructionism is abnormal. Why?

Ironically, even though Jackson is once again the major strategist in the 1975 race, his political operation, which showed some promise in 1971, is not improving. According to Leon Davis, the man who designed the movement's political education program and left PUSH in 1972, "Although at one time our organization looked promising, it has declined. I built a strong political program, which would have provided a basement organizing effort. Unfortunately, I have to admit that the PUSH implementation is very weak. In fact, it has dissipated. What PUSH can actually do, in voter registration, precinct organizing, and creating a war chest is very disproportionate to the rhetoric at the top. The sad part is that PUSH has the numerical potential for being a political force. In 1971, we could have been a force. Today, there are just a lot of unanswered questions."

In 1971, while Jackson was verbally challenging the Mayor, the chairman of his board, the Reverend Clay Evans, endorsed Daley. On Jackson's board are big businessmen, most of whom had to play ball with Daley to make it big, before Jackson came to town to make them bigger. Some of Jackson's businessmen still depend upon the Mayor for city contracts. Board member Theodore A.

Jones, for example, is the Daley loyalist who, along with Dawson, gutted the NAACP in 1957. Jones, until June 1974, was an executive of the WJPC radio station owned by John H. Johnson. Johnson, also a Jackson booster, endorsed the Mayor in a full page editorial in *Jet* magazine in 1971. Is it possible to praise Caesar and bury Caesar—concomitantly?

How can Jackson give the pretense of providing citywide leadership necessary for a mayoral race when his efforts do not extend to the west side—where nearly half-a-million blacks live? West-side blacks are the cushion of the Daley machine. According to Richard Barnett, a PUSH political education graduate and a west-side organizer, "Since 1973, I have repeatedly called on Jackson to aid us by sending troops into several key congressional aldermanic and state races. Once he reneged on a promise, once he sent one person and on another occasion he sent a message back that he had more important things to do than help us. In the 1974 state legislative race, our own grass-roots organizing among the poor elected a Democrat in the primary. Our candidate, Jesse Madison, won the state legislative race without Jackson's support. But we still need Jackson's people because we have so little to work with. From the time I was in PUSH in 1971 to now, only three years later, Jackson has retrogressed in Chicago politics, rather than progressed. And I can't help but raise the question of why."

Why?

The obstacles to effective,
unified black action are about
the same as those of people of
every race when they try to join
in a cooperative effort: lack of
vision, unexamined prejudices and
concentration on personal desires
at the expense of the common goal.

Congresswoman Shirley Chisholm, *The Good Fight*

Nineteen seventy-two washed in with the politics of blackness. Like the birth of any new ideology, the baby screamed, kicked, stumbled, but as a revisionist national spirit, as the most definitive statement of black power, it captured the essence of the times.

Black power politics at the local level had established itself as the New Frontier around 1967, differing from what other ethnic groups had perfected only by its candor. During the last hundred years, the Jews, the Irish, the Italians, and the Poles had quietly gone about acquiring ethnic power and building political and economic institutions. And so had blacks, but the Hayes-Tilden Compromise of 1877 had destroyed the black political beachhead. After a blackout of some ninety years, black power politics was on the rise again, aided by the Voting Rights Act of 1965 and the voter registration drives of SNCC, SCLC, CORE, and the NAACP, which enfranchised more than 3 million blacks in the South. Unlike the ethnics, who surreptitiously did their own thing while assuming the public posture of America first, blacks new to the game sidestepped the melting pot mythology and called it like it was.

By 1972, blacks had elected thirteen congressmen, eighty-eight mayors, 780 city councilmen, 140 judges and magistrates, 204 state legislators, and about 675 black school board members. Although the more than 2,000 black elected officials constituted only three-tenths of 1 percent of the total 521,760 elected officials in America, the gains were a great leap over 1968's total of 475. By 1974, black elected officials had moved to 2,991, with black mayors numbering 108 and black congressmen eighteen, according to data from the Joint Center for Political Studies. And that was black power. Blacks took pride in saying so, although it was considered most un-American not to attribute the successes to the gratuities of a pluralistic society.

In 1972 black power politics was to undergo the most Spartan test in its youthful history. Blacks were challenged to disprove the often quoted theory of Daniel Patrick Moynihan, former White House counselor: "The Negro is only an American and nothing else. He has no values and culture to protect." The politics of blackness was a crusade, a call for unity, an unparalleled soul-love fest construed to destroy all ties with party bosses and party labels. The single motivating force in 1972 was to be the commonality of blackness, a national effort to organize around the self-interest of race. Emotionalism—a drum beat to the masses—was at its peak. "The hands that picked cotton in 1964 will pick a president in 1972," cried Jesse Jackson. To depict the new mood of independence, Congressman Bill Clay of St. Louis coined the phrase, "No permanent friends, no permanent enemies, just permanent interests." To the mayor of Gary, Richard Hatcher, it was a time "when blacks ain't in nobody's hip pocket now."

If the new politics was to live up to its creed, it should have meant only one thing to the men at the top. The brokerage system would undergo a massive over-hauling. Assuming the new black leaders were not white bosses in black faces, the black vote would be brokered by blacks for blacks. And the price tag would run high. Depending on which black leader was doing the horse-trading, black loyalty to a presidential candidate in 1972 meant: cabinet positions, a black vice-president, adoption of the Jackson Movement's Economic Bill of Rights, the Gary National Convention's Black Agenda, the Congressional Black Caucus' Black Bill of Rights, 20 percent of the 583 decision-making jobs in federal government, and a hodgepodge of other demands. Although some demands were unrealistic, running counter to the mood of a country lumbering heavily to the right, they were all intended to change the position of more than 23 million blacks from pawns to rooks, if not knights, on the national chessboard—or at least this is what the rhetoric implied.

No less abundant than the shopping list of items to be purchased from the presidential contenders were the strategies to ensure that the brokerage system worked. Ideas like seeds were tossed into the political winds where hopefully one would take root, serving a unifying platform for the black leadership at the national conventions and beyond.

Georgia State Legislator Julian Bond advocated black favorite sons or daughters entering the 1972 presidential primary elections in selected states with high black voter population. The ultimate goal of the strategy, Bond said, "was to have at least 1,200 official black convention delegates at Miami to form a 'power block' that would seek to wrest concessions from the national Democratic party and from the presidential aspirants. There should be no one leader or group of leaders. The delegates will likely form groups among themselves, meet with all of the presidential candidates to tell each of them what he must agree to in order to get their votes." Prophetically, Bond said, "It's dangerous to have one spokesman, because there is always the danger that he will sell the others out when he meets behind closed doors."

Another advantage of Julian Bond's strategy was that it would be less expensive than fielding a single black candidate and it would lead away from the ever-present danger of personality politics that plagues many black politicians.

Phrasemaker Bill Clay rhetorically pursued the Mau Mau philosophy of black politics, that of annihilating a political party by taking away the black voting bloc. Clay pointed out that Dick Gregory received more than 500,000 presidential votes in 1968 although his candidacy was less than serious. And since Hubert Humphrey had lost by less than 200,000 votes, the black "take away" vote remains formidable, if directed properly, Clay pointed out. And Manhattan Borough president Percy Sutton, an astute pragmatist, stressed the independency of black delegates. "Most of the '68 delegates were controlled, selected, and elected by the white political machine and are beholden to it. Few black delegates have ever been black sponsored, black appointed or black elected and black controlled. If we don't represent a power bloc in the selection of the president or his running mate," Sutton said, "the post-election granting of cabinet posts to blacks—if there are any—would be more a concession to imagery, rather than a response to power." (Speech at Gary National Convention, March 11, 1972.)

Early in the game, the ideologies were straining to emerge from a consortium of abstractness into a concrete blueprint, using the power of the black vote as the cutting edge to make a dent in the two-party system. In essence, the thought leaders were—rhetorically at least—on the route to organizing a black third force. But Jackson consolidated the theories, taking them all one step further. If the politics of blackness meant anything at all to Jackson, it meant going beyond conservative intraparty adjustments— Bond, Clay, Sutton, and Hatcher are all Democrats, independent to a degree. With no elected constituency, no party label, Jackson was in the best position to bring pressure militantly on both parties.

But few were prepared for the next card Jackson had up his sleeve. On March 28, 1971, Jackson quickly moved back onto page one. The *Chicago Sun-Times* headlines: "A Black for President among Jesse's Goals." Jackson announced that he was extending his leave from the movement to organize a third party—the Liberation party—whose membership would be made up of blacks and liberal white elements. Although the party would be created for the specific purpose of nominating a black for president in 1972, Jackson said, the party also might bargain for the nomination of a black as vice-president at the Democratic National Convention. Stressing the potential of black votes, Jackson said, "In 1968, 2 million blacks did not vote and in 1968 Nixon won by 500,000 votes. There are more unregistered black voters in Chicago than there are black people in Mississippi. We are going to get these people on the books." As a token gesture to whites, Jackson said whites could be included on the slate of candidates for national office. "I estimate that the new party could siphon off more than 10 to 12 percent of the vote in a national election and would be a phenomenon that both major parties would have to seriously consider. It could even force Senator Edmond Muskie and Senator

George McGovern to seek a black for the vice-presidential nomination. The new party will be a kind of Populist bread-and-butter party with a platform based on programs designed to respond to the basic needs of the poor in America and the national call for peace in Indochina," Jackson said. (*Chicago Sun-Times*, March 28, 1971.)

White reaction to Jackson's announcement included shock, incredulity, and a feeling that Jackson had leaped out front at least ten years too soon. Others gauged Jackson's strategy as a bit whimsical, engineered as another headline-grabbing stunt. For example, *Chicago Daily News* columnist Mike Royko perused Jackson's moves throughout 1971 and concluded:

> One of the most dynamic new figures on the political scene today is the Reverend Jessie Jetstream.
>
> At a press conference yesterday, the Reverend Jetstream disclosed his latest plans.
>
> "I wish to announce at this time," he said, "that I am in orbit. There is no way I can be stopped."
>
> What are you running for? someone asked.
>
> "I have not decided that yet," the Reverend Jetstream said leaving the room.
>
> He returned in a few minutes, wearing a change of bell-bottoms and fringed vest, and said:
>
> "I have made my decision. I am running for mayor of Chicago and there is no way I can be stopped."
>
> But you just did that, somebody said.
>
> "Hmmmm," he said, "Excuse me."
>
> He left the room, but returned in a few minutes wearing tailored fatigue jacket and a medallion.
>
> "I wish to announce at this time that I have

withdrawn as a candidate for mayor, but I am issuing an ultimatum that the mayor appoint blacks to head all city agencies."

What if he does not accede to your demands?

"Then I shall support his opponent and defeat him."

But he just won.

"Hmmmm," the Reverend Jetstream said. "Excuse me."

He left the room and returned in a few minutes wearing tailored jumpsuit and alligator work shoes.

"I have an announcement to make," he said. "I have decided to support a black candidate for governor of Illinois in the next election."

Can you name the candidate?

"Yes. Carl Stokes."

But he is from Ohio.

"In that case, I am withdrawing him as a candidate for governor of Illinois, and I am supporting him as a candidate for vice-president of the United States."

Which party?

"Both parties."

But he can't do that.

"Hmmmm, excuse me," he said. He left the room and returned in a few minutes, wearing a 25-button dinner jacket with a fringe, and a medallion.

"I have an announcement to make," he said. "I am issuing an ultimatum that the President appoint a black attorney general of the United States."

What if he doesn't?

"Then I shall withdraw my support of him."

But you didn't support him in the first place!

"In that case, I wish to announce that I am going to endorse Richard Hatcher for governor of Illinois."

But he lives in Indiana.

"Then I announce that I withdraw my support from him as governor, and I shall support him for vice-president of the United States."

But you are running Carl Stokes for vice-president.

"I have decided to support him for President."

Which party?

"Both parties. We can't be stopped."

But you can't do that.

"Hmmmm. Excuse me."

He returned in a few minutes, wearing a diamond-studded smoking jacket and five medallions, and said.

"Since both political parties have ignored us, I am announcing the formation of a third political party. We can't be stopped."

Who will your candidate be?

"I shall run for President."

And your running mate?

"I shall be my own running mate."

But who is going to run for mayor?

"Ralph Bunche will run for mayor."

But he doesn't live here.

"In that case, he will run for President, and I will run for mayor."

Do you have any further announcements?

"Not at this time. The next press conference will be in minutes. Now excuse me, I must change." (*Chicago Daily News,* May 24, 1971.)

Jackson fumed at the thought his announcement was not taken seriously. "A black for president of this country is certainly not a joke. It would give people a choice between two evils, the Republican and Democratic parties—that snake with two heads."

Nevertheless, in the ensuing months, Chicago became the hub of political activity as members of the Congressional Black Caucus, black mayors, and other elected officials answered Jackson's call to mount a strategy for 1972. Among national black political leaders, Jackson is held in high esteem. Through lending the magical Jackson name and oratory to energize voter registration and fund-raising drives, he has aided countless black and white politicians in their bid for office. After the basic campaign organizing is done, there is no one better equipped than Jackson to lend credibility to a candidate, as well as to pack in the crowds for political rallies. His popularity among a cross section of blacks and whites around the country prompted former Cleveland Mayor Carl Stokes to say of him, "There is a growing feeling among blacks that if you want to run for a high political office, you'd better have Jackson's support. In my two mayoral campaigns I sought and received the help of only one man—Jackson. Jesse can draw more people than the candidate himself. Of all the groups I know, politicans have the biggest egos; I don't know of any man that could draw all these conflicting egos together behind a single candidate but Jesse." (By 1974, his national image had been blemished by reports of his flying in on election night just in time to be seen on national television with Mayor Maynard Jackson of Atlanta, although he had done little to aid him in his win. Also in 1974, Jackson was accused of soliciting $70,000 in expenses for his staff in exchange for aiding

Detroit Mayor Coleman Young. Jackson did not endorse
Young. He also denied the charges.)

In secret sessions held in and around Chicago in
September 1971, a search for a front candidate was
discussed as well as the political reality of Jackson's
third-party movement.

Defending his position, Jackson argued, "Throughout
history, divergent groups have formed third parties. These
parties have decided the outcome of elections many times
at the state and local levels and twice at the national level
in presidential elections. For those who dare to question
the historical logic of a black political party, know that
with 450,000 more votes in just three states in 1968,
George Wallace would have thrown the election into the
U. S. House of Representatives; that the mayor of the
largest city in America, John Lindsay, was elected in 1969
on a third-party ticket and one of the senators from New
York, James L. Buckley, was elected in 1970 on a
fourth-party ticket. Wallace, by organizing a third bloc,
had tremendous influence on the Nixon administration.
The first two candidates suggested for the U. S. Supreme
Court were from the South, bussing declined as a national
priority and oil and farm subsidies were prevented from
being killed. Since we have more numerical strength than
the Wallace followers, then it is only logical that we follow
the route of bloc voting to accomplish those things
relevant to blacks."

Because the subject of a third party is an issue that
will no doubt reappear in 1976 as a result of growing
dissatisfaction among some blacks with the two-party
system, more detail is provided from a study of the black
vote by Mark R. Levy and Michael S. Kramer.* It should
be emphasized that no one in 1971 had a crystal ball

---

*The Ethnic Factor: How America's Minorities Decide Elections
   (New York: Simon and Schuster, 1972).

forecasting that the white vote would go so heavily for Nixon in 1972 or that the black vote would be as irrelevant as it was in 1968.

Levy and Kramer maintain: "If an independent black candidate can carry between 20 and 30 percent of the black vote, it will be virtually impossible for the Democratic nominee, whoever he might be, to carry nineteen states representing 285 electoral votes. These nineteen—all states in which black voters play a key role—account for more than half the nation's 538 electoral votes. Thus even if the Democratic nominee could win all thirty-one remaining states, among them the staunchly Republican bastions of the Midwest, he would fall short of an electoral majority. An independent black candidacy will depress the Democratic vote below its already depressed levels in the Deep South. In 1968 Hubert Humphrey won roughly one-quarter of the votes cast in Alabama, Mississippi, and South Carolina. A substantial majority of the Humphrey vote came from black voters. An independent black candidate who polls 20 percent of the black vote will likely force the Democratic portion below 25 percent in each of the six states. Black voters are in an enviable position for 1972. The Democratic nominee cannot expect to win without the black vote, so he must attempt to stop any movement for an independent black candidacy."

On the minus side, Julian Bond spoke for the need for coalitions to make the third party movement work. At the same time he rejected their workability: "Coalitions between blacks and other groups have yielded largely negative results for blacks because whites have tended to dominate."

There was the additional concern over the conservative nature of the black vote. In 1972 most blacks were so locked into the one-party system, especially in Chicago, that voting Republican on a local level was revolutionary. If a split ticket vote is earthshaking news in some quarters, a third party would seemingly be a takeoff into the outer limits, it could be argued.

The third-party notion, billed by the theorists as the panacea for black voting impotency, wanders through a maze of imponderables and a jungle filled with "ifs." Only if certain other conditions were valid would a black political party be valid in this decade:

1.   If blacks who have risen to top positions in federal, state, and local electoral and appointed positions would sacrifice their stake in the proven for the unproven. However, this group, needed to provide the technical assistance, would only defend the two-party system, and destroy a third-party effort.

2.   If most black campaigns were not financed by whites.

3.   If blacks—especially in lower economic groups— saw politics as an avenue of improving the quality of their lives.

4.   If other factors, such as status, employment, religious, social, professional, and labor associations were not, in the final analysis, often a stronger bond of commonality than race.

Perhaps the best counsel on the third-party strategy was offered by former Cleveland Mayor Carl Stokes. Although Stokes was probably not referring to Jackson, his friend, it would have done Jackson well to have taken note. As Stokes pointed out, until someone has proven capable of organizing a local precinct it might be premature for him to tackle the nation.

Stokes argued that before a black party can function nationally, it must organize effectively on the local level. He cited his brother Lewis' Twenty-first District Caucus in Cleveland, the National Democratic Party of Alabama, the Mississippi Freedom Democratic Party, and the United Citizens Party of South Carolina as examples, but he pointed out that those third-party efforts were isolated local cases of success. "You can't win by wishing and hoping, by television posturing, by someone telling the nation how to run a presidential campaign, while losing local elections by leaving 50,000 registered black voters at home. Demonstrate your grasp of basic politics at home first before pursuing or even entertaining national ambitions. Rhetoric will never substitute for work in professional politics. We live in an age of rhetoric and self-proclaimed experts. That is one of the things that has held America back and held black people within America back even further. The proper focus is on basic mechanics, issues, procedures, and organization. Personalities come and go, flashing briefly before us. But the issues and the processes go on. In this process of developing and expanding our meaningful participation in the political processes, I would suggest that you look to those who have had experience and who have demonstrated political and organizational success. This is not a game for the personally ambitious. This is not the civil rights struggle repeating itself. Obviously I am not advocating or proposing a third party. George Wallace has that. Or a fourth party. The history in this country of minority parties is not a history of success and success is what we mean to have." (Address at Chicago's Robert's Motel, September 30, 1971.)

Still the black third-party notion gathered steam and U. S. Representative John Conyers, from Michigan, was suggested by Jackson to head the national ticket. Explaining his choice, Jackson said, "He's a lawyer, a veteran of eight years in Congress, he's handsome, he's a good speaker, and he's a skilled politician."

Conyers seriously considered the offer but was slapped down by the Congressional Black Caucus, composed then of the thirteen black members of the House of Representatives. The April 9, 1971, edition of *Newsweek* showed that the caucus was miffed at both Jackson and Conyers. The Periscope item stated: "Most of the Black

Caucus is very unhappy with the Reverend Jesse Jackson, who is being talked of as the successor to Martin Luther King, Jr. Focus of the discontent is Jackson's plan to create a new political party. The Caucus considers itself the political arm of the 25 million U. S. Blacks and sees Jackson's idea as a move to supplant them. The Congressmen are also angry with Michigan Democratic Representative John Conyers (a caucus member), whom Jackson has spoken of as a possible presidential candidate of the new party. This they think is a grandstanding idea on Conyers' part." (Black resentment over Jackson's third party move was partially because it was perceived as a tactic to emerge as the top powerbroker at the Democratic Convention. If Jackson had pulled it off, that is exactly the position he would have secured. Watch for a similar development in 1976, which would launch Jackson into the spot of dispenser of patronage, especially if the Republicans lose control.)

As if the year of black political unity was not starting off badly enough, Conyers passed the ball to Stokes, but it was intercepted by New York Democratic Congresswoman Shirley Chisholm. She stole the black kingmaker's thunder by announcing her own bid for the presidency. All the months of secret caucusing suddenly went out the window. Chisholm upstaged them all. By entering the race, she could be the queenpin at the Democratic National Convention. If she did well at all in the primaries, she could use the amassed delegate strength to bargain at the Democratic National Convention. Privately, the menfolk condemned her as a pawn of New York Mayor John Lindsay, as a spoiler, as a feminist who forgot she also had a race. But publicly, they were at a loss for words. They could not posture themselves as male chauvinists by openly attacking her; neither could they run anyone against her. In private meetings she refused to retract her decision, as well as to allow the black inner circle to control her moves. Forgetting that white women are still white, she trotted along with feminists Gloria Steinem and New York Democratic Congresswoman Bella Abzug, both of whom would abandon her when the choice came down to black or white.

In an attempt to patch together some modicum of political unity, Jackson invited Representative Chisholm to the October Black Expo in 1971. But the spunky, ninety-pound dynamo sank her spurs further into the male egos in retaliation for their put-downs at the Women's Day program on October 3, 1971. "Brothers, please get off my back. I am not here to compete or to fight with you, brothers, I am here for you to help to use me as an instrument. Brothers, brothers, please stop criticizing me unjustly. I say to you that Shirley Chisholm is just a little tired of some of the things that are constantly being thrown at her. Because were I to tell you the whole truth, and nothing but the truth, you would understand at times that those who say they are fighting to liberate us are also at times exploiting us."

Had Mrs. Chisholm been pushed into a corner, she could have clearly pointed out which of the brokers were in the political ball game for the people and which were for themselves—a distinction some could not clearly make about Shirley Chisholm.

By the time the black political leadership issued its call for unity to the masses at the Black National Convention held in Gary, Indiana, in March 1971, solidarity among the front runners, if not dead, was seriously crippled. Although Gary's theme was "unity without uniformity," there was no solid unifying plan. The more than 8,000 delegates and spectators who made the historic trek to Indiana from as far away as Hawaii came seeking direction. What role would they play as delegates? What role would they play as voters? What had happened to the third party? Was an endorsement of Shirley Chisholm going to be made? The kaleidoscope of ideologies was masterfully held together by writer Imamu Amiri Baraka (Leroi Jones), Michigan Congressman Charles Diggs, and Mayor Richard Hatcher. However, so much went wrong that even the evangelical spirit, the talk of political emancipation, and the imagery of the black tribes of the nation united under the Kenyan red-black-and-green banner— the black flag—could not obscure divisiveness. Before the opening gavel could be sounded, NAACP's Roy Wilkins' emissary, the late Dr. John Morsell, denounced the gathering as separatist and refused to support it. The Congressional Black Caucus, which by all rights should have been the convener of the convention, sent several members but withheld its offical endorsement. Hatcher made an eloquent speech denouncing the two-party system as evil but ended with a plea to give the Democrats one last chance. Even though the election was but eight months away, Jackson continued with his call for a third party immediately. Delegates, in no mood for sophistry, irreverently booed, as they again did when Jackson repeated the call at the Little Rock National Convention in 1973. U. S. Representative Chisholm was somewhere else, although the bulk of the delegates would have endorsed her, if she had made a showing.

But the saddest paradox was that while all the talk of political emancipation was free-flowing through the convention hall, many of the leaders had already committed themselves to Democratic candidates, largely because of the lateness of the hour. John Conyers, Coretta King, and Julian Bond were stumping for George McGovern. Charles Evers, then mayor of Fayette, Mississippi, was backing John Lindsay. Representative Louis Stokes of Ohio had joined Humphrey and almost ran over Conyers for going into his Twenty-first Congressional District on behalf of McGovern. Jackson held off until the end of April, 1971, to endorse and campaign for McGovern. Even then he tactfully proposed that Representative Chisholm be McGovern's running mate. (*Chicago Today,* May 23, 1971).

The Gary convention did live up to its purpose in part, although no single strategy emerged to guide the leadership or those there to be led. The delegates carved out their aspirations in an impressive National Black Agenda, whose acceptance was supposedly to be the prerequisite for the black vote. But even the agenda was subjected to a hatchet job by the Congressional Black Caucus, which watered it down in order to divorce itself from two items: an anti-Israel resolution and an anti-bussing proposal, commandeered through the convention by CORE president Roy Innis. Many thought Innis was sent to Gary by President Nixon. The diluted agenda compiled by the caucus was renamed the Black Bill of Rights. Thus presidential contenders had a choice: they could support Jackson's Economic Bill of Rights, the Black Agenda, or the Black Bill of Rights. If the contenders had accepted any one of the three, they would have only created more enmity. Thus McGovern gave lukewarm acceptance to all three, but he would publicly endorse none at the Democratic National Convention.

Jackson surveyed the dishevelment, grumbling: "If black politicians would just get off each other's backs, it would be a real revolution." (*Black Enterprise,* February, 1973.) He then turned his attention to the business of dethroning Chicago's Mayor Daley at the Miami Convention. The delegate challenge would be just as chaotic; only the menagerie would contain mostly whites.

Millions of TV-viewers may think they caught the biggest spectacle of 1972—the Democratic National Convention in Miami—a ragtag assortment of hippies, yippies, blacks, Latins, intellectuals, meaty housewives in shorts and halters, and middle-aged teeny-boppers. But the best performance of the season had already unfolded before a

select audience in Chicago. Almost every delegate seated
there had been through a series of dramatic episodes that
would be bleeped if the scenes themselves were ever
reproduced for public consumption. The saga of the
Chicago delegation, however, would never be produced for
the screen. The public would think it was fiction. People in
real life don't experience fire bombings and death threats
or engage in fisticuffs just to sit down on some folding
chairs in a Miami convention hall. And the Lone Ranger,
Punch 'n Judy, and Hizzoner all appearing together in one
flick is a bit too camp. But if anyone had dramatized the
Chicago delegate challenge, the written text might go
like this:

The Characters: The Reverend Jesse Jackson, dressed in
star-spangled blue denim suit, red, white, and blue T-shirt,
and medallion, shares the spotlight with Alderman William
Singer. Singer's most famous credit before the Miami
Democratic Convention was a city ordinance against dog
littering. But this achievement, coupled with a nurtured
political organization, has prepared Singer for a serious
shot at the 1975 mayoral election. White reporters in
Miami are calling the thirty-one-year-old Singer the star.
Meanwhile black reporters are calling the thirty-one-year-
old Jackson the star. Both men engage in serious debates
over which one of them really is the star. Mrs. Carmen
Chico and Alderman Anna Langford of Chicago are also
heavies, but since they are only women, they are barely
billed as supporting actresses. Mayor Daley and Company
are pictured as cigar-chomping bosses plotting havoc in
smoke-filled rooms. The Mayor doesn't smoke, but a cigar
has to be stuck in his mouth as a prop to lend credibility
to the plot.

The Plot: The Jackson-Singer or Singer-Jackson entourage
file a challenge to the Democratic National Convention

Credentials Commission complaining that the selection of Mayor Daley's fifty-nine "uncommitted" delegates and thirty-one "uncommitted" alternates was in violation of the McGovern Commission's reform rules. Mayor Daley has been quoted as saying, "We'll elect our delegates as we always have. Why the hell should we let those people in Washington tell us how we should elect them? I don't give a damn about the McGovern rules."

The rules state that if the party involved itself in delegate selection, it must do so at open meetings and must not secretly slate candidates. The rules forbid the use of party money and resources for its favored candidates. Also, the party was to take all possible steps to achieve representatives of minorities as delegates in proportion to their presence in the population. True to his opening line, "The hell with the rules," the Mayor disobeyed them all. Selection was held in secret, sample ballots were printed so the people would know who they'd better vote for, and most of those slated were party pros, ward committeemen, and the Mayor's pals. The slate was short by nine blacks, five Latin-Americans, twenty-three women, and thirteen persons age thirty years or younger. It is important that Mayor Daley operate in his usual manner. How else could he control all the supposedly uncommitted delegates, brokering their votes and emerging as the kingmaker at the convention, as he has done in the past?

Scene 1: The Hearings: Mrs. Patricia Harris, credentials chairman from Chicago and former ambassador to Luxembourg, dispatched a hearing officer to find out why people in Chicago couldn't seem to do anything right. Alderman Thomas Keane pressured the hearing officer into disqualifying himself. After the referee quit, the Daley team thought the case was closed. But Mrs. Harris, a black woman, not to be outdone, this time dispatched a Harvard-trained lawyer, Cecil Poole, from San Francisco,

who was also black. That their fate was going to be
decided by a black man had the Daleyites almost swallow-
ing their cigars. To make matters worse, Cecil Poole didn't
act like a Claude Holman, Cecil Partee, or any of the other
domesticated blacks that the party regulars thought were
the only kind around. Some of the dialogue at the hearings
between the Daley team and Poole went like this:

After Poole had finished overruling the twenty-third
motion of the machine Democrats, Alderman Thomas
Keane strolled over to Poole, saying, "I want to make sure
that you and I are on the same wave length." (In Chicago
this means, "Cool it baby, name your price.")

Poole glared back at Keane, saying, "We are not on
the same wave length, Mr. Keane."

Holman jumped up: "I've got something to say here.
I've got lots more to say."

Poole: "You are finished as far as I'm concerned,
Mr. Holman."

Alderman Edward Vrdolyak butted in: "I feel like
I'm being stifled."

Poole: "Funny you don't sound at all stifled,
Mr. Vrdolyak."

And on it went with Poole treating the world's
notorious Chicago organization like a minor league basketball team composed of paraplegics. However, Poole made
it clear he was not showing favoritism when he allowed
Jackson to undergo an embarrassing grilling from a battery
of Daley's lawyers, including the Mayor's son, Michael. It
was the first time in Jackson's career that he had appeared
in public forgetting to bring his brain along. Jackson
admitted he did not know his cochallengers or his
attorneys; he did not know the requirements for being a
delegate; and he did not know the racial makeup of Mayor
Daley's delegation, although he had previously condemned
it as unrepresentative. However, when Jackson admitted
that he, the leader of men, had not voted in the last

primary, a stunned hush fell over the hearing room. Jackson had just defined one of the goals of his movement as registering and educating people about voting and he, himself, was not a voter. A check at the Chicago Board of Elections showed that Jackson had never voted in a Democratic primary election, according to former Election Board Chairman, Stanley Kusper.

Jackson's admission left him open to an onslaught of caustic criticism. One columnist wrote: "In accepting Jackson as a delegate . . . the reform rules have achieved the ultimate generosity: they have given a voice to the person who doesn't bother to vote. If they are going to open up the party to the person who doesn't bother to vote, then they would be wise to also let in delegates like Vito Marzullo, who is capable of getting two votes out of one voter. That way, Marzullo could compensate for the Jackson-type nonvoter." Commenting on Jackson's conduct at the hearings, another columnist wrote: "Jackson, the leadoff witness for the challengers, was, to be brutally frank, terrible. In short Jackson was ill-prepared and showed it. But he was impeccably dressed." Findings from the Poole hearing substantiated the challengers' complaints that the Daleyites had been disobedient. Poole recommended that the Daley slate not be seated, which was the green light for the Singer-Jackson, Jackson-Singer duo to elect their own delegation.

Scene 2: The Democratic Process Hardly Working: On June 22, 1972, Jackson and Singer announced eight locations where voters could elect a new delegation to the convention. Lawyer Andrew Leahy was one of the first to arrive at the election meeting held in a Chicago Catholic Church in the Fifth Congressional District. Leahy gives this account of what happened: "When I first got there, no one else had arrived. The Mayor's son, Richard M. Daley, was there. He said nothing but he had a strange look in his eyes. Suddenly the church was inundated with Daley loyalists, about 300 or 400 of them. Some of them must have been bussed in. I thought they had lost their marbles. They came in, taking over like a Mack truck. Young Daley jumped up and started yelling, 'Point of order.' Booing started. Things got so bad we adjourned to the rectory. I feared for the women and young electors' safety." Over in the Second Congressional District, things were worse. An attorney for the challengers, Wayne Whalen, tried to control the Daley mob who arrived with bull horns to disrupt the election. Whalen said about thirty people rushed him, including Alderman Vrdolyak. They grabbed his rules material, tearing it in half. When he reached down to pick up some torn paper, somebody punched him to the floor. At the Seventh Congressional District meeting, an airline employee was pulled off an elevator as he was heading for the election and punched by about a dozen persons. At the Third Congressional District meetings, Daley supporters shouted at Alderman Singer: "Get the dirty little Jew. We want the Jew." The only meeting not disturbed was the one Jackson was presiding over at a residence in Hyde Park. The next morning at the election rescheduled at the Chicago Sheraton Hotel, Jackson arrived leading a group of more than a hundred of the meanest, toughest-looking blacks to be found in the city of Chicago. Requests for police protection had been denied Jackson. If the Daleyites wanted to play rough, they had met their match. Although the black men were unarmed, they had their hands in their pockets, appearing as though they were going to turn the Sheraton into a shooting gallery. The Daley mob tinkled a few cowbells and meekly excused themselves. Although the election was imperfect because of the gangster-type tactics confronting the Jackson-Singer forces, finally Chicago had its new delegation. It was composed of twenty blacks, five Latin Americans, twenty-nine women, and twenty-seven young people—a victory for the McGovern reform rules and for the democratic process, in spite of itself.

Nevertheless the travesty for Jackson was far from over. Shortly after the delegate elections, Daley retaliated by removing Jackson's Chicago police bodyguards. Subsequently, the minister's offices were fire bombed twice. After his office switchboard was flooded by callers threatening that he would never reach Miami alive, Jackson moved his family out of the city and secured the protection of a black detective agency—W. L. Lillard. And Singer's office windows were smashed by a hail of bricks.

Scene 3: My Lap or Yours? After the Democratic Convention Credentials Committee had accepted the Poole report, voting 71 to 61 to oust Daley's slate and seat the new delegation, Jackson infuriated members of his group by calling on Daley to compromise. While the other three cochairmen were in Washington lobbying with the credentials committee, Jackson issued a surprise statement that he was willing to *share* seats (both delegations would have a half-vote) with Daley in exchange for reforms in the black community, such as a civilian police review board. Others from the new delegates argued that there was no reason for the victorious to extend an olive branch to the vanquished. Singer stood firm: "We are the delegates now." Alderman Langford maintained: "It is a moral question of whether the reform rules stand or whether it is politics as usual."

Some journalists criticized Jackson's stance. *Chicago Tribune* columnist Vernon Jarrett immediately dubbed Jackson "the Lone Ranger," not so much for his compromise position but for his unilateral decision. Ethel Payne, veteran columnist for the Sengstacke publications, reported: "Jesse Jackson has a lot of folks bothered about his role in trying to be the compromiser in the Illinois credentials fight. He's accused of running with the hares and hunting with the hounds." However, I thought the idea of Jackson and Daley sitting on each other's laps in Miami was amusing but it also was wise politically. The issue at hand was the nomination and election of a president, not the defeating of a mayor. And Jackson, growing in astuteness, never failed to keep his eye on the prize. In 1960 John F. Kennedy had personally given Daley credit for winning the election for him. (Others, privately, congratulated the Mayor for stealing it.) In 1968, Daley had been accused of dismissing Hubert Humphrey as a loser and forsaking the national ticket in order to hold his own power base together by getting the vote out for Edward V. Hanrahan, the state's attorney. If Daley had not sat on his hands, Humphrey might have carried Illinois, the legend goes. In Cook County, Hanrahan ran 200,000 votes ahead of Humphrey, the same margin by which Humphrey lost.

The question in the minds of many was: If Daley were ousted from his eminence in the party, would he work for McGovern? The conjecture that Daley might retaliate mounted to a near paralysis when one of Daley's spokesmen leaked the word to the press that Daley might use his legal machinery to knock McGovern off the Illinois ballot if his slate were not seated in Miami. McGovern's campaign lieutenants were running scared over the fact that the man who could deliver Illinois' electoral college vote because of his ability to deliver more than 1 million Cook County voters would be left standing out in the cold. Sizing up the alternatives, Jackson perceived that the new guard was expendable. Jackson said, "Given the choice between crushing Daley and elevating McGovern, I would elevate McGovern. We cannot major in a mayor and minor in a president. Being anti-Daley is not the same thing as being pro-black. I am not as committed to destroying the Mayor as he has been to us. Knocking down the Mayor may be necessary, but the major thing is electing a

Democrat against Richard Nixon. The new guard and the old guard of the Democratic party can either live together like people or die apart like fools."

McGovern had promised Jackson that he would support the movement's Economic Bill of Rights, which, among other points, called for a tightening of tax loopholes, thus giving the government an extra $40 billion for the poor, and a guaranteed minimum annual income of $6,500 for a family of four. A moment of glory in Miami was not worth the risk of four more years of agony for 23 million blacks under the "benign" neglect of Nixon, Jackson felt. However, despite Jackson's repeated overtures to Daley, the offer of compromise was not accepted. The Daleyites held to the winner-take-all position, preferring to debate the no compromise position in a minority plank before the full convention in Miami.

Scene 4: The End? Suddenly it was all over. The magic moment had arrived. Laughs, hugs, shouts, sobs. By a vote of 1,486 to 1,371, Daley was out, the Jackson-Singer delegation was in. The unexpected happened, the experts said. But the dethroning of King Daley by a bunch of near-juveniles was not so unexpected. The Jackson-Singer delegation had the kids and those who didn't believe in cruelty to kids on their side. In 1968, Daley's men in blue had beat hell out of the kids outside the Democratic Convention Hall in Chicago. The police had chased them, maced them, clubbed them, and tossed some in the lagoon, mostly without provocation. Four years later, the kids had grown up, moved inside the convention hall, and were obsessed with beating the hell out of Daley.

Also because of Richard Hatcher's demands on the Democratic party leadership and the McGovern reform rules, there were 452 blacks there at the convention, more than double the 209 attending in 1968. With the young innocents who had blazed the Kennedy trails and civil rights activists who marched with King for black political enfranchisement, an eclectic force had converged. These groups were fighting not so much for the defeat of Daley as for the defeat of what he stood for: a Northern Bull Connor, the back room boss, the plantation slavemaster. What really mattered was that morality lived and it would be carried on the shoulders of the conventioneers. It was an explosion of idealism, a sterling victory of right over wrong. At the time, if anyone had suggested that McGovern would sell both groups short, eating his own reformism to return to the political center, he wouldn't have been believed.

The national press ignored a significant point contributing to the ineffable upset: Charisma has its legitimate function when it is connected to a call for action, when there is no time lapse for the emotional stimulation to escape. The podium in the convention hall was the proper place. An address just before roll call on the fate of the Illinois delegation was the proper time. And no other man in the nation could have activated this set of circumstances any better than Jackson, the greatest public speaker in America today. Jackson stood before the convention with the countenance of a prince, displaying all the magnetic qualities of a Kennedy or a King. Through him, the idealism and the righteousness of both martyrs lived. His call that "It's time truth speaks" energized, electrified, mesmerized his audience and transformed the convention hall into a ground swell of approval.

However, the national press refused to give Jackson, a black man, his share in the momentous Daley defeat. The headlines boomed, "Singer Did It—Daley Defeated" and "Singer Defeats Daley." All along, the national press had been calling the delegation the Singer-Jackson team. Now when the moment of glory came, Jackson, who usually has no difficulty in making headlines (and this time deserved the recognition) was pushed out altogether. Probably the most unheralded contributor to the Daley ouster was the plain simple fact of timing and organization. Jackson, Singer, Al Raby, Leona Black, and a host of other activists simply out-propagandized the old political pros at a time when liberalism was straining to be heard.

The effect of Daley's missing his first Democratic convention in thirty years was traumatic. Daley could not even set foot in the convention hall to plead his case for fear he'd be booed. Weeks following the defeat, sources close to Daley said he spent most of his time in his Grand Beach, Michigan, summer home alone, sometimes avoiding even members of his family. On the few occasions persons other than his family saw him, Daley was described as "obviously angry." (*Chicago Today*, July 17, 1972.) And there was one report that "he was pacing back and forth furiously like a caged lion." Headline writers chopped into him with unheard of vengeance. "The King's Crown Tilts," "Daley and Democrats in a Stew," "Daley's Machine in Twilight." A *Tribune* editorial went so far as to say, "as a national public figure, as the man to whom presidents paid homage and before whom congressmen groveled, as the whole ball game in the Democratic Party, Richard J. Daley has lost his clout. . . . " (July 12, 1972.)

On his own front, Jackson was hailed as a hero. For a time, there was a move for a Jesse Jackson Day which Jackson modestly squelched: "Don't worship me from afar. Work with me up close."

At Daley's moment of ignominious defeat, it is a safe bet the Mayor wished he had hired Jackson when he had the opportunity. When Jackson came to Chicago in 1964 he innocently went to the Mayor, asking for a job. He arrived with a letter of reference in hand from the governor of North Carolina. Instead of grabbing up the potentially formidable young man and corrupting him with power, the Mayor looked upon him as just another black. A job as a toll collector was offered, but Jackson declined. Imagine all that charisma and talent wasting away on some lonely highway.

However, Daley's dark clouds from the convention would soon float away. Although he had been knocked down in Miami, his political kingdom is in Chicago and Cook County. It did not take long for most to see that there he was still king. They were soon knocking on his door, begging to pay homage again.

At the same time that Jackson was leading the New Chicago Delegation, he was still involved in the national "politics of blackness." This had been unraveling the year long, and by the time of the convention it was hanging by a thread. By the eve of McGovern's nomination even that thread had snapped. One week before the nomination, the pace quickened over which black leaders would emerge as the major powerbrokers. Who would worm their way into the position either to appoint others to major posts or to get in on the gravy themselves?

For a while it appeared as if Walter Fauntroy, the nonvoting congressional delegate from the District of Columbia, and Michigan Congressman Conyers would be crowned black kingmakers. The pair, along with other Congressional Black Caucus members, delivered ninety-six black uncommitted delegates to McGovern, who immediately proclaimed that the black bloc would put him over the 1,509 mark to assure victory on the first ballot. But before the day had ended, the size of the black bloc had eroded to seventy-five. By the end of the week, because of a duplication of names and individual delegates withdrawing from the "delivered bloc," the count had narrowed down to about fifty-seven.

Conyers retrospectively assessed the move as "imperfect." It was imperfect because many of the uncommitted black delegates across the country whose names were included in the bloc delivered to McGovern had not given their approval for Fauntroy or Conyers to broker their votes. It was also imperfect because caucus members had not touched base with other black politicians outside the nation's capital before making their move. Jackson attempted to smooth over his friends' preemptive moves by stating that since a bandwagon movement was swelling around McGovern so fast, the black leaders had to move hurriedly before McGovern clinched the nomination without them.

However, nothing black men did was as dramatic as the last ditch effort of New York Representative Shirley Chisholm, who reportedly had joined the Stop McGovern Movement on the promise that she would become secretary of HEW (Health, Education, and Welfare) if Humphrey received the nomination. At a Sunday meeting of 452 black delegates in Miami, at which all presidential contenders appeared, pleading for the black delegate vote, Mrs. Chisholm upstaged them all. She also tore into Jackson, Hatcher, and all the other black leaders who hadn't supported her. With tears streaming from her eyes, Mrs. Chisholm said, "Some of these people who are calling this meeting are doing it for a price because they are in The Man's pocket. Those who are delivering you have personal contracts for jobs and money. They want to be kingmakers. The nerve and audacity of them to call people here and play the game that they can deliver the black vote. You came here to participate and not be delivered. If you wanted to be delivered, you should have stayed at home. And I am here to tell you that I am the only one among your so-called black friends that has the balls to stand up for you." Mrs. Chisholm ended her speech by asking the delegates to allow her to replace her accusers as the chief powerbroker. "I am asking that you go with me on the first ballot to give the candidates time to think of how significant you are. If you can't do that, at least stay uncommitted."

After Mrs. Chisholm's speech, pandemonium broke loose. The black delegates, with tears in their eyes, felt they were being used, sold out. Many wanted to switch from McGovern to Chisholm. Mississippi Mayor Charles Evers proposed a resolution which would have released black committed delegates from any prior promises to other candidates, so they could swing their support to Mrs. Chisholm. Humphrey had also released his black, but not his white, delegates to Mrs. Chisholm. Only by the skillful manipulation by Representative Diggs and Jackson, who tabled both proposals, was a black stampede for Chisholm intercepted. The tragedy of Mrs. Chisholm's campaign was that she did not turn to blacks until there was no place else to turn. And all the while, it was the black rank and file who loved her. But Mrs. Chisholm started on the wrong foot with the women's lib group and ended on the wrong foot with the Humphrey-Wallace-Mills-Muskie alliance to elect anybody but McGovern.

The year of black unity missed its mark in 1972. Perhaps it will do better in 1976. In its first try, there was not much ethnic solidarity to make the politics of blackness anything more than a bluesy beat for the same old lyrics—"What can I get from whom for me."

The love affair between McGovern and black leadership also began hitting a sour note the day after the South Dakota senator won the nomination. Senator Thomas Eagleton, a Democrat from Missouri, had just been selected as McGovern's running mate, so I ran over to the Doral Hotel, McGovern's headquarters, and asked the black leaders their opinions of the vice-presidential nominee. The blacks had been sequestered for hours debating who their choice would be. Although they were sitting there with a list of names in their hands, which included Democratic Chairman Lawrence O'Brien, Pat Harris, and Moon Landrieu, mayor of New Orleans, McGovern had not requested or accepted their recommendations. They did not know of McGovern's vice-presidential choice until the announcement flashed on the television screen. Only one man among them admitted that they had had no input. Jackson said, "I want black people to know that their leadership has been humiliated and violated, but I am not too embarrassed to tell the truth. Let the others act as if they were in on the decision, but I say McGovern has been dishonest. I hope this is not the sign of worse things to come." McGovern's exclusion of black king pins from the vice-presidential selection was a bad omen, a preview of what Jackson hoped would not happen. The worst was indeed yet to come.

Once the nomination was pocketed, McGovern concerned himself with the practicalities of getting elected. That meant mending fences with Daley, whose organization he needed to win Illinois. McGovern pulled out all stops to woo Daley, even apologizing for the upset in Miami: "I really very much wanted you and your delegates to be seated. It had been my hope that some kind of convention arrangement would have been worked out." (*Chicago Today*, August 23, 1972.) McGovern also reluctantly agreed to support the entire Illinois ticket, a pledge which hung like a noose around McGovern's neck because State's Attorney Edward V. Hanrahan was on it. Because of Hanrahan's indictment in the Black Panther raid, Illinois U. S. Representative Ralph Metcalfe convinced Daley to snatch back the slating of Hanrahan in the primary. But Hanrahan had run against the machine candidate and won. So there he was back on the ticket again. Hanrahan was one wedge among many that kept McGovern and Jackson from being the great duo they were before McGovern won the nomination. McGovern had to give lip service to Hanrahan to keep Daley's support. For reelection Jackson was supporting Hanrahan's Republican opponent, Bernard Carey; a Republican governor, Richard Ogilvie; and a Republican senator, Charles Percy. Thus Jackson's independent stance was considered a liability to Daley, who had no intentions of working with Jackson, because if by chance Jackson had registered any votes they would have been anti-Hanrahan, and in some cases anti-Democrat. Given a tossup between Daley and Jackson, McGovern made his choice perfectly clear on August 23, 1972, after one of a series of meetings with Daley. "No, I have no plans to meet with Jackson," he told me.

McGovern's statement was crucial because it settled a running feud that had been erupting since the convention between Jackson and machine black aldermen, who were parroting the Mayor's viewpoint. On August 1, nine prominent national black leaders telegraphed McGovern: "If you come by to see Daley you had better stop by to see Jackson first. You are to make no deals with Mayor Daley that are not agreeable to Reverend Jesse Jackson."

McGovern was thrust in a cross fire on August 3 when seven black Democratic ward committeemen wired McGovern, stating that if he came to Chicago, he'd better see *them* first. Alderman Claude Holman, the most vociferous of the Daley black pack, said, "You [McGovern] had better think twice about who you see. Jesse Jackson couldn't get ten votes in my ward. Let it be known that any national candidate visiting Chicago must meet with the duly elected black leaders who always deliver huge Democratic majorities in their respective wards. Elected black leaders speak for real Democrats as distinguished from self-styled leaders and phonies. If you come to Chicago and see Jesse Jackson, we'll vote for Nixon." Ward committeemen who signed the McGovern manifesto were: James Taylor, Bennett Stewart, Eugene Sawyer, John H. Stroger, William H. Shannon, and Claude Holman.

Jackson is a proud man, not one to take public ridicule lightly, whether it's from the press or from a presidential candidate. Since Jackson considers himself a symbol of black self-esteem, he viewed the McGovern snub as a slap in the face to thousands of other blacks. Still Jackson said if McGovern had handled himself with more diplomacy, a breech might have been avoidable. Jackson told me, "When McGovern needed black support, he called twice from Wisconsin, came to Operation PUSH, the Family Affair banquet, and personally encouraged me to speak for him in the primaries. Since he won, I've seen and heard less and less of him. He has seen Daley three times and said publicly three times he has no interest in seeing representatives of the movement. I have not changed, McGovern has changed. He was for reform, now he is for accommodation. Before Miami, he was all for us, now he is all for Daley. George is blowing it. If he had come to me and told me confidentially that he had to gain Daley's support and play mine down to win Illinois, I would have simply moved from Chicago and won votes for him nationally, but I had to read his opinions of me in the newspapers, which was an insult."

McGovern's snub of Jackson, personally, was something Jackson initially tried to forgive for the sake of unity. But after McGovern reportedly began reneging on promises made to blacks, Jackson blasted him with verbal rockets hitting page one of newspapers across the nation and causing many blacks to have second thoughts about McGovern. McGovern had promised black participation in campaign management decisions and the selection of state campaign leadership, yet the Illinois campaign coordinator was white, as well as most of his underlings. "They call twenty-six year old Eugene Pokorny, the coordinator, a young genius," Jackson said, "Well, I happen to know a couple of black young geniuses who could have handled the job. The failure to select blacks as state campaign leaders is not happening just in Illinois, but across the country."

However, black leaders locked into the system were

in no position to call McGovern's hand on his failure to name blacks to important campaign jobs. Another thorny situation evolved on August 19 when the announcement that Jackson, Richard Hatcher, Congressman Louis Stokes of Ohio, and Julian Bond were being considered for cabinet or subcabinet posts was widely disseminated by the media. The South Dakota senator made the disclosures while filming television campaign spots and commercials at a motor factory in Milwaukee. No sooner than the word was out, it was retracted by Kirby Jones, McGovern's press secretary. "The senator has never made any commitments to Jesse Jackson, Richard Hatcher, or any other black leaders concerning cabinet posts. At this point in the campaign, the senator has duties that take priority over cabinet appointees," Jones said. "I'm sure he has no intention of talking with Jackson or Hatcher when he meets Mayor Daley next week." Although Jackson said he had no intention of accepting anything from McGovern ("I find the movement more interesting. I wouldn't exchange the Black House for the White House"), the on-and-off statement didn't score any points with Jackson.

The issue that perhaps loomed most important was McGovern's about-face on his promise to earmark 40 percent of the Democratic party's funds for black voter registration. In dollar terms, the percentage should have amounted to about $2.5 million that would have gone to black political leaders across the country for massive voter registration drives. This matter was something Jackson didn't wish to talk about. I checked with Yancy Martin, who was a top aide to McGovern, to find out what happened to the voter registration monies that were to be distributed to Jackson. Rumor said they had been ripped off. I checked the rumor out with several McGovern aides and it was invalid.

Martin, who is now executive director of the Southern Elections Fund in Atlanta, said, "Black leaders started out asking for $2.5 million for voter registration, but we had much less money than the press led people to believe. The figure was finally narrowed down to $1 million, which was very inadequate. But I am awfully sorry that blacks didn't even get that much. I don't remember Jesse receiving any funds at all for voter registration. McGovern made a lot of promises he could not keep. For example, the McGovern campaign didn't deliver any get-out-the-vote money to New York until the day before the election. My argument was that whenever there was a priority analysis on how to spend what funds we had, the blacks had the lowest priority. Almost everything, even printed material, received funding before any money was allotted to blacks. I am as disappointed with McGovern in that phase as Jesse was. At first I thought Jesse criticized McGovern much more than he should have but in the long run he was on the right track."

Commenting on McGovern's rejection of Jackson, aide Martin said it was the other way around. "McGovern made every attempt to talk with Jackson. All kinds of calls went into him. We even used Nancy Wilson, the singer, and John Conyers to act as a go-between with Jackson and McGovern. There were damn few times that McGovern came to Chicago that he did not try to get Jackson to appear in public with him. Jackson never lost favor with McGovern. Jackson was the one that ignored McGovern and he had some very valid reasons for doing so. The McGovern campaign had initially planned to use Jackson and Daley to get out the vote, but it just didn't come off that way."

Regardless of which one out-snubbed the other, Jackson made his position clear as to where he stood on McGovern. "I don't owe either party anything, but both of them owe us something. The political realities are such that they won't run me into the Nixon circles. I will cast my personal vote for McGovern, but I will not work enthusiastically for McGovern." (*Chicago Today*, September 29, 1972.) Other blacks inside the party, however, took a different position at Black Expo '72. Conyers said he had been involved in the last three presidential campaigns on behalf of the Democrats. He said he felt that McGovern was the most progressive candidate and was more apt to deliver on his campaign promises than anybody he'd seen in a long time. Representative Louis Stokes echoed a similar view. "Those of us who are elected officials see no other alternative than to commit ourselves to the overwhelming defeat of Richard Nixon."

Nevertheless, Jackson bowed out, wished McGovern well, and pitched himself into some important key local races.

At the top of Jackson's agenda was the defeat of State's Attorney Edward V. Hanrahan, a hero in some white communities and a symbol of hatred in some black communities. Jackson had continued a constant vigil for three years against the state's attorney, whose police used overkill tactics on the Panthers in a shoot-in during which 100 shots were fired to the Panthers' one—and there was a doubt about that one. A report conducted by a study group headed by former U. S. Attorney General Ramsey Clark revealed that Fred Hampton was in comatose state at the time of his "execution." It was also later revealed that an FBI informant had been in charge of Panther security. Hardly a Saturday morning passed that Jackson didn't impress upon his audience and radio listeners that any black who voted for Hanrahan was signing his own death warrant.

When Hanrahan was reslated for office, Jackson was there. At the slate-making session, Jackson pleaded with Claude Holman and Ralph Metcalfe not to vote for Hanrahan for another term. Jackson confronted Daley: "What you're doing is building a bridge to the Republicans. We're going to see to it that every black person in Chicago gets instructions on how to vote a split ticket." Jackson was alone at the slate-making meeting. Where were the NAACP, the Urban League, the scores of other black leaders, who knock down Jackson's upfront position? "Why was he alone?" *Chicago Today* columnist Dorothy Storck asked. Answering her, Jackson moved his hand wearily in front of him and then let it drop at his side, saying, "They don't understand. Next week they'll be out there protesting and all that. But next week is not the time. We've got to try to do something now to stop it."

Jackson could not pull it off by himself. Within hours after Jackson had threatened Daley, Hanrahan was on the Democratic ticket again. But Jackson had apparently softened up Metcalfe, who, in his characteristic role as a behind-the-scenes fighter, would help turn the tables around.

Over Claude Holman's assurances that Hanrahan would win in black wards, despite the Panther tragedy, Metcalfe, who was preparing to break from the machine, convinced Mayor Daley to reconsider. The new Metcalfe told me how the decision was overturned. "When we met in the inner, inner circles, we argued for hours and I told them they were making a serious mistake going with Hanrahan. I told them that Ed was becoming a national figure, he was being discussed on the floor of Congress, and he was going to be a national campaign issue, plus the fact that he was not acceptable to blacks, as Jesse had said. I suggested that Hanrahan step aside until his case was out of court. [At the time of the slating, Hanrahan was under indictment for conspiracy to obstruct justice in connection with the Panther raid.] Then he could come back and write his own ticket.

"Well, anyway the motion was passed to endorse him. The slate-making committee was also getting ready to dump Representative George Collins for Representative Frank Annunzio, but since I was raising so much hell they felt they couldn't slap the blacks in the face twice. So they decided to keep Collins in Congress, as a concession for

slating Hanrahan. Two weeks later or so, I got a call that
the inner-inner circle was meeting again. Mayor Daley told
us that the state candidates were complaining that they
could not campaign because people were asking them
where they stood on the Hanrahan issue. Hanrahan was
then asked to step down. He refused and there we were
stuck with this recalcitrant member who could not be
budged because he had the support of Holman, Marzullo,
and Keane. Finally, the inner-inner circle sent for Hanrahan. I told him, 'Ed, you say you love the party and I
don't question that, but if you love the party as you say
you do, you'll step down because you're hurting the
party.' He again refused and that's when he was dumped. I
was asked about a replacement and I suggested Traffic
Court Judge Raymond Berg. He was a good candidate and
if the ward committeemen and the Irish had supported
him instead of Hanrahan he would have been our nominee
in the primary, but he wasn't," Metcalfe recalled.

On October 25, 1972, Hanrahan was acquitted of
conspiracy charges and was warmly received back into the
party ranks by the Mayor. Daley even admitted he had
made a mistake in removing Hanrahan's name from the
regular Democratic slate prior to the March primary. "This
is a great lesson to all of us. Not to be willing and anxious
to believe charges, but instead to wait until there is a full
hearing of the facts."

Jackson, who had argued that Hanrahan should be
indicted for murder instead of conspiracy, declared
angrily, "Everything Hitler did to the Jews in Germany
was legal. History is replete with instances where the
courts have been used to wash clean the crime of the ruling
class. We maintain that Hanrahan should step aside, and no
acquittal of technical charges can erase the level of
incompetence which has characterized the state's attorney's office under his administration."

Jackson then spun into action:

- A fund-raising campaign was initiated to collect at least $500,000 for the Hanrahan offensive. "Just a great black hope won't do it. We need money, timing, and strategy," Jackson rallied. (Less than one-fourth of this sum was actually raised.)

- Richard Barnett, Anna Langford's former campaign manager, who was trained by the movement's political education division, was dispatched to the west side to teach the split-ballot routine. Jackson taught the technique on the south side in such a way that there was no way the process could have been misunderstood: "Take one of those ole brown paper bags, the kind you carry your lunch in or roll you hair up in, and write the candidates' numbers down that I tell you. Anybody that has ever played policy or the numbers knows how to split a ticket. Don't think Democrat or Republican, that's too confusing. Go by your number. It's like going to see the Cubs play. When you go to a baseball game, you don't worry about the whole section. You just look at your number and go to your seat and sit down. Don't worry, I repeat, about Democrat and Republican, you ain't neither one, you're black, and you're trapped. White folks been saying black folks ain't sophisticated enough to split tickets, well they just ain't been speaking our language. Now remember, Tuesday ain't no hollerday for drinking, eating, and laying around. It's a holy day set aside for doing something sacred like running Hanrahan out of office. Am I clear?"

- Jackson called for 1,000 of his Saturday morning benchwarmers to move from the pews out into the streets to knock on doors, distribute literature, and propagandize against Hanrahan.

- According to Jackson, more than 40,000 new voters were registered. Just as the Mayor registers those more inclined to vote for the machine, Jackson registered blacks and whites who were antimachine.

The anti-Hanrahan offensive was not a one-man show. As always, hundreds of blacks and whites participated, including Dr. Charles G. Hurst, formerly head of Malcolm X College, Don Rose, Ralph Metcalfe, Leona Black. Some made larger contributions than others, but still all acted as a team.

On November 8, 1972, at 6:03 P.M., three minutes after the polls closed, NBC's John Chancellor declared what the political polls had been threatening all along. It was four more years with Nixon. Blacks in Chicago, for the most part, remained indifferent. There were more important matters to settle, like life or death under a state's attorney who some blacks thought would just as soon blow them away as the Panthers.

By 8 P.M., the south-side black ward reports started rolling in. Cousins' ward: Bernard Carey, 15,183, Hanrahan, 9,631; Langford's ward: 8,299 to 4,368; Metcalfe's ward: 7,118 to 4,961. And no black west-side wards, the cushion of the Cook County Democratic machine, delivered overwhelming pluralities to Hanrahan, as was expected. Overall, Carey received 62 percent of the vote in the fourteen black wards, which contributed to his countywide margin of 129,000 votes. If Hanrahan had run as well in the black communities, he could have won reelection by about 70,000 votes. Black voters showed a never-before sophistication, splitting their votes not only for Carey but also for Senator Charles Percy and Attorney General William Scott. The creeping independence that had been gathering on the south side finally connected with the west side, uniting them at last in their own self-interest.

Many whites were flabbergasted. Blacks fighting back at the polls like whites? They thought it could never happen here. But the Hanrahan defeat showed that blacks were growing in the delicate art of punishing their enemies if not yet rewarding their friends. The black vote was the man-in-the-street's way of saying that the slain Panther leaders, Fred Hampton and Mark Clark, had not been forgotten. However, Hanrahan's defeat was not justice. Hanrahan lost an office. The Panthers lost their lives.

After the historic upset, black and white leaders had much to say about the Hanrahan defeat and what it meant. Jackson took off on Hanrahan's famous last line: "I shall return." The implication was that he might run for mayor in 1975. "Wherever you turn up, Ed, we will be there to defeat you. You will have a long time to consider why you lost the election. For the first time in decades, the emergence of a new citywide independent black voting bloc will result in bargaining leverage for the black community, since both parties will have to compete for the black vote. The attitudinal winds have shifted. It is no longer fashionable to say, 'I'm a Democrat.' It is more prestigious now to say, 'I'm an independent.' However, don't get too carried away, the new state's attorney is still a white man and white people only respond to blacks from pressure. Since we elected Carey, it is now time to give him our assignment for jobs and investigations we want conducted." (Hanrahan lost the congressional race in the November, 1974 election, but we still haven't heard the last of him.)

Alderman Langford commented: "The anti-Hanrahan vote was a question of survival. The threat of losing welfare checks or being kicked out of public housing didn't mean anything. Blacks were really afraid for their lives. They felt that if the Panthers could be killed, so could some of them. I think we have the beginning of a black independent organism. For many blacks, it was their first taste of victory through electoral politics."

The future would prove the dumping of Hanrahan was a one-time shot. From 1972 to 1974, several key black congressional and aldermanic seats were lost to the Daleyites. All the independents had Jackson's verbal backing, but the prophecy that he would work for the candidates was not borne out. Under the threat of death, blacks proved they can kick someone out of office.

Another victory lauded by the black community was the election of grass roots candidate Mrs. Peggy Smith Martin to the state legislature. Aided by the tremendous advantage of gaining the top spot on the ballot, high voter identification, Mrs. Martin became the first elected official who allowed the movement to claim sole credit. "Everybody who worked for me, except two people, came from the movement. In both the primaries and the general election, Jesse sent over hundreds of people to work with me. And it was not money that got me elected. I won both races on a shoestring of $2,100. It was the movement who supplied the workers and Jackson's Saturday morning platform, helping me to reach the people that made me a winner." Also making Mrs. Martin a winner was her own propensity to endure. Four times before she had run for the same legislative seat. She never gave up until she won it. The chances of Mrs. Martin returning to the state legislature are slim. She lost in the March 1974 primary. She had very few PUSH workers in her campaign. And published financial statements showed Jackson gave $10.00 to her campaign. She was also ruled off the general election ballot.

With Hanrahan retired from state office, with Mrs. Martin, the movement's singular victory, in office, with Metcalfe's turning black, and with the Jackson-Singer forces disproving the invincibility of Daley, Chicago blacks had more to stick out their chests about in 1972 than they had had since anyone could remember. Spectacular. Maybe not elsewhere. But in Chicago. And for Chicago blacks, considering what they're up against and the tactics they're using, it was a very good year. In fact, 1972 may long be remembered as the movement's best year.

*Jackson is a man who arouses
loyalty and love, but also distrust
and enmity, a man who seems to be
sometimes on the right hand of God
and at other times on the right
hand of the devil.*

Calvin Morris, former Jackson aide

A sleazy rodent eases around the corner driving an
Eldorado. He is the pusher. Everybody knows where to
find him, especially the police. Sisters in big straw hats
bustle off to church to give the preacher what little money
they have as a down payment on the Promised Land.
Leaning on a stop sign is what once was a woman. The
despair around her is mirrored in her face and in her stare.
A child plays at midnight. His mama and daddy are
somewhere else. The streets will raise him and probably
kill him before he becomes a man. An eviction here, a
killing there, gang bangers here, police beating heads over

there. Sirens. An occasional scream. A shot fired. And in a small tavern someone is singing the blues.

Welcome to Crisis City. It is not that city typified by Picasso sculptures, tinted-glass luxury apartments in the John Hancock Building, or the chic boutiques that line the fashionable "magnificent mile" on North Michigan Avenue. Crisis City is one of the Chicago-land wonders not scheduled on the sightseeing bus tours or included in the slick brochures hawking Chicago as the convention capital of the world. Crisis City remains invisible to the powers who could change it, including the executive editors on the metropolitan press, the majority of whom live in the suburbs. When Chicago hosted the 1968 Democratic convention, Mayor Daley put up red fences to conceal its ugliness. And he also manages to blot out Crisis City psychologically when his speeches laud Chicago as the most "wunnerful city in the world."

Although it is seldom seen or heard from, Crisis City exists. It is another world located on parts of the west and south sides of Chicago. Life there is one continuous scream of misery for many of its 1.5 million inhabitants: evictions, police brutality, dope, gangs, bad meat at high prices, rats, roaches, filth, Jewish and Irish control of slum housing, which when no longer profitable mysteriously burns down. If people just happen to be trapped in the flames, the slum landlords mourn briefly on their way to collect the fire insurance. And the educational system has become so unmanageable that in ghetto schools, children in the twelfth grade are reading at the eighth grade level.

Today the Jackson Movement is a captive creature of its own environment in coping with the gut concerns of all of Chicago's black problems. No longer does it operate under a neat set of goals such as the Ministers Fight for Jobs and Rights, business development, or political enfranchisement. Rather than completing any one mission (such as building viable economic institutions or organizing a tough counterforce against Mayor Daley), the movement, following along behind its leader, has evolved into a multi-faceted crisis center. As its leader hopped from issue to issue, crisis to crisis, so did the organization, becoming more crisis oriented than solution oriented, more visible than effective. Breadbasket, the all-purpose leader, became the singular force in Chicago with its finger in the dike, holding back the flood of crises spilling over into the black community. But once it turned its attention to another area, the floods would still come. For example, two years after Breadbasket pressured Mayor Daley into opening up free dining centers, they were surreptitiously phased out. Overburdened with the problems of day-to-day black survival, Breadbasket implemented no mechanism for constant vigilance and follow-through that would enable it to hold on to the victories it had won. While on the one hand, Breadbasket was able to increase its mass following with service in a multiplicity of areas, the approach also diluted what it could have accomplished in dealing with the root causes of black misery. Its approach of fighting on the tip of every front often staves off the immediate, but since the basic structures remain the same, the problems often recur. In effect, the movement soon reached the point where, despite its high profile position, it was realizing diminishing returns.

In any given year, whether the movement is called Breadbasket or Operation PUSH, the issues that confront the organization are mind boggling. They almost always divert the operation from its primary goals.

Take 1971 (Breadbasket), for example. A partial work log of Jackson and his staff included: staving off welfare cuts at the state capital; a repeat of the demonstrations which staved off welfare cuts in 1969; the massive organizing efforts necessary for fund raising through the movement's Family Affair Banquet and Black Expo Trade Fair; an attempt to organize a nationwide workers' demonstration in condemnation of President Nixon's wage-price freeze; pressing for an immediate investigation of the arrest of H. Rap Brown, former leader of the Student Nonviolent Coordinating Committee; election to the board of Common Cause, a national citizens' lobby; an attempt to organize nationwide demonstration to protest shifting of postal operations into white suburbs; involvement in the Chicago Plan to desegregate the building trades; testifying before a federal commission against population control; acting as spiritual advisor to imprisoned Angela Davis; boycotting A & P food stores because of their refusal to honor the movement's covenants on hiring and promotions; forcing the reinstatement of seventeen nurses who had been suspended from a hospital for organizing a union to improve working conditions; helping pull black homeowners out of the trap of contract buying; picketing the board of education to upgrade teaching standards; and organizing the Saturday morning meetings. These activities were carried out along with Jackson's more than 100 speaking engagements and television appearances, in addition to his involvement in the 1971 aldermanic and mayoral races.

PUSH defines itself as a "civil economics program organized in a religious setting." However, as in Breadbasket, goals are multifaceted. The PUSH fifteen-point program follows:

1. PUSH for a comprehensive economic plan for development of black and poor people. This plan will include status as underdeveloped enclaves entitled to consideration by the World Bank and the International Monetary Fund (development of a plan to finance and share in the equal system for distribution of wealth).

2. PUSH for humane alternatives to the welfare system (money invested in education

Dr. King and Al Raby, leader of the CCCO, carry trash
from Dr. King's west side Chicago apartment,
1550 S. Hamlin.

Dr. King and his aides deplane at
Memphis for a meeting with striking
garbage workers. Left to right: Andy
Young, now a Georgia congressman,
Rev. Abernathy, Dr. King, and
Bernard Lee, now administrative
aide to Abernathy.

Dr. King addresses a crowd of more than 50,000 at Chicago's
Soldier Field for the Campaign to End Slums, July 11, 1966.

The day before the Tragedy of
Memphis, Jesse Jackson, Dr. King,
and the Reverend Ralph D.
Abernathy pose for
photographers
on the balcony
of the Lorraine Motel.

Jackson addresses the Chicago City Council, April 5, 1968,
wearing a turtleneck sweater said to be smeared
with the blood of Dr. King.

Senator George McGovern appeals for black support through the Reverend
Jesse Jackson at an August 24, 1968, Operation Breadbasket meeting
in Chicago. Before the 1972 Democratic Convention, McGovern would
speak at PUSH, then he and Jackson would part company.

"Cut us in!" Jackson tells A&P executives. A&P in Chicago was the only clear-cut victory SCLC-Operation Breadbasket won in its boycott of the supermarket industry.

Jackson gives a clenched-fist salute from a police van after he and eleven others were arrested in a sit-in at the Atlantic and Pacific Tea Company offices in New York, February 2, 1971. Jackson's first attempt to nationalize the economic boycott was not successful.

Phase II of the Poor People's Campaign, led by Jackson, winds through
Southern Illinois. Grasping Jackson's right arm is the Reverend Calvin Morris,
a former aide. On Morris's right is the Reverend Jesse "Ma" Houston, who
operates a one-woman campaign for penal reform.

(Wide World)

Jesse Jackson leaves the December 4, 1971, SCLC executive meeting investigating Breadbasket's alleged improprieties connected with Black Expo. A dispute over money subsequently leads to a split and the forming of Operation PUSH.

A ten-year-old at PUSH Expo '72 holds the banner of black self-esteem.

(Chicago Today)

Mayor Max Heller of Greenville, S.C., gives a homecoming award to Jackson.

Jackson and "Pharaoh" Daley exchange a soul shake at Black Expo '71.

(Wide World)

Jackson chats with Hugh Hefner
at Hefner's mansion in
Chicago, September 1972.

Jackson shakes hands with
President Nixon at the 1972 Black
Republican dinner in Washington.

of the mind will generate productivity over and against long term welfare dependency, e.g., $25,000 for education per person will produce approximately $300,000 earning power over a 20-year period rather than expenses of $100,000—at $5,000 a year for 20 years in welfare payments).

3. PUSH for the revival of the labor movement to protect organized workers and to organize unorganized workers.

4. PUSH for a survival Bill of Rights for all children up to the age of eighteen guaranteeing their food, clothing, shelter, medical care and education.

5. PUSH for a survival Bill of Rights for the aging guaranteeing adequate food, clothing, shelter, medical care and meaningful programs.

6. PUSH for full political participation including automatic voter registration as a right of citizenship.

7. PUSH to elect to local, state and federal office persons committed to humane economic and social programs.

8. PUSH for humane conditions in prisons and sound rehabilitation programs.

9. PUSH for a Bill of Rights for veterans whose needs are ignored.

10. PUSH for adequate health care for all people based upon need.

11. PUSH for quality education regardless of race, religion or creed.

12. PUSH for economic and social relationships with the nations of Africa in order to build African-Afro-American unity.

13. PUSH for national unity among all organizations working for the humane economic, political and social development of people.

14. PUSH for a relevant theology geared to regenerating depressed and oppressed peoples.

15. PUSH for black excellence.

In 1974, PUSH continued moving on a multiplicity of fronts, some of which were unconnected to their stated goals; others showed signs of becoming major phases but would disappear. Still others were rhetorical objectives.

A partial list of PUSH activities for 1974 follows: involvement in congressional hearings in Atlanta, Washington and Indiana on President Nixon's budget cuts in social welfare programs; participants in Chicago Children's March on Day Care; sponsored a conference on tax reform; entered into a formal agreement with a large black southern farm cooperative in Epes, Alabama, to open up lucrative northern markets; a major symposium on the black consumer; participants in a Chicago march for Jobs and Economic Justice; sponsored a revenue sharing conference; marched on Standard Oil of Indiana to protest freezing out black gasoline dealers; secured scholarships for a black high school basketball team; sponsored a Hank Aaron Day to bolster the spirits of the Atlanta Braves outfielder, who had been getting hate mail; held a PUSH revival-crusade for Christ; led the fight for a black contractor to build the Carter G. Woodson Library on Chicago's south side; held the third annual PUSH convention in Memphis; talks with President Gerald Ford on the state of the economy; involvement in the drive for black mayoral candidates; and an attempt to gain a black superintendent of schools, followed by an attempt to gain a black superintendent of police.

One area new to PUSH is involvement in African affairs, which shows signs of becoming a permanent concern. However, at this writing it is unclear what form the link with Africa will take, other than the exchange of information. On November 20, 1972, Jackson led a delegation to Monrovia, Liberia, to develop a plan where American blacks could acquire U. S.-Liberian citizenship, an arrangement currently enjoyed by the U. S. Jews in Israel. Since under Liberian law only citizens could own real estate, formalization of the proposed pact would have enabled American blacks to own property in the African state.

A statement issued by the Liberian Ministry of Information said both sides agreed that the outcome of the talks was perhaps the most significant development ever in relations between an African government and black Americans. It added that several other far-reaching measures were discussed during the talks and "drew a warm reaction from President William Tolbert and members of his cabinet."

In a press conference in Monrovia, Jackson said he would use his influence to open the U. S. market for goods made in Liberia. "It is high time for the nearly 30 million American blacks, who have a gross national product of some $42 billion, to start moving from lip service to ship service with Africa, which means black Americans buying products made in Africa, in Liberia in this case, and exchanging a variety of skills with African countries."

A U. S. State Department official said the agency is not overly concerned about the possibility of dual U. S.-Liberian citizenship. "We are relaxed about the idea," the source said. And at this writing the plan seems to have been scuttled.

Another venture in Africa did produce results. Six nations—Chad, Mali, Mauritania, Niger, Senegal and Upper Volta—are undergoing the worst national catastrophe in their history. Unlike America's urgent response to Israel during the Mid-East crisis, the government was strangely sluggish in shipping supplies to the African nations where more than 10 million people were threatened with starvation and sickness caused by a five-year drought. This steady decline in rainfall had cut farm production in half and killed some 60 percent of the countries' livestock by September, 1973. Not only did Jackson make an impassioned plea for a U. S. commitment at the United Nations, but he also spearheaded a national drive of his own. Solicitations from white businesses, such as Quaker Oats, General Foods and Jewel, all of which had been muscled into morality by the Jackson forces in the past, helped produce more than sixty-five tons of food and medical supplies for the starving nations. In addition, Jackson's national call for donations produced $92,000, which was turned over to Niger Ambassador Abdoulaye Diallo at PUSH Expo in September, 1973.

Jackson's performance not only satisfied an urgent need, but it helped educate blacks to their responsibility for supporting their mother country, as the Irish take care of Ireland and the Italians take care of Italy. Jackson's action in the African drought, again, pointed up the role he plays best—throwing pebbles into a pond creating waves larger than he is. People in Columbus, Ohio, for example, both white and black, were touched by Jackson's appeal. This usually aloof all-American city contributed $43,000. And Lawrence Auls, who turned over the money at a

PUSH meeting, admitted: "We wouldn't have thought of this ourselves. It was Jackson who forced us to be accountable and created the excitement for our effort."

Peering ahead, on the civil rights front, there is a chance—though slim—that the old labor coalitions, which packed up and went home after the election of President Richard M. Nixon, may be returning to the Movement folds under Jackson's leadership. Early in 1973, Jackson and labor leaders discussed the regrouping from which the Coalition for Jobs and Economic Justice emerged, operating out of PUSH headquarters. Although the Jackson-Labor coalition is engaged in dialogue at this writing, no traceable change has been reflected in the labor unions' exclusionary policy toward the black worker.

The crises of the city land on the movement's doorstep basically for three reasons: Mayor Daley's insensitivity toward blacks; the passivity of other civil rights groups compared to the activist role of Breadbasket/PUSH; and the compassionate and charismatic nature of the leader, Jesse Louis Jackson.

Since the political impotence of blacks has been elaborated on at length, only the last two points require discussion. On the civil rights front, there are only two citywide organizations left among the proliferation of acronyms prevalent in the 1960s. The NAACP, directed by Andrew Barrett, is fighting valiantly to build a viable organization from the hull it became after the machine Democrats gutted it in 1957. Two years earlier, the militant group had vociferously condemned the late Congressman William Dawson. He had not taken a stand on the Emmett Till lynching, and he had opposed the amendment of the late Congressman Adam Clayton Powell to bar federal aid to segregated schools. However, when the NAACP overstepped the acceptable boundaries of litigation and lobbying techniques and started picketing Dawson's office, the late congressman crushed them.

Precinct captains packed the 1957 presidential election and outvoted the regular NAACP members, enabling the Daleyites to install their own leader. Their kind of NAACP president, Theodore Jones, was in marked contrast to the dedicated labor leader he ousted. The retiring Willoughby Abner reflected the encroaching militancy of the era. Dawson, who controlled the black Chicago submachine and who was credited with the election of Daley in 1955, ran the NAACP so tightly through Jones that its lawsuits became increasingly spineless, ignoring the critical areas of police brutality and school desegregation. From 1957 on, until Barrett's election in 1971, the NAACP was under strict domination of the machine. But even at best, the NAACP's dependence on white funding and its white influence at the top will ensure that it cannot assume a reformist or revolutionary posture in the black liberation movement.

In 1971, the Chicago Urban League's executive director, Laplois Ashford, also flexed his muscles at the Daley machine. At the league's annual banquet, attended by all the prestigious, acceptable blacks and whites in the city, Ashford ripped the city's segregationist practices in education and housing. Mayor Daley, an honored guest at the speaker's table, was visibly shaken by Ashford's innuendoes. Subsequently, Ashford resigned. An ad hoc group charged that Ashford was forced out of his post. The group also accused the league of dumping Ashford because he was too militant for its conservative interracial board of directors, especially one who had ties to Daley. Ashford was replaced by a competent administrator, James Compton, the nephew of the late Whitney Young, who is low keyed and sticks to the basic roles of research, social welfare programs, and job placement. But since the Urban League acts on the principle of good faith, lacking muscle to back up its requests, its successes are moderate. Edwin (Bill) Berry, who was the executive director of the Chicago

Urban League for more than a decade, once admitted that "the League had played it so safe that we are well behind the safety zone." This is the role the league continues to play.

What happens, though, when blacks need assistance other than legal counsel or job referrals, which are the staples of the NAACP and the Urban League? What happens when their needs are not met because they live in a neighborhood without political clout? They call on Jackson because he is the only leader in Chicago with a force under him capable of militantly demanding that black people be respected. Many black critics of Jackson have denounced him until they became embroiled in trouble, looked around, and found that there was nobody else in sight to run to for help. Jackson, a nonbureaucrat, doesn't call a board meeting to study a problem or pass a resolution for him to act. He just runs out the door.

For example, at racially troubled Gage Park High School in 1973, black children were being intimidated by whites, as white police watched dispassionately from their squad cars. A student called. Jackson immediately appealed for 100 black men to stand up and protect the students. Presto, it was done. Months later, the Urban League reacted with an impressive study of the tensions prevalent in changing neighborhoods which sparked such outbreaks. But it was Jackson who stopped the rock throwing.

On one level, Jackson responds to every crisis affecting black people in Chicago because he is compassionate. He feels compelled. When accepting the Humanitarian Father of the Year Award in 1971, in Washington, D.C., Jackson spoke about his so-called "gadfly role." "As a father of four children, I am a biological father. I am also a domestic father inasmuch as I must protect and provide for them and be a companion to their mother. But another role is to be father of the broader community. A father must protect that community, must try to heal wounds, to bind it together if it has fallen apart, to see for it if it is blind, to give it direction if it is lost. This country is a civilization in crisis. Somebody has got to respond."

In another interview (*Penthouse*, April 1973), responding to a similar question, Jackson said, "You can call me a gadfly if you wish. The job of a doctor is to show up where sick people are. The job of a concerned person is to show up where desperate people are. Jesus was once challenged by a group of people who said he couldn't be a righteous man because he hung around whores and various other unsavory characters. He argued that a doctor should be around sick people. So when the people of Cook County are in trouble, I go. They call. And sometimes when they don't call, I go because many times people are in trouble and do not realize it. Congressman George Collins did not call and ask for us to help him get reslated. But we knew that we needed a black congressman from the west side of Chicago rather than a white man. A lot of people who want to join the struggle are not abreast of the critical issues. They don't know where to show up or when. The gadfly has to know where to be and when to be there and why he is there and he has to be on strong moral grounds."

The other level points to the role he plays: a charismatic leader leading a charismatic movement. As German social scientist Max Weber put it: "By its very nature, the existence of charismatic authority is specifically unstable. The holder may forego his charisma: he may feel 'forsaken by his God,' as Jesus did on the cross; he may prove to his followers that 'virtue is gone out of him.' It is then that his mission is extinguished and hope waits and searches for a new holder of charisma."

Weber stresses the response of the followers as the crucial test of charismatic gifts of grace. "To be a charismatic leader is essentially to be perceived as such.

Such recognition of charisma on the part of the followers must be reinforced from time to time by the leader's demonstration of charismatic powers. He must furnish 'signs of proof' of the exceptional qualities for the sake of which his followers render him their personal devotion. If he fails to do so over a long period, his charismatic authority may disappear."

Unless Jackson is able to transcend this role he remains locked into a position akin to a magician forever expected to pull rabbits out of a hat. Thus, to attract and hold on to a heterogeneous massive following, he must prove himself in a variety of ways. To the businessmen, the economic pillar of the movement, he is a dollar sign. To black youth, he is a neon light, beckoning: Follow Me. To the religious groomed in the Baptist tradition, his sermons offer an emotional cleansing of the soul. They leave the Saturday meetings feeling through Jackson that they are spiritually rejuvenated. To the intellectuals he must demonstrate the ability to move ahead of the ideological tides. To the politicians he is a crowd drawer. To those in need of a savior pro tem, he the Reverend Super Jess creating an image of holding back danger, allowing the protected the option of aiding him in the struggle or doing nothing, content that somebody else is minding the store. To blacks still suffering an identity crisis, he gives rituals, "I Am Somebody"; he must also demonstrate that he, too, is the superlative somebody. To the altruistic, he must provide the opportunity to serve a higher principle than materialism or self-aggrandizement. Thus, his movement is a workshop to realize the dream of his mentor, Dr. Martin Luther King, Jr.

Ideally, by coalitions and a division of labor among other community and civil rights groups, Jackson's role could be made less overwhelming. Since Jackson often describes his posture as that of a tree-shaker, other groups could pick up the fruit. For example, as the Jackson forces ran ghetto gougers out of the black community, some group could have organized the economic resources of blacks to purchase and operate the businesses the whites left behind. As Lerone Bennett, black historian, wrote: "If we pooled our resources and energies, if we correlated all our forces and created one black superpower, we could end this thing in a few weeks or a few months. A united black community, speaking with one voice and acting with one will on issues, in politics, welfare, education, and housing, could turn this country upside down."*

Cooperation, communications, and coordination between groups are concepts all pay lip service to, but they still remain an elusive goal.

Thus, the onus is placed back on Jackson to structure his own organization if he is to carry out his multiplicity of roles with any degree of efficiency. However, although the organization has grown by leaps and bounds from its one-dimensional objective of forcing open employment for blacks, it has not developed past the point of one man decision making. Whether the structure underneath Jackson is called Breadbasket or PUSH, it still operates like a band of disciples following the inspired directives of the leader—a carry over from SCLC. Although SCLC moved on one front at a time, the Jackson movement is still organized around the leader instead of around a logical order of programs. As Gary Massoni's book* vividly points out, at one level, the expansion of the organization and the role of Jackson are complementary. It is Jackson's vision that shaped the organization and his analysis of the black condition that strengthened it. But on the other hand Jackson and his organization are in profound conflict.

"This tension is between the need on the one hand for systematic organization to fulfill specific, defined goals

The Challenge of Blackness (Chicago: Johnson Publishing Co., 1972).

and to cope with the requirements of an expanding operation and, on the other hand, the need for immediate response to the creative ideas and spontaneous directives of the inspirational leader. Systematic efforts to accomplish particular goals or to maintain some continuity in programs have frequently been broken by creating an entirely new program thrust. On the one hand, Breadbasket attempts to become a significant organization which exercises power to achieve particular concrete results in terms of community development. On the other hand, Breadbasket remains a kind of charismatic movement under the direct, personal control of the leader," Massoni wrote.

In order to make sense of what often appears to be a chaotic, contradictory relationship between the leader and the organization, perhaps it is best to illuminate the Jackson modus operandi by pointing out what it is not, using the Weberian concept of "legitimate" authority as a basis of analysis.

According to Weber, an organization's claim to legitimacy (a belief that the formal structure of power is valid) is based on the "pure types of" legal, traditional, or charismatic authority.*

Clearly Jackson's organization could not be pigeonholed under the classification of legal authority because there are few arrangements of functions in a coherent order governed by rules. Departments and divisions come and go depending on the interests of the leader. Between 1968 and 1970 there were more than forty subgroups crowded under the Breadbasket umbrella. (In PUSH as of June 1974, there were twenty-three.) They dwindled as the leader's interest dwindled. Functions placed under a particular division are not a matter of a rational determina-

*_The Theory of Social and Economic Organization_ (New York: The Free Press, 1947).

tion within a logical order but more a matter of the personal discretion of Jackson. For example, direct action campaigns will be the responsibility of the ministers' division. In another instance they will fit under the special projects division or perhaps the black-men-moving group, which is not even a division but a semi-autonomous organization. Even more intriguing, in a moment of inspiration, Jackson may snatch a function out of a division, assuming the responsibility himself, or he may create a situation which will make the execution of the expected function impossible. The Reverend Richard Lawrence, former chairman of the Walgreen's negotiations team, explains how the conflict between the leader and the organization can lead to disruption of specific goals:

"This particular Saturday we were supposed to picket Walgreen's. All week my group had been announcing over the radio we were going to picket them. We worked hard getting leaflets printed, designing picket signs, stapling them to sticks, and recruiting troops. But in the midst of the big boycott scheduled, Jackson announced from the pulpit that he had decided to picket the Board of Education. He said that he wanted 100 faithful folk to go with me and the rest of the Saturday morning flock to go with him. Naturally everybody followed the leader and nobody went with me. I was so furious I threw those picket signs all over the Capitol Theater. I just blew my stack because nobody picketed that day and before long Walgreen's stopped taking us seriously."

Another characteristic Max Weber assigns to legal authority relates to the specification of functions in a sphere of competence. This involves a sphere of obligations as part of a systematic division of labor with the necessary authority to carry out a function. In Breadbasket/PUSH there is some semblance of a division of labor, but it is not well defined, partly because of a shortage of paid staffers. The communications director, for example, may also be responsible for fund raising, membership drives. He may fly across the country acting as an advance man for the leader, or he may carry out whatever plans the leader thinks of at any particular occasion. Still the communications director must find time for issuing a stream of press releases, for speech writing, and for setting up media appearances for the leader.

Delegation of authority is another obstacle. Jackson does not transfer his power of authority to anybody beneath him. Everybody responds immediately in a precisionlike manner to his command, but staff members do not like obeying orders of a lesser individual because there is little division of authority. All the administrative staff feel they are all on the same level; there is nobody capable of being above them but Jackson.

This dilemma was one of the reasons for the staff changing from mostly white to mostly black between 1966 and 1970. Although the first three Breadbasket staffers were white, it was inevitable that there would be conflict between the black and white personnel with the increasing emphasis on black self-determination. Most of the whites within the organization held top echelon positions, feeling that was their right because they had administrative backgrounds. Blacks felt that the whites were trying to take over the organization and were exerting too much control. Organizational rivalry became so heated at one point that Jackson threatened to resign if the whites were driven out. In any event, by 1970 all whites had left except the Reverend David Wallace. However, Calvin Morris stated that the white exodus had a deeper meaning. "The whites on the staff symbolized white America's ability to follow the *one* selected black leader, but they were not about to take any orders from anybody else who was black."

Thirdly, Weber points out that in a system of legal authority "administrative acts, decisions, and rules are formulated and recorded in writing, even in cases where oral discussion is the rule or even mandatory." Most decisions are communicated between the leader and individual staff or within staff meetings in Jackson's organization. As Massoni, as well as I, soon found out, it is impossible to reconstruct an accurate history of Breadbasket/PUSH on the basis of recorded decisions.

Finally, probably the most essential element of an organization's claim of legal authority is missing since the Jackson Movement does not base its claim for leadership on any valid form of enactment by the black community. Jackson has often pointed out, "There'll be no voting here." On other occasions he stresses: "I am anointed, not appointed." To argue this point would require an interview with God. Thus few blacks ever challenge the legitimacy of Jackson's leadership. However, the "divine" nature of Jackson's leadership does raise imposing questions concerning how the black community can hold him accountable for his actions. Blacks did not vote him into his position. They cannot vote him out. The only conceivable check and balance on Jackson is his following, who perceive his acts as right or wrong. If they did not like what he did, his followers would dwindle. He would then have to shift his actions in order to attract his people back. At this point, I can think of no act of Jackson's that has been perceived as wrong by the majority of his following.

Charismatic leaders who flaunt their virility never fall from grace because of their amorous indiscretions.

There is an acute lack of financial accountability to the public. Requests by the press for full financial disclosures are viewed as intimidation. When requests are answered, records are obfuscated or incomplete. The movement's practice of begging publicly but keeping its records private has not been vigorously challenged by anyone. If his national PUSH board, which Jackson appoints, would ever have the audacity to depose the leader, there simply wouldn't be any organization, unless someone with more charisma were to emerge. The emergence of such an exceptional individual was not possible under Breadbasket and, so far, not under PUSH. Jackson was crafty enough to submerge or oust any other charismatic personality who posed a threat to his leadership. Jackson never allows any one individual to hold much power for long unless the individual's tenacity is more cosmetic than real.

Traditional authority à la Weber is based on the sanctity of traditionally established relationships and powers of control as they have been derived from the past. Furthermore, the person exercising authority is designated according to traditionally transmitted rules and he claims personal obedience by virtue of the traditional status. This type of authority again is not primary in PUSH, although there are more nuances of the traditional than there are of the legal.

The Jackson Movement bases its claim to legitimacy, in the traditional sense, partially on its ties to Dr. King. In death, as in life, King institutionalized the qualities of man's humanity toward man, the Christian ethic, brotherhood, and self-dignity. It was felt in some quarters of both the black and white communities that Breadbasket and now PUSH is the legitimate institution to carry on the tradition of Saint Martin. That Breadbasket, and not SCLC, was perceived as King's authorized legacy stemmed from the ability of Jackson and the press to perpetuate the myth that Jackson was King's heir apparent. They also spotlighted shortcomings in the Abernathy personality.

People obey commands issued by Jackson not only because it means incorporating themselves into Dr. King's legacy but also because the movement draws much of its tradition from the black church. Ministers from Baptist churches, the strongest institution in the black social order, have always presented autocratic leadership. Black ministers, for the most part, rule their churches. There is no question of who is in charge. In some churches, the ministers become gods themselves. Their word is law and often goes unchallenged, even though the black gods of the metropolis may not themselves practice the piety they preach. The authoritarian pattern spills over into PUSH intentionally and provides the basis both in and outside of the organization for some people to accept the authority of a leader who operates in a church setting. In the Baptist church tradition, ministers receive the greatest amount of respect in the black community, and Jackson, the Country Preacher, who is thought to be the successor of King, receives the greatest respect of them all.

An entrenched attitude in the movement is that criticism, no matter how well intentioned, is disunifying. Dissent is not allowed to catalyze substantial action: "You're either for or against Jesse." Most critics resign from staff positions suddenly silent rather than risk social ostracism.

The distinguishing factor in charismatic authority, the overriding characteristic in PUSH, is the concept of charisma, which Weber describes as: "A certain quality of an individual personality by virtue of which he is set apart from ordinary men and treated as endowed with certain supernatural, superhuman, or at least specifically exceptional powers or qualities. These are such as are not accessible to the ordinary person, but are regarded as of divine origin or as exemplary, and on the basis of them the individual concerned is treated as a leader."

A dominant theme in Weber's definition is the language of deification, and it is true that some of Jackson's followers and staffers perceive him as godlike or Messianic, much to the irritation of many other black intellectuals. Weber tells us that charismatic leaders have been the natural leaders in times of psychic, physical, economic, ethical, religious, and political distress. In short, the key to the response that the charismatic leader evokes is the distress that the followers experience. Furthermore, the charismatic leader is one who convincingly offers himself to a group of distressed people as peculiarly qualified to lead them out of their predicament toward salvation. After the assassination of Dr. King, whom some looked up to as a Black Moses, certain factions of the black community were "savior desperate" in their extreme suffering. The time was ripe for Jackson's entrance. In fact, between 1966 and 1968 he was already building a small, charismatic movement of his own. However, had there been no King, there still might have been a Jackson—the Messiah. Since the black community is always in a profound state of crisis, there is always a steady stream of saviors.

Robert C. Tucker writes in an essay entitled, "The Theory of Charismatic Leadership," in the summer 1968 issue of *Daedalus*, "All charismatic leadership is specifically salvationist or Messianic in nature." On one occasion of extreme upheaval within Jackson's new organization, I asked some of Jackson's aides how he was responding to this particular crisis. The aide, who is highly intelligent, said, "Jesse is going through a transgression comparable to Jesus in the Garden of Gethsemane." Followers often refer to him as their "Black Jesus." Not only do some of his aides perceive of him as "divine," but from time to time Jackson himself reinforces the Messianic motif. In some instances, Jackson will deemphasize his status, asserting that he is only an ordinary man with extraordinary commitments. He will garble his speech, using the language of the streets, dress in a mod style, as compared to the suit and tie uniform of Dr. King, in order to present himself as a leader his followers can relate to horizontally. Yet on other occasions Jackson will compare himself to Jesus or to the Biblical characters David, Moses, Daniel, or Ezekiel.

In 1972 black journalists—usually a tame breed in

Chicago—spoke out with unprecedented rage against Jackson's exploitation of the Christ imagery. That year, the Jackson-the-Messiah malarky was at shrill pitch. At Black Expo, he was introduced as the Black Messiah. An album by that name, composed by Cannonball Adderly, had been dedicated to Jackson, and at a Saturday morning meeting, Jackson had intoned, "I am only a mortal man," as if anyone would disagree. Also in 1972, Jackson was fostering the notion that those who disagreed with him publicly were Black Judases. (In 1974 at the PUSH Family Affair Dinner, Jackson walked on stage to the musical introduction, "Jesus Christ, Superstar.")

Mrs. Lillian Calhoun, a former writer with the *Chicago Journalism Review* and now an editor of the *Chicago Reporter,* lashed out in the February 1972 issue of *CJR:* "Jesse Jackson came to fame through his association with Dr. King, a man of tremendous power followed by millions. King's oratory stormed at bigotry, ignorance, and hatred but his way was 'moral redemptiveness.' His power was the power of love. Whatever Doc, as King's men called him, said of others behind closed doors, he never said a hateful word in public about anyone or any group. The complete absence of malice in his nature was one characteristic of his greatness. If Jesse Jackson is to really wear that mantle, he'd better make sure it will go over his head."

For good measure, she added, "makes one wonder if he now spells Jesse—J-e-s-u-s."

Vernon Jarrett—social-historian and columnist for the *Chicago Tribune*—said, "It's important that we seriously ponder the historic [Booker] Washington-Du Bois confrontation, particularly when at this moment we are witnessing the construction of a self-destructive Messiah Machine . . . one must not only be fair, one must shout 'Hosanna' when one mentions Jackson's name."

Yet, the Messianic motif emanating from Jackson is

somewhat secondary in relationship to a second theme within Weber's definition: the charismatic leader is set apart from ordinary men because of exceptional qualities. There are men on Jackson's board who are millionaires. Some of his staff members are attorneys and political scientists. To suggest that all his followers, the affluent and cerebral, attribute this Messianic quality to Jackson would be ludicrous. Men with money and wisdom do not need saviors. However, it is unusual even for them to take serious issue with or disregard a command of Jackson. On Jackson's board are men and women much older, more experienced, and more astute than Jackson. Jackson's ability to serve the self-interest of this particular group, as well as his exceptional personality, allows him to assert his will. In board meetings, he dominates without ever giving the appearance of dominating. Often Jackson walks into the room with his strategy already mapped out. Yet he may pose a question, poll his board for solutions, and sit quietly while ideas are thrown into the hopper or until discussion flounders. Then he may gratuitously thank everyone for their input and offer what he might call a minor suggestion. By the time the board meeting is over, his point has become the major strategy, with most everyone in agreement. Jackson has created the impression that they, not he, are the decision makers. On other occasions Jackson listens and simply synthesizes the best opinions into one approach that still allows his board the opportunity to contribute. Still other times, his immense persuasiveness in argument, the precision of his logic, his perfection of comic but stern "put downs," his ability to turn dissent into consent are the extraordinary qualities by which Jackson retains control over those whose needs are not salvationist. In other words, Jackson's reasoning just sounds rational to the trained ear. The consenting board is in marked contrast to those status-worshipping followers who would not think of disagreeing with him on the most trivial point. But the end result among both groups is the same—total fidelity to a Jackson directive.

The same extraordinary personality, coupled with underlying strains of the Messianic motif, forms the basis of authority from which Jackson achieves strict obedience from his staff. To work with Jackson is considered a privilege. It is viewed as answering the call to fulfill the Dream which Jackson projects. Jackson's employees are not preoccupied with career, promotion, or salary in the bureaucratic sense. The job itself is its own reward. Their career is working with Jackson. Jackson's own enthusiasm, conviction, and commitment act as a type of energy, fueling up his staff, pushing him, as well as his employees, to the extreme limits of human endurance. Although staff functions are nonbureaucratic, they are highly disciplined—as long as the leader is around. When the offices were housed in the old Capitol Theater, it was not unusual to see Jackson staffers running down Halsted Street to punch the time clock before 9 A.M. Jackson, a strict disciplinarian, has been known to dock staffers two weeks' pay for tardiness. After work begins, there is no set time for it to end. Jackson, when in the city, often works an eighteen hour day, with the staff following his model, often running on the fuel flowing from the Jackson personality and a sense of mission. This sense of mission, transferred from leader to employee, has often resulted in many staffers putting their sense of duty to Jackson ahead of their family, health, and financial obligations. Jackson, as well as several staff members, has been frequently hospitalized, families have been broken up, and in the early days, because of the low pay, many were just one step away from bankruptcy.

My view of Jackson's staff is consistent with Max Weber's statement: "The corporate group which is subject to charismatic authority is based on an emotional form of communal relationship." Organizational work often merges with personal duties for the leader. It is not unusual for a member of his administrative staff to run his bath, wash his Lincoln, drop his children off at school, or run to the grocery store for him. Some of Jackson's aides berate this as a master-servant relationship, but others say it is more familial, because the Jackson household is also the "dropping-in" place for eating, relaxing, and exchanging ideas for his staff and others who have worked themselves into the Jackson inner circle. However, the fact that his staff and others of his following often operate in a family structure does not make it ideal.

Since charisma is a value-neutral concept, it should not be assumed that all those around him conceive of him as an admirable individual. Some former aides have depicted Jackson's charismatic light as demoniac, often burning the human worth from persons he has drawn close to him. The damaging quality of Jackson's charisma is usually experienced by men more than by women; females are not called upon to prove their femininity to the extent that men must prove their masculinity. The most frequent comments voiced are:, "Jackson expects me to submerge my ego into his," "I am as much a man as Jackson," or "He tried to make me feel less than a man."

One aide said, "I have seen good people working in the movement and somehow come to Jesse's attention. He pulls them into his inner circle and in two or three months these people have gone from good picket captains or organizers to carrying suitcases, and answering his doorbell, and taking his children to the bathroom. They lose all commitment to any kind of movement and become only centered around him. Jesse tires of people very quickly, but when he dismisses them from his presence people conceive of themselves as limited. The light that draws people to Jesse is in one sense a very good thing, but it can also be very debilitating."

Another negative effect of Jackson's influence I have

observed is that many of Jackson's followers perceive of people as right or wrong strictly in terms of Jackson's perception. Under the formidable mental persuasion of Jackson, values often become twisted, all minds become locked into one, and there is a paralysis of analysis. The awe of power, hero worship, and acceptance of Jackson's "word" blinds people from trusting their common sense as the final determination of what is flim and what is flam.

Since the movement has grown so large there is intense competition among groups and staff members to be the closest to the leader. According to Massoni's thesis, this has resulted in cliques within the staff rather than in a cohesive staff community. Because the leader is the center of the staff's work routine, when he is away, the discipline vanishes. Some assume more authority than their positions entail, others drift away, and still others fail to obey any commands until the leader himself is back to issue them. Other problems existing in the charismatic leader-organization are outlined by three of Jackson's former top lieutenants. They were all fervent loyalists until the tension between Jackson and his peculiar institution drove them away. Interviews with Noah Robinson, Jackson's brother, the Reverend Calvin Morris, who until 1971 was Jackson's number two man, and the Reverend David Wallace, Breadbasket's first staff member, who resigned in 1973, add insight into the tension and the need for change.

In 1970, Noah Robinson ran off with the Breadbasket Commercial Association (BCA), just as in 1971, his brother would run off with the whole organization. Even though there was a battery of lawsuits filed to keep Robinson from using the name BCA (because it implied that it was still connected to the Jackson Movement), the move could not be blocked because Breadbasket had not been incorporated as a legal entity. Today Robinson still runs the Breadbasket Commercial Association, performing the same function he did for Jackson: obtaining contracts for producers, builders, scavengers, and exterminators, as well as providing management consulting advice. Robinson also distributes several products, such as milk and wax, under his own label.

Robinson offered two observations, one concerning an internal ploy used by Jackson to overpower possible contenders for his throne and the other concerning the need for the organization to concentrate its efforts in fewer areas.

"Calvin Morris and I were always at each other's throats. We fought each other hard. But one day we sort of got tired of being each other's antagonists and sat down, compared notes, and were shocked at what we found. Calvin told me, 'Before you came here Jesse told me that you were a smart nigger, a fast mover and if you weren't held down you would steal our thunder. I was told that I was supposed to put the brakes on you to hold you down, every time you wanted to do something I was supposed to slow you down.'

"Jesse had told me, 'I don't trust Calvin. He is trying to scheme on me. Since you're my brother I am depending on you to watch my back. You have to block Calvin because he is trying to take over the organization.' So Calvin and I fought like cats and dogs, each carrying out our orders against the other. It was a brilliant move on Jackson's part. With me blocking Calvin and Calvin blocking me, Jesse was free from any threat of power-grabbing from his brightest lieutenants. But what was so sad, most of Jackson's fears were imagined. Both of us knew we couldn't have displaced Jackson as the leader, even if we had a mind to. Another problem we had also focused on is Jesse's insecurity. When the businessmen would come up to Jesse and tell him how pleased they were with me, they thought they were making Jesse proud, but what they were doing was making Jesse afraid of me. The closest Jesse ever came to telling me how he felt was one day when he said that I had become an emotional liability to him, but he never told me why. And I didn't act right either.

"One day Jesse walked out of his office and called me. I kept walking. He told me something. And I called him a liar. He kept following me and I called him a bunch of names in front of the whole staff, which was bad for the morale of the staff. But I got so emotionally involved in some of the wrongs I saw Jesse doing that I would forget he was my boss and relate to him like he was my brother. But I found nobody cusses Jesse out in public and is forgiven, not even his brother. Today he won't make peace with me no matter what I do. Probably the day Jesse and I will come back together is the day our old man dies and that's what I don't want to happen, plus I got this deep-seated feeling that something is going to happen to Jesse and I don't want it to be with us on the other end of the poles."

Commenting on the organization, Robinson said, "There is a real philosophical conflict there. Jesse has to decide whether he is going to concentrate on a few things and do them well or do a lot of things, capturing a lot of notoriety but doing nothing of substance well. You see, what is important is not how many battles you engage in, but how many you win or lose. People look at all the motion, never considering it is results that counts. All the things Jesse has claimed he has done and the press has given him credit for doing he could have done, but Jesse is just too damn insecure to gather any supertechnicians around him."

Calvin Morris served in various positions, including associate director with Jackson for four years. One of Morris' major concerns was that Jackson was not building any second string leadership, not only to function efficiently in his absence but also to continue the movement in the event of his death.

"For four years, I tried to systematize the organization, trying to arrange it so it could operate smoothly while Jackson was carrying out his national responsibilities. On many occasions he would come off the road and call a staff meeting or talk to personnel one by one. Often I would have issued assignments and Jesse would countermand them. The staff would often go around the designated person in charge and feed right back into him. Rather than his sending them back to their immediate superior he would intervene for them. So there is always that continuous struggle over who will have access to the leader and no matter who is number two, he is going to have trouble with molding a staff because nobody wants to relate to anybody but Jesse. And Jesse is not always available, nor does he have the kind of personality that can go day-by-day through mundane kinds of staff decisions. He has a great sense of things not going right. He will come in after a trip, call a staff meeting, and he will preach for hours, calling people by name, telling us what we are doing wrong. But things only go right when he's there. In another sense, he intentionally sets up situations where the regular staff will resent whomever he places in the second slot. But he needs somebody there because he can't carry his staff as a family any longer as his national commitments grow.

"Still Jackson is like Dr. King in a way. He can attract good people around him, but I am not sure he has the internal security that Dr. King seemed to have to let people really sprout wings. Jesse sets up too many situations where people expend energy seeing each other as enemies rather than doing their jobs. When I think of what could have been accomplished all those months that Noah and I were fighting each other, it is pretty disgusting.

"There was a verbal concern on Jesse's part that the systematic part of the organization be broadened and I really think he believed what he was saying. But in another way that was in conflict with a part of his personality. He wants the system, but he also wants to be able to charismatically swoop in and change everything," Calvin Morris concluded. (Morris is now executive director of the Martin Luther King, Jr., Center for Social Change in Atlanta.)

The Reverend Dave Wallace had been Jackson's closest friend and assistant, following him from theological school to Operation Breadbasket and finally to Operation PUSH. He resigned suddenly in May 1973 to form a public relations firm with another Jackson aide, Paul Walker, a chemist, who also resigned. Wallace was the kind of staff person who most assumed had no further ambition than to follow Jackson. He always remained in the background, never vying for an outfront position, quietly carrying out all the many other tasks assigned him along with his duties as communications director.

"Last summer on July 19, 1972," Wallace said, "Jesse told us in a staff meeting that there was no place for us to move vertically, that we needed to concentrate on growing spiritually. It was my opinion that there was plenty of room to grow in the organization. But if you live in some kind of fear of your staff overshadowing you, then you won't let them grow. What bothers me so is that Jesse's fears are so unfounded. Most of his staff were not in competition with him. I know I wasn't. If we couldn't grow inside the organization, he should have used his contacts to help people to move out. For example, a guy like Richard Thomas who organizes a Black Expo, why couldn't he use his influence to get him on with Motown or Columbia Pictures? That way people leave with a great sense of gratitude, a sense of loyalty, and a working relationship that feeds back into the organization, helping him to extend his power base. But if you tell a guy he can't grow, it stunts his growth psychologically. I simply left because I had to grow, programmatically, intellectually, and financially. There wasn't anything else left for me to do. And nowhere else for me to go."

Commenting on the leader-organization, the Reverend Dave Wallace said, "Jesse believes in 'divide and rule,' in terms of all relationships, flowing from him and to him. He believes in being the nucleus, with no middle man. He gives the praise, the rewards, plays on people's weaknesses, and their strengths, working mostly on one-to-one relationships. Working on a one-to-one basis, Jackson finds it easier to get people to perform more by encouraging them to compete against each other. It is also easier to pit one against the other if the occasion demands it. In a structured organization, Jesse would have to delegate authority, but in his organization, he delegates responsibility, but hardly ever authority. For example, you give a Richard Thomas responsibility for putting on a Black Expo, but you do not give him the authority to spend funds or make decisions. This means people still have to feed back to Jesse, although Richard may be doing the job. Jesse feels it is better to be feared than loved. That's why he keeps everybody responding and answering to him.

"Two observations I made about Jesse in an organizational setting is that he gets bored easily. He doesn't have much patience. He will bring up a lot of issues, but they are usually general propositions. They are all great, but turning them into specifics is hard, hard work, taking a lot of follow through. If you are not a good administrator, you should delegate problems to an administrator, and Jesse could lend his charisma to attract the talent to obtain solutions. But like I said before, Jesse delegates responsibility, but not authority.

"In PUSH, there are few problems we had that didn't follow us from Breadbasket. I still don't see much follow-up; for example, the business development program is declining through lack of follow-up. And Jesse is still not building any second string leadership. Attorney Thomas

Todd, who replaced Calvin as the number two man, tried for a while to build a second string, but I don't think he has succeeded. In fact, today, so many staffers have left that there are only two program staff members still with Jesse," Wallace said.

Since 1971, Jackson has lost all but three of his key people: the Reverend Mrs. Willie Barrow, who on October 11, 1973, was named vice-president of program operations, is a dynamic orator and organizer, and a graduate of the Moody Bible Institute and the Warner School of Theology; James Fields, one of the key organizers of Expo, was named controller-administrator; George E. Riddick, one of the top researchers in the nation, has been promoted to staff vice-president for research and negotiations.

Those who have resigned are: the Reverend Calvin Morris, Noah Robinson, Arthur Perry, the Reverend David Wallace, Richard C. Thomas, Paul Walker, Lucille Conway-Loman, who later returned, Alice Tregay, Harold Sims, David Potter, Ron McDuffy, and Attorney Thomas N. Todd.

In November, 1973, eight days before PUSH's latest financial crisis broke out into the open, Todd, who replaced Morris as Jackson's top lieutenant, resigned not only from his staff position but also from his board position. Todd, a Northwestern University law professor, said publicly that he left to spend more time with his family and to pursue his legal career.

Expecting a rift between Todd and Jackson, since both are strong personalities, I asked Todd on March 10, 1973, under what conditions he would leave. At that time, he told me: "I have made it quite clear that I am an individual in my own right but I don't seek to replace Jesse. We have tried to project the needs of the organization before the needs of our egos. Thus far, our egos are operating on a plane of peaceful coexistence. The organization is first, allowing the superiority of PUSH to emerge.

When that is no longer possible I will move on." Todd was the man who gave Operation PUSH its name.

In the March 1974 issue of *Race Relations Reporter,* writer Robert McClory asked Jackson about his diminishing staff. "Everyone doesn't join the movement as a lifetime career. Some serve a few years and move on to other things." That every one of his protégés has not developed his own sphere of influence he attributes to the Peter Principle. "Shit," Jackson said, "I can't keep people's wings flapping forever."

In a third attempt to build a support cadre, which would free him to pursue his plan of establishing national chapters in major cities, on August 19, 1974, Jackson announced a reorganization. The Reverend Wilbur Reid replaced Todd as number two. Reid, pastor of the St. Stephen A.M.E. Church, is president of the Chicago Chapter of PUSH. Mrs. Frances Davis, former community services director, was appointed executive director of the Chicago chapter and Issac Singleton of Joliet, Illinois, became state coordinator. When announcing his staff changes, Jackson cautiously pointed out that Reid and Singleton would serve in their posts for only one year.

Max Weber's discussion of pure types of authority shows that of the three legitimate forms of authority, the charismatic is the least stable because it depends so much on the health, energy, and vision of just one man. Furthermore, the tensions between the creative, exceptional personality and his dependent organization are not compatible with Jackson's style of fighting on every front in Chicago, as well as with his overwhelming national responsibilities. The analysis also leads to the inevitable question of what happens to the organization when the leader dies.

In pursuing the first point, one could apply a Weberian theory called "routinization of charisma." "Indeed, in its pure form charismatic authority may be said to exist only in the process of originating. It cannot remain stable, but becomes either traditional or rationalized or a combination of both." In other words, charismatic leadership undergoes transformation from an extraordinary and purely personal relationship into an established authority structure that is no longer necessarily dependent upon personal qualifications of the incumbent leader.

At this writing the transformation of Jackson's organization into a more stable entity is in the realm of the possible. The only stable functions are those relating to fund raising. However, at this juncture, the best anyone can do with Jackson is what his attorney does. Robert Tucker calls Jackson up at 6 A.M. each day to see if he has had a "vision" that would change the directions of decisions made the day before. This is hardly the type of "routinization" that is described in the Weber doctrine. Yet, since Jackson is only thirty-three years old, it would be too presumptuous to say the transformation could never occur. It has happened with other charismatic leaders. For example, the Reverend Leon Sullivan started in the early sixties in Philadelphia to lead a charismatic movement for jobs. Later he developed the movement into a worldwide manpower training program. However, the routinization or depersonalization of charisma did not occur within Dr. King's organization, whose style Jackson comes closer to emulating.

If Jackson sees the need for exchanging superficiality for substance and durability, there are at least two approaches he could take.

On the one hand, he could subdue his ego, admit he needs help, and call on the many qualified blacks in the nation to organize a pragmatic thrust at each issue that he alone can only scratch the surface of. If Jackson issued the call, the talented tenth would come. In fact, they are already there on his national board of directors. By a division of labor, Jackson could unite blacks locally and nationally in one program of advancement around each crisis affecting the well-being of blacks. If the effort were organized around programs and not around Jackson, the superstructure would find itself on the offensive, instead of the defensive; it would be solution oriented instead of crisis oriented.

For example, since inferior inner city school systems are not just a Chicago problem, one wing of the superstructure would do nothing but focus on education. Perhaps the solution would be alternative schools, in which children in the ghetto would receive three hours of additional tutoring and confidence-building courses after their regular school day. Any solution would be better than the Jackson approach of marching around the board of education and running to Washington (to get federal funds cut off only for the Daley clout to have the funding turned on again). Jackson's setting up Freedom Schools for students when the teachers go out on their perennial strikes only results in the students returning to the same educational cesspools. All the Jackson approaches to education produce only temporary results; they do not in any way change the educational structure. One coordinated, sustained, permanent effort at ameliorating the schools also might not change the system, but an alternative system could at least reduce the drop out rate and raise the standards of education with a program of reinforcement.

The superstructure would use Jackson's charismatic ability to attract and coordinate while the talented tenth turned to administration and implementation. Jackson, like King, is not a brilliant administrator. This is no blemish on his record because administrators can always be found; but a creative fountain of ideas, the strong point of Jackson, is rare in any race. This approach could be workable only if Jackson realized that other men also have superegos. The superstructure should have no leader, as such; rather competent theorists should devise programs to be implemented through a cadre of administrators, locally and nationally.

The superstructure model would also require Jackson to surrender his coveted position that allows him vis-à-vis the establishment press to be the spokesman for the approximately 25 million blacks on everything from politics, to economics, to art, to medicine, to space travel. The superstructure would force the establishment press to deal with blacks as it deals with its own. When a white journalist seeks a top authority on labor, he does not go to the Reverend Billy Graham; he goes to a George Meany or a Frank Fitzsimmons. The same illustration is applicable to other disciplines. No one man speaks for all whites, and it is the epitome of asininity that the establishment press does not recognize the expertise of innumerable blacks in a wide range of disciplines. Under the superstructure, the white press would be forced to consult the proper expert and thus be forced to recognize the versatility and heterogeneity of the black race. It would only require Jackson, when he is called up to speak on education, for example, to relinquish his position and to refer journalists to the proper expert. Then the practice of one man authorities would end as journalists grew accustomed to dealing with sources other than Jackson. This tradition, which began with Booker T. Washington's being assigned by the establishment press to speak for millions of his race, should have ended with Booker T. Washington. But it takes a bigger man to terminate this tradition than it does to continue it.

Jackson also needs to act as if he believed he is a mortal man and that he is not God nor father to the black nation. In spite of the epidemic of crises calling for response, Jackson simply cannot do all things for all people. He cannot be Milton Friedman, Mayor Daley, the Country Preacher, Socrates, the New King, W. Clement Stone, and so on. While he might receive less press coverage, he could achieve more substance by carving out a tiny piece of the black landscape, building institutions on it, and encouraging others to take on the work left undone. For example, Jackson could satisfy his urge to climb more mountains by concentrating on Chicago. He could then focus all his efforts on building his own political power base into a force capable of wresting control from Mayor Daley. However, at this stage, politicking is a seasonal performance of Jackson's. He tries to blend it into all his other roles while he continues his treks across the country. Jackson, perhaps, should study Daley. The Mayor seldom leaves home. Daley realizes his empire is Chicago and not the world.

Institutionalization of the movement also poses a solution for the future of Jackson's organization in the event of his death. But as it stands today, the permanence of the movement is tantamount to that of Jackson. Jackson, the man, is an emerging institution. Emerging in a form that only one black has held in this century.

The new King?

Some people see what they are compelled to see. Others would see what is there.

*If you leave a man alone
and give him enough rope,
he'll hang himself.*

A black southern adage

On December 18, 1971, hundreds milled around in the streets, trying to join thousands more who jammed into the Metropolitan Theater on Chicago's south side to witness the unveiling of the Reverend Jesse L. Jackson's new organization. A curtain snapped, revealing a satin banner which announced the title as well as Jackson's personal motto: PUSH. It was Operation PUSH, an acronym for People United to Save Humanity.

Never had the Jackson Messianic motif asserted itself with such audacity. He told the crowd that he was holding his first meeting in a drafty old theater because after searching Chicago, he had found no room in the inn for the birth of his new baby, which would be officially christened on Christmas Day. Yet never had thousands responded so approvingly to Jackson, the Messiah, to Jackson, the leader of men, who had just transferred the meat—staff, board of directors, his following, and perhaps some SCLC funds—from SCLC to his new organization. Thus he handed back to his former boss, the Reverend Ralph D. Abernathy, a well-stripped skeleton.

Even the sacred aura of Dr. Martin Luther King was bundled into the package, removing the only tie left that might have enabled Abernathy to hold on to some remnant of national leadership. "There is no man of whom Dr. King was more proud," former Cleveland Mayor Carl Stokes said of Jackson. But whether outsiders respect or disrespect Jackson, one fact seemed unalterable. Mrs. Fannie Lou Hamer, director of the Mississippi Freedom Democratic party, wisely summarized this fact: "Power is in the people. And as long as Jesse got the people, he got the power and cannot be destroyed."

Jackson's split from SCLC ended a tasteless internecine struggle for the mantle of national leadership, a drama that unfolded in Memphis only hours after King was shot. Through the press, Jackson had succeeded in convincing thousands that he had been King's closest aide, that he had cradled the dying giant in his arms, and that he was King's successor. All the while the national press was perpetuating the myth, Abernathy, Dr. King's legal successor, remained silent. Abernathy had never left King's side from that historic beginning of the Montgomery bus boycott in 1955 to the evening of April 4, 1968, when he cradled the Dreamer as he lay dying on the balcony of the Lorraine Motel in Memphis. To challenge Jackson publicly would not dignify Dr. King, whom Abernathy followed, and was the perfect complement to, for thirteen years. The only option was to become embroiled in controversy, scarring his best friend's memory by letting the truth speak; so Abernathy chose to let the twisted myth live.

However, there was no denying that Jackson had

piled up an array of brilliant victories in Chicago, making Operation Breadbasket the most impressive and exciting program under the SCLC umbrella. Jackson had completed a mission that not even King had accomplished, by establishing SCLC firmly in the North where, because of its institutionalized subtleties, fighting racism was more difficult than in the South. Also because the contest for King's mantle was based primarily on charismatic appeal rather than administrative ability, it took little effort for Jackson to completely overshadow his boss, reducing Abernathy to the tragic figure of a king without a court.

Over the years, the internecine struggle for power was played down by the two for the sake of black unity. But sporadically the tensions would spill over into the public sector, with black writers watching and wondering wearily how and when the dissension would end.

The first major confrontation erupted during the Poor People's March in Resurrection City, one month after King's assassination. Abernathy had led thousands of the nation's poor to Washington, D.C., in an effort to force the federal government to provide jobs and a guaranteed income. But the "city" reflected the frustrations of its inhabitants, drawn from the squalor of the ghetto and the rural slums. Drinking, brawling, theft, and rape in the plywood encampments destroyed the dignity of the poor people's legitimate demands. Heavy rainfall turned the "city" into a six-inch pit of mud. The morale of the poverty pilgrims sank to the depths of the mud, because no single figure emerged to heighten their hopes or rally them around a single objective. Jackson seemed on the verge of creating order out of the chaos by forcing the tough street-gang members into line: "Now let's get something straight," the twenty-six-year-old former star quarterback demanded over a bull horn. "I'm a preacher but I can talk that talk and walk that walk just like you can. There ain't going to be no takeover of this camp. I have been named mayor of this city. I'm moving in today. I'm going to run things and I can tell you now that all this 'down home' and 'on the block' hell raising is over. We are on the Lord's business and every living one of you is going to get in line."

Surprisingly enough the dissenters obeyed. Jackson appointed some of the gang members his deputy marshals, assigning them the responsibility of keeping peace in the "city"—which they did.

But no one knows whether Jackson's leadership qualities could have saved the "city" from such overwhelming ruination. Abernathy, who had been staying at the Pitts Motel because of the lack of phones and the seclusion to map strategy, showed up at the "city" and demoted Jackson to city manager. As SCLC lawyer Chauncey Eskridge told it, Abernathy was only joking with Jackson when he proclaimed him mayor. "Ralph said it in an offhand sort of way. But Jesse immediately went down to Resurrection City and called a press conference and took it over, totally took it over. He went wild for the headlines . . . like I was standing there at the time when TV stars Bill Cosby and Robert Culp walked in the gate. Jesse looked over the crowd of newsmen and said, 'Here come my boys' and grabbed them into the press conference. The next week he had them speaking at Operation Breadbasket."

SCLC's Hosea Williams said Abernathy's reaction was also based on the fact that previously Jackson had argued bitterly with King against the Poor People's March and then he turned around and tried to run it. "Anyway after Jackson was demoted, he said he was sick again and took off to Chicago. But a couple of days later, we saw him on a TV show emanating from Los Angeles," Williams recalled.

Before Jackson left Washington, D. C., he managed further to incense his boss by leading a group of marchers over to the Department of Agriculture building and letting them run up a $292.66 lunch bill. Then refusing to pay, he said that the amount was a token of what the nation owed the poor. Jackson characteristically overstepped his authority, but at least his move was an exercise of creative thought, something noticeably missing among the upper-echelon leadership of the pilgrimage. Although Abernathy succeeded in bringing the issue of poverty to the attention of the nation, the Poor People's Campaign failed to shake any funds loose from the federal lawmakers. In fact, in a display of total disrespect for Abernathy and the cause he represented, the government demanded that SCLC pay more than $10,000 for the removal of Resurrection City's instant slums. In the final analysis, Abernathy's demotion of Jackson worked in Jackson's favor. Abernathy's first test of national leadership would never be compared with King's march on Washington, Selma, Birmingham, or Montgomery. So, because Jackson was pushed out of the spotlight, he could divorce himself from the Resurrection City fiasco. The Poor People's Campaign became Abernathy's flop, not Jackson's.

The cold war between Jackson and Abernathy smoldered under the surface until 1971. In public, the two continued to congratulate each other and act out the role of perfect harmony. In private, Jackson couldn't refrain from hitting Abernathy with a string of below-the-belt one-liners: "Ralph says all the right things, so what if he doesn't say them well," or "For a man extremely limited, Ralph performs extremely well." Although Jackson periodically denounced all claims that his game plan was to wrest the baton of SCLC's national leadership from Abernathy, thousands of reprints of a *Playboy* article in which Jackson was proclaimed King's heir apparent were circulated to the throngs of spectators attending Black Expo 1970. Several staff people were fired because their loyalty to Abernathy exceeded their loyalty to Jackson.

In April of 1971, Abernathy again tried to check Jackson's growing popularity, by ordering Jackson to leave Chicago. Operation Breadbasket was to move to Atlanta where all other SCLC national offices are headquartered. With the pulling in of Jackson's reins, he would be easier to watch and control, it was thought. Jackson summarily dismissed the directive, saying, "Just because the offices are moving, it doesn't mean the officers are moving." Abernathy's strategy touched off a minor rebellion among Chicago loyalists, with Jackson expertly manipulating the move to create sympathy for himself among his supporters. Not only did Jackson easily thwart Abernathy's strategy to crush his power base, but he also united his followers in a solid wall of resentment against Abernathy. This enabled him to continue to run Operation Breadbasket as he chose, with little fear of further intervention from Atlanta.

What manner of man was the Reverend Ralph D. Abernathy? How did he become stuck with the irreverent title of the "Charlie Brown of the Civil Rights Movement?" Was he an honored prophet in his own hometown as Jackson was in Chicago? Was Abernathy's demise more than another case of the white press picking leaders for blacks or was it also a reflection of his inability to lead? Why couldn't Abernathy grip the reins of SCLC leadership tightly enough to hold Jackson in line?

The stream of questions demanding answers apart from those spoonfed to Chicagoans by Jackson led me to Atlanta.

On first impression, Abernathy seemed to fit into the prophetic wisdom of an ancient Chinese proverb: there are two ways to destroy a person, either by digging a hole and letting him fall into it, or by building a mountain, perching him on top of it, and allowing him to fall off.

The mountain awaited Abernathy. But he could not reach the mountain top as Abernathy—the ordinary man

with extraordinary dedication—because the demands of
human aspiration were crying out for the second coming
of a Christ figure. Not being able to balance himself against
the heightened expectations of the masses created by the
man who went before him, where else could he go but
down?

From cab drivers to office workers, to professionals
gathered in Paschals, Atlanta's fashionable black-owned
hotel, the commentary was the same. "Well, there is
nothing wrong with Abernathy, he just isn't like Dr.
King." "Dr. King lived with us. He could have lived
anywhere he wanted, but he lived with the poor. Abernathy lives with the rich folks. He has forsaken the
movement for material gain." "I know Abernathy's not a
King, but at least he could try to measure up." "I don't
know much about SCLC since Dr. King died." "No,
Jackson ain't no King, ain't nobody no King, but it was
King who appointed Abernathy to follow in his footsteps
and he just ain't doing it."

When Martin Luther King was alive, he and Abernathy functioned as balanced opposites. King once described his relationship to Abernathy as that of an alter
ego. As Lerone Bennett defined their roles in *What Manner
of Man*:* "Though markedly different in personality and
outlook, King and Abernathy were perfect complements as
leaders and speakers, King taking the high road of
philosophy, Abernathy taking the middle road of Baptist
fervor, King exalting a crowd with Hegel and Gandhi,
Abernathy moving a crowd with humor and earthy
examples."

Al Sampson, a former SCLC staff member, said,
"King saw something in Abernathy that he didn't see in
the rest of us. Abernathy has a rare blend of humility,

*(Chicago: Johnson Publishing, 1964).

patience, and integrity. Martin had to know what he was doing or he would have never insisted that Abernathy succeed him. King once told us that no man knew his philosophy better or had the stability to hold the staff together as Abernathy did. Most of us agreed."

But once King died, it became clear that he had been correct only up to a point. King had always praised Abernathy as his most trusted follower, a man who asked nothing more than to walk at his side during their thirteen-year pilgrimage through the moral wilderness of the Southland. However, do good followers make good leaders, especially when the claim of leadership was based on charismatic appeal? Inadvertently King had left an impossible legacy by institutionalizing himself instead of his organization. In a structured setting such as the Urban League or General Motors, Abernathy's honed administrative ability and sense of commitment, along with a loyal board, would have been enough for him to carry out a smooth changing of the guard. But in a systemless movement based on charismatic appeal, Abernathy could not cling to the mountain top. Personal charisma is not transferrable.

Thus, Abernathy became trapped in a role. Neither could he answer the masses' cry for a new King, nor could he be himself. On occasions when the two identities would strain to merge into one personality, Abernathy would often come off confused or lacking in confidence.

Abernathy often displayed his insecurity by his frequent comparisons of himself to King, as well as by his constant reminders to himself that *he* was the leader. In Memphis, he said, "Don't ever get it in your mind that it was Martin Luther King's dream only, it was Ralph Abernathy's dream, too." In Atlanta: "Dr. King had a dream but I have a vision." In Chicago: "I don't have to tell you that I am the leader, Baby, I am going to show you." A leader never has to remind anyone that he is the leader. A leader just leads. Everybody knows Jackson is in charge because that's the way he acts.

Another disturbing characteristic of the Abernathy personality is his frequent reference to martyrdom, as if he hoped to gain the historic stature Martin Luther King achieved in death but which Abernathy does not seem able to claim in life. Before engaging in the most harmless of confrontations he often quotes the Biblical passage: "If I perish, I perish" to his followers as if to evoke sympathy or respect for his daring. Another is: "The Lord is my light and my salvation," a passage which Abernathy said arms him for the "inevitable"—his own martyrdom. Jackson also often uses the martyrdom motif, but to evoke a different response. A favorite line is "Character assassination precedes physical assassination," which wards off public criticism. Hosea Williams, a long-time SCLC staff member, added: "The things that that man has gone through during the last couple of years have really torn him apart. He once told me, 'Maybe I ought to give my life for the poor?' He went on a fast and was going to fast until death. It took all of us to stop him."

The most revealing portrait of Abernathy, condensed from an interview with Hosea Williams, provides an explanation of why he was not capable of coping with Jesse Jackson, a man with little respect for timidity, and one who is quite adept at exploiting the weaknesses of his antagonists.

"Ralph Abernathy is the right man for SCLC, but he just doesn't have the toughness. Dr. King used to define a leader as a man with a tough mind and a tender heart, but Abernathy has a tender mind as well as a tender heart, even though he is one of the top executives in the country. A man with a tough mind and a tender heart like King understood us, was sympathetic with our shortcomings, was able to change things that could be changed, and could accept our deficiencies that could not be changed. But at the same time, King demanded that we give SCLC top priority. For example, in the old days Andy Young, myself, and others got so frustrated trying to thrash out problems that we used to throw chairs and tables during staff meetings. Dr. King would sit there like he wasn't paying any attention to us but when he heard what he thought was the right idea, he would simply call for order and we'd all settle down. Remember we were all in our twenties then.

"But Abernathy can't seem to gain the same respect. Jesse just kept chipping away at Abernathy's authority, breaking all the rules in the book, but his tender mind and tender heart could never bring him to the point where he could demand from Jesse that certain organizational policies not be violated. Because of Abernathy's tenderness, he is indecisive; he allows himself to be pressured. For example, Abernathy never wanted to move into the expensive Collier Heights area of Atlanta. He wanted to live with the poor like King did, but he gave in to family pressure. Another difference I've noticed is how people in the streets look upon Abernathy. In Chicago, King would walk into a pool room and try to act like any other cat. But as soon as he was recognized, people would stop talking, lower their voices, starting to speak in respectful tones. But the biggest bum in the street will run up to Abernathy and throw his arms around him and say 'Where the hell you've been?' I am not saying that something special about King and that sense of commonplaceness about Abernathy are good or bad. I'm just telling you the way it is."

From Jackson's point of view, since he had proven himself the more capable of the two men—an excellent fund raiser, quick-witted, tough, the greatest public speaker in America, a builder of men, a bridge over troubled waters for blacks—he could think of no reason why he should not aid Abernathy in his plunge down the mountain side.

Jackson's constant image building via the media and

his nurturing of his own power base in Chicago reduced Abernathy to the titular head of SCLC. Jackson also plotted two other strategies to weaken Abernathy's position: one was through the SCLC structure and the other was his own vehicle created for the sole purpose of escape.

SCLC, like Jackson's own organization, offered little opportunity for advancement. As Abernathy so often said, "I was named to my position by King and God." (In 1974, the same claim would be implied by Jackson.) Either mandate was enough for his board to consider Abernathy's position a lifetime office. Furthermore, the thirty-three-members of the SCLC board of directors were much older than Jackson, who was only twenty-seven when he began demanding that the coveted post pass to him. Most of the board members had been with the movement before Jackson was out of high school and they were not inclined to hand over the control to a young upstart. In his first plea for the SCLC presidency, Jackson was scoffed at. The board considered him rather amusing.

A board member at the SCLC 1970 convention in Atlanta described the dialogue: "Jesse said, 'You old men have to make room for a young man. You have to find a method by which you can do this.' It was so shocking, we all laughed. Nobody took him seriously, which really angered Jesse. 'No, don't laugh at me, I mean it. If I had gone to work for a large corporation, I'd be an executive by now, probably vice-president or something. I demand the same respect for my abilities in this organization. At least make me a national vice-president, if I can't be president.' We just told him there was nothing in our bylaws or administrative hierarchy for a national vice-president and he certainly couldn't be president. Besides there were many others in the movement who had served longer and less selfishly than Jesse. If we had created a new position, it certainly would not have gone to him. After we told him no we thought that would be the end of it."

However, in 1971, at an executive board meeting in Detroit, the same subject was raised, only with more persistence. Jackson, reportedly, made personal contacts with several of the board members prior to the meeting, attempting to persuade them to lead the power struggle for his intended promotion to either vice-president or president. At the meeting, the board members did not back Jackson. Still he made an elaborate plea: "If I am to return to SCLC, I must be given a post that is consistent with my national and international position." (Jackson had been on leave in order to change an Illinois law making it difficult for an independent to gain a spot on the mayoral ballot.) After the board again refused his request, Jackson then threatened to extend his leave of absence indefinitely.

As a counter-move, a spokesman for the board told Jackson that he could remain on leave if he wished and that SCLC and Breadbasket could get along without him. "If SCLC survived the death of Martin Luther King, Jr., then I'm certain we can survive if one individual ups and decides to leave the organization." Then, faced with the possibility that Jackson might not resume his leadership post in Breadbasket, Calvin Morris requested that the board name him national director of Breadbasket, replacing Jackson. Jackson quickly reconsidered and informed the board that he would return to Breadbasket. After Jackson's plan was scuttled, an SCLC board member admitted that he was glad Jackson had remained: "We hope we can save him because we need each other. But Jesse is young and energetic and he has a big ego problem."

SCLC's Al Sampson, now an executive with the Chicago United Builders, lent understanding to Jackson's dilemma: "There is an old Baptist syndrome that you are always a boy preacher to the old folks. You can use the SCLC title to branch out, but you can't go up. Abernathy had the humility to stay in the basement of SCLC for thirteen years, but the young guys just don't have that kind of patience. Most of the original SCLC young men on the executive staff left after King died: Hosea Williams, Andy Young, Kim and Jim Bevel, Walter Fauntroy, Leon Hall, Bernard Lafayette, Randolph Blackwell, Bill Rutherford, and myself. Most of us used the SCLC name to promote ourselves to bigger things. The only difference between what we did and what Jesse did was that we didn't attempt to take the whole SCLC organization with us."

Considering the alternatives governing his mobility in the civil rights movement, Jackson saw that the only course of action left was to start his own group. He could not rise through the SCLC ranks. The Breadbasket Commercial Association, according to his brother, Noah Robinson, was the intended vehicle by which Jackson could make his break.

Robinson said, "We secretly incorporated BCA as a separate entity from Breadbasket. We were not pushing the name because we didn't want SCLC to know about it, because Jesse thought he might have to leave and he wanted BCA to be underground, so we could get up and run if we had to. When we decided to make the break out the door, we would have a concerted effort because the businessmen would underwrite the new movement. But somehow the word got back to Atlanta and Abernathy called us down there. All during the meeting with Abernathy, I heard later, Jesse denied that BCA existed. Since I have a habit of talking too much, Jesse had made me sit out in the hall, so I wouldn't spill the story."

Hosea Williams attributed Abernathy's willingness to believe Jackson and not discipline him for violating organizational policy to Abernathy's "tender mind and tender heart." "That BCA thing about a department of SCLC setting up a separate corporation was a major violation of the organization. Noah and Jesse never told us one word about it. They had even obtained a federal grant

[BCA applied for, but did not obtain, a federal grant] although SCLC never accepted grants from the government. Jesse's other violation was that he solicited funds nationally in one of the magazines. He asked people to send $5 to an organization called Resist, one that he had set up without asking anybody. He had Abernathy's signature on the letter and Abernathy didn't know anything about it. Then we get a call from the Internal Revenue Service saying the SCLC tax exemption was in jeopardy because one of our top executives was running for mayor in Chicago. Again we didn't know about Jesse's running for such an office. So we asked Jesse to withdraw. The point is that during all of these violations, Ralph never stood up to Jesse. He should have taken direct action as soon as he heard about BCA. That would have nipped Jesse's other stunts in the bud."

The clandestine activities surrounding Black Expo '71 shoved Abernathy so far into a corner that he had to respond. Even then Abernathy's strong-man image emerged not so much because Jackson had once again demonstrated his disdain for SCLC organizational policy and its leadership but because a black reporter, Angela Parker of the *Chicago Tribune,* forced him into a position in which he had to either confirm or negate Jackson's latest impropriety. Once he had confirmed the violations, Abernathy was compelled to take action to save face and also to prove that he, not Jackson, was in command.

Angela Parker handed Abernathy two documents: one showed that on September 29, 1970, Black Expo was formed as a foundation and later as a nonprofit corporation on September 14, 1971. According to a December 2, 1971, *Chicago Tribune* article, Black Expo never registered as a foundation with the Illinois Attorney General or the IRS, as required by law. "The foundation . . . was ordered dissolved by the Secretary of State's Office on November 15, 1971." As usual, Abernathy was totally unaware of the

Jackson machinations in Chicago: "This is most unusual. I find it difficult to believe. Although there may not have been any mishandling of funds by this move, still if it is true, it was wrong. Black Expo should not have been incorporated without approval and knowledge of the board of directors and the SCLC president. If this is true, the Reverend Mr. Jackson had no right to direct the founding of either a foundation or a corporation. No department had that right according to the policies of the national organization. It cannot make any legal moves without the approval of the president and the board of directors of the national office. We cannot, at this time, allow a department to get out of line. It can hurt the entire organization," Abernathy said.

Answering for the first time in print (*Chicago Tribune*, November 30, 1971) why he consistently allowed Jackson to abuse SCLC, Abernathy stated: "In previous instances I have avoided confrontation with Jackson about not following policies of the national organization because the freedom movement was at stake and that's all the white power structure would need—to see internal strife within the most vibrant civil rights organization in the country.

"I have considered the liberation of the black and the poor people much more important than dissipating energies and resources seeking to deal with organizational structure with Reverend Jackson or anyone else, which often ends up in a hassle which is not always understood by the public. We have been bogged down with matters of getting America to feed its hungry, house its poor, and redirect its national priorities. This has had to take precedence over everything else."

This public disclosure of Jackson's typical inability to be governed invigorated Chicagoans. But others found another item buried in the *Tribune* story far more intriguing, causing many to suspect that a large portion of

Black Expo funds had been misplaced, lost, or otherwise unaccounted for.

According to a formula worked out between SCLC and Operation Breadbasket, 25 percent of Black Expo funds were to be funneled back to the national office. The funds were to be distributed and shared with smaller SCLC chapters that did not have the resources for self-sufficiency. The *Tribune* article revealed: "Abernathy reported that in 1969, the national office received $60,000 as its share of the Black Expo proceeds. In 1970, however, the SCLC share had dropped to $11,000."

Two months after the 1971 Black Expo, no report had been made to SCLC concerning its 1971 divvy. However, the *Tribune* stated that an estimated $450,000 gross from the Black Expo '71 fund-raising event held at the amphitheater from September 29 to October 3 had been reported by Breadbasket officials. (On February 19, 1972, an audit report prepared by Washington, Pittman, and McKeever, Chicago accountants, showed that gross receipts, which included booth sales, for Black Expo '71 amounted to $500,270.57.)

A gross of $400,000 to $500,000 was impossible, concluded many fairgoers, exhibitors, and participants. Skepticism was a natural by-product of media reinforcement of a 700,000 crowd figure in the public mind. The media dutifully reported attendance figures fed to them by Jackson's press agents and other movement officials. In fact, the Reverend Ed Riddick, research director, on a note of enthusiasm, told *Chicago Today* that crowds would pass the 750,000 mark by the end of the five-day event.

Once that crowd figure of 700,000 was accepted, however, a gross of $400,000 to $500,000 became unacceptable. How was it possible for 700,000 adults and children to pass through the exhibition gates at $1 and 50¢ a head, and for 66,000 more to attend the six performances of the star-studded entertainment at $4 a head and still gross no more than $500,000? Absurd—scandalous—ridiculous, were among the various reactions.

Whispered indictments of theft, malfeasance, and exploitation follbwed in the wake of the public disclosures. Responding to pressure from the press, neat, impressive graphs and charts were presented by Expo businessmen, the financiers. Their focus was on the net amount. In this area, the businessmen went to great lengths to explain how funds were spent, but circumvented questions on the gross. But the journalists were particularly interested in ticket sales since they were all cash transactions. If there were missing funds or monies skimmed off the top, ticket sales offered a handy hiding place, it was surmised. According to the audited report, ticket sales during the five-day affair from both the exposition hall and shows amounted to $339,824.70, which formed the bulk of the gross. How could the gross be so paltry when Black Expo was billed as the greatest show on earth by Jackson himself? After attempting to wrest an answer from Jackson, James Fields, Expo accountant, attorney Robert Tucker, Expo general manager Celious Henderson, and anybody else who even looked knowledgeable, journalists, lay mathematicians, and other nonbelievers took it upon themselves to figure out the Expo puzzle. On August 15, 1974, Henderson said, "For three years you have bugged me about Expo monies. The public doesn't care. It's just you nosey reporters." Jerry Bell, Expo aide on loan from the U.S. Department of Labor, said bluntly, "No. The public does not have the right to know." Neither, of course, cooperated. Without help from Jackson or his assistants, all the armchair auditors produced disastrous conclusions.

Theory 1: This method involved adding the 700,000 crowd figure, used in every major newspaper, radio, and TV report in Chicago, to the number of people attending the entertainment and multiplying by admission fees. The shows were overwhelming successes. Most of the entertainers performed gratis, but were paid for expenses. Each night performers such as Aretha Franklin, Roberta Flack, Kim Weston, the Jackson Five, Issac Hayes and Stevie Wonder performed back-to-back. Nowhere else in the country could an audience enjoy such a galaxy of stars for only $4. Even police estimates—always low—stated that 25,000 people and about 8,000 cars tied up traffic the night of the Jackson Five performance. I attended all six shows and each time there was standing room only. But more specifically, Larry Caine, general manager for the International Amphitheater, described a packed house as 11,000 persons seated. The number does not include 1,500 "obstructed view seats" which Richard Thomas, Expo '71 director, said were given away. The total receipts for the six shows would amount to $264,000 (11,000 x 6 @ $4). Giving the movement the benefit of the doubt by saying that half of the 700,000 who passed through the exhibition hall were children, paying half price, the exposition gate sum would have been $515,000. The gate fees would amount to $779,000. This would push the Black Expo gross up to $939,445.78, assuming the other figures used to compute the gross were correct. By this method of computation, an estimated $439,175.21 would remain unaccounted for.

Theory 2: Another method for unraveling ticket sales was to accept Jackson's explanation. "There were 500,000 people at the trade fair and about half of them were let in free." That Jackson's assistants would let 250,000 people in free seemed implausible, because the event was a fund-raising affair. In any case, using Jackson's 250,000 figure would produce a gross from the exposition hall of $187,500. Adding this figure to the entertainment receipts would equal $451,500. The total gross would then be pushed upward to $611,945.78 with $111,675.21 still left unaccounted for.

Theory 3: By talking with trade fair experts, using an empirical analysis, and an examination of the age-old game of crowd inflation, I have a theory, which could put the gross well within the perimeter of credibility. However, without factual documentation from movement officials or IRS agents, who were adding up the figures along with everyone else, my conclusion remains merely a theory— and no more than that.

The first step included dispensing with the movement's 700,000 figure, or anything close to it. Putting 700,000 people in the amphitheater in five days would be like rounding up every man, woman, and child in the state of Hawaii, or Montana, or Idaho and positioning them 35,000 at a time on 585,000 square feet of space. 700,000 people attending the amphitheater in five days, during the sixty-two hours in which the exposition was open, would mean 11,290 people passed through two gates every hour, or 186 people a minute. And it was not a stampede. It was a walk-in trade fair. In time, space, and size, 700,000 people at the amphitheater would be in line with what Expo Director, Richard Thomas, himself said, "The figures given out to the press were as far off as the moon is from the earth."

Although Thomas, who resigned in 1973, did not help matters by giving a realistic crowd count or documented substantiation of the gross, he did say that if there was any mishandling of monies, his former boss, Jesse, had nothing to do with it. "Jesse never signed checks or handled any Expo money. I was responsible, but I never put a finger on it either. I used an accountant to handle the money, who reported directly to the treasurer. If monies were missing, it came because of an inability of those of us to function properly, not because monies were misappropriated or stolen. It is only fair to assess the situation in terms of the newness of putting on something that blossomed beyond our wildest dreams. Personally, I don't think that there was much of a discrepancy between what came in and what was accounted for."

However, trade-fair professionals, all of whom prefer to remain anonymous, did put the Black Expo imbroglio into some perspective.

An International Amphitheater executive said that if 20,000 people jammed the exposition hall in any one day, the scene would be wall-to-wall people. That figure was also consistent with Chicago Convention and Tourism Bureau information. In fact, a bureau spokesman remarked, "I can't imagine what could draw 700,000 people to the Expo. I don't see how the first floor could hold that many people unless the event ran more than a month, instead of five days."

Another tradesman in the exposition industry said, "Lay people don't understand that an announced figure is just an announced figure, which might be announced at any number. Sometimes I think we'd all be better off if we did not announce an attendance figure. But there is one thing that the professionals never get caught doing. We would never announce a crowd figure and a dollar figure in the same breath, which is the trap Black Expo people got caught in. We could get away with giving crowd figures and dollar figures out better than a show like Black Expo because our events are sponsored by trade associations. Black Expo is a more publicly owned event than a product-line trade fair. A dog show we put on at the amphitheater drew 5,000 a day, which we considered a good crowd, but remember a trade show is interested in quality not quantity. But there would be no way to get more than 20,000 people a day in there."

Thus, accepting a 20,000 daily crowd figure would bring the five-day exposition attendance figure to 100,000.

Assuming again that one-half the paid admissions were for children, the exposition gate would have totaled about $75,000. Added to the total receipts from entertainment, the two gate fees would equal about $339,000, which in round numbers compares evenly with gross ticket sales shown on the audit report. Using this method of computation, one finds the $500,000 gross figure wholly acceptable. Plus, tickets were cashiered by union ticket agents and receipts were taken to the bank by Brinks Security, leaving little room for error.

There are enough skeptics in Chicago who would swear that a 20,000 per day crowd at Black Expo was impossible. Their skepticism is aided by Jackson and his lieutenants, who still have not learned from their mistakes of Black Expo 1971. In 1973, Jackson once boasted that crowd attendance at Black Expo '72 almost topped the one-million mark.

It would not be surprising if one day Jackson manufactured crowds gathered around him larger than the population of the People's Republic of China.

It would all be such a tidy ending, if the point of all these arithmetical exercises were to prove that armed with bits of fact, one can add up a balance sheet that justifies Black Expo '71 finances against charges of malfeasance. No, if anything, the many loopholes involved prove how easily a case could be built against the movement—not only around Expo finances but also other loose money matters—if there were a proper motive.

The larger questions, then, are what facts do the IRS and the Daley Democrats have, and if there is incriminating evidence, could it be used as political ammunition? Would that use result in the government's leading the civil rights movement, with Jackson only adding the flair? Watergate proved to the unaware how the IRS machinery can be used to "screw political enemies." It was all laid out in testimony before the Watergate Senate Hearings by John Dean III, former White House counsel. Even before the Nixon regime, the late Congressman Adam Clayton Powell, reportedly, found himself locked into an IRS entanglement, which resulted in his endorsing Dwight D. Eisenhower for a second term over Adlai Stevenson in 1956.

If the IRS has not built a case against Jackson, it is not because they were not diligently trying, while at the same time issuing disclaimers that they were investigating Black Expo.

IRS auditors never stop at the obvious. Often they dig into records from the day one. If the IRS applied this approach to Operation Breadbasket, they most likely have found a dubious digit, because in the organization's early stages, accounting was not a high-priority item. If this is a true conjecture and the evidence is strong enough, Jackson himself is not in jeopardy, only those who depend on him for direction. Jackson is white America's most valuable mouthpiece. To lock up a gold-plated larynx would be ludicrous, but to harness it would be logical.

After Black Expo, three occurrences add weight to the allegation that Jackson may not be the same free spirit he once was. Consider the White House Enemies List and the harassment that was to go into effect after Watergate had blown over. Abernathy, Bill Cosby, and twelve black members of the House of Representatives appeared on the coveted Enemies List. Jackson did not. Does this mean that Jackson, the vociferous champion of black nationalism, is less of a threat to American internal security than Cosby, the comedian, or Abernathy? Jackson's being overlooked by the paranoid Nixon staff, who even considered Barbra Streisand a menace, could be explained by his independent political stance, which usually favors Republicans over Democrats in Illinois. But it also could be explained as the result of Jackson's making peace with the federal government to loosen the noose the IRS may have tightened around his neck.

Another anomaly was brought to light by an August

13, 1972, item in an Evans-Novak column tagged, "Jesse Jackson's Ways Puzzling." The columnists reported: "This was Mr. Jackson's story: The Internal Revenue Service had dispatched an investigating team to Chicago and was flinging unjust accusations at him. But the IRS agents offered to leave him alone if he endorsed Republican Governor [Richard] Ogilvie in his campaign for re-election." The columnists, however, went on to dispute the story by saying that sources in the Justice Department had said that there was no special investigative team checking out Jackson, which, of course, is not true, according to other sources. Even Jackson admitted there was an investigation.

Jackson's ways really were puzzling as the gubernatorial election approached. October 7, 1972, Jackson endorsed nine political candidates, including the new Ralph Metcalfe, Republican Senator Charles Percy, and Republican ally, Attorney General William Scott. Because of the cold war between Jackson and McGovern, the presidential endorsement of the Democratic South Dakota senator came on November 1. But it was not until three days before the election that Jackson gave the nod to his long-time pal Governor Ogilvie, who badly needed black support since he was running against a so-called Independent Democrat, Dan Walker. The day that Jackson gave Ogilvie his political blessing, something most unusual transpired. The week before, Jackson had conducted what was said to have been a random sampling of the black community to determine who their gubernatorial choice would be. Never before had Jackson sought the counsel of the black community prior to making a political endorsement. Yet, in this critical election, he had to let it appear that it was the black community speaking, not him, endorsing Ogilvie, when it was Ogilvie whom Jackson had wanted to endorse all along. It was clear to many that Jackson's hands were tied from actively supporting the man who had aided his appeals for staving off welfare cuts

and advancing business contracts with minority entrepreneurs.

In the wake of the Evans-Novak revelations, which
had spread quickly in black and white political circles,
Jackson had to back off from aiding a valuable ally. Ogilvie
lost the election, which is not to imply that he would have
won if Jackson had worked for him.

Shortly after Expo '72, Jacksonian watchers noted
that while he had never captured the Chicago political
world by storm, even his waves were becoming shallow. In
several key anti-Daley elections, Jackson made endorsements of the machine opponents but sent no troops. In the
Cardiss Collins congressional race in 1973, I spotted a
troop of one from the movement dispatched to help
Mrs. Collins' opponent, who badly lacked campaign volunteers. Although Jackson himself rarely sets foot on the
west side, among the poorest of poor folk, in the past at
least he would send aides to assist in key political races.
But by the summer of 1973, Jackson's easing away from
key anti-Daley political races burst out into the open.
Richard Barnett, campaign manager for a west-side independent aldermanic candidate, said that Jackson reneged on a promise to send precinct workers into the
predominantly black machine stronghold. And not only
that, but Jackson also "sought to recruit what few
campaign workers we did have to join in a movement
demonstration at another location." Barnett, who was
trained by the movement's political education division,
suggested that the word "political" be removed from the
movement's membership cards. Jackson's answer to the
criticism was "there are other things to conquer besides
the twenty-ninth ward."

All the conjecture, speculation, and rumors about
Black Expo and its aftermath could have been avoided if
the movement had opted for accountability to the public
it serves.

But movement money matters are about as open as a

Swiss bank account. And the gnomes of Zurich are probably less irked when that embarrassing question about money is raised. When a financial scandal hits the press, only then will the Jackson businessmen pass out financial reports. But these are never complete, nothing like the ones leaked to the press by those on Jackson's board who do not share the attitudinal travesty that anybody who questions the movement's handling of public money is committing treason or sabotage. The practice of begging publicly for funds while keeping accounting private was touched on by the Reverend David Wallace, Jackson's former staff member.

"The Black Expo matter was a question of stewardship. It raises a sound theological question, that those in power should not only resist evil, but should also avoid even the appearance of evil. Blacks have been misused so much by business, government, and even churches that the movement should be conscious of that fact and demonstrate both sincerity and honesty. Bookkeeping must be as meticulous as the preaching. Records for the public should be kept. Although their product is an intangible, their honesty must be tangible. It would have been wise to answer all questions about Black Expo, even before they were raised, and then the questions would not have been raised," Wallace said.

Legitimate questions of stewardship and accountability surfacing with Black Expo would hound the movement, growing increasingly ominous. Reasons vary: few checks and balances from the Chicago media, the drying up of funds for all civil rights groups, perhaps making the use of unorthodox schemes necessary for movement survival and isolation from the skepticism in which the movement is viewed by many at the bottom. Erosion of public trust in some quarters coupled with questionable actions providing fuel for the numerous surveillance groups' "cloaking 'n daggering" the movement poses a grave threat to its prosperity. The enigmas—minutiae to some, monumental to others—are answering questions lingering in the minds of many. What does the Jackson Movement have to do with the King Movement? Can the Jackson Movement stand above the times to fill the vacuum of moral leadership or will it become just like the times?

Examples follow:

• Save the Black Colleges was the theme of Expo 1973. Jackson said in the July 31, 1973, issue of the *Chicago Sun-Times*, "This year we will focus on black colleges because there's a rather definite move in this country to eliminate them from the face of the earth. PUSH is committed to carry out a national campaign to save black colleges by obtaining financial and legislative support."

Did PUSH help save the black colleges?

Well, it appeared it was the other way around, according to United Negro College Fund officials. UNCF supports more than forty private black colleges.

In a letter written on November 26, 1973, to columnist Vernon Jarrett, a UNCF board member, Ernest E. Fair, Sr., wrote: "I was really appalled when I found out earlier that PUSH, using the slogan 'Save the Black Colleges,' in turn charged those institutions and/or alumni that wanted to participate. Of course, the figure you quoted ($13,400.00) doesn't represent the additional money spent for staff who came and represented the Black Colleges at Black Expo '73. Please be assured that I am upset because some of my colleagues allowed themselves to be used by PUSH. P.S. Does PUSH publish an annual report?"

On June 4, 1974, I checked with another top official of the UNCF to see if Jackson's climate setting had helped, if there has been legislative support, or if Jackson followed through on obtaining financial contributions.

"Off the record, a PUSH official presented us with what the audience thought was a check at Black Expo '73. Actually, the envelope contained nothing but a pledge that we would receive 3 per cent of the sales from the sound track of the movie, 'Save the Children.' This was supposed to amount to about $5,000. To date, the UNCF has received nothing. I had grave concerns about the whole thing. I discouraged alumni from participating because we needed money so badly. We had none to give away. But many believed in the cause and went ahead. Now they all know they have been used. The amount of money we received has not increased as a result of Black Expo."

It would avoid confusion if Jackson's altruistic slogans were not taken literally. 1972 Expo's theme, "Save the Children," was used as the title of a motion picture produced with a $750,000 loan from the Ford Foundation. If the movement's main priority was "saving children" would the Ford funds have gone into a movie, in which Jackson received top billing or, perhaps, to an inner city pre-school development program?

•   Secrecy surrounding the PUSH Foundation is another instance of the Jackson inner-circle appearing needlessly suspect because of their defensiveness and their "we are above reproach" attitude.

Reporters wanting to gain access to foundation files found that movement officials have grown in sophistication—although not in their adherence to legality.

Organized on March 21, 1972, as a trust, using the name PUSH Foundation, it has the customary two-year probationary tax exempt status under section 501 (c) (3) of the Internal Revenue Code.

The foundation address is 33 Public Square, Cleveland, Ohio, in care of Attorney John Bustamante, said to be one of the best foundation lawyers in the country.

As of June 5, 1974, the Foundation remains in violation of both Illinois and Ohio law.

Paul Miller, in the Attorney General's Office of the State of Ohio, said, "I have no record of any registration by either PUSH or the PUSH Foundation. They are definitely in violation. We have sent forms requiring them to register with us. The forms were sent by registered mail on May 8, 1974."

In a letter dated April 19, 1974, William H. Gerster, corporation division of the Office of the Secretary of State of Illinois, said: "An examination of the records fails to disclose a corporation, foreign or domestic, by the name of the PUSH Foundation." Illinois officials have also sent letters of compliance.

According to Michael Rotman, Chicago corporation lawyer, "The Foundation violates the Charitable Contributions and Solicitation Act of Illinois. A public accounting must be given for charitable contributions collected or solicited in excess of $4,000. This relates to anybody collecting funds in Illinois. They cannot do business in the State of Illinois without registering. If nothing else, they are guilty of very sloppy management."

Each year nearly 10,000 people pay $30 per plate to attend Family Affair—a fund-raising dinner—where proceeds go to the Foundation.

Yet, though the Foundation is public and it collects public funds, Foundation officials hedged, resisted, and in some cases would not give a public accounting, supposedly because, like Jackson, they had no knowledge of the financial details.

Celious Henderson, president of the Marion Business School, is the Foundation manager.

In Henderson's office on June 5, 1974, he was cordial. He supplied data, but subsequently admitted they were "incomplete." He said, "I agree that since it is a public foundation, our records should be open. If the Board agrees, I'll get back to you." As the book goes to press, there has been no word from Henderson.

Efforts to contact Bustamante failed. Phone calls made on April 19, 20, 21, 29; May 15, 16, 30; June 1, 2, 3, 4, 5 and 6 were not returned.

Form 990, filed with IRS for 1973, showed total

assets: $769,526; total liabilities: $757,969; net worth: $11,557. The bulk of the money was the Ford Foundation loan, all of which is audited by the Peat, Marwick and Mitchell accounting firm.

Taking into consideration that the movement's foundation was not registered with the federal or state authorities in 1971, their ignoring state procedures could be considered an improvement, since they are in compliance with the IRS. In Chicago, the foundation would not be viewed with suspicion if the Jackson inner circle published the location and finances. Because they have not, the foundation is another example of the innocent looking guilty, not because of their actions, but because of their "public be damned" attitude.

• As PUSH launches national satellites a trail of suspicion follows—always as a result of confusion over money matters.

On October 4, 1973, the Greenville *Piedmont News* heralded Jackson's homecoming to raise money for Happy Hearts Park, the first erected for blacks in South Carolina. Jackson used to play there as a child. "While he is here to help raise money for Happy Hearts, Jackson's appearance here is also expected to initiate a local PUSH chapter."

On November 21, 1973, a curious reader wrote to the Greenville *Piedmont News* Action Line: "How much money did Happy Hearts Club receive from proceeds of Jesse Jackson Day activities? Advertising stated that all proceeds were to go to Happy Hearts Club. Who received proceeds from those events and how much profit was there?"

Answer: "According to James A. Carter, Happy Hearts Club coordinator, after expenses which included paying a motel bill of approximately $1,000 for Jackson and around 30 other people, PUSH-Greenville received $1,005.19. Happy Hearts received $5.30."

Carter later told me, "About $22,000 was raised, $13,666.50 of which was paid to 'Soul Train' star Don Cornelius—in cash, at the request of Reverend Jesse Jackson."

Piedmont reporter Dale Perry outlined the cash transaction in the May 17, 1974, issue, but added:

"Out of the money raised members of the Park Association felt they were going to make a sizeable amount to spend on upgrading the park. When the Don Cornelius "Soul Train" show was suggested by Jackson as a benefit for the Greenville young people, the local leaders were led to believe most or all the talent would be donated or at least done for a small amount.

"The Greenville auditorium manager wrote Carter a check for $13,666.50 and then Cornelius asked Carter to pay him in cash (check number B1060 Southern Bank and Trust Co.). Initially, Cornelius figured show expense at $19,650.04, but Park officials protested, because considering their investment they would have gone in the hole. A lower figure was then settled on. Carter did not want to go along with the cash transaction because the Park Association would have a cancelled check proving for tax purposes it had received the money. But Carter went along, endorsed the check and paid Cornelius in cash because Jackson, his friend, asked him to do so.

"Cornelius was contacted about the incident. 'As a nationally known entertainer I certainly don't have to make my living ripping off Greenville, South Carolina,' Cornelius said.

"Local reaction to the Happy Hearts incident was guarded—most all the local leaders involved are friends of either Jackson or his family. However, Carter said, 'Although I do not believe Jesse did anything wrong a lot of people feel let down. A lot can be assumed but nothing can be proven. I just would not get involved again.'

"Dr. W. F. Gibson, local NAACP president and a

homecoming official, added: 'So many people were disappointed. I certainly was. None of the local leaders were made aware of the arrangements between Jesse and Cornelius until the concert was about over. We were under the impression that a lot of the talent would be free or at a low cost.'

"Jackson said that Cornelius reaped no financial benefits from the show and actually the entertainer lost money. The real value of the weekend was that attention was turned on the park."

Among some Greenvillians, there is no bitterness, just sadness. I attended the celebration and talked at length with Miss Dorothy Brockman, who founded the park in 1949. She had talked to me enthusiastically about how the fund-raising events would help so many young people. Miss Brockman, a dedicated civic leader, is the type of woman whom it would seem difficult to disappoint.

She is the one who diligently organized the Jesse Jackson Day activities that produced tons of publicity for Jackson. Like many other Greenvillians she was unaware of the "arrangements" used by professional promoters. Often, as in the Greenville situation, contracts are verbal commitments and entertainers performing for "free" often charge more in "expenses" than would have been earned by a straight fee.

However, both Cornelius and Jackson are "old pros" at the promotion game, since they, too, have a quid-pro-quo agreement. For example, on Cornelius' Saturday "Soul Train" show on CBS-TV, he often encourages fans to write in to obtain PUSH membership cards. Cornelius' involvement with the Happy Hearts Park is not so reprehensible. He is a businessman. But Jackson calls himself a moral leader, which carries an implied responsibility to protect the unwary. Since Happy Hearts received $5.30, there was nothing illegal about it. But was it ethical?

• Money problems appear to be behind the stagnation of PUSH East, established in Harlem. According to a PUSH 1972 unaudited report of the "Soul Picnic," a fund-raising event launched to open the New York office, income was $18,522.35. An audited report showed that monies were transferred into operating expenses for New York expansion. The Harlem office opened in May, 1973. By August, Herold Sims, the New York regional vice-president and head of the Harlem office, had resigned and was $5,000 in debt. Sims, who had introduced Jackson as the Buck Rogers of the super-industrial age when PUSH was organized, said, "I spent $5,000 of my own money to make the program work. I received no pay. No expenses. The money came out of my personal pocket and that of the late Jackie Robinson's.

"Harlem didn't want Jesse. Jesse's life was threatened here. I had to risk my own credibility, sacrifice friends, family and health to ward off threats to Jackson's life. But I never knew what was going on. I was never brought into Jackson's confidence.

"Part of the problem here was that people felt there was a kind of prostitution going on. All the suspicion in the air over money has created a bad impression. But black folks just aren't going to help somebody do something that doesn't help black people. They are tired of self-aggrandizement. His friends in New York are turning against him. They used to tolerate him, saying at least he scares white America. There was so much turmoil here a group of black journalists met with him. They told him they were ready to overlook a lot of stuff, but if pushed at some point role would override their race. They told him they didn't need any more race bandits. At this point, I have no idea whether or not PUSH East will survive."

Sims is presently director of corporate affairs for Johnson and Johnson in New Brunswick, N. J. Sims, former acting director of the National Urban League, is

working to turn a company around from the inside as
Whitney Young did from the outside.

  •   Jesse Jackson is known for his headline grabbing
and requests for handsome donations for his services, but
few compared to the $70,000 expense account Jackson,
reportedly, asked for in return for his support of Detroit
Mayor Coleman Young.

According to Phil Smith, a Chicagoan and one of
Young's campaign aides, "Jesse was at a speaking engagement at Michigan State University. After Jackson's speech
one of the faculty members re-introduced Jackson to
Coleman and asked Jackson for his support.

"Jackson said, 'I've got rings. I've got jewelry. I've got
a car. I got a house. I don't need nothing, but my staff has
needs and they have to live. And I don't see how my staff
could help what you're doing for less than $70,000.'

"At this point, Coleman thanked him and left the
room. Black faculty members were mad as hell because
they knew Jackson was hustling."

Mayor Coleman Young had no comment.

However, on November 4, 1973, Jackson was denied
a seat at the speakers' table during the pre-election
banquet for Young at Cobo Hall where Mrs. Coretta King
and Senator Harold Hughes of Iowa were guest speakers.

Jackson denied the charge and said he declined to
support Young or any other candidate in the primary
because he did not want to be involved in a black-on-black
contest. (*Chicago Tribune,* November 18, 1973.) (In
Chicago, most of the local candidates Jackson endorses are
in black-on-black contests.)

  •   December 8, 1973, opened with winter re-runs
of defense strategy used after the brouhaha over Black
Expo '71 monies. At a press conference the same inner
circle was there defending the leader. Attorney Robert
Tucker labeled published reports leaked to the press by
PUSH board members, pointing to possible fund mismanagement, as "unmitigated lies."

Before the leak, executive board members had called for a meeting with the leader. For the first time the committee balked at being a rubber stamp for Jackson. One board member, who was promised anonymity, reported: "The meeting was held in Reverend Claude Wyatt's basement. We opened it by telling Jesse we didn't want to hear any of his sermonettes. He sat through the meeting and didn't even cough.

"He was told that we didn't want him running all over the country anymore, that we wanted him to do more in Chicago. We told him to quit quoting those outlandish crowd figures at Black Expo. Somebody raised the question that some people were beginning to feel the Movement had little to do with Dr. King. The poor were getting poorer and the rich were getting richer and people were beginning to see this."

Relating specifically to money problems, the board member said, "Some shocking things for a struggling civil rights group were reported. There was this exorbitant air travel bill for $13,000. Some of those bills we thought were paid in honorariums from his speaking engagements. It seemed that he was either being paid twice or was going places unconnected to PUSH business and charging it to us. [Jackson travels about 200,000 miles a year, usually with an entourage and always first class. In the 1972 audit report by Washington, Pittman and McKeever (see Appendix) travel was $85,985.53, which includes lodging.] We found there were people on the staff payroll we knew nothing about and we also found we were broke."

The unresolved cash crisis made front page news. (*Chicago Tribune,* November 8, 1973). "PUSH . . . is on the verge of financial collapse. The board members, who asked not to be identified, said PUSH had a bank balance of less than $6,000 with debts of more than $51,000." The *Tribune* also pointed out that PUSH had realized a profit of $163,195.00 at Black Expo, held in September, only two months before. "The public is going to ask what has happened to all that we have raised." Board members stressed in the article that they believed the fund shortage stemmed from "mismanagement of funds, not misuse."

Jackson denied the charges of his board. All civil rights groups are in financial difficulty. And Jackson said PUSH problems were no different from those suffered by the NAACP and SCLC. "PUSH faces a financial crisis stemming from the crisis in the American economy and from a historical dilemma. Civil rights has always found fund-raising difficult. This is nothing that started yesterday. I do not gain from PUSH. Since early 1973 my annual pay is $1.00. My income is derived from preaching and lecturing." (Jackson's lectures and talent fees, such as his commentaries on WBMX-FM radio in Chicago, are paid to the Freedman's Bureau, which, according to a close aide, nets more than $100,000 annually.)

At the December 8 press conference a sketchy report of PUSH income was released. No detailed report of operating expenses was given. But a fund-raising drive to make up a $598,140.48 deficit in the 1973 budget was announced. Jackson did not show up for the press conference. Why? For the same reason he hadn't shown up in 1971. He does not sign checks and he knows little about PUSH money matters, reporters were told.

The press conference ended with: "We have every confidence in the organization's leadership under the direction of its brilliant and dynamic president, Reverend Jesse Jackson. He has and will continue to have our total support."

Jackson later skillfully turned the reports of mismanagement around into a successful appeal for public financial support, launched a scathing attack on the reporters who wrote the articles from information given to them by his board members and went into a tailspin to villify those among them who were "in a conspiracy against him with the press." The uprising among the palace guard was defused. The "kill the messenger" motif was evoked and today the lid is on at least temporarily.

Money matters, posing a problem for the future, set the stage for the break with the past.

In light of the serious questions being raised about Black Expo, Abernathy rode into Chicago for the last confrontation. On a snowy December 3, 1972, SCLC leaders and eleven members of Jackson's executive committee set up quarters at the Marriott Motel near O'Hare International Airport for the reckoning day. This was no longer a rift; it was a major showdown. If Jackson didn't have a sound explanation for his shenanigans, he would be soundly lashed. The whip would be double-wrapped, because the High Noon setting was designed to dramatize Jackson as the bad guy and Abernathy as the tough good guy, finally riding into town to put Jackson down.

But Abernathy was in Jackson country. Picketers greeted Abernathy's arrival with a pointed statement of their affection: "Don't get messy with Jesse." Some black newspapers called for Abernathy to get out of town, while some white newspapers behaved like mischievous magpies pecking away at both from the sidelines.

The Inquisition, as it was called, got off to a choppy start. Jackson appeared at the conference room door, portfolio in hand, prepared to present his case. Each time Abernathy turned him away, saying, "We are not ready to see you now. Wait until you're called." This stern-father-scolding-the-naughty-son routine infuriated Jackson, the leader of men. Once he was so angered by the colloquy that he wheeled around, knocking two women reporters to the floor. They were leaning, pressed against his back, trying to capture the dialogue inside because they, like Jackson, were personae non grata in the top-level discussions.

Three hours later, Abernathy called for the recalcitrant Jackson, who by then was so enraged he made a historical statement to the press—"No comment."

The verdict handed down by the tribunal was that

Jackson would be suspended for sixty days with pay. Despite all the tough talk, the SCLC leadership still meted out the lightest sentence possible because the point was to punish Jackson, not to lose him. He might have broken all the rules, but none among them could match his act.

Once back among his followers at the Saturday morning meeting, Jackson circumvented his "fall from grace." Because of the suspension, he was banned from all SCLC-related activities, but he nimbly side-stepped that little technicality by showing up as guest speaker. All signs of humiliation had disappeared. In fact, he was jubilant because he was shrewdly turning the issue around from his misconduct to the irresponsibility of the press. Compared to Jackson, Spiro Agnew's scathing condemnation of the media rings like an effete tinkle. Jackson is at his best when he is on the defensive. No matter what the journalists say, Jackson will mold Biblical parables, Southern anecdotes, and jests into a firebomb that explodes in the critics' faces, and he escapes through the smoke. The issue was no longer Black Expo, possible missing funds, or corporations formed illegally, but a black female reporter who proved her paganism by reporting facts. "Dr. Abernathy is not the problem," Jackson told a highly receptive audience. "The issue is that last Friday a black woman reporter left Chicago with her mission being to separate great black men. She took a plane from the Tribune Tower to Atlanta. Now you know who your enemy is."

What about his wrongdoing? As if daring anyone to ask, Jackson thrust forth his leonine neck and roared: "My record needs no defense. We don't owe the IRS anything, but in case we do, we're not going to pay." Unbelievable as the performance was, the real culprit in the Black Expo matter was not Abernathy, the accuser, or Jackson, the accused, but the reporter who was denounced as a Judas because she dared to report the facts. Also incredible but predictable was the crowd reaction. Jackson's spiel was bought in toto. And, at the conclusion of the performance, after most had stood up and cheered the leader, people walked away at least knowing who the enemy was. It was that reporter, because Jackson himself had said so.

A more palpable defense did follow, however, with the Black Expo board of directors moving center stage to clear Jackson of any knowledge of the trade fair's incorporation. The press conference called by Jackson's business associates was not attended by Jackson. Why? Because Jackson, who usually knows something about everything, was unaware of the legalities governing Black Expo, so there was no reason for him to be present.

The businessmen explained to the press that Jackson's only involvement in the operational procedures of Black Expo was that the trade fair was Jackson's brainchild. Their statement made on December 9, 1971, follows in part:

> Structurally, the relationship of the sponsoring businessmen and women to one another, as well as their relationship to SCLC's Operation Breadbasket, has remained essentially one of informal mutual cooperation and help. It is here that we would wish you to be informed that at no time did Reverend Jesse Louis Jackson incorporate or direct the incorporation of the Minority Business and Cultural Exposition under the name of "Black Expo Foundation," "Black Expo Inc.," or under any other name.
>
> In September 1970, a committee of the sponsoring black businessmen and women decided to explore ways and means to assure the continued existence and possible interstate expansion of the Black Business and Cultural Exposition. Consideration was given, at that time, to institutionalizing the exposition, and to

qualifying the exposition to receive tax deductible grants and contributions from all legitimate sources throughout the world. It was in this connection that in September of 1970, legal counsel was authorized to obtain authority from the State of Illinois for the establishment of the "Black Expo Foundation" as an Illinois charitable organization. Subsequently, it was decided by this informal association of black businessmen and women that a controlled expansion of the exposition concept to other states and territories of the United States would not be administratively feasible; that charitable or "foundation status" would unduly restrict proposed expansion of program format; and further that concentration upon the Chicago community and skillful implementation of the exposition concept in the City of Chicago would not only attract national support, but would also render the exposition self-sustaining. For these reasons, no additional steps were taken to further structure or render "Black Expo Foundation" operational.

The Jackson businessmen also presented a rubrical accounting of Black Expo, which explained the net, but still obfuscated the gross. To most reporters, however, the movement's explanation was satisfactory. The next day's news heralded: "Jesse Cleared in Expo Case." Jackson was tried by his friends and found innocent by his friends.

All that had transpired was a trial balloon set off to test the allegiance of his followers and to clear away any lingering cobwebs of suspicion from the public mind. Then, the game plan became escape, something that Jackson had longed for since early 1969, after weighing the reality that he could never officially replace Abernathy. It was around that time that feedback from the

press as well as from many around him concurred in thinking that SCLC needed Jackson far more than he needed
them. As some saw it, Operation Breadbasket had become a
case of the young, ingenuous mind trying to stimulate SCLC
—a feeble body, too brittle to respond, but yet too senile to
give way. To Jackson, SCLC had become a drag. He had
carefully nurtured the businessmen into the movement's
major financiers, yet large portions of Breadbasket monies
had to flow back to Atlanta. His power base was his alone.
He had developed that too. Yet Atlanta never innovated,
they merely criticized. All over the country, politicians,
actors, athletes, and businessmen owed him favors, but all
they owed Abernathy was respect as Martin Luther King's
official standard-bearer, an honor which Jackson never felt
his boss was capable of carrying. Now Expo had set him
free of the dissension. It provided just the right excuse to
mark the final beachhead. Since sixty days was too long to
be away from the movement, he summarily resigned,
taking his staff, board of directors, in fact, the whole
movement, with him. His telegram statement to the
Reverend Abernathy on December 12, 1971, follows:

> Gentlemen:
> Since 1966 under the appointment of our
> late president, Dr. Martin Luther King, Jr., I
> have worked as a paid employee of the Southern
> Christian Leadership Conference and served as
> the national director of its economic arm,
> Operation Breadbasket.
> It is a position I have held with deep
> humility and great pride. I have worked hard
> and tried to carry out to the best of my ability
> every assignment given to me.
> Since the time has come when I cannot any
> longer give my active service to the organization,
> and since it is not my desire to stand in the way
> of progress, I consider sixty days too long for

this vital work to be endangered by my "leave of absence" and hereby submit my resignation for the good of the organization effective Friday, December 17, 1971.

I hasten to add that my work with the SCLC has been most valuable and fulfilling, and I deeply regret now to break my connection with it.

As we go separate roads, I pray that our goals will remain united. We must feed the hungry, clothe the naked, and set the captive free.

Respectfully yours,

Jesse Louis Jackson, The Country Preacher

The surprise announcement was a complete turnabout from what Jackson had said on March 22, 1971, shortly after the death of Urban League director Whitney Young in Lagos, Nigeria, where both leaders had been attending an Afro-American culture event. A move had been precipitated for Jackson to succeed Young in the Urban League post. At that time, Jackson publicly scuttled any notions about his leaving SCLC: "Dr. King left a legacy behind when he established SCLC and I'm going to stick around and reap the dividends of that legacy. I'm not going to leave SCLC to start my own civil rights group as some have suggested. Nor do I intend to join another existing civil rights group because it would not accomplish anything meaningful for the Civil Rights Movement. Jumping organizations doesn't alter the quality of human life. Although there is a degree of conflict within the organization and occasionally my leadership is challenged that is no reason for me to walk off. Divorce is seldom the answer to conflict. Civilized men resolve conflict by communication and confrontation, not by resorting to suicide."

That Jackson's public pronouncements were contradictory did not mean that he was in conflict with himself. Leaving SCLC was his declaration of independence, his passport to freedom, perhaps a more manly thing to do than his prior efforts of sabotaging rather than supporting Abernathy's attempts to perpetuate King's legacy.

Summing up his own feelings about the resignation, Jackson said, "I have good reason to leave. I need air. I need room to breathe. To live is to suffer and I stuck it out to that point because I had to find myself. But when it becomes clear that two people can't work together, they should amicably divorce. If the baby stays in the womb too long, it destroys both the parent and the child. I leave in peace. I'm not going to say anything unkind about Abernathy. When I was around twenty, I left home to get married. I sometimes visit my folks but I don't stay too long because I'm grown now. That's how I feel about leaving SCLC. But let's not talk about a split. Let's just look at it as the movement marching on."

Yet, Jackson's resignation was received with bitterness, as if it was better to be joined in misery than for either to be free to live separate in harmony. The unpalatability of Jackson's act was also a result of the hard realization that SCLC had lost its brightest star, its greatest fund raiser, its most articulate spokesman, even though Jackson's efforts in these areas were always highly criticized. But once removed, what was left?

For these reasons, as well as for those included below in SCLC's response, despite Jackson's being looked upon as a belligerent-arrogant-but-kicking-egotistical pain-in-the-ass, Abernathy and his board initially refused to accept his resignation.

Initially, on December 16, the Reverend Abernathy said, "We will not accept the resignation of the Reverend

Jesse L. Jackson until he gives an accounting of hundreds of thousands of dollars and explains the operation of Black Expo. Mr. Jackson must clean his house before he leaves. I never thought it would come to the point that a brother would quit and walk out on the movement started by the late Dr. Martin Luther King, Jr., rather than to deal forthrightly with the issues. I cannot in good conscience, at this time, accept Mr. Jackson's resignation since so many matters are pending and yet unresolved."

Later, a more temperate response was sent via telegram by the Reverend Joseph Lowery, SCLC board chairman: "Jackson is choosing to abandon the movement started by the late Dr. Martin Luther King, Jr., which all of us as a team have tried to carry on. While we have long been aware of Jackson's impatience with the restraint that organizational discipline dictates, we hoped that his concern and commitment to the movement would override his personal ambition and we could continue to move forward in an effective crusade against poverty and injustice. We regret that he wishes to quit in the midst of so many unanswered and unresolved questions, one of which involved the establishment of corporations under his leadership as an employee. We regret that he wishes to quit and to lead members of the Chicago chapter to quit in the midst of these unanswered questions. As we stated in our advice to Jackson on Friday, December 3, we were compelled to put him on leave with pay, while we met with him and officials of the Chicago chapter to clarify all matters related to the SCLC program and structure in Chicago. We regret he wishes to quit rather than deal realistically and forthrightly with these matters. In our efforts to include him as a member of the team, we have held several meetings with him, calling attention to his repeated violations of organizational policy and discipline. One such instance was establishment of another corporation in 1970 under his leadership without our knowledge

or authority. Breadbasket Commercial Association resulted, to say the least, in a serious cleavage in the ranks of the
Chicago movement.

"In spite of our continued efforts to work with Jesse
as a valued member of the team, he continued to violate
organizational policy and now he has responded to our
attempt to firm up our differences and to clear up matters
relating to SCLC by refusing to work with us and quitting.

"We tender our regrets to Mr. Jackson, however, in
the spirit of love and nonviolence, and we will continue
our struggle, to help the poor in this nation. In the spirit of
our founder, Dr. King, we hold our arms open to Jesse to
remain and of course work within the rules and policy of
our organization as a part of a redemptive fellowship of
concern to liberate the oppressed. If, however, he insists on
leaving, we can do none other than wish him Godspeed. If
he and members of SCLC Chicago chapter insist upon
quitting and his attempt is to serve the needs of the poor,
our executive committee has determined that we turn over
to him the members of the Chicago chapter, the building
now known as Dr. King's workshop, where the offices are
located and which we obtained at our expense upon the
request of Mr. Jackson."

And finally, Abernathy resigned himself to the
inescapable. If SCLC did not now move forward as a viable
organization, could Jackson still be held culpable? After
three years of attempting to hold the threat to his
leadership in abeyance, the menace was gone. Abernathy
said, "I've received many calls from Chicago from people
expressing their confidence in me. No person is indispen-
sable. There will be a movement in Chicago."

The pleas, the insinuations that Jackson was transferring illegal funds into his own movement, the allegation
that he was turning his back on Martin Luther King's
legacy, all fell on deaf ears. With his Chicago support
firmly intact, the fast-stepping Jackson, by December 18,

had successfully lined up national support, pulling in his countless IOU's.

On Christmas Day, 1971, in the Metropolitan Theater, a child was christened. It was a day of jubilee. It was not the time for considering rights or wrongs or for searching for deeper meanings. Somehow anything less than applause seemed sacrilegious.

But the irony of it all still strained for recognition. Shortly before his death, Dr. King had angrily told Jackson: "If that's what you want, for God's sake, go ahead and carve out your own niche." Did Dr. King ever dream that Jackson would take his advice literally, severely crippling the organization that King had founded as Jackson pursued his own personal ambition?

11

*I accept this award in the spirit of a
curator of some precious heirloom
which he holds in trust for its true
owners—all those to whom beauty
is truth and truth beauty, and in
whose eyes the beauty of genuine
brotherhood and peace is more
precious than diamonds or silver
or gold.*

**From Martin Luther King, Jr.'s acceptance speech,
Nobel Prize ceremony, December 10, 1964.**

Tears traced the heavy furrows of his face as he fondled
the crypt of his ardent confidant, whom death had
released from the pathos that had been his alone to bear,
but which he could not bear. The Reverend Ralph D.
Abernathy turned to reporters, invading the sanctity of
that private moment, and pleaded for solitude: "Let me
be, I must talk to Martin now."

Hours before, the president of the Southern Christian
Leadership Conference (SCLC) had sent shock waves
across the nation by announcing his intention of resigning.
On July 6, 1973, after sixteen years of service in SCLC,

Abernathy could no longer ignore the thunderous silence of black America.

It was as if all the glowing shibboleths of the sixties had been irreverently hurled back on SCLC's doorstep for self-examination. The weight of change had detoured it from its once evangelical mission of redeeming the soul of America. Now one could only hope that SCLC could redeem itself. Whereas the black-and-white-together movement people had once locked arms in the face of danger singing "We Shall Overcome" with stamina and conviction, the lyrics were now phrased in skeptical interrogatives: "Can we overcome—ourselves?" And blacks were singing it alone.

Once the Jackson personality was removed from SCLC, the eye was no longer astigmatized by the extraneous. Robbed of Jackson, who refracted analysis away from SCLC to himself, one could gaze deeply into its marrow.

Stripped of its glamorous deception, the once premier organization had become old and wizened, with a spirit and the wherewithall to survive in the 1970s held by the very few. If SCLC were not dead, its signs of life had become so faint that an obituary should at least be readied.

On the national front, it seemed as if Abernathy had never left King's Atlanta grave site, as he continued to linger in morbidity on July 6, 1973. Forever reaching and looking back to Martin Luther King, Abernathy had tried to organize the black poor with the emotional instruments of sentiment and reverence for the memory of Dr. King. He hardly ever emerged as his own man, with his own style and programs. On the other hand, the Reverend Jesse Jackson used the King imagery to assist in the transference of emotional dependency and to obfuscate his ascendance. Today he is gradually shifting the symbolism to the background.

When Whitney Young died, the Urban League contin-

ued into the next era under Young's successor Vernon
Jordan. When Martin Luther King died, instead of canoniz-
ing his legacy into a framework of new ideas, for the most
part SCLC allowed King's memory to stagnate, making
dwarfs out of them. Not until the summer of 1973 did
SCLC seem to be emerging from its somnambulistic
stumblings when Hosea Williams challenged the organization to "incorporate the era of Dr. King into the era of
Ralph Abernathy. The late Martin Luther King, Jr., was
the greatest man who trod the earth since Jesus Christ, but
he is dead now and that is a fact of life that we must
accept. We must carry on the legacy that he left us."
Williams is now a Georgia state legislator.

For five years, SCLC and Breadbasket had been mired
in a succession of irreconcilable conflicts over the leader.
At no point in their post-King history had the organizations
focused with such frenzied intensity on where they should
be going. The mission. And without missions what good
are men?

As in any social evolution, change creates both
victims and victors. Abernathy became the prey of
progress as the movement forked. One branch moved
ahead building political and economic beachheads on the
inroads established in the sixties. The other lumbered in
place. Where Abernathy stood, to the left and to the right
nothing was intact. SCLC arrived at this juncture by not
arriving. As history zigzagged tumultuously forward, SCLC
stood still, dazzled by its string of victories, all belonging
to the past.

The past—an ebullient era of black revolt and white
response—was synonymous with SCLC. With King at
SCLC's helm, it shook loose the Civil Rights Act of 1964,
the Voting Rights Act of 1965, and days after King's
assassination, President Johnson muscled through the 1968
Housing Bill. Thus, under the coalition leadership of
Martin Luther King, Jr., blacks had made more legislative

advances in a decade than had been made since Reconstruction.

And in the most cruel set of ironies, SCLC joined the legions of the vanquished simply by not leading the trends the organization itself had created. As SCLC drooled in a dazed fixation on the past, Ralph Abernathy became the victim instead of the victor as the movement gained momentum, literally running over him. Black people soon forgot the connection of events which brought them to a point where they could be seated more than 400 strong at a 1972 Democratic Convention. Perhaps it is the tendency of all people to applaud not what was done for them yesterday but what is being done for them today.

Needs are the basis of organizations and bring them into existence. Use sustains them. To survive they must remain necessary, which SCLC failed to do. Bernard Lee, administrative assistant to the Reverend Abernathy, admitted as much: "The kind of organization Dr. King left at his death was not sufficient to deal with the problems of today and they were never updated. We needed a refurbishing of the whole system. We should have reorganized ourselves to deal with the economic and political needs of the 1970s. Our greatest value to this country was to reorder the priorities of this nation, but so far we have failed to do so."

Noah Robinson, who replaced his brother as national director of Operation Breadbasket, added: "The men who yesterday were effective at leading protest marches may not have been able to adjust to the modern requisites for organizational survival and relevance—mobilizing masses to secure economic gains."

Coupled with the problems of being an anachronism in a movement in which it once was the innovator, SCLC, with the loss of Jackson, its most glamorous figure, and Breadbasket, its most relevant program, floundered without substance or style. As detailed earlier, SCLC could have functioned quite well without a charismatic leader, if it had been organized within the framework of substantive programs. But SCLC was organized around the persuasive personality of one man—Dr. King. Once the magic and mystique of King were removed, followed by Jackson, and the lack of programs became acute, Abernathy could hold on to neither staff nor supporters.

Caught between the national blackout on civil rights and the attitude of many blacks and whites alike that SCLC was a dying organization, donations to SCLC declined to the point that by early in 1972, twenty-one staff members were forced to resign. Two key national SCLC staffers, Stony Cooks, executive director, and Tom Offenburger, director of public relations, joined the campaign staff of the Reverend Andrew Young, to aid in his successful bid for Congress. By the summer of 1973, SCLC's budget, which had often before soared past $1 million annually during the peak of King's career, enabling it to employ 175 full-time staff members, had dwindled to a $75,000 yearly deficit and only twenty staff members remained. Abernathy himself offered several reasons for the financial crisis.

Speaking in Philadelphia in August 1973, Abernathy said, "Whites who formerly contributed large amounts of money to the support of the SCLC movement when it emphasized 'peaceful resistance' have become disillusioned with the negative civil rights rhetoric—'cries against integration and against nonviolence.' They have lumped all civil rights organizations together regardless of ideology and cut off their financial support."

The strained relationship growing between Abernathy and King's widow, Coretta, surfaced when he said that if Mrs. King had donated more money to SCLC instead of funneling donations into the Martin Luther King, Jr., Center for Social Change, "we wouldn't be in such a bind." But Abernathy quickly added, "I don't blame Mrs.

King for anything, I wish her well in all she's doing." (Mrs. King has, understandably, stayed aloof from both Abernathy and Jackson since the power struggle.)

As Hosea Williams explained it, although Coretta King did pay some of SCLC's bills, the multimillion dollar King Center in Atlanta, which Mrs. King is building as a monument to her late husband, drained much of the contributions intended for SCLC. "When he was alive, it was an honor to write a check made out to Martin Luther King, Jr. I would say that 40 percent of our funds came in that way. When he was killed, he had made one great mistake. He didn't leave a will. After the murder, donations poured in. So we immediately got our lawyers working on setting up a Martin Luther King Foundation. And we put every dime under the foundation account. But, Mrs. King got everything, including all the funds set aside in the foundation.

"There are many people today who still write checks in the name of Martin Luther King, Jr., or the foundation in his name. But what they don't know is that SCLC, which was entrusted with carrying on his work, does not get one penny of it. It all goes to Mrs. King, who is trying to build a $40-million edifice."

When in Chicago on July 21, Abernathy also lambasted the black middle class as a contributor to SCLC's budget woes. "The trouble with blacks who have a good job and live on the lakefront is that they forgot the bridges that brought them across. But you'd better know that the Jews never forget Israel. The problem is that black people are just giving lip service to Martin's movement. They take a trip and look at his tomb and then go on back to business as usual. I'm tired of blacks spending their money on dope, liquor, big cars, and fabulous furs. If poor people are unable to finance the movement but can and will supply the troops, then certainly the middle-class black people who have 'arrived' and now receive fairly decent salaries should supply the finances."

Although Abernathy's attack upon the nature of the black middle class seemed justified, his remarks were strongly criticized by Chicago civic leaders, people such as Edwin (Bill) Berry, veteran civil rights leader and the past executive director of the Chicago Urban League. Berry said, "I think he's wrong, very wrong. I don't think blacks have abandoned Ralph. I think he simply failed to carry out a professional fund-raising program. Folks won't give you money without being asked. They won't even pay a gas bill unless you send them one. I worked as a fund raiser for SCLC for five years during King's leadership. But since then, I have not been asked to do one thing, even though Ralph knew the role I had played. If he missed me in Chicago, he must have missed a lot of others. Ralph is disillusioned, bitter, hurt, and probably suffering from battle fatigue. Battling this whole business of race relations can be as bad as the mud of Vietnam."

Certainly the Reverend Ralph Abernathy has been dragged through the muck and mud of humiliation and frustration enough times to snuff the fire of any man. Abernathy said that in his eighteen years in the movement, he had been imprisoned thirty-six times; his home had been bombed; his church dynamited; he was being sued for $3 million; his automobile had been taken away and sold at public auction, and some property inherited from his family had been taken away and sold in an effort to satisfy an unjust judgment.

Consequently, when Ralph Abernathy announced on July 6, 1973, that he would make his resignation official at the sixteenth annual SCLC convention held in Indianapolis, on August 16, most people believed him. He was tired. Public and financial support had severely waned and certainly he had paid enough "dues" to leave with honor. But if anybody had listened closely to his words, delivered at a mass rally in his honor in Chicago, it would have been evident that Abernathy, like Jackson, had a flair for the dramatic, and was merely setting the stage for a comeback, hoping to win a vote of confidence from black and poor Americans. In Chicago, Abernathy had told a dismal turnout of less than 200 supporters: "I do not see an individual on the horizon at this point who is dedicated enough to the welfare of the poor to take over SCLC." Seemingly on cue, one of his aides stepped forward and shouted, "No one but you," a chant that was suddenly picked up by the crowd. On TV that night, the staged performance reaffirmed that Abernathy did, in fact, have mass support.

Before leaving the podium, Abernathy didn't fail to take a swipe at Jackson. Once, since the split, he had appeared at Operation PUSH, which convinced many that the ill will between him and Jackson had been resolved. But that night Abernathy, without mentioning Jackson's name, told how he really felt, "No super black cat riding an ebony charger is going to ride in, swinging his sword to guarantee your freedom. You are your own leaders. I don't see another leader with enough integrity for me to put my stamp of approval on him to take over SCLC. Every leader I know is trying to get rich himself. And they're so full of trickery. They are all scheming and trying to make headlines and get on the cover of *Time*."

Abernathy's cut at Jackson was intended to quash a movement that was swelling among some SCLC board members to elect Jackson the new SCLC president, if Abernathy could be convinced to follow through on his announced resignation. Jackson's name was widely circulated as one of the leading contenders for the SCLC post, along with Walter Fauntroy, a nonvoting congressman from the District of Columbia, an SCLC board member and a director of the Martin Luther King, Jr., Center for Social Change in Atlanta; the Reverend Wyatt T. Walker, an SCLC board member and former administrative assistant to vice-president designate Nelson Rockefeller; and King's widow, Coretta. Both Fauntroy, who was not likely to step backward from Congress to civil rights, and Mrs. King quickly refused the offer. Popular support called for Jackson, with about half the SCLC board members agreeing that Jackson should assume the presidency, or at least merge PUSH with SCLC. Although it pleased Jackson that some of the board members had finally come around to agreeing with what he had told them all along—that he was more capable of leading SCLC than Abernathy—he adopted a wait-and-see attitude. Privately, he told supporters on the SCLC board that he was interested, but publicly he said, "I'm not looking for something to be president of. I am president of PUSH, which is already in fifteen cities. And it is growing." This was Jackson's way of not pushing for the presidency if Abernathy's resignation was just grandstanding, which it turned out to be.

As expected, on August 16, events at the SCLC convention ran close to script. Since Abernathy's announced resignation in July, his aides had been scurrying across the country drumming up support for Abernathy's retention. On the convention floor, his aides continued to work for his support among the 1,000 delegates attending the convention. In light of the enthusiasm among the conventioneers, the SCLC board of directors voted not to accept Abernathy's ·resignation. Many of the delegates burst into applause at the news. Eventually pandemonium broke loose. The call for Abernathy lasted for a full hour, with the SCLC president imbibing every dram of the long-awaited feeling of being needed. Few could begrudge him his joyous intoxication after so many years of public neglect. Finally, making his way through the mayhem to the podium, the rejuvenated leader leaned over to the mike and intoned: "I feel now, that not only do I have a mandate from Martin and from God, but also from Black America."

Perhaps the who-is-the-leader controversy plaguing SCLC since the death of King was at last reconciled. But

since the more essential question of what-is-the-program
had not been settled, it may well mean that nothing had
been settled. The proper equation seemingly attached to
civil rights groups is either substance or style. SCLC had
neither. Unless it can develop one or the other or ideally
some proper blend of both, SCLC seems destined to being
run over by the very parade it started.

In Chicago, SCLC never got off the ground after
Jackson's departure. Although there were many problems,
the most stubborn logjam was just as SCLC nationally
could not move forward from the shadow of King, so too
did SCLC in Chicago become frozen in place under the
shadow of Jackson.

There was also a hardly genteel, near vulgar, squabble
over where the mantle of King belonged—SCLC or PUSH.
The dispute was often disgustedly referred to as "fighting
over the robe," as the Romans did after the Crucifixion.
Almost forgotten in the local scramble for self-importance
was that the nobility of brotherhood knows no organizational boundaries. And it seemed that the principle itself
had grown too large for SCLC— and PUSH, as well.

Abernathy named Jackson's brother, Noah Robinson,
director of Operation Breadbasket; the Reverend C. T.
Vivian, former director of SCLC affiliates under Dr. King,
was named executive director, and the Reverend John
Thurston became president of the Chicago chapter.

Initially, SCLC soared on a spirit of hope and
commitment. Abernathy pulled together a coalition of
more than seventy ministers with large congregations to
provide troops and financial support. The ministers, many
of whom had been displaced by the businessmen in
Jackson's movement, seemed adamant in their determination to aid SCLC in continuing as a living memorial to
King in Chicago.

SCLC's programs for Chicago were ambitious, but
even at the outset announcements of intent always carried

an underlying preoccupation with Jackson, who had completely detached himself from the SCLC picture, busying himself with launching Operation PUSH.

Noah Robinson had indicated on April 10, 1972, that the programmatic thrust of the new Operation Breadbasket would not include the shortcomings existing in his brother's movement. "Ours will be a seven-day-a-week program, rather than a once-a-week-Saturday-morning production. Our program will provide jobs, bid minority contractors, speak to inadequate housing and health. In short, it will include everyone and not operate where just four or five black businessmen get rich and the rest of the black community acts as just consumers. We are trying to take the difficult road of building a systematic structure instead of concentrating on charisma. What you will never see from us is publicity for publicity's sake."

Correct to a point in his assessment of his brother's imperfections, Robinson soon proved that while he would not imitate the mistakes of Jesse Jackson, he was quite capable of initiating some blunders of his own.

With all the social, political, and economic crises festering in the black and poor communities of Chicago, blacks watched in disbelief as SCLC embarked on a narrow, self-defeating course of proving their worth by attempting to upstage Jackson.

One such effort was the decision to hold mass meetings on Saturday mornings at the same time Jackson was holding his, only a few blocks away. While crowds at PUSH were numbering in the thousands, SCLC had difficulty attracting more than one hundred supporters. Because the meetings were poorly organized, unimaginative, and slow paced, the crowd soon dwindled to twenty followers. Its radio broadcast was summarily canceled. And after the meetings began to be preempted by gang members and other undesirables, they too were quietly phased out. It seemed ludicrous at the outset to attempt to beat Jackson, the master promoter, at a game in which he had perfected the rules. After five years of attending Jackson's Saturday morning forums, I had become accustomed to near perfection. Once provided with a basis of comparison, I, at least, gained more appreciation for the inspirational and informative community forums Jackson provided.

In the sum total of things, how many followers SCLC could draw was irrelevant. The issue should have been, "How many could they serve?" The few direct-action programs which had been launched fizzled. SCLC complained about Jackson not following through on supermarket covenants promising jobs and upgraded employment opportunities, which again was a correct evaluation. However, when SCLC declared war on Jewel Tea food stores, not more than twelve picketers showed up, and the boycott was soon dropped.

The Chicago SCLC chapter also suffered from a severe leadership and financial crisis. A top SCLC official resigned under a cloud of charges of missing funds. A board member, Mrs. Katherine Ladner, complained, "We had worked so hard to raise money, but by the time the minister left, we could hardly pay the staff. I am not accusing anyone, just wondering where the money went. That money could have been used to pay the workers' salaries." But salaries had not been paid, forcing the lower echelon workers to resign after picketing SCLC in a futile attempt to receive back wages.

Noah Robinson also resigned. Although he had organized the only successful fund-raising event to keep Chicago SCLC afloat, he was thrust into a position of double jeopardy because he was Jackson's brother. Handsome, articulate, aggressive, with an inflated ego easily punctured, he was too much like Jackson to be trusted, some SCLC officials felt. "Blood is thicker than water and he might sell us out, if the choice came down to SCLC or his· brother. One member of the Jackson family is enough," a board member said.

Robinson's presence prompted haunting visions of his turning into a Jacksonlike superstar, who would use the organization and the symbolism of King as a springboard for self-promotion and glory. As a result of the unfounded suspicion, Noah Robinson was gagged and bound into such a low-profile position that neither his rhetoric nor his technical talents could be utilized to help push SCLC along. After Robinson bowed out and returned to his business, the Breadbasket Commercial Association, the SCLC chapter was administered temporarily by Ben Branch, a Chicago musician and bandleader. Today, it matters little who the leader is because there is nothing of substance to lead. The Chicago SCLC chapter is still traveling on a collision course with overinflated egos, misdirected priorities, and an overall lack of leadership and purpose. Periodically statements are issued promising a revitalization, but nothing concrete emerges. All that remains is hope wearing thin from the black masses, especially on the west side, who remember what Dr. King and SCLC stood for in the past.

12

*He . . . must not be hindered by
the name of goodness, but must
explore if it be goodness.*

Ralph Waldo Emerson

And what of Jackson?

As it stands today, his mountain top is within reach.
Jesse Jackson may well become the singular most powerful black man in America since Booker T. Washington.

In Washington's famed Atlanta Exposition address of
1895, he appeased the conscience of the Post-
Reconstruction South with: "In all things that are purely
social we can be as separate as the fingers, yet one as the
hand in all things essential to mutual progress." After the
speech, in which Washington also urged Negroes to "cast
down your buckets where you are," he was immediately
projected as the undisputed leader of 10 million of his race

by both the Northern and Southern press. Washington's speech was made at a time when bitterness between the North and South, stemming from the Civil War and Reconstruction, had ended. On the question of race, the U.S. Supreme Court, along with the proliferation of Jim Crow laws, cemented the pervading mood that suffrage and social mixing had been a grave mistake. By advocating that Negroes should sacrifice political and social equality for advancement through industrial education and business development, Washington eloquently parroted the view of his Age, at a time when America was emerging as the leading industrial nation in the world.

As he captured the spirit of the mercantile age, Washington's career as a race leader blossomed into a potent force wielded by no other black man. The crux of his power was: (1) Since he was a "safe and constructive leader," he had the complete cooperation of the white press. His activities were so fully reported in the white press that he became one of the best known Americans of his day. In 1901, his autobiography *Up From Slavery* was translated into at least a dozen languages. He was in such demand as a public speaker that he spent a substantial part of every year on the lecture circuit, with his pronouncements widely disseminated in white journals as the Gospel. He was frequently characterized as the Moses of his people and portrayed as almost a saint. (2) Washington showed a remarkable capacity for winning white financial support for the Tuskegee Institute, which during his reign became the capital of the Negro nation. One of Tuskegee's biggest donors was Andrew Carnegie, who bestowed upon Washington a gift of money which guaranteed him and his wife an income for life. (3) While presenting himself as a modest, self-effacing leader, Washington controlled the flow of white philanthropy, and few Negro institutions could receive grants without his sanction. (4) During Theodore Roosevelt's administration, he not only controlled considerable political patronage of blacks, but also of some Southern whites. (5) A fierce in-fighter, he coopted the Afro-American Council, the leading civil rights group of his day. (6) As founder of the National Negro Business League, which claimed 300 chapters across the country, Washington was lauded as a black business expansionist. But most important, Washington's Tuskegee machine was able to squash most opposition from blacks by using the Negro press against his critics. "Through the influence of strategically placed friends, by judicious use of advertisements and subscriptions and subsidies for special issues, through control over the Negro Press Associations, in some cases by supplying actual editorial copy, in half a dozen instances by substantial cash contributions and in two cases by securing part ownership in a journal, Washington exercised wide influence."*

A hard look at Jackson, in six major areas, shows why he is almost home.

First, Jackson has mastered the art of evoking fierce racial pride, looking militant, acting militant and at the same time accommodating white power, from which he marshals vast support.

No better illustration of Jackson's adroitness in maintaining the allegiance of white conservatives, while at the same time appealing to the passions of his race, is a statement given page-three prominence in the prestigious *Chicago Tribune,* Sunday, May 19, 1974.

"Neither blacks nor whites really want integration, the Reverend Jesse Jackson said, and the time has come to abandon the fight to establish a racially integrated society . . . .

"People resist that. White people don't like to relate to it because of strong sexual overtones. They resent the

*August Meier, "Booker T. Washington and the Rise of the NAACP," *The Crisis* (Vol. 61, Feb. 1954).

thought of their daughter not only marrying a black person, but marrying a Japanese person or a Catholic person or any number of different persons. That's a hangup.

"A lot of blacks have a hangup, too, because integration suggests we are inferior and only by sitting next to white people, having white teachers, can we be somebody. . . . "

The date and the placement of Jackson's statement are significant. Jackson's go-slow-on-integration commentary appeared two days after the twentieth anniversary of the *Brown* vs. *Topeka Board of Education* Supreme Court ruling which held that "separate educational facilities are inherently unequal."

Jackson's conciliatory stance serves as a concession to turning the clock back on decades of hard-won legal gains by civil rights activists, including Dr. King. It did, however, win friends in the conservative belt, providing fuel for whites pleased with the status quo.

Ired by the can of worms Jackson opened, which prompted ultra-conservative commentators, such as Phyllis Schlafly—CBS "Spectrum"—to support his position, Ethel Payne, laureate columnist for the Sengstacke publications, was one of the few who took issue. In a May 28, 1974, column in the *Chicago Daily Defender*—"The Odd Couple—Jackson-Schlafly," Miss Payne wrote:

"The whole dialogue is patent nonsense. Mrs. Schlafly is eagerly signing up allies for her campaign to return the country to the status quo of pre-May, 1954, when the Supreme Court handed down its historic ruling. Wittingly, or unwittingly, I'm not sure which, Jesse Jackson has provided her with some fresh ammunition.

"It is dangerous because his rationale is so fuzzy. It is clear that he did not consult with people who have been involved in the battle for more than 20 years, like the NAACP and the Legal Defense Fund. Had he done so, he might not have gone off shooting from the hip on the subject, guaranteed to do nothing, but give him one more headline and create more mischief.

"Unfortunately, the whole issue of desegregation and bussing has been so politicized and used by demagogues on both sides to promote their own interests that too many of us can't see the forest for the trees. The victims are the children, black and brown and white, undereducated, unprepared for life, learning only to hate and distrust one another . . . .

"Jesse Jackson is smart and bright and able. But when the majority media anoint him as the Guru for Black People and he begins to believe his own press notices, then I worry and so do a lot of other folks."

Returning to 1895 gives reason for worry. One year later, the Supreme Court handed down *Plessy* vs. *Ferguson*—"the separate but equal doctrine." As Rayford W. Logan wrote: "The author of this book hazards the guess that Washington's Atlanta compromise address consoled the consciences of the judges of the Supreme Court who in *Plessy* vs. *Ferguson*, the following year, wrote into American jurisprudence one of its least defensible doctrines, the constitutionality of equal but separate accommodations.* "

It took fifty-four years to reverse *Plessy* vs. *Ferguson* to bring blacks to *Brown* vs. *Topeka*.

In interviews with a number of white politicians, corporate leaders, law enforcement agents and newspaper executives, who choose to be anonymous, I recorded the following attitudes:

1. "Jackson is not violating the public interest in any way. It is questionable what is done with PUSH funds, but

---

The Negro in American Life and Thought (New York: Macmillan, 1965).

contributions to it are give-away money from whites and the other is black people's money. Now in a sense he is immune from scrutiny—yes, perhaps, even from the IRS. Black money going back and forth is not a great concern. The white community is concerned with protecting itself from the black community. Protecting blacks from blacks is not a white priority."

2. "Off the cuff. Those covenants are the whitest demands I've ever seen. They are the best PR a company would want. We look good. PUSH looks good. And when somebody asks about progress we give our own employment statistics, the same data PUSH uses. Then we might buy some tables or supply some money for his PR purposes. See, we're looking ahead. At some point in time, we can get a lot of other black groups off our tails. When they come to us begging for contributions for this and that cause we can say we gave to PUSH. You know, the 'we gave at the office' type of thing. In the covenants they ask for x-amount for black philanthropy. Okay, we're giving, but through PUSH. It makes it easier for everybody. No, I'm not worried about what Jackson does with the money. He could paper his walls with it for all I care, as long as there are no boycotts. And look how long there hasn't been a boycott—since the late sixties, I think. So there are a lot of people who feel like I do. He's not asking for much. Jackson is a very reasonable man."

3. "I look at Jesse in terms of cause and effect, what are the odds, what are the options. It's not that I am dispassionate or cold, but I just think my approach is more calculating. While others seem to believe the words, I look at the effect in dollars and cents. I'll say this for the man, I don't know why he talks all that country talk on Saturday mornings when he sure knows how to talk our language. He could write his own ticket as an advisor on corporate affairs. But nobody has been able to persuade him to do that. I believe he is basically an honest man. He just knows

how to play two ends against the middle. Nothing wrong
with that."

4. "To me Jackson is doing at least three things
right: he is not pushing for open housing in the suburbs, he
is not pushing hard for jobs in the labor unions, and the
political machine that keeps the Loop and the business
district flourishing is by no means jeopardized by Jackson's rap. Chicago is no place for heroism. As long as he
stays on target Jesse is good for Chicago, the same way
Daley is. Twice I've heard about the Mayor showing up at
Expo giving Jackson a soul handshake. Well, if I was the
Mayor, I'd be happy with Jackson's performance too.
Daley and Jackson have much more in common than most
people think."

That Jackson is a safe and constructive leader in the
eyes of the white establishment is not necessarily a
disdainful criticism. Rather it points to the ugly reality of
the tightrope he must walk in order to be of assistance to
any segment of his race. In America, there is a thin line
between heroism and martyrdom.

On the road Jackson is traveling, the only way for
him to make it is to play it safe. But at the same time it is
important for other blacks to see what is in the realm of
the possible for Jackson in order that they may work
around him and the problem. Jackson's role-playing
creates the aura of comfortableness in the minds of blacks
and whites, when in reality none of the basic power levers
have changed since Dr. King came to Chicago in 1966.

On the political stage, Jackson's actions, for whatever
reasons, are ineffectual and in some situations obstructionist, as pointed out earlier. On the economic front, he is
in step with the times. Black capitalism was a program
pushed by Nixon. As in the era of Booker T. Washington,
black capitalism is seen as a panacea to the race problem.
It is in line with the work ethic. And there can be a
plethora of individual "success" stories that create the
impression that blacks are making great strides when the

masses are standing still or at worst going backward. And then there is open housing—a civil right yet to be realized in Chicago, which Jackson does not touch. Remember the bad press, the bloodshed, the explosion of white rage that Dr. King, whom few thought of as militant, stirred up by pushing on that issue. It is still one of the most incendiary issues in Chicago. It becomes increasingly crucial as the Chicago public school system follows a pattern of separate and unequal instruction and as industry-related jobs— 90,000 since 1960—continue shifting to the suburbs. Jackson's leadership says to blacks "cast down your buckets where you are" in your own businesses and in your own neighborhoods. Most whites agree.

White capital, as it was with Washington, is a growing source of Jackson's influence. Washington's white benefactors were Andrew Carnegie, John D. Rockefeller, the president of Standard Oil, and Julius Rosenwald of Sears, Roebuck and Company. In Jackson's era they are Hugh Hefner, the Jewel Tea Company, the Gulf Oil Company, Sears, Roebuck and Company, and the Ford Foundation.

No other black man in America, except Washington, has been given the green light by the media czars. Where have you not seen Jackson's face? On the cover of *Time?* Full-length in *Playboy, Penthouse,* the *New York Times, People?* On TV specials on all three networks. In Chicago, if a week goes by and Jackson's name is not in the news, he is calling on the print executives for an explanation. His is a household face. Why?

As J. Saunders Redding wrote in a critique of white media treatment of Booker T. Washington, "From white America's point of view, the situation was ideal. White America has raised this man to power and it was in white America's interest to keep him there. All race matters would be referred to him and all decisions affecting the race would seem to come from him."* What was true for

They Came in Chains (Philadelphia: Lippincott, 1973).

Washington is also true for Jackson. Would the white
media project and protect something that was against their
self-interest?

Washington hobnobbed with the white publishing
barons, which in return evoked certain unheard of gratuities. Jackson performs this role in grand style, although
the reporters at the bottom he can barely stomach.

A column by Frances Ward in the March, 1972,
Chicago Journalism Review accurately portrays Jackson's
role with his media "angels." Ward, a writer for the *Los
Angeles Times*, reported:

> Back in December 1968, most of the top
> executives and editorial personnel of Field En-
> terprises, Newspaper Division, held a meeting in
> the seventh floor dining room with one of
> Chicago's up and coming leaders—the Reverend
> Jesse L. Jackson. Jackson brought along to the
> meeting his trusted associate, the Reverend
> Calvin Morris. Every important Field executive
> was on hand.
>
> The session lasted more than two hours.
> When it was over, the Field execs were ecstatic
> with praise. One memorable comment came
> from *Chicago Sun-Times* Associate Editor Bob
> Kennedy. "Reverend Jackson," he intoned,
> "though I'm a conservative, I can live with you."
> Kennedy went on to tell everybody how easy it
> was for him, a confirmed economic and political
> conservative, to accept Jackson's program.
>
> Jackson, for his part, had simply outlined
> how he thought black communities could em-
> power themselves economically by stabilizing
> part of the wealth created there by consumer
> spending, then placing it in black-controlled
> financial institutions which presumably would

use it to further build the community. Another important facet of Jacksonian economics was the then-familiar Buy Black campaign, using the theory that if black consumers bought from black businesses, considerably more wealth could be generated for community betterment. And more jobs would be simultaneously created, thereby increasing the numbers and strength of black consumers.

Toward the end of the meeting, Jackson had warm words of praise for Irv Kupcinet [*Sun-Times* columnist] "for all the things you've done for us, Kup." It wasn't quite clear then what all the things were, but anybody who reads Kup's column these days surely knows. Hardly a week goes by without a couple of mentions of something from—or about— Jesse Jackson.

And that's the surest sign of change at the Field papers, for since that meeting, both the *Sun-Times* and *Daily News* have taken kindly to just about everything Jackson and Breadbasket have done. (By contrast, Jackson scores heavily with his Saturday morning audiences by flailing away at the white press for alleged sins of commission and omission.)

Jackson fails to note, however, that it has been the white press, which he frequently argues is "out to get him," that has been most generous to him. Most national publications, including *Time, Harper's,* now-defunct *Look,* and *Newsweek,* have done features on him, all overwhelmingly favorable.

A steady stream of favorable local stories, especially in the Field papers, have aided Jackson and PUSH incalculably in building a favor-

able image. In fact, Jackson has closer personal
relationships with more white media executives
than any other black leader in modern times—
including Whitney Young and Roy Wilkins.

And because of Jackson's militant-but-safe role, as
well as his adroitness in making friends in the right places,
the gratuities are well at hand. According to several
newsmen in Chicago, a WLS-TV official helped to provide
free "promos" for both an Expo and Family Affair
dinner in 1973. The offer to Jackson, according to some
WLS-TV employees, was "anything you want I'll give
you." On another occasion several writers—nationwide—
were contacted by a national network willing to pick up
the tab for a full-time public relations person for Jackson.
During PUSH Expo '74—September 25 through 29—WBBM-
TV, a CBS affiliate, underwrote the opening day breakfast
at a cost of $3,000. The station also gave a $10 dinner to 150
high school students, who assisted as volunteers. WMAQ-
TV, an NBC affiliate, "produced free promotional spots
for sixty-five stations across the nation," said Miss Ella
G'sell, press manager for WMAQ. "Although I can't quote
you a figure, when you count production costs and 'dubs'
in six different segments, the cost is astronomical." The
major networks cooperate with Jesse, promoting him on
TV specials and doing little favors for him so he won't stir
up flack from the FCC.
     Jackson is shrewdly squashing criticism and earnest
evaluation of him by the black press and those black
journalists who are employed by the white press. In his
day, Washington simply bought off some black publishers,
used others against his critics, and screamed traitors to
those blacks who dared challenge his authority. Some
Jackson tactics are right out of the Booker T. handbook
on how to deal with pesty journalistic nuisances. However,
Jackson has added a novel imperative: manipulation of the

Black Code. The Black Code à la Jackson comprises two elements: negation of Jackson, the symbol of blackness, is negation of the race and self; and criticism is disunifying, as if it is wiser to topple off a cliff unified than argue over direction and perhaps avoid the plunge. Blackness is one of those emotional codes that nobody can be against if he is black. But who is supplying the definition? Who is the highest authority on the Black Code? Jackson. What is Jackson's definition? It can mean anything depending on the occasion.

The black journalist in a white institution is in double jeopardy. Racism within is not a subject for debate; it is a truism. But demagoguery without, using the Black Code as a cudgel, is also a truism. Jackson has successfully managed to twist both perversions around by propagating the impression that any black journalist in a white institution is a pawn of the establishment. Of course, there is a way to disprove this: write articles lauding Jackson, the so-called symbol of blackness. Other novel additions to the Black Code for journalists are the labels Judas, traitor, enemy, or conspirator with the FBI or CIA. Propaganda being bandied like this destroys credibility, creates confusion, and could build up the atmosphere for personal injury. It takes only one hard-core zealot to use his own imagination to act out what is thought to be perceived by the leader as correct. Thus, the whole system works like Skinner's conditioning for mice. Reward the "good" journalist with adulation, which easily elevates him to celebrity status in some circles of the black community. Punish the "bad" journalist who analytically criticizes with "personal attacks."

Although interpretive criticism is the worst sign of treachery, a straight news story—balanced, taking no stand—causes severe retaliation. Although there are many examples, the case of Angela Parker is the best.

Ms. Parker broke the Expo '71 story by flying to

Atlanta to confirm or deny rumors surrounding the trade fair. It is significant to note that several other black reporters had the same information but chose not to release it.

After breaking the story, Ms. Parker walked into the Saturday morning meeting and was greeted with a hail of boos. For fifteen minutes Jackson talked about the treachery of black women, how she had gone to Atlanta to divide black men, and compared her to the woman who stabbed Dr. King in New York in the early sixties. All this produced thunderous approval from the audience. Later she received threatening phone calls, picketers arrived at her apartment, and finally she moved. Three years later the public and personal abuse continues.

Thus, Ms. Parker became the "whipping girl"—a lesson to any other black reporter who might dare step out of line. Today most black reporters on the white establishment press have been frozen into *omerta.* Knowing a noose awaits the Judas, many reporters circumvent Jackson by performing as expected.

Today, out of fourteen black journalists on the Chicago establishment press, there is only one black man fighting to invoke the public's right to know, using his forum to call for financial and programmatical accountability to blacks from Jackson, the leader of blacks. He will report accurately—the favorable as well as the unfavorable on the Country Preacher. Vernon Jarrett, a social historian and lecturer at Northwestern University, has seen the black intellects of the era come and go—W. E. B. Du Bois, Paul Robeson, Langston Hughes, et al. He can tell the real from the unreal. His sense of history spots what some of the younger journalists are seeing for the first time. He is a man hard to fool. But more than that, Jarrett analyzes contemporary white leaders with the same depth of perception, providing a model for other young blacks who must cope with both demagoguery and institutional racism.

Here are samples from two of his columns that deal
with the climate:

> Historically, black journalism has been un-
> der pressure from two formidable sources: Pow-
> erful white interests that used the denial of
> advertising income as a threat, and "powerful"
> black leaders of organizations who wanted to
> use black papers and writers for promotion-
> al purposes.
>
> Unfortunately, there are black writers in
> Chicago who respond fearfully to such pressures,
> especially when they know that some jive self-
> proclaimed "prophet" is given free time every
> Saturday morning to browbeat and slander any
> journalist who insists on taking the truth to the
> people—including the disregarded black masses.
>
> But that is not their only fear. They know
> something the public does not know. The
> Reverend Jesse Jackson has established a beauti-
> ful relationship with the big people who run
> several of our major newspapers, television
> channels, and radio stations. These are the
> people who helped make him a national leader.
>
> These concerned writers know that Jesse is
> acting out the big lie when he struts around
> trying to convince blacks that the white man
> doesn't like him.
>
> I firmly believe that the big white establish-
> ment fears the National Association for the
> Advancement of Colored People more than it
> does the potential of a Jesse Jackson. This
> example explains why:
>
> When it was revealed that the jobs of
> 16,000 black postal workers would be threat-
> ened if the work at the main Chicago post office
> were to be distributed through the suburbs,

guess who in 1971 was given the freedom to parade through the central post office? Big *bad* Jesse, who promised to save the black workers.

After all that *bad* talk he dropped from the scene. The Chicago branch of the NAACP had to take up the fight to the tune of $65,000 already spent in legal costs to really try to save these jobs which bring $243 million into the black community annually.

It is understandable that the men who control the Postal Service would prefer dealing with a loud-talking Messiah than grapple with the masses quietly organized to fight back. (*Chicago Tribune,* November 21, 1973.)

This is an open letter to a soul sister, a good and sincere woman who I am proud to look upon as a friend of many years. She is genuinely disturbed over my public criticisms of a nationally-known black personality. In substance, she asks this very common question: "Why should black people do their laundry in front of the enemy?" Here is my answer:

Dear sister: I understand your anguish and concern, for it is a problem that has plagued black people since the first black newspaper was launched over 146 years ago.

Secrecy and hidden agendas are the enemies of the common masses whether black, brown, yellow or white. Show me any movement wherein the leadership is overly protected from public observation and I will show you a movement that ends up as a disaster.

I'm sorry, sister, but in the specific instance of your anguish for me to remain silent about the often disgraceful conduct of your leader would mean my betrayal of the black masses who, like their misinformed white brothers and sisters, don't learn the truth about their leaders until some calamity occurs.

When your leader, the Reverend Jesse L. Jackson, visits the editors of daily newspapers for the implied threat of a picket line or boycott just because their black writers dare say what their white writers refused to say, then I must speak my piece.

When Mayor Daley issued Jackson one of those proclamations that he just recently denied Dick Gregory and Jackson later invited Daley to make a speech during the opening breakfast meeting of Expo '73, several young black journalists knew that Jackson had broken an agreement made among all the black organizations and leaders supporting U. S. Representative Ralph H. Metcalfe's Concerned Citizens for Police Reforms.

The agreement was that all of these supporting organizations would ignore Daley until he gave the black community the respect of meeting with Metcalfe and the CCPR on the south side. Daley thumbed his nose at all of us, but there he stood making a big speech at the opening of PUSH Expo '73, and the hand that thumbed his nose was clasping that of your leader, big, baaaad Jesse.

Two young black writers innocently wanted to check out just who authorized Jesse to make this move. On second thought they began to consider the vengeful reaction of both Jackson and Daley. The inquiring articles were never written.

Soul sister, I value your friendship but I'll

just have to risk losing it if you insist that I
remain quiet in such a climate and encourage
young black writers to make that awful detour
from the great tradition of forthright journalism.
(*Chicago Tribune,* November 23, 1973.)

Regardless of who is right, personal attacks on the
leader and by the leader are hardly justifiable. Sporadic
time-consuming diatribes, often escalating into vendettas,
deter both from performing more worthwhile objectives.
Ideally, both could aid each other in exposing and
addressing the pressing concerns of the black poor, the
elderly, and all other neglected minorities. However, it just
doesn't work that way. The Mayor runs the city. Jackson
runs around the city. Neither can be ignored. And since
Jackson speaks out on all issues, moves on all fronts, too,
often he becomes "the issue," making ideological head-on
collisions unavoidable.

In the establishment press, few white reporters cover
Jackson. In the few that do, Jackson most often is able to
surface bigotry or confusion. Many white reporters are not
certain whether or not they understand the "race problem." Often Jackson is able to reach into their psyches and
touch whatever confusion or prejudice that does exist.
Either because he has exposed the truth or in an effort to
prove to Jackson that he is not a racist, the white
journalist often justifies his or her "liberalism" with
favorable stories about the leader. Mike Royko, a *Chicago
Daily News* columnist, is a notable exception.

From the black journalistic institutions there is
overwhelming support. On the one hand, the Black Code
adhered to by the black press calls for projecting and
protecting most legitimate black leaders, including Jackson. On the other, Jackson has generously included the
bulk of the black press in his economic covenants
(see National Tea—Appendix). Since there are twelve

black newspapers fighting for the black market, the flow of ads Jackson directs their way is not an inducement to find fault with their benefactor. Thus either because of the economic quid pro quo or the adherence to the Black Code, the end result is a double gag. Except for the *Chicago Daily Defender*, balanced stories on the leader are the exception, rather than the rule.

In the past, the Negro or black press had a noble history of truth-slinging. Despite Booker T. Washington's awesome power, freedom writers such as Ida B. Wells Barnett, (editor of the Memphis *Free Speech*), William Monroe Trotter (editor of the *Boston Guardian*), and W. E. B. Du Bois checked and balanced the Tuskegee machine. Robert S. Abbott, founder of the *Chicago Defender*, criticized Marcus Garvey. Garvey, publisher of the *Negro World*, challenged Du Bois. There was a time when no one was sacrosanct to the crusading black journalist. There was a healthy balance which kept black leaders on their toes because they knew they were under the scrutiny of journalists who were fierce in their protection of the black masses. Although they vigilantly scrutinized black leaders, the black writers were not deterred from the main target—white racism. Hopefully, this tradition of the black press will be revitalized.

The Johnson Publication empire—WJPC radio, *Ebony, Jet, Black World*—aids Jackson's image making, although it is guided by somewhat different principles than those governing the black newspapers.

John H. Johnson had made his millions when Jackson hit Chicago with his Buy Black inducements. It has always been the tradition of Johnson to spotlight the attractive side of black America—its entertainers, its politicians and athletes. Thus, Jackson fits neatly into Johnson's framework. Rarely a week passes that Jackson does not appear inside the cover of *Jet*, if he is not featured on the cover. His Saturday morning broadcast is aired over WJPC radio, with Supreme Beauty Products, a Johnson subsidiary, serving as one of Jackson's sponsors. But oddly enough, Jackson's "exclusive home," according to the daily advertising hype, is WMBX-FM—a white-owned, automated "soul" station. His daily commentary, fed to forty-one other cities by the Black Audio Network, is heard on WMBX, and Jackson is the host of a weekly phone-in hot line, called "Jackson In Touch," the brainchild of his Chicago ad agency—Proctor and Gardner—which handles a sizeable chunk of Jackson's image making.

Splice together all the media fragmentations and one finds that the passions and prejudices existing in both white and black print institutions cancel each other out. The incredible end result is that Jackson has checked and balanced the press. He has authority without accountability to his race—the only group he is in the position to help or not help.

Du Bois warned Washington about an almost identical situation in his *Souls of Black Folk:* * "But the hushing of the criticism of honest opponents is a dangerous thing. Honest and earnest criticism from those whose interests are most nearly touched—criticism of writers by readers, of government by those governed, of leaders by those led—this is the soul of democracy and the safeguard of modern society."

Jackson reigns without opposition from his race. Within and without his organization he has countered all challenges to his leadership—imagined or real. From without, Jackson reigns unopposed through his ability to bring the affluent sectors of the black community together and to block areas of criticism from dissenters—most of whom are the unorganized black poor.

Washington's most scathing condemnations came from the talented tenth or the black intelligentsia. In

*(Chicago: A. C. McClurg & Co., 1903).

Jackson's case, the talented tenth—those blacks whose opinions are respected—are his greatest supporters.

The support for Jackson is threefold:

First, so much of the criticism surrounding Jackson comes from other displaced demagogues, the jealous, the envious, from narrow minds, often leading some to just ignore it all. No one respects accomplishment more than those who have striven to accomplish themselves. Jackson's braggadocio, his oratorical skill, his self-reliance, his intellectual cunning have made him a folk hero in many corridors. Those attributes alone, which are so much a model for black youth, perpetrate the attitude to forgive and forget whatever else he does or does not do.

Second, Jackson, a man who started out fighting the establishment, has become an establishment figure. Jackson directs the flow of millions to black corporations. He is positioning himself as the orchestrator of philanthropy to black institutions. An undying loyalty to Jackson makes good business sense, in the minds of many business leaders.

Third, from Jackson's immediate constituency there is strong adherence to the Black Code. In a real sense, Jackson has become Alpha and Omega. Nobody but nobody argues with the Prince.

What happens when it becomes inescapable that something is wrong? Is constructive criticism acceptable? No. To Jackson there is only one type of criticism—conspiratory. So what is the alternative? The following drifts away, Jackson's charismatic appeal attracts fresh blood. The staff leaves, usually in bitterness. And the board—usually people with prestige, status, position—leave in silence, resigning quietly, because they cannot afford the controversy that open disagreement, no matter how constructive, would cause. Board member Dr. Arnita Boswell, the sister of the late Whitney Young, resigned in 1974, following the proper movement protocol: silence, except to ask that her name be removed from

PUSH stationery. Lerone Bennett, noted historian, re-signed in silence. The only other method of criticism by board members is through leaks to the press. And depending on what member of the press the leak is dropped to, it may not be printed.

Echoing from the poorest section of Chicago is an extreme undercurrent of disillusionment. The black poor do not ask for much; yet they receive less. Their value is that, too often, they exist to serve the ends of politicians, poverty programs, and an assortment of black leaders who rise to prominence by being experts on their misery. The black poor do not ask much from Jackson. They ask only that they not be misrepresented. They ask that the media and all others leave them out of Jackson's constituency. Jackson and the talented tenth have not created any significant programs which, in their opinions, meaning-fully affect their lives. The sentiment is that the more Jackson is seen and heard, the more invisible and inaudible they become. And most detest being thrown into the constituency of a man, without his first earning their allegiance. Why are they not heard? Simply because in Chicago, Jackson is regarded as their voice. However, here is some commentary from the disregarded masses, as well as movement officials:

• Mrs. Anna Moore, a west-side housewife: "Jack-son is no hero to us. He couldn't draw a crowd of twenty people in Lawndale. Jackson doesn't want to be bothered with us. We're too poor. He gravitates around people with promise. Not us."

• Clarence Grant, unemployed: "Jesse Jackson says he represents us but I have never seen him address our needs. We need housing, jobs, our schools are falling down. We never see him and can't even contact him personally to help us."

• A welfare mother: "The only leader that walked among us was Dr. King. He lived with us. He touched us personally to attempt to lead better lives."

- A south-side tradesman: "Jesse leading the poor? Is that right? I didn't know he was leading anybody but black businessmen."

- Barbara Eubanks, an assembly line worker: "Jesse Jackson says he represents me on the west side but I have never seen him over here. So how can he represent me or the west side?"

- Richard Barnett, who lives and works on the west side: "The newspapers project Jesse as a poor folks leader, but he is not, although he could be. The newspapers can make him anything he wants to be, since he is a media creation."

- Leon Davis, former PUSH political education director: "The movement is not as sophisticated as the poor people. We should talk to the poor people and share with them our expertise so they could develop their own resources. The King movement developed leaders in different communities. But is it as important for Jesse to develop leaders as it is for him to project himself as the only leader? That's a good question."

- A south-side woman, who was interviewed at PUSH headquarters: "I give my five dollars and to me I am just as important as the people who give $1,000. When it was Breadbasket, people like me could sit anywhere. Now we are pushed further and further back. Our seats are given to the big brass. I have called PUSH to ask for help at least ten times when I was evicted. I never got through to anybody important. They told me 'I ain't got time.' Since I contributed they could have least given me some advice. I still come 'cause it's Dr. King's workshop."

- Dempsey Travis, PUSH board member and president of Sivart Mortgage Company: "In terms of the poor, I think, we are definitely missing the boat. For example, each year we pack 10,000 people into McCormick Place for a dinner. As a board member I deliver $2500 worth of tickets. If Jackson wants me to sell tickets, I'll sell tickets. But if his vision was expanded to build recreational facilities for children or any other kind of tangible service to the poor, I would do that too. Out of the political arena, Jackson is the only effective leader in America today, but, often, I can't identify with where his leadership is going. Those religious, collective, spiritual revivals take us backward. An hour of that is like an hour in bed. You should get up and go on to something else. If we can attract 10,000 people to McCormick Place it should be for an economic fund-raising dinner, which could provide tangible services to the poor. I have made my concerns known to Jesse. I have told him that the spirit of the times is with him. Instead of buying that old synagogue, we should be about the business of building institutions that serve people."

Among the many fallacies of Jackson's one-spokesman's role is that Booker T. Washington could have never gotten away with projecting himself as the number one honcho of his race without showing some demonstrable evidence of service. At least there was the Tuskegee Institute to which Washington's white benefactors could point as justification of their support. Jackson has produced no concrete evidence of service, except several black millionaire corporations which have now reached multimillionaire status. His approach to the poor is "Let them eat rhetoric."

And, finally, Jackson has cloaked his drive for power and control as the titular president of black America in the noble imagery of Dr. King, operating on both an overt agenda and a sub rosa agenda simultaneously.

Power in its rudimentary stages must not be self-revealing.

In order to complete the cycle, most often motives for self-aggrandizement must appear altruistic, benevolent, or even sacred.

And what is more sacred to blacks in America than

the memory, the mission, the mantle of Dr. Martin Luther King, Jr.?

Pictures and art work position Dr. King and Jackson side by side to reinforce the legitimate transference of leadership in the public mind. Three ad oriented firms handle Jackson's image making: two in Chicago and a white firm in Beverly Hills that promotes Cutty Sark and other commodities deemed attractive to the black market.

Rhetorically, Jackson, as the leader of PUSH, stations himself as the one individual given the mandate to carry on the Dream: "We believe that God has given us a vision and that the nation of black America has granted us a mandate. We are now charged to make the provision for our people to be led to that promised land seen so clearly in the eyes and soul of Dr. Martin Luther King, Jr."

Neither public relations gimmickry nor noble prose can obscure, forever. Eyes and ears can be betrayed, but the soul—never.

Who is that man behind the imagery of Dr. King?

He may well be called the new Booker T. in Blue Jeans, a Madison Avenue-Playboy Enterprises-multimedia production.

*I have talked to you — maybe
not officially — more than any other
journalist in America. If you can't
present me properly, who can?*

Jesse Jackson

Two minutes before flight time in Chicago. Everyone is
on board but him. Where is the man? Has something
happened?

Well. Finally. There was the familiar Afro bobbing up
and down above the throngs pushing forward to the
loading gate. An aide scampered at his heels balancing
three flight bags and a box of hot dogs. "Come on,
Reverend," I called over the crowd, "or the plane will
make it to Albuquerque without us."

Hadn't he heard? Why was he strolling so leisurely?
Why was he stopping near the gate at the pay phone? The
ticket agent looked at me and I looked at her, wondering

what she expected me to do about him. He was chatting on with every assurance that the Big Bird would wait. "Oh, would you make it brief, Mr. Jackson? We are past departure time. Brief, please," she purred.

Jackson acted as if Continental needed him more than he needed Continental. Perhaps he thought the angels would open up the heavens and fly him in on a cloud. But whatever he thought, the reaction was the same. Jackson acts like Numero Uno, and, of course, that's the way he is treated.

Twice before I had observed this supereminence reduce the peerless to plebes. In June 1971, at the Congressional Black Caucus dinner, a group of dignitaries were solemnly queued around the lobby of Washington's Sheraton-Park Hotel. After brief moments of silence interspersed with banalities, Senator Edward Kennedy strode over to the Reverend and extended his right hand. The senator acted like a man running for president. Jackson, who was twenty-nine, acted like a man who was president.

And the chance meeting with President Nixon at a black Republicans banquet in 1972 was a pathetic twist of irony. Here was the president—a hollow Howdy Doody doll—reaching up to the black commander-in-chief without portfolio. Jackson was standing ramrod straight, glaring down a look of condescension. A photographer froze the moment for those who needed a psychological uplift after those depressing pictures of a grinning Sammy Davis holding on to the coattail of Nixon at the 1972 Republican National Convention.

Having held up 105 other passengers who would have been more than irritated if they had known a black man was responsible for their ten-minute delay, the Reverend sprawled casually into the first class section and threw his muscular legs over the seat in front of him.

Two white stewardesses overexerted themselves making Jackson comfy. One was fussing over his seatbelts. The other was sputtering about how much she admired his medallion. As the stewardesses became aware there were other passengers aboard, Jackson whispered, "Barbara, you know I have never liked white women. I never met one yet that I thought deserved me." I said, "Well, at least there's something I like about you." What was meant as a joke prompted, "Well, that's one of the many things I don't like about you. You are disrespectful. And you have no grace."

My private thought had clumsily tumbled out. He rarely finds unsolicited one-liners amusing. A joke on Jackson is funny only if he tells it.

Although often moody and cryptically aloof, at times it appears as if Bill Cosby is his understudy. He may lean into a Fat Albert stance, belly thrust out, and deliver a comic monologue on President Nixon: "Nosuh, he ain't guilty of stealing. Thas what common folks do. He guilty of em-bezzzzzzz-elment. Thas mo 'spectable'. It's like when we was little kids stealing blackberries—'no, mama we ain't been stealing no blackberries and all the time we looking at her with purple all over our faces. . . . Ole tricky Nixon jumps on television and makes it perfectly clear that good Americans turn their thermostats down to 68°. Then he runs out the back door of the White House and jumps on a plane to Florida. . . . "

For those who want to remain on his good side, it is best to laugh at him by permission only. And most around him laugh at his jokes, funny or not.

Despite his own delicate sensibilities, Jackson is a man who takes great pleasure in ridiculing and mimicking others, putting particular stress on their weaknesses. "That crippled [vulgarity expunged]" he once labeled a Chicago journalist. The mere mention of Abernathy around 1971 evoked remarks which would have made scorching copy for *Smut* magazine. Black journalists and Abernathy fit into a special category. What kind of minister would he be if he loved his enemies and cursed his friends? Why not curse enemy as well as friend, which Jackson invariably does?

Once after introducing a college president as the "modern Socrates of our time" he walked off stage and typically quipped, "You know I think that punk is a mental midget." Jackson's standard repertoire is a collection of public glorifications laced with private condemnations. In fact, the private man seems capable of only two kinds of behind-the-scenes praise: flattery that invokes competition ("I respect that journalist because he writes about the issues rather than people") or flattery which indirectly flatters him ("When I met her, she was nothing but an evangelist screaming her head off in some storefront church. But since she's been with me, she's a national personality."

Even Dr. King, the man who he says was unequalled by anyone in the twentieth century, is given faint praise in comparison to what he showers upon himself. Characteristic comments are: "I doubt if King could have held on to national leadership had he lived," or "Dr. King was into economics but not with the depth I have."

"Water, please," he demanded politely from a passing stewardess, who cooed that rules were rules and no one is served until airborne. To Jackson rules must serve some sane purpose, and remaining thirsty until 30,000 feet up was not sane. The stewardess brought the water. Although I knew they wouldn't hold a jet for me, I at least thought I deserved a Coke once the rules had been cast to the wind for the Reverend. But he chided, "Don't drink those things, they poison your kidneys. Drink water, it purifies your body."

The Coke had merely been a pacifier to dull the nicotine demon. Jackson severely scolds those around him who drink, smoke, or eat pork, since he doesn't. Those cursed with these abominable vices go to great lengths to

conceal them out of respect. His wife chain smokes, but
not in front of her husband. Although he is packaged as a
sizzling hulk of pop art, he has always seemed straitlaced
to me. Yet, I have always wondered when he pals around
with Hugh Hefner and the psychedelic crowd, is he still the
autocrat or is he more like the aphrodisiaCat?

"Why do you always ride first class?" I asked. "Why
shouldn't I?" his expression said, but he explained, "I
often fly over 200,000 miles a year, more than some
pilots. When I'm flying I need thinking room to read, to
write, and reflect. Do you see anything wrong with that?"
I didn't, but a lot of others have, especially the time when
we were winging our way to the Miami Democratic
National Convention and all the Daleyites boarded and had
to pass Jackson and his staff to get in their coach seats.
"That's where they belong, in the back of the plane," he
said of the Mayor's pundits.

As the 707 ascended, Jackson began quarreling again
about my writing a book about him without his permission. Immediately, I blotted it all out for the more
pleasant temptation of musing over how incongruous it is
for a man so sensitive about his image to settle into first
class accommodations and then to munch hot dogs from a
cardboard box. I remembered how once he had blown up
when I threw into a magazine piece a personal note that he
was playing pool in his basement while planning a strategy
meeting. Dr. King used to shoot pool in sleazy west-side
pool rooms, feeling it was good for his image. But Jackson
resents any innuendo that he is jiving instead of taking his
mission seriously—a case which couldn't be built even by
his staunchest critics. The man generally works eighteen to
twenty hours a day. Sleep has become a luxury.

Out comes the tape recorder and over the monoto-
nous hum of the twin engines, I try to squeeze out an
interview, which, lately, he has been avoiding.

A skilled rhetorician, he races around questions with

a flurry of statistics, eloquence, and sheer brilliance. The interviewer usually feels Jackson has satisfactorily responded to the issues when often, substantively, he has not. Jackson's masterful elocution once tied archconservative William F. Buckley into verbal knots on the television talk show, "Firing Line." After Buckley had held a fifteen-minute exchange with Jackson, his aristocratic nose, which has an upward tilt, actually angled to the straight line of a commoner—perhaps a body language sign for "I cry uncle." Buckley ended the debate simply saying, "I agree. Agree with everything you've said."

Me? I am past the point of trying to twist the Reverend's arm to admit a fault or back away from a position. Even if all the facts say he is in error, the Reverend will indubitably turn the facts around in his favor or fix the blame elsewhere. He rigidly clings to his convictions, trusts his inner ear, and firmly believes that come what may he will always end up on the right side of history. To me, almost everything the Reverend says sounds perfectly logical, irrefutably correct. Somehow it takes distance and effort to cut through and sift out the crap disguised under moral purpose and noble prose.

Q.   *I have the feeling you are trying to prove something. Whatever you are trying to prove, are you convinced, yet, you have proved it?*

A.   At first in my early life I might have been trying to prove a personal point. But now my point is public. I'm not excited any more about being on TV and in the newspapers. I've been in the newspapers since I was thirteen years old. I was trained by one of God's greatest ministers [Dr. King] to deal with the public. It doesn't excite me any more that I have fifteen honorary degrees—I can't eat them, I can't sleep on them, and my people can't eat them either. I've been a

star since high school. I was never lacking
anything. I was the best quarterback, as well as
the best scholar, and could still get my favorite
ladies. I'm beyond proving anything personal. If
I am proving anything at all it is a public point.
Where I used to preach for reputation, I now
preach for edification.

Q. *Why is there so much mystery about PUSH
funds? Why are financial reports so incomplete
and are usually issued only after allegations have
been made? How can PUSH ask publicly for
funds, but keep full financial records private?*

A. First, it is not my fault if people think we are
hiding something, but we have so little money to
operate on we don't have much to hide, if that
was our purpose. You are asking the wrong man
when you ask me about PUSH finances. I don't
even sign checks. Right now I only accept a
dollar a year. My speaking engagements provide
my income. We have a bookkeeper and a
treasurer who keep our records. For the last five
years the IRS has been in my books. But we got
a clean bill of health obviously, or you'd have
known about it. They went into my personal
books as far back as 1966 and they wound up
owing me $842. Any significant figure in Ameri-
ca, white or black, is constantly under IRS
surveillance. The first time they tried to chop
down Dr. King, in 1957, was on an IRS situation. They tried to get Carl Stokes, they tried to
get Mayor Hatcher, and they tried to get me.
But if my books are sufficiently correct for
them they should be sufficiently correct for
you. Besides, too much is made of PUSH
finances. You black journalists would be doing
more public service if you would go bug the

Mayor about his billion dollar budget than harassing me about our measly budget, which is less than one million dollars. Why don't you go ask Elijah Muhammad what he does with the Nation of Islam's money? But you wouldn't do that because you're scared.

Q. *Is there anything you dislike about being a leader?*

A. Not much, I enjoy my role. I was born to lead. But some things disturb me. For example, black people have a way of praising the dead but crucifying the living. Many people today are praising King but they crucified him publicly, which I think set the climate for his assassination. In many cases, I will be asked to a city to help with a particular problem and I will have to spend half my time trying to keep down jealousy. People sometimes hold this misplaced notion that I am trying to come in to take over—when often there is nothing to take over. People always view you with mixed emotions. One is that they want you because they need you, but on the other hand they resent the fact that they need you. That's always the case. But there are ways of keeping that anxiety reduced, which I learned to do.

None of our problems is the result of the lack of black leadership. It's the lack of white leadership. Black leaders don't have the power to save our people. By and large, black leaders can only raise hope so as to keep our people from giving up. White leaders have the power of the budget. They have the military, the judges. You look at war or peace, bad housing, slums, overcrowding, misappropriations in the federal budget, bad foreign policy. All these are the problems of white leadership. Also it is disturbing that a guy like myself is always compared with white leaders who are sixty or seventy years old.

They won't compare me at thirty with Mayor Daley's son, who is my peer. They compare me with his daddy, who is seventy. They won't even compare me with Ted Kennedy. They compare me and his daddy.

Q.   *Why do you play the role of the one black leader?*

A.   It is possible to have one spiritual leader. The Germans at one point had one leader—Hitler, who embodied the demonological qualities of an era. DeGaulle in France and FDR, from his wheelchair, both embodied the principles of their countries. So I see nothing wrong in embodying the spiritual and moralistic qualities of this nation. And with white national leadership sinking this proves more and more that a black man can symbolize the moral principles of a nation. You can't say Ford does. To give Nixon a pardon was not morally sound. People can embody principles. And furthermore, I resent your choice of words—"role playing." What I am doing is not play. It is serious.

Q.   *How many members does PUSH have?*

A.   We have 60,000 members nationally in twenty cities. But that number is really inaccurate. I have grown into the hearts of thousands of nameless, faceless people who are far removed from the towers of influence.

Q.   *How do you respond to the criticism that your political forays have not accomplished much and that you do not have an organization to pull votes—which is the measure of political efficacy?*

A.   In the Bible there is a statement, "In the beginning, there was the word and the word was with God." Before you organize people you've first got to educate them, wake them up, and turn them on. I am not but one man. I must aid people who have the will to do precinct organizing. I can't organize no precinct. Daley don't organize precincts. Dan Walker doesn't organize precincts, Nixon doesn't organize precincts. . . .

Q.   *That may be true, but their troops do.*

A.   PUSH does too. But then, Governor Walker inherited an army that puts people on payroll in patronage jobs. I don't have any payroll. Daley has a patronage army which includes police, firemen, and 25,000 other civil servants. I don't have any such paid army. But in spite of that we have begun to wake people up and the people in Newark, Cleveland, or Gary, they would suggest to you that in addition to our rhetoric we have organization. You see, the whole thing about we don't do anything but talk never takes into account the odds. We don't know how many elections we have won in Chicago because we lose because of political corruption. We may register 50,000 voters, but the Mayor's machinery may take off 100,000 voters. No one at this point knows how much organization we have done. Daley is in charge of the rules in the City of Chicago and the County of Cook.

Q.   *Were your plans to push a black man to the forefront for president in 1972 ruined when Shirley Chisholm entered the race?*

A.   It must be made clear that I was not running anybody for president. I was the host for a group of others who were talking about running a black for president. We pulled top-flight leadership from across the nation into our political strategies. Now Shirley did not come out of that group. She came out of a white women's movement orientation. I think she felt that blacks would vote for her because she was black and in fact could be intimidated into doing so. But there was never a real attempt on her part to pull together black folks. As a matter of fact her position remains that. She assumed that her black brothers would support her so she spent her time working on the white folks. But that ain't necessarily so. You don't love less the ones you need the most. You don't take your base for granted. You organize your base if you never get with the bird in the bush. You cannot get around being accountable to people that support you.

Q.   *Who are you accountable to?*
A.   I am a minister in the service of the Lord. I am accountable to Him. I am just an imperfect instrument trying to do God's will. Do you think I am concerned about whatever news you may be writing about me? I'm doing my own book. The only reason I'm giving you this interview is because I may not live to finish my own. And I want people to know me as I am.

Q.   *But this is only one interview, the third for the book. The only way I could have presented you to the people the way you wanted to be presented was to have been your ghost writer. I can only present you as I see you, I . . . .*

A. I have talked to you—maybe not officially— more than any other journalist in America. If you can't present me properly, who can?

Q. *But you want me to define you by your words, when I can only portray you by your deeds.*

A. Well, that's your problem, not mine. My good works speak for themselves.

Q. *You mentioned you may not live to finish your own book. . . . Have you had any premonitions about assassinations?*

A. No, I haven't. I have no subconscious dreams of martyrdom. I want to live. But a man must be willing to die for justice. Death is an inescapable reality and men die daily, but good deeds live forever.

Q. *Along with Reverend Abernathy, you were among those marked for death by Marcus Chenault. Do you have any comments on your concern for your own personal safety, as well as the tragic murder of Mrs. Martin Luther King, Sr.?*

A. I have always believed the assassinations of the Kings and the Kennedys were a part of a conspiracy. Look at the J. Edgar Hoover memo, which wasn't released until 1974. The stated goal was to prevent the rise of a black Messiah who could unify and electrify the militant Black Nationalist Movement. The Hoover memorandum was dated March 4, 1968—one month to the day before Dr. King's assassination. I am convinced the FBI figured prominently in the assassinations of the Kennedys, Dr. King and Malcolm X, and possibly Mrs. King. Mama King was killed at a time when racial violence had already hit Atlanta. As a result of the assassination blacks could have started rioting, law and order troops could have waded in to save the people, all of which would have diverted attention from other national concerns. It is possible Chenault could have been a paid agent for whites. Many blacks who are afraid of whites channel their rage inward. The conclusion of self-hatred is to destroy your own people. As I said before, I am confronted with the possibility of death daily. In the final analysis I have one protector—and that is God.

Back to what we were talking about you digging around in my personal life. No white reporter tells it all and neither should you. It is crucial that you understand this. For example, one American president died in bed with his girl friend—a heart attack. That wasn't revealed until many years later. There are personal things about John Kennedy or Bobby Kennedy that we won't know until the year 2,000 or later. Remember what happened to that black female *Tribune* reporter who busted up our organization? Her drive to gain the world was so strong that she did not know what it meant to lose her soul. You just don't tell it all.

Q.   *Do you mean to tell me that just because she reported fact, she lost her soul?*

A.   Not only that, but today she can't hold her head up in her own community. Now, I wouldn't want that to happen to you. Boy, am I going to tear you up. I'm going to have a ball helping you make a fool out of yourself.

Q.   *What are your plans for the next decade or so?*

A.   We want to become a unified national indepen-

dent political force. We want to posture ourselves as the conscience of America. And we want
to amass the national structure which is necessary to confront national crises. A local group
cannot fight a national issue. We will be able to
move simultaneously in at least twenty cities.
The nature of our problem is international. The
nature of our offensive must be national and
international but with local bases and personal
expressions.

Q. *Some people have said you are really profiting
from the movement. In fact, they say you are
getting rich off the poor and have amassed a
large fortune. What is your yearly income from
all sources?*

A. I'm not a Daddy Grace or a Father Divine. My
value system is such that I don't have to live
ostentatiously. They put the white leader in the
White House. Why would anyone expect me to
live in a mud hut? At least I deserve a Black
House. There was a time when movement
leaders were pushed so tight by the public that
we couldn't even get a house, we couldn't get a
change of suit, we couldn't even go to the
movies . . . . Well, I am committed to helping
myself as well as others. . . . You see I don't
think . . . . I think . . . . My house . . . . I don't
think . . . .

As he turns away from the mike, my first thought is:
"Ah! He is feigning illness to gracefully dodge the question
of personal finances." Emotions are strings of catgut, to be
strummed for the proper effect. Fear, love, envy, eth-
nicity—and sympathy, especially in women—are easily
surfaced and manipulated by Jackson. Is this what is being
done, I wonder. But I ease the callousness to the

background as I concentrate on his contorted facial expressions. Thin blue lines form around his temple. His forehead wrinkles to ease the tautness. I notice his eyes are the pinkish haze of a sloe gin fizz. He holds his head in one hand, the other rings for help. The stewardess brings three aspirins.

Before the trip is over, she brings two more. Dizziness and headaches always follow high-altitude climbs, an apparent side effect of his sickle cell anemia trait. Yet, he makes no less than six flights a week.

Flight illness is one of the many unglamorous side-effects of an all-purpose leader, small by comparison. Sleeping has given way to nodding in airports between flights or on airplanes between public appearances. He is shadowed by the FBI, the IRS, the U. S. Army Intelligence, plus surveillance groups yet to be publicly identified. It is quixotic for him to even chat unguarded over the phone—although he does. Dr. King was wiretapped. Why not him? He is extremely sensitive about any of his four children being photographed—and can you blame him? And then there is the racial strait jacket. He knows a white man of equal cunning, courage, and intellect would be aiming for the presidency, but his options, as open as they may seem, are still limited compared to his capabilities. If he does show up for an event of national import, he is accused of scene-stealing. If he does not, he is accused of deliberately downplaying the event's significance. Then there is the constant inner drive to update his image, his strategies. When a man at thirty-three has risen so far, so fast, the term "has-been" threatens his equilibrium. He has locked himself into the role of a miracle-worker, and the fountain of new ideas, schemes, must keep pouring out. They can never run dry.

Despite the paradoxes surrounding him, his spartan schedule, his mental state is one of imperturbability. He may hurl a string of obscenities, but his temper flare-ups are sequels—something unleashed after he has handled a crisis, almost always with incredible cool. In fact, when nothing earthshattering is going on is the time when he appears irritable. During brief interludes of tranquility, he seems possessed by wanderlust, at a loss for something to do.

His egotism is often referred to as a neurosis. But while his galloping egotitis can be a personal liability, a lesser portion would be beneficial to the entire race, if suddenly there was an epidemic.

It is not his mental stamina but his physical condition that raises the question of how long he can stand the pace. Despite his athletic appearance, he suffers from recurrent respiratory illnesses, gout, and he has a bad back. At age sixteen, he caught pneumonia for the second time. By age thirty-two, he had fought off five more pneumonia attacks, brought on by his propensity to work past the point of exhaustion. Yet not once have I ever heard him complain about his personal illnesses—about anything except media coverage, which he feels is never fair or enough. His passion to fulfill his mission—whatever it may be—is his own self-replenishing antidote.

Almost instantly, it seems, he drifts away. The tape recorder picks up a distorted mix of grunts and snorts. As he sleeps, I use the opportunity to stare at him without his knowing it. Interesting. It is not only the esthetic contour of his face that is intriguing but the enigma of which face or faces I am seeing. His personality is squeezed out of a toothpaste tube, oozing out in different forms, depending on the environment, the occasion, or the person. Of all those who swear they are the ones he "really" listens to or who swear they are closest to the leader, the wisest among them will ask, "Which Jesse are you talking about?"

On one day, he will launch a vituperative attack on the FBI. Yet moments later make national headlines shaking hands with law-and-order Governor Ronald Reagan, saying, "Really, we're saying the same things." In Chicago, he is blasting the Watergate gang, but in Washington he is lunching with H. R. Haldeman. He turns on the crowd by threatening to tumble the walls of Jericho down on Pharaoh Daley, yet he is often seen chatting amiably with the Mayor on the fifth floor of City Hall.

He says he is a moralist, but his decisions are political, coated with morality. McGovern wasn't the only one 1000 percent behind Tom Eagleton. So was Jackson. The day the story broke about the senator's mental condition, Jackson said, "I prefer to stick with a man who has sought help, than with a madman like Agnew who needs help." The following day, though, Jackson called a press conference with his pal, Dr. Alvin Poussaint, to stress that Eagleton did not have the mental stamina to be "a heartbeat away from the presidency."

He demands publicity, but howls about public scrutiny. He keeps reporters at bay by burying them in their own racial confusion. To a white reporter he says: "The fundamental character of racism in America is so congenital it is impossible for white folks to perceive reality. I don't know how capable you are of getting my story straight, your world is so different from mine." To a black reporter he says: "The brainwashing of white America has been so complete that by your so-called constructive criticism you have become a part of the enemies' plan to destroy PUSH and myself."

Jackson seems a ball of confusion. However, under close scrutiny, there may be inconsistencies but Jackson is a very purposeful man. He knows exactly where he is going and every move, even the slightest seemingly unconnected act, has been weighed and studied for effect.

Since he is an actor who compartmentalizes his personality, few have seen a composite Jackson. The private dimension I see is a man so personable, disliking him would take practice. He is the kind of man that babies instinctively kiss. When he is around, the neighborhood hound who barks at everyone wags his tail. I remember the tender things. Once while following him around, I lost my notebook. It was filled with personal gush from his many adversaries. He found it and gave it back. "Barbara, I don't know what kind of super-sleuth you're going to be if you keep losing the evidence," he said. We argue. He scolds, cajoles, threatens, but the moment he is treated unfairly I am often surprised that I will rush to the typewriter to defend him. With all the miserable models of manhood existing in both races, his positiveness and self-assuredness are qualities I have grown to respect.

He brags. I enjoy it. Sometimes I help him brag. On one occasion he walked into the board room of Standard Oil and intellectually whipped six of their top white executives. That day, I spent the balance of it bragging about Jackson's T.K.O. to a couple of white reporters at my paper who didn't want to hear it. Bragging is therapeutic.

The most disturbing feature of his personality is his Messianic complex. He prays and fasts for the strength to carry out what he believes is a God-appointed mission. Since God appointed him, he cannot be wrong. On May 16, 1974, I received a blistering phone call from Jackson. "Why do you insist upon calling me a demagogue?" he demanded. "Because you are a demagogue," was the best answer I could think of. Undaunted, he said, "Don't you realize Jesus was a demagogue?" I said, "Excuse me, Reverend, but I fail to see the comparison." He changed the subject. When the Reverend "transcends," I postpone discussion until he re-enters the zone of mortality. It's one thing for others to be convinced he is a Messiah, but when he begins believing it, I worry.

I cannot help but marvel over why the writers are so fascinated with his clothes. So he is wearing a creamy beige tailored suede suit with John Wayne leather insets, a brown striped knit T-shirt and spit-polished brown leather boots. So what? I remembered the time at a press conference a reporter dashed back to the phone. Thinking I had missed some spectacular statement, I asked the reporter what had happened. "Oh, I forgot to report what the Reverend was wearing," he said. I only wish the city editors would be more concerned with the effectiveness of his programs rather than encouraging "blue-jean Jesse" stories, which seriously debate whether his blue jeans are, indeed, tailored or picked from the rack.

Admittedly, though, the fact that he is a sensuous male—an extremely sensuous male, who wears tight pants—has acted as a distraction, especially to female reporters. Although he complains about media people being out to get him—there is always an uprising in the palace—most women, both black and white, feel compelled to protect him. Middle-aged women, the matriarchs, tend to cover him with the cloak of vicarious motherhood. The younger ones seem mesmerized by his charm and sex appeal. And the white male reporters are easily intimidated by Jackson, who evokes racial guilt by making them feel whatever unfavorable impressions they write are the results of their bigotry.

As he continues to sleep, I journey into his home without him. His fifteen-room Romanesque home is located in a racially changing neighborhood on Chicago's south side, next door to composer-musician Ramsey Lewis.

The front door is for dignitaries, media-types, businessmen, attorneys; those in formal quid-pro quo relationships with Jackson. They are greeted by aide-bodyguard St. Clair Booker, who has the personality of an armadillo. It may take him five years to get around to saying hello without looking tortured. His role is to protect, keep his mouth shut, and keep those who don't "belong" away from the leader, all of which he does well. Those on official visits are seated by Saint in the State Room—which is tastefully decorated with red crushed velvet drapes drawn together by black velvet tapestry. There are red and black French chairs to match. Soft black leather couches, a baby grand piano, art pieces shipped in or selected from the family's trips to West Africa complete the decor of stately elegance. The official aura of the room evokes hushed, modulated tones.

Through the back door streams a steady flow of movement people, relatives, and friends. They are regulars and move about the Jackson household as they please. Most will break up in small groups to talk out some particular project. Some gather in a small anteroom, adjoining the kitchen. It is decorated in psychedelic purples with bamboo curtains. Others gather around a shellacked picnic bench in the dining room. It is a remnant of the leaner days when Jackson was a seminary student living in a crowded walk-up flat. Copper pots decorate the wall, giving the room an antique flair in line with Mrs. Jackson's taste for "things old and functional." A few regulars may recess from a strategy meeting to the basement to listen to Jackson's collection of favorite gospel music or shoot a game of pool. Pool is about the only amusement allowed in Jackson's household. He expects those around him to be serious, involved, busy. No drinking or dancing is allowed.

After a three-hour wait, Saint gives the nod. The Reverend will see me now. He is holding court in his bedroom, a common practice when his personal physician, Dr. Andrew Thomas, confines him to bed.

The stairway is darkened, perhaps purposely. Many celebs—Isaac Hayes, Bill Russell, the Reverend James Cleveland—may be the Reverend's houseguests, and their privacy must not be disturbed. Two full-sized portraits, one of Dr. King and the other of JFK, are all that can be distinguished in the dimly lit second floor hallway.

The endless surge of gran personas streaming in and

out of the Reverend's bedroom is remindful of a Cecil B. De Mille epic. Out dashes Ms. Victoria Sanders, his black, flamboyant but cerebral stockbroker. Clad in suede jumpsuit with mink trim, she is tra-la-ing off to Lake Tahoe to ski. In comes publicist Harry Dale, smiling affably through diamond-studded dentures, small compared to the flash of diamonds in his stickpin and on his pinky. An unknown enters to deliver some apparently unsolicited information about the seedier side of a well-connected Chicago political figure. This secret, of course, would never leak out unless the politician got in Jackson's way. The Reverend Clay Evans, chairman of his board, checks in for his orders saying "Hi, Leader." A couple of entertainers Jackson is promoting stroll in, so does his doctor, and the stream of other deal-makers, favor-seekers and sincere loyalists continues into dawn. A bedside audience with Jackson always improves the status of an individual within the black community. To say with authority, "The Reverend wears sexy navy-blue silk pajamas, the same color of his plush bedroom rug," earns respect.

Six of his eight phone lines are lit. His first conversation is through the intercom with his wife, Jackie, whom he requests to bring up some orange juice. When she sets it down on the night table, he thanks her formally, too formally, it seems. Another button tunes in an athlete who is having troubles with his manager. He calls several benefactors. The movement needs money again. Black service station operators are buzzing. The big oil firms are attempting to make pawns out of them in the energy crunch. Will he stand up for them? "Soul Train" star, Don Cornelius, is having a problem. Can they meet? Although his phone number is unlisted, it still must be changed twice a year. He is the neutralizer between blacks and whites and there are plenty of problems to neutralize.

By the time he turns his attention to me, I am

running out of anger. I had walked six blocks to his house in zero weather to make certain that anger would not thaw. I came not to ask, but to demand an apology. In front of a listening audience of 94,000 people and the thousands that attend the Saturday morning meeting he had deliberately lied. There was no excuse for his saying that I used white ghostwriters. He would apologize to me, if I had to become a permanent houseguest. He apologized so graciously and so sorrowfully that I instantly forgave him. It would not be until I had walked the six blocks back home that I became angry with myself. Of course, he would apologize in private. I should have asked for a public apology. The blunder would remind me of a Jacksonian phrase: "So many people walk away empty-handed from confrontations because they don't know what to ask for," he often says. Many others walk away empty-handed from a Jackson bedside chat. The impression—whether staged or real—is here is a man, so exhausted from pushing for solutions to the black condition that his doctor orders him to bed. Yet, his mind churns on. Under his bed are piles of legal pads, where he is constantly scribbling notes to himself, ideas for speeches, plotting his next step. When he can't sleep, which is most of the time, he disturbs others with predawn phone calls about his latest hot ideas, a vision or a suggestion about what others should be doing. In light of his burdens, the sweat marks staining his collar, whatever was monumental soon becomes microscopic. Sympathy and empathy soon replace anger and dissatisfaction.

Few people have seen him relaxed. He plays basketball, supposedly for relaxation. But an aide who plays him on the family backyard court calls it "an outrageous outpouring of fury." "I don't see how he calls basketball relaxing. I am nearly five inches shorter than he is. Yet he runs me all over the court like it's a big stakes tournament game, pushing, shoving, and once he poked me in the eye.

Everything he does he does to win. Maybe it's relaxing to
him, but it sure as hell ain't relaxing to me."

A sudden jolt ends the reverie. An air pocket is
shaking the descending aircraft into a frenzy of burlesque
turbulence. The stewardesses are strapped stiffly in their
seats. (Something metal slams to the floor.) I look around
into the faces of other nervous passengers. Only the
Reverend seems unperturbed.

I laugh quietly at my thoughts because normally I
would be petrified. Now I am not. I feel the plane would
not dare crash with the Reverend on it. And as ludicrous as
the muse sounded in retrospect, it is important to the
understanding of the personal magnetism of a charismatic
leader. This sensation of fearlessness, of strength flowing
from Jackson to his following underscores the point that
Jackson could be a real threat to the establishment. But
real threats become martyrs. Jackson does not minimize
the cold reality that no matter how much he wants to do,
there is little he, alone, can do—and live.

At the airport, his arrival is a spectacle, an event.
Some famous men have to send advance men to create
excitement. Not Jackson; the excitement is there awaiting
him. Everyone loves a hero. There is a lust for a Paul
Bunyan in everyone, and the Chicanos, Indians, and whites
who absorb him are no different. He is a household face,
courtesy of the mass media, and no one among them will
not repeat to all who will listen that he has shaken Jackson's
hand. It is the burden of the journalist to ponder. But it is
the delight of the crowds to accept on face value. They see
what they like and that is enough.

At the National Brotherhood Conference at Albuquerque's main auditorium, Jackson finds a quiet place to
change out of his rumpled clothing into a leather suit with
fringed jacket. Before 1973 his speeches were often
prepared by two white journalists, the Reverend David
Wallace and Don Rose, a Chicago political expert and

newspaper publisher. But on minor addresses I see he is perfectly capable of writing his own. Since he has a photographic memory, his notes consist of a few scribblings of important landmarks, dates, and names of local leaders. In minutes, he is before the audience. The visible signs of fatigue are gone from his face, but the beads of sweat remain. He always fascinates the crowds with his fusillade of remembered facts and homespun wit. He tells of how many people were killed in the Vietnam war compared to what is spent on food for the poor. For the benefit of the Latinos and Indians he recites incidents from the Spanish-American war and dates of treaties America has broken with the Indians. His brain is a computer of information. He acquired mental discipline long ago when he used to fill his mind with new words by studying the dictionary.

A leader of the American Indian Movement, who led the Wounded Knee uprising, follows Jackson at the podium. But as Jackson descends from the stage, he notices people are following him. By returning to his seat, he encourages people to stay and listen to the Indian leader. He knows he can steal the show now but this is not the place.

As I study the reaction of nonwhites to Jackson, the reality of his potential for organizing a coalition of poor whites, blacks, and browns is not lost. There is no greater threat to democracy than democracy itself—the dispossessed breaking through their superficial class barriers to gain a piece of this country's wealth. But Jackson, who is spread so thin, is not likely to serve as this catalyst. When he leaves, there will be no vehicle to turn this desire, this excitement he generates, into effective action. Few will remember his proposals or solutions for change. All that will be remembered is that he came.

Back at the airport, he is told that all planes are grounded because of a snow storm in Denver. A woman passes a note to him, boldly telling him there are much better ways to spend a snowy evening than pacing about an airport. He politely demurs.

As soon as he is settled into a nearby hotel, he places a call. Cradling the phone, he tells me, "It's one thing to be in love, but it's quite another to be so in love."

I return to my adjoining room, closing the door, assuming he is talking to his wife, Jackie.

It is no secret among the movement people that the Reverend's name is occasionally linked with entertainers. On a 1969 TV show a Hollywood gossip columnist leaked the news that Jackson had formed a close relationship with singer Nancy Wilson.

The latest rumor bandied about from the West to the East Coast is his close friendship with singer Roberta Flack. Gossip about the pair continues to gush, not only because of frequent public sighting of the two orbiting together, but also because of their "musical compatibility." On Ms. Flack's 1971 Atlantic recording *Quiet Fire,* Jackson received a credit for the song, "Go Down Moses," containing phrases such as "Am I clear this morning y'all?" which Jackson uses at the Saturday morning meetings. However, on the singer's 1973 album entitled *Killing Me Softly,* there is a torrid love song entitled "Jesse." Violins moan melancholily in the background and among other things, the song gives many good reasons why Jesse should "come home."

In 1974, Ms. Flack sang "Jesse" on two national network shows, one on which the set oddly enough resembled the staircase in Jackson's house. All of the public crooning was creating quite a stir inside the movement. A press aide told me, "All right, now how am I supposed to cover when the press starts asking the obvious?" My suggestion was to simply ask, "Jesse who?" After all, the name "Jesse" is a common Southern name. There must be a million Jesses. Or maybe Jackson should ask "Roberta who?" if pushed, I suggested.

On February 2, 1974, Jackson was asked, "Ms. Flack keeps singing about a man called Jesse. Are you that Jesse? Are there any romantic attachments?"

His answer: "This rumor is the Adam Clayton Powell syndrome. I refuse to be intimidated by it. Until such time as I'm ready to concede some formal relationship I refuse to deny it. I'm not going to plead the Fifth.

"About that song, I am flattered by the thought. But Cannonball Adderly has a song out entitled, 'The Country Preacher' and we ain't got nothing going.

"I guess what I'm proudest of in my personal life is that I have maintained enough discipline to keep all things in perspective. Roberta is a close personal relationship and I refuse to have it muddied. Roberta is intelligent, independent, she has her own spirituality. She doesn't have to pursue me.

"I have a very enviable home situation. Jackie has made me secure in many ways. She understands me. She gives me rope, but I haven't hung myself."

His wife, Jacqueline, braves gossip about her husband with unbelievable self-assurance. She, more than anyone else, realizes how impossible it would be for her husband to work nearly 120 hours a week and still run in and out of all the romantic entanglements of which he is accused.

"I understand other women wanting to be around Jesse. I can understand them even being attracted to him. They join me and plenty of others in our admiration for Jesse," she said.

"I am not a slavemaster over his body or his commitment and neither is he over mine. Jesse loves and so do I. We don't just exist. Living means being creative, not destructive, which results when we trap and bind people. Our need for each other is that of good friends. Friends who know each other quite well and appreciate a total experience with each other. It is a needing in a more spiritual sense; more than in the nine-to-five situations where I need him to fix the television or need him to pay the bills. Jesse is rarely home. But I am not like most lonely people who require their husbands to punch a time-clock so they can use them to satisfy the feeling of loneliness. I give him no ultimatum on when to return. He returns because he wants to. And when he does I am happy to have him back."

Mrs. Jackson has such a pliant, saccharine voice her phrases seem to be rolling out of a honeycomb. She is petite—5'1", 108 lbs—and the lightness of her steps gives the impression that a choreographer is designing her movements. She is an articulate conversationalist, whose reading material ranges from Sartre to Nietzsche, from Richard Wright to Emerson.

Although she prefers to stay out of the public spotlight—she is a bit shy—gradually she is moving to the forefront, not necessarily as Mrs. Jesse Jackson, but as an individual who has her own concerns and involvement. Her cultural exhibits, one depicting the rise of the black man from slavery to producer, have been shown at PUSH Expo, Tuskegee Institute, and in New York City. She is best described as an involved black woman—into everything from making her own curtains, to metaphysics, to politics, to being a professional student. "Don't box me into any one function," she cautions. "I'm not just a name for fund-raising, somebody's wife, or just somebody who does something in a house. Maybe I should be, I don't know. But that's certainly not who I am."

The only function Mrs. Jackson allows herself to be "boxed" into is that of mother of four children. Motherhood is the one role she says she enjoys. All her children are beautiful and bright. Santita is ten. Jesse, Jr., is nine. Jonathan Luther, who carries Dr. King's middle name, is eight, and Yusef DuBois is three. All the children relate to their father's work, watch his moves closely on TV, and it is clear he is their hero. "Their father creates so much excitement in their ears that they may someday become the new revolutionaries," she says.

Mrs. Jackson calls media treatment of her husband artificial. "Jesse and I are human beings—sometimes I think we are more human than most, because we know the good in people as well as the bad. Yet everything I read about us makes us seem superficial people. Just images, not real. I relate to Jesse in terms of his message, not what the media have made out of him."

Her fears concerning her husband are that wherever he goes, he may not come back safe and well. Late phone calls sometimes warn that there is a bullet waiting with her husband's name on it. An assassination plot was uncovered in 1969 and another in 1974. Threats against his life are continuous and unnerving. Yet, she is beginning to accept the possibility that he may meet the same fate as Dr. King. "I'm never relaxed when he's gone. And I can't say that I'm unafraid, but I have disciplined myself to function while I am fearful."

Flights are being rescheduled now. At the airport Jackson cajoles, "C'mon, you want to know all there is to know about me. Well, in the morning there's Detroit, later that night it's Philadelphia. Tuesday, we're heading back to Los Angeles, then it's. . . ."

For five years I have followed the leader. Now I smile, wave, and wish him well, as I go off in another direction.

Appendixes

Operation PUSH
Convening Board of Directors
January, 1974

Officers
REV. CLAY EVANS, Chairman
Chicago, Illinois
REV. JESSE L. JACKSON, President
Chicago, Illinois
ATTORNEY THOMAS N. TODD, Executive Vice-President
Chicago, Illinois
JACKIE ROBINSON, Vice-Chairman
New York, New York
CHARLES HAYES, Vice-Chairman
Chicago, Illinois
WESLEY SOUTH, Vice-Chairman
Chicago, Illinois

ATTY. A. BENJAMIN JOHNSON
Philadelphia, Pennsylvania
GEORGE JOHNSON
Chicago, Illinois
JOHN JOHNSON
Chicago, Illinois
GEORGE JONES
Chicago, Illinois
THEODORE JONES
Chicago, Illinois
QUINCY JONES
Beverly Hills, California
DR. D. E. KING
Chicago, Illinois
REV. BILLY KYLES
Memphis, Tennessee
ATTY. ERNEST LaFONTANT
Chicago, Illinois
ALD. ANNA R. LANGFORD
Chicago, Illinois
RUBY LAWSON
Chicago, Illinois
JOHN LEVY
Los Angeles, California
PETE LONG
Teaneck, New Jersey
ROBERT MARTIN
Chicago, Illinois
DWIGHT McKEE
Chicago, Illinois

REV. OTIS MOSS
Cincinnati, Ohio
DR. ALVIN F. POUSSAINT
Boston, Massachusetts
DIRECTOR WILLIAM ROBINSON
Chicago, Illinois
BILL RUSSELL
Los Angeles, California
HON. CARL B. STOKES
Cleveland, Ohio
HON. PERCY SUTTON
New York, New York
DR. ANDREW L. THOMAS
Chicago, Illinois
DEMPSEY TRAVIS
Chicago, Illinois
REV. FRED WALL
Chicago, Illinois
ALBERTINA WALKER
Chicago, Illinois
ALLENE WALKER
Chicago, Illinois
BERNADINE C. WASHINGTON
Chicago, Illinois
PROF. ROLAND WIGGINS
Amherst, Massachusetts
REV. CLARENCE WILLIAMS
Brooklyn, New York
DORIS ZOLLAR
Chicago, Illinois

B

The Kingdom Theory
by
Rev. Jesse L. Jackson

A slum develops any place where the people who reside in the area have no control of the economic resources or over the political decisions which affect their lives. Money must travel in a circle just as blood does, no clots, no anemia. By this definition, an area would not need to comprise tenements or slum shacks to be a slum. Any place in capitalism with no capital leaves just the "ism" or socialism without social benefits or sharing. A slum could develop in an affluent community where people lack the wherewithal to deal with their basic problems.

The Kingdom Theory is an attempt to address those problems. It is premised upon an understanding of the ghetto as an economic and political colony, rather than as some aggregate of slum housing. In a colony, people are directed from without—to use the terms of

David Riesman, they are "other" directed rather than inner, or self directed.

The Kingdom Theory rests on other assumptions also. First, that as blacks and non-whites, we control, potentially, the margin of profit on most of the consumer items and nearly all of the basic consumer items in the nation. A report of the Conference Board, formerly the National Industrial Conference Board, sustains this position. As consumers, we consume far out of proportion to our percentage in the population; as the major marketing firms have stated, we are "heavy" users of most products we consume.

If this is the case, the issue for black and non-white people is to discipline their appetites in such a way that they can demand respect of large corporate giants who control the production and distribution of the marketable items in this nation. This presupposes that aware black people will always take inventory in their communities.

For example, any given chain store markets between 8,000 and 15,000 products on average. A vast proportion of these products will be brand names. Let us assume that one of those brand names is Carnation Foods, and we are attempting to secure jobs and other economic benefits from that corporate organization. Failing to gain an entrée for negotiations, what is our next step? If Carnation is on the shelf of that chain store (and it most likely will be), is it feasible for us to demand from management that it be removed? If a disciplined cadre of 12-15 persons takes a picket line around that store, it can gain the attention of the surrounding community. When that happens, no Carnation moves. When no Carnation brand-label moves, the milk and other products sour and are of no use to the management or to the parent company, for that matter.

Moving from such *units* as a store, the Kingdom Theory seeks to explain basic control of each marketable product, and in fact, the store itself. Control of the store means determining who will be clerks and bookkeepers, and who will have such monetary awarding jobs as butchers and meat manager roles within the store. By that same token, it is also to determine the amount of shelf space which that community feels should go to the products of black producers; who is to do the exterminator, janitorial and scavenger services in the store; when the store chooses to expand, who will secure the construction and remodeling contracts; which banks will the store transact its financial operations in; who conducts the collection services for the store; with whom does the store have transportation business; does the store maintain transactions with black farm co-operatives for its vegetable supplies.

At the same time this principle applies to all other institutions in the community.

Public schools should insure their athletes with black and non-white insurance companies, and black suppliers should have their products in social rooms and restaurant vending machines; black and non-white stationery supply firms should deal with black distributors, etc.

Black youth should be able to secure jobs through the retail outlets in the community. This is especially needed in an area like Chicago where unemployment among teenagers is over 67% this summer.

Real estate dealers should use black managers for apartments and have them serviced for extermination, janitorial work and scavenger work by black and non-white companies. Black contractors should paint, refurbish and remodel buildings in the community. Black banks should be the source of financial transactions; black mortgage bankers should provide mortgage in the community, and black insurance firms should carry the casualty or fire and property damage insurance. Black savings and loan associations should share the mortgages on homes in the community.

The purpose of gaining this accountability is to utilize the results of our inventory in and for our own interests.

An example of this type of accountability can be applied to a PUSH protest presently taking place at 95th at South Halsted Street in Chicago and concerning the Carter G. Woodson Library.

This library is located in the very heart of the black community. Operation PUSH has maintained the position that a black builder should construct that building and should be the general contractor over total building operations. The Chicago Library Board, acting at the instance of the Public Building Commission, has awarded the contract to a white contractor who lives on Chicago's Northwest side. Despite this, we have evidence that a qualified black builder, whose bid was only 3% more than the winning low bid, can and is prepared to build that library. The worth of the project is in the neighborhood of $2.8 million.

No matter how he may present his bid, a white contractor

cannot serve the purpose since he has no basic investment in the community he is building in. He does his banking transactions in a white area; he is insured by a white company; all of his commercial business is done in the white community. Thus we must ask, what is his stake in the local community apart from exploiting that community?

While some wages paid out may go to blacks, the largest portion of the dollars go to the white community. In this particular instance, the black contractor had offered in his bid not only to include black sub-contractors, but to bring them in on the major money making trades (cement, brick masonry, carpentry, plumbing, etc.) and to share the profits with them. The white contractor, whose first submitted bid included black sub-contractors for only $20,000 worth of work, made no attempt to include black sub-contractors in the profits. The point here is that the big buck will leave the community.

In this instance the library's being built by a white contractor is inconsistent with what Carter G. Woodson, a leading black historian (who founded Black History Week), was all about.

It is also inconsistent with our goal to bring economic viability to the black community. Moreover it insults qualified black contractors by presuming them too ignorant or incompetent to handle the job—and by extracting profits to take to another alien community when the money is needed in the black community.

It was very interesting to note that the white contractors who bid on that job came from as far away as Alsip, Rolling Meadows and Naperville. But the two black contractors who bid on the project would hardly expect to secure work in those areas.

Opportunities gained by black contractors (or any other black businessmen) tend to create more opportunities for others within the black community. This is what can be roughly called the multiplier effect of economic activity.

This does not take place when whites build in our communities. Most of the traditionally high paying jobs, from the top level trades to supervisors, foremen, architectural draftsmen etc., are monopolized by whites through custom or restrictive unions. Blacks may inch into these slots, but seldom can they claim their proportionate share of them. Thus, the prime dollars in even the hired categories are claimed by whites when whites are in charge of a project.

Time and time again, one can observe in the black community the very debilitating sight of whites being employed (from window washers and painters, to electrical fixture (street light) adjusters—while blacks sit idle and unemployed. This is what we must be prepared to march on and protest.

Kingdom Building Means Protecting the Gains We Secure:

A major part of the task of Kingdom building is protecting the gains that have been secured. This is why we must enter politics with a determined and disciplined understanding of the objectives political involvement serves.

Speaking from a national perspective, black people now hold 2,621 elective offices in this nation. This is an impressive figure taken, say as a comparison to the 500 we had only 5 years ago. But it actually represents 1/2 of 1% of the total elected officials in the country, for there are 521,760 elective offices in the nation.

There are 21 states with fewer than 30 black elected officials. The largest bloc of blacks, some 1,119, have been elected in the south. Although we are the most urban of any ethnic group in this country, only 47% of the blacks holding public office hold office at the municipal level. Although there are more blacks in the north than in the south, there are only 579 blacks in office in northern states; only 585 in midwestern states and 178 in far western states. All of these states have far more blacks than does the south.

If we can read anything into the implications of some significant Supreme Court decisions concerning redrawing Congressional and state legislative districts in the south, there will be more black representatives at all levels in the south. But to effectively build the Kingdom, we must deal with gaining more aldermanic, Congressional, state legislative and county representative districts above the Mason-Dixon line.

It should not escape us that of the 14 or 15 black congressmen and congresswomen, at least five (5) are threatened by remap of their districts. The United States Census Department now admits that it *grossly undercounts* black people, which in itself constitutes a conspiracy to prevent blacks from having adequate representation and from securing their proper share of such funds as those coming from Revenue Sharing entitlements.

The issue of Revenue Sharing is closely related to the matter of securing adequate representation. Revenue Sharing is replacing the previous block grants which the Federal government provided states to meet the needs of hard pressed budgets, particularly in the area of social services. Because the President has announced the elimination of some programs and impounded funds for some categorical grants, revenue sharing has now become a subterfuge for avoiding some programs most in need of federal supplementation.

Most mayors and governors have used Revenue Sharing funds for Public Safety (including law enforcement and fire protection), for environmental protection projects, or for reserves in lieu of increasing property taxes. People priorities such as Social Services for the poor and aged have been subordinated to the above decisions.

The result is that black people in particular are deprived of their share of the entitlements. As blacks, we must become familiar with these complicated schemes and workshop our community people to deal with the legal "loopholes" which local officials take advantage of to evade the issues of people priorities.

Summary:

In summary, we are stating that black people must understand themselves as having the authority of kings and that their dominions are their communities. An informed people is a well armed people in this struggle.

Taking inventory means becoming informed of the people who benefit economically from our community but have no real investment in that community. It means replacing those people and companies with those from our own community.

It means seeing our money remain within our community instead of entering and leaving at an acute angle (i.e. within six hours). It means providing the base for a circular flow of dollars in black communities. It means monitoring local chain stores, local schools, local apartment buildings, local services (there is no reason why the City electrical department should send whites to black areas to adjust the street lights—that is a well paying job and should go to a black person; by that same token, the Board of Education should contract with black companies to do its window and landscape maintenance; policemen in black communities should be black for the most part as this is a very sensitive type of operation. The transit authority should not only hire black drivers, but black claims adjusters to deal with accidents in the black community caused by faulty transit equipment.) Utilities such as the phone and gas and electric companies should do contractual business with black building contractors as they expand their operations in the black community. These are a few examples of what we look for in the total process of Kingdom building. For Kingdom building represents a strategy for developing a community and fueling it with the economic wherewithal and the political resources to sustain and continue its growth.

We must understand very clearly that black people not only deserve to survive but to thrive in a nation that has taken so much from them.

National Tea Co.
Review of Covenant with
Operation Breadbasket
April, 1970

This report reflects 33 stores (21 nationally) with 50% or more black trade
(12 DEL FARM)

BLACK PRODUCTS ANALYSIS

Product	1970 Avg. Monthly Purchase Cost	1969 Yearly Purchases	Availability No. of Stores
Joe Louis Milk	$36,000.00	174,973	25
Baldwin Ice Cream	3,300.00	25,414	23
Grove Fresh Orange Juice	3,000.00	15,809	31
Out Clean Corporation	1,600.00	11,556	All Stores
Conway Products	1,200.00	14,419	All Stores
Argia B. (Mumbo Sauce)	1,700.00	12,684	All Stores
Fifty-Fifty Corporation (Stewarts Bleach)	1,200.00	11,686	All Stores
Rual Products (Diamond Sparkle)	1,000.00	7,644	All Stores
Atlas Broom Company	1,200.00	3,140	All Stores
Silver Cup Bread	15,800.00	186,504	All Stores
Parker House Sausage	8,800.00	65,037	All Stores
Metropolitan Sausage	4,300.00	34,166	All Stores
Dixie DeLuxe Sausage	1,400.00	8,562	All Stores
Hinduscheen	190.00	2,181	All Stores
Bins Company	50.00	540	All Stores
Carson Chemical Co.	160.00	1,843	All Stores
Fuller Products	130.00	1,593	All Stores
Johnson Products	1,700.00	20,992	All Stores
Magnificent National Products	120.00	1,424	All Stores
Soft Scheen Products	200.00	2,451	All Stores
Supreme Beauty Co.	400.00	4,606	All Stores
*James Bennett—Cool Summer (Black Christmas Cards)	292.00	292	30

*Seasonal item — Standing agreement with company to feature item during
appropriate season.

EXTERMINATORS AND SCAVENGERS
JANITORIAL SERVICES

A. Scavenger Services	Stores	Avg. Cost per Month
Assc. Disposal Contractors	6330 S. King Drive	
(Corp. of Smith & Pyramid)	4759 S. Calumet	
	5020 S. State St.	
	600 W. 63rd St.	$600.00
Al's Scavenger Service	411 S. Kedzie	
	420 S. Pulaski Rd.	$520.00
E & D Scavenger Service	7811 S. State St.	$ 70.00
W. Amerine Scavenger Service	3924 S. State St.	
	3425 W. Roosevelt Rd.	$415.00
Paul Clay Scavenger Service	7739 S. Exchange	$124.00
Bert Jones Scavenger Service	8558 S. Cottage Grove	$175.00
Howard Scavenger Service	7162 S. Exchange	$100.00
I & D Scavenger Service	2323 E. 95th. St.	$120.00
Nash & Jones Scavengers	1346 E. 53rd. St.	$ 36.00
Associated Scavenger Service	9341 S. Ashland	$100.00
	6611 S. Halsted	$200.00
	9001 S. Halsted	$150.00
	90 E. 103rd. St.	$150.00
	751 W. 79th St.	$ 10.00

B. Exterminating Services

Scott Exterminating Company	6339 S. King Drive	$6.00 per
	600 W. 63rd St.	month per
	5024 S. State St.	store.
	3920 S. State St.	
Petty Exterminating Company	11525 S. State St.	$6.00 per
	4905 W. Madison St.	month per
	213 N. Pulaski Rd.	store.
	7443 S. Racine Ave.	
	6830 S. Stony Island	
	6611 S. Halsted	
	9001 S. Halsted	
	2346 E. 79th St.	
	8246 S. Stony Island	
	8558 S. Cottage Grove	
Berry and Sons Exterminating Co.	801 W. 119th St.	$6.00 per
	10815 S. Halsted St.	month per
	90 E. 103rd St.	store.
	2325 E. 95th St.	
	9341 S. Ashland	
	8325 S. Ashland	
	1312 E. 79th St.	
	7162 S. Exchange	
	1346 E. 53rd St.	
	4666 S. Halsted	

C. Janitorial Services

Emerald Janitorial Service	3924 S. State St.	$1,160.00 per
	3425 W. Roosevelt	month
Great Lakes Janitorial Service	4759 S. Calumet	
	4701 S. Cottage Grove	
	5020 S. State St.	
	800 W. North Ave.	
	3425 W. Roosevelt Rd.	
	6330 S. King Drive	
	420 S. Pulaski Rd.	
	600 W. 63rd St.	
	7811 S. State St.	
	5314 Lincoln, Skokie	
	1120 N. State St.	
	4905 W. Madison St.	
	215 N. Harlem, Forest Pk.	
	1312 E. 79th St.	
	8558 S. Cottage Grove	
	6820 Stony Island	$6,415.00 per
		month
Clark Janitor Service	4060 S.W. Hgwy., Hometown	
	8821 W. 87th Hickory Hills	
	6620 W. 111th, Worth	
	7546 W. 63rd St., Argo	
	2120 S. Mannheim, Westchester	
	16725 Oak Park Ave., Tinley Pk.	
	561 E. Cass St., Joliet	
	950 Jefferson, Joliet	
	2142 Sauk Trail, Sauk Village	$7,000.00 per
		month

D. Security

Lilliard Detective & Investigation Agency	$9,500.00 per month

CONSTRUCTION

Robert Martin Construction Company
    Store Address — 3425 W. Roosevelt
                    9001 S. Halsted

Smith Construction Company
    Store Address — 4759 S. Calumet

W. Thomas, Vice-President of Real Estate, is currently working with a Black Real Estate group regarding a store site at 69th and Wentworth.

BANKING

Independence Bank of Chicago	Store	Avg. Balance per Month
	6330 S. Park Ave.	$13,700.00
	600 W. 63rd St.	$14,900.00
	7811 S. State St.	$ 8,000.00
	5020 S. State St.	$11,300.00
	6820 Stony Island	$11,711.00
Seaway National Bank		
	9001 S. Halsted	$28,369.00
	8240 Stony Island	$22,161.00
	2346 E. 79th St.	$19,232.00
	1312 E. 79th St.	$17,741.00
	8558 S. Cottage Grove	$12,512.00

The Division Controller is presently considering stores that can be added to those handling banking procedures through the banks listed above.

ADVERTISING

Newspaper

Chicago Crusader	$ 704.00
Gary Crusader	$ 900.00
South Suburban News	$ 680.00
Chicago Defender	$1,732.00
Chicago Courier	$1,344.00
Chicago Gazette	$ 800.00
West Side Torch	$ 400.00
Chatham Citizen	$1,400.00
West Side Observer	$ 500.00
Black Truth	$ 201.00
Vista News	$ 350.00
Auburn Gresham Advertiser	$1,600.00

ADVERTISING (Continued)

Radio Advertising
WBEE   30 Second Spots   Monday through Friday (5 per week)

*WVON   996 - 60 Second Spots
            432 - 30 Second Spots = plus 44 in-store appearances
*WGRT   1110 - 60 Second Spots
            240 - 30 Second Spots

*Since December, 1966, we have spent a total of <u>$69,846.14</u>

TRAINING

Outside Source	Proposed Training
1. O.I.C.	Male — Management
	Cost $7,800.00
2. MARION BUSINESS COLLEGE	Male — Female
	Cost $17,500.00

Both programs are presently under consideration by the Company.

Internal Source of Training
Checkers   — 2 day school — Continuous courses
Bookkeeping   — 2 day school — Continuous courses
Above instruction is handled by Company employed trainers on a full-time basis.
        Management Development Program — monthly meetings at Company's
                                          expense and time.
        Office Training   — On-the-job training.
        In Depth Training   — Delores Ware
                                 Leonard Robinson

EMPLOYMENT DATA – NATIONAL TEA CO.

W/E JANUARY 31, 1970

Division Classification	Total No. of Employees by Class 1-31-70	Black Emp. by Class as of 10-66	Black Emp. Required by Oper. B/B 10-66	Blacks Currently Employed	Salary
OFFICE**					
Mail Clerks	12 (3)	6	0	6	$70.00-90.00
Clerk Typists	19	1	4	5	75.00-105.00
Multh. Operators	6	1	1	1	75.00-105.00
Junior Clerks	31	2	6	8	75.00-105.00
Acct. Clerks	38 (10)	1	7	6	83.00-130.00
Steno.	14	1	1	2	83.00-119.00
Sr. Comp. Operator	17	1	3	2	83.00-119.00
Key Punch Operator	16	4	0	8	83.00-119.00
Tab. Operator	4	1	0	1	83.00-119.00
Ad. Layout Man	5	1	0	1	115.00-165.00
Secretary	15 (5)	1	3	3	93.50-150.00
Draftsman	4	1	0	1	115.00-165.00
Cafeteria	12	1	0	1	134.50
Totals	193 (18)	22	25	45	
RETAIL					
Store Managers	97 (28)	10	14	9 (9)	$192.31-346.15
Market Managers	97 (28)	8	16	6 (9)	173.00-201.00
Asst. Managers	92 (24)	12	8	6 (11)	166.80

Division Classification	Total No. of Employees by Class 1-31-70	Black Emp. by Class as of 10-66	Black Emp. Required by Oper. B/B 10-66	Blacks Currently Employed	Salary
Prod. Managers	91 (23)	11	9	9 (11)	164.80
Cashier Bookkeepers	92 (23)			7 (18)	140.30
Checkers—F.T.	637 (155)	136	99	80 (73)	105.30-129.80
Checkers—P.T.	425 (104)			54 (48)	2.22-2.67 P. Hr.
Gro. & Prod. Clerks—F.T.	630 (185)	174	92	95 (77)	109.80-138.80
Gro. & Prod. Clerks—P.T.	420 (123)			63 (51)	2.22-2.67 P. Hr.
Journeyman	257 (70)	17	43	11 (28)	171.00
App. Butchers	92 (52)	39	0	23 (23)	100.00-133.00
Meat Helpers	39 (29)	26	0	13 (17)	75.00
Security Guards	17 (3)	0	0	0 (3)*	95.00-125.00
Totals	2894 (842)	433	281	376 (378)	
WHSE. & TRANSP. (CANAL ST.)					
Gen. Workers	43	39	0	35	98.00
Receptionists	4	1	0	1	90.00
Totals	47	40	0	36	
WHSE. & TRANSP. (SO-FRESH)					
Gen. Workers	90	56	0	26	95.40

Division Classification	Total No. of Employees by Class 1-31-70	Black Emp. by Class as of 10-66	Black Emp. Required by Oper. B/B 10-66	Blacks Currently Employed	Salary
MAIN WAREHOUSE					
Car Unloader	31	23	0	16	$148.00
Machine Operator	59	19	0	27	156.00
Checker	32	5	0	5	147.00
Inspector	4	1	0	0	149.00
Order Picker	165 (7)	40	0	66	146.00
General Workers	13	11	0	5	120.00
Truck Loaders	41	4	0	17	146.00
Office Clerk	16	1	4	3	134.00
Elevator Oper.	10	0	0	2	141.00
Drivers	205 (10)	4	35	40 (1)	166.40
Drivers Helper	33	4	4	7	143.00
Washer	5	8	0	4	121.00
Gasser	3	3	0	3	121.00
Tireman	2	1	0	1	136.00
Lugger—Comm.	13	11	0	9	116.00
Janitor	5	3	0	2	111.00
Scaler	7	1	0	5	116.00
Stockman	8	0	0	6	152.00
Mechanic	21	0	5	4	162.00
App. Mechanic	2	0		1	138.00
Banana Proc.	1	0		0	151.00
Butcher—Comm.	1	0	0	0	128.00
Totals	677 (17)	139	48	223 (1)	

Division Classification	Total No. of Employees by Class 1-31-70	Black Emp. by Class as of 10-66	Black Emp. Required by Oper. B/B 10-66	Blacks Currently Employed	Salary
MANUFACTURING					
Machine Operator	66	4	0	8	$140.00
General Work	43	6	6	6	136.00
Totals	109	10	6	14	
BAKERY					
1st Hand Baker	13	1	2	3	$125.00
2nd Hand Baker	11	7	0	7	123.00
Bread Helper	7	6	0	5	113.00
Bread Packer	13	1	2	3	123.00
Carton Maker	1	0		0	126.00
Bread Checker	2	0		0	129.00
Machine Operator	7	1	3	1	130.00
Order Picker	6	1		4	126.00
Truck Loaders	4	1		2	126.00
Shipline	3	0		1	130.00
Working Foreman	2	0		0	131.00
Brew Masters	2	0	0	0	129.00
Stockman	1	0	0	0	131.00
Janitors (Cake & Bread)	8	8	0	5	108.00
Cake Helpers	14	7	0	12	113.00
Cake Wrapping	13	1	3	3	126.00
Elevator Operator	1	0	0	0	130.00
Totals	108	34	10	46	
GRAND TOTALS	4118 (877)	734	370	766 (379)	

Division Classification	Total No. of Employees by Class 1-31-70	Black Emp. by Class as of 10-66	Black Emp. Required by Oper. B/B 10-66	Blacks Currently Employed	Salary
KEY PERSONNEL					
Marshall Benny	District Manager		Supervises 10 Stores &	250 People	Promotion
DePlessie Drew	Meat Specialist		Supervises 10 Stores &	50 People	Promotion
Marvin McKeever	Product Specialist		Supervises 10 Stores &	40 People	Promotion
Darryl Brazil	Personnel Dept.				Promotion
Jessie Johnson	Human Relations Rep.				Promotion
James Clifton	Asst. Supt.		Supervises 47 Warehouse Workers		Promotion
John Smith	Foreman		Supervises 25 Bakery Workers		Promotion
Sylvester William	Whse. Supv.		Supervises 75 Warehouse Workers		Promotion
Mrs. B. Whiteurst	Coordinator Community Affairs				Promotion
St. Clair Booker	Management Trainee				Leave of Absence
Columbus Dunn	Management Trainee				Hired
Leonard Robinson	Coordinator Minority Training & Development				
James Jones	Warehouse Security Supv.			Supervises All Warehouse Security Guards	Hired
Delores Ware	Checker Trainer				Hired
Annie Williams	Price Check & Audit				Promotion
House Cathey	Foreman	80 Stores	•Supervises 25 Warehouse Workers		Promotion
Raymond Ogletree	Security Rep.				Hired

Salary Range
Key Personnel — $ 9,000 min.
15,000 max.

D

Covenant between
Miller Brewing Company
and
People United To Save Humanity

This covenant is entered into this _____ day of _____ , 1973, between the Miller Brewing Company and all of its subsidiaries and divisions (hereinafter called MILLER) and People United To Save Humanity (hereinafter called PUSH), as a mutual commitment to expand relations between MILLER and black, nonwhite and other minority communities, and to help develop practicable solutions for their economic problems.

This covenant is an affirmative measure proposed jointly by MILLER and PUSH in recognition that total economic opportunity for black, nonwhite and other minority people is essential if we are to weave the fabric of a healthy nation in which all people share the benefits of economic viability and social strength.

MILLER considers this covenant as consistent with its own steps to assure racial equality in its total operation.

In signing this covenant MILLER reaffirms its desire to join PUSH to bring these goals to early realization. This covenant, moreover, involves a mutual moral commitment on the part of both MILLER and PUSH to join forces and bring their resources to bear upon the task of eliminating inequities in our economy.

PUSH acknowledges the steps already taken by MILLER to effect solutions to these problems and both parties see this covenant as consistent with the goal of further expanding opportunities for blacks, nonwhites and other minorities.

Therefore, acknowledging the significance of this moral covenant and the aims and objectives it projects, MILLER pledges to exert every reasonable effort to realize the following goals for black, nonwhite and other minority people in the following areas of Employment, Purchasing, Economic Development and other business activities of MILLER.

Employment

MILLER agrees to employment and promotional goals in all categories and classifications for blacks, nonwhites and other minorities as follows:

As of December 31, 1972

	Total Employment	Black, Nonwhite and Other Minority Employment	Black, Nonwhite and Other Minority Emp. Goals
Officials & Managers	462	24	55
Professionals & Technicians	91	4	11
Sales workers	67	6	8
Office & Clerical	248	24	30
Craftsmen, Operatives, Laborers & Service Workers	1,588	106	190
	2,456	164	294

MILLER's goal is to attain a minimum of 12% of black, nonwhite and other minority employees with an eventual goal of 15%.

MILLER agrees to continue and intensify its employment program for the recruitment of black, nonwhite and other minority workers, utilizing such resources as those placement and employment agencies which specialize in black, nonwhite and other minority recruitment.

MILLER will also take steps to establish a management intern recruitment at black, nonwhite and other minority colleges.

MILLER will also take steps to establish a management intern program with black colleges—as a further contribution toward the development of black industrial leadership in the nation.

Business Development

MILLER agrees to increase the level and dollar volume of business done with black, nonwhite and other minority vendors in all categories in which it contracts with outside suppliers.

MILLER's immediate goal for the purchase of that portion of its goods and services which can be provided by black, nonwhite and other minority companies is 12%. MILLER's eventual goal for the purchase of that portion of its goods and services which can be provided by black, nonwhite and other minority companies is 15%.

Insurance

MILLER agrees to request its insurance carrier to reinsure 15% of its group life insurance with black, nonwhite and other minority-owned insurance companies. MILLER agrees to investigate placing a portion of its casualty insurance with a black, nonwhite or minority brokerage company.

Medical Care

MILLER will investigate the use of black, nonwhite and other minority physicians and such paramedical personnel as industrial nurses—and the utilization of accredited medical clinics owned and operated by black, nonwhite and/or other minority physicians.

Legal Counsel

To meet its legal needs, MILLER will take steps to engage black and nonwhite law firms, as well as those firms which employ black, nonwhite and other minority lawyers. The Company will also seek to hire a black lawyer for its own legal staff.

Transportation Services

MILLER will strive to have its lessor of cars and trucks purchase an increasing share (up to 15%) of MILLER's automobile and truck fleet from black, nonwhite and other minority dealers. MILLER will strive to use up to 15% of its trucking and delivery services which can be provided by black, nonwhite and other minority companies.

Distributorship

MILLER understands the significance of developing black, nonwhite and other minority trade outlets through the utilization of black, nonwhite and other minority independent businessmen and distributors or wholesalers for the company's product.

To this end, MILLER will endeavor to increase its use of black, nonwhite or other minority wholesalers, especially in those cities where there are large black, nonwhite and other minority populations. MILLER will cooperate with black, nonwhite and other minority financial institutions by referring such prospective wholesalers to such financial institutions for financial assistance. MILLER also agrees to render whatever additional assistance is necessary and permissible toward the development of a viable distributorship.

Advertising and Public Relations

MILLER recognizes the strategic importance of advertising in increasingly literate and aware black, nonwhite and other minority communities. It also realizes that advertising dollars represent critical significance for media specifically addressed to and owned by black, nonwhite and other minority people.

MILLER agrees to increase its advertising in black, nonwhite and other minority owned and managed print and radio media. MILLER agrees to increase its use of black models in its advertising. MILLER will seek to use a black, nonwhite or other minority owned advertising agency.

MILLER agrees to investigate the possibility of utilizing the one black TV channel in the Detroit area and to direct special attention to those ways in which it can creatively employ more black, nonwhite or other minority print media for advertising purposes.

MILLER will continue to utilize the services of black, nonwhite and other minority public relations companies for up to 15% of its outside public relations consulting needs, including its current black, nonwhite and other minority public relations consultants.

MILLER will also consider black clothing manufacturers for the design and manufacture of the promotional apparel.

Banking and Finance

MILLER agrees to continue its program of utilizing black, nonwhite and other minority financial institutions for 15% of its bank deposits. MILLER will develop a total financial institution strategy directing an increasing share of its deposits into black, nonwhite and other minority banks. These will include tax deposits and, where possible, payroll accounts.

Construction

MILLER will seek out black, nonwhite and other minority contractors and sub-contractors for up to 12% of that portion of its construction, demolition and facilities renovation which can be provided by such contractors and will exert every reasonable effort to realize 15% of that portion of such projects which can be provided by such contractors and sub-contractors as an eventual goal.

MILLER will contractually require all prime contractors to make every reasonable effort to provide, where possible, for the employment of an equitable proportion of black, nonwhite and other minority laborers, journeymen and apprentices on the jobs which they perform for MILLER.

MILLER agrees, where feasible, to consider utilizing the services of black, nonwhite and other minority architects.

MILLER will consider contractual allocations to black, non-white and other minority landscape professionals.

Philanthropic Donations

MILLER agrees to provide at least 15% of its philanthropic gifts to IRS qualified programs, organizations and institutions which benefit the black, nonwhite, and other minority communities.

MILLER pledges to give particular attention to constructive black, nonwhite and other minority institutional programs which have demonstrated by their services a wide ranging value to black, nonwhite and other minority peoples.

MILLER agrees to consider developing a relationship with black, nonwhite and other minority institutions of higher learning that will include the awarding of research grants, where such are feasible, consistent with its goal to make these institutions both visible and viable as they continue to render invaluable service to the nation in general, and to the black, nonwhite and other minority communities in particular.

It is understood that PUSH does not seek to participate in the philanthropic gifts of MILLER.

Policy Development

MILLER believes the input of black, nonwhite and other minority Americans at the policy (or Board) level of company decision making is consistent with its overall objectives of involving blacks, nonwhites and other minorities at all levels of the corporate operations of the Company.

MILLER currently has a black member on its Board of Directors and will make every reasonable effort to continue the practice of having a black, nonwhite or other minority on its Board of Directors.

MUTUAL RESPONSIBILITIES OF THE COVENANT

MILLER and PUSH have entered this covenant intending that it serve as a moral commitment, rather than a legally binding contract.

This covenant shall be applicable to all of MILLER's U. S. operations, including all subsidiaries and corporate divisions whether or not under the Miller Brewing Company name.

MILLER agrees to communicate this document throughout its corporate complex nationwide and will utilize its full resources to insure the implementation of this covenant. The foregoing provisions shall be implemented within a reasonable period of time by the parties involved in this covenant.

MILLER agrees that, within thirty days of the signing of this covenant, an initial review meeting between MILLER and PUSH will take place and again within ninety days, to further monitor initial action in the fulfillment of the covenant. Within six months of the signing of this covenant, a full scale review of the progress of the covenant should take place. A meeting will then be scheduled at intervals of no longer than six months to review and monitor progress of the covenant.

All communications regarding any aspect of the fulfillment of the terms of this covenant shall be made only through MILLER's Corporate Personnel Officer and PUSH's Director of Research & Negotiations or their designated alternates.

MILLER and PUSH will agree in advance through the above designated representatives to any publicity released to the general public.

FROM OPERATION PUSH

PUSH pledges its full support in the implementation of this covenant and it will direct favorable attention to the positive posture of MILLER and its commitment with PUSH to the black, nonwhite and other minority communities throughout the nation.

Subject to MILLER's prior approval, PUSH will publish this covenant to all of its local and national satellite organizations and will cooperate as requested in any reasonable matter relative to implementing this covenant by providing appropriate information to facilitate the smooth execution of its provision.

MILLER will not be expected to violate any law in attempting to comply with the provisions of this covenant.

MILLER BREWING COMPANY   PEOPLE UNITED TO SAVE HUMANITY

by _____ by _____

by _____ by _____

                            by _____

                            by _____

Black Expo '71
AUDIT REPORT
February 29, 1972

WASHINGTON, PITTMAN & McKEEVER
Certified Public Accountants
2400 South Michigan Ave.
Chicago, Illinois 60616
Telephone 326-2477

April 16, 1972

Members of the Board of Directors of
Southern Christian Leadership Foundation
110 South Dearborn Street, Suite 1500
Chicago, IL 60603

Gentlemen:

In accordance with your instructions, we have examined the statement of financial condition of Black Expo '71, as of Febru-

ary 29, 1972, and the related statements of income and fund balance
for the period July 6, 1971 to February 29, 1972, and now submit
our report thereon together with the statements enumerated in the
index prefixed hereto.

Black Expo '71

STATEMENT OF FINANCIAL CONDITION

February 29, 1972

EXHIBIT A

ASSETS

CURRENT ASSETS
Cash on Hand	$ 350.00	
Cash in Bank	78,314.33	
Accounts Receivable — Trade	6,925.00	
Accounts Receivable — NSF Checks $2,035.00		
Less Allowance for Doubtful Accounts 2,035.00	—	
Loans Receivable — Employees	330.00	
Total Current Assets		$85,919.33

OTHER ASSETS
Deposit — International Amphitheatre	$ 1,000.00	
Deposit — IBM	250.00	1,250.00
TOTAL ASSETS		$87,169.00

LIABILITIES AND FUND BALANCE

CURRENT LIABILITIES
Accounts Payable	$ 1,704.82	
Estimated Liability for Lost Paintings	845.00	
Total Current Liabilities		$ 2,549.82

FUND BALANCE
Balance, February 29, 1972	$ 9,619.51	
Reserve for Tax Escrow	75,000.00	84,619.51
TOTAL LIABILITIES AND FUND BALANCE		$87,169.33

Black Expo '71

STATEMENT OF INCOME

For the Period July 6, 1971 to February 29, 1972

EXHIBIT B

INCOME
  Booth Sales

Allied Booths	$65,000.00	
Selling Booths	18,225.00	
Display Booths	53,720.00	
Government Agencies	8,375.00	
Community Organizations	2,650.00	
Total Booth Sales		$147,970.00
Ticket Sales		339,824.79
Expo Trade Directory		3,300.00
Donations		16,646.00
Concessions (Canteen Corp.)		1,780.28
Total Income		$509,521.07

LESS – REFUNDS

Booths	$ 1,325.00	
Tickets	7,925.50	9,250.50
INCOME AFTER REFUNDS		$500,270.57

OPERATING EXPENSES

Publicity and Advertising	$47,581.97
Show Production	64,145.78
Facilities Rental	25,649.50
Booth Set-Up	51,126.80
Floor Services	36,158.35
Cultural Booths	19,139.26
Other Minorities	157.00
Decoration and Expo Theme	26,973.40
Businessmen's Breakfast	1,546.31
Music Workshop	11,521.40
Political Workshop	482.20
African-Afro American Conference	847.90
Printing (Expo Directory)	4,155.00
Printing (This Is OBB)	3,610.75
Printing (Cultural)	1,004.50
Printing School Participation	737.53

		(EXHIBIT B cont'd)
Travel	10,745.14	
Telephone	6,230.53	
Tickets	3,493.75	
Office Equipment Rental	911.71	
Office Salaries	1,550.00	
Office General Expenses	3,921.73	
Insurance	5,149.91	
Booth Sales Promotion	1,603.28	
Black Expo Newspaper	400.00	
Damages to Exhibition Merchandise	300.00	
Brinks, Inc.	1,015.00	
Damages to Amphitheatre	4,002.48	
Legal and Professional Fees	1,882.92	
Staff Lodging	3,472.07	
Dr. King's Award	775.00	
Patron Ticket Prizes	317.57	
Bank Charges	94.85	
Bad Debts	2,986.00	
Total Operating Expenses		343,688.59
NET INCOME		$156,581.98

Black Expo '71

STATEMENT OF FUND BALANCE

February 29, 1972

EXHIBIT C

BALANCE — July 7, 1971		$ 4,211.49
ADD:		
Net Income from Black Expo '71		156,581.98
Total		$160,793.47
DEDUCT:		
Transfer to SCLC — OBB	$65,400.00	
Transfer to SCLC Foundation	5,625.00	
Payment of Breakfast Committee Loan	5,148.96	76,173.96
BALANCE — February 29, 1972		$ 84,619.51

In the following paragraphs, we submit comments on the principal items in the Statement of financial condition at February 29, 1972:

ASSETS

Cash in Banks The cash in banks was verified by certificates received direct from the depositories. The amounts in the respective depositories are as follows:

Independence Bank of Chicago, Chicago, IL	$ 3,132.25
Independence Bank of Chicago, Chicago, IL	71.30
Independence Bank of Chicago, Chicago, IL	75,000.00
Seaway National Bank, Chicago, IL	110.78
Total	$78,314.33

Accounts Receivable Accounts receivable represents amounts billed for ticket and booth sales as of February 29, 1972, which were unpaid at that date, and are summarized below:

	Feb. 29, 1972	Portion Since Paid
SCHEDULE I — *Accounts Receivable*		
City of Chicago Human Resources	$ 400.00	
Loyola University Afro-American Student Association	500.00	
FHA and HUD	350.00	
Tilmon Productions	925.00	
Johnson Publishing Company	1,825.00	
Roberts Enterprises	1,525.00	$1,525.00
Odie's Morgan Mattress	325.00	
Champion Sales Agency	325.00	
City of Gary	425.00	
Social Security Administration	325.00	
Totals	$6,925.00	$1,525.00

SCHEDULE II — *Accounts Receivable — Returned Checks*

Richard H. Newhouse*	$ 200.00
Metropolitan Wrecking Company	625.00
Black Educational Development	425.00
Jackson R. Champion	100.00
C. Delores Tucker	2.00
James E. Holman	8.00
Michael Fields	50.00
Nud Company	425.00
Lanfrey L. Boyd	100.00
Lanfrey L. Boyd	100.00
Total	$2,035.00

*Check from Richard Newhouse returned for a second signature. Check was given to Mr. Newhouse for that signature.

Insurance Black Expo '71 was covered by the following described insurance policy:

Insurer	Description	Coverage
Yosemite Insurance Co.	Owners' Landlords' and Tenants' General Liabilities	$100/300/25

Contingent Liabilities Black Expo '71 has a few legal claims pending against it resulting from various personal injuries suffered by patrons. We have not been able to determine the status or amounts involved and accordingly have not shown any liability for these items on the statement of financial condition.

EXHIBIT IV — SCHEDULE OF TRANSFERS TO SCLC OPERATION BREADBASKET

9-22-71	SCLC Operation Breadbasket Program Fund	$ 6,000.00
10-15-71	SCLC Operation Breadbasket Program Fund	20,000.00
11-22-71	SCLC Operation Breadbasket Program Fund	10,000.00
12-02-71	SCLC Operation Breadbasket Payroll Fund	17,400.00
12-16-71	SCLC Operation Breadbasket Payroll Fund	12,000.00
	Total Transfers to SCLC Operation Breadbasket	$65,400.00

Transfer to SCLC Foundation On January 27, 1972, American Airlines advised Black Expo '71 that the $5,000.00 due for display booths was sent to their office November 14, 1971, addressed to Dr. Ralph P. Abernathy. This mail would have been sent directly to SCLC in Atlanta office. To date no official notice has been received from that office confirming receipt of this check. Photostats of the cancelled check have been issued by American Airlines.

Payment of Breakfast Committee Loan Black Expo '71 fund paid the SCLC Operation Breadbasket Breakfast Committee of Black Expo loan of $5,000.00 plus interest of $148.96. The loan was obtained from Independence Bank of Chicago to finance the Black Expo's Businessmen Breakfast.

The scope of our examination did not include an audit of the SCLC Operation Breadbasket Breakfast Committee of Black Expo account.

Black Expo, Inc., has not received its exemption from federal income taxes. In the event that a determination by Internal Revenue holds that the entertainment net income is "unrelated business income" under provisions of the Internal Revenue Code, $75,000.00 of the fund balance has been appropriated for this purpose. It is impossible to determine Black Expo, Inc., liability, if any, at this time. No provision has been made for this contingent liability.

Notes Payable Certificates of deposit in the amount of $75,000 were pledged as security for various bank loans made at Independence Bank of Chicago during the year ended December 31, 1972.

The following is a schedule of the various notes payable:

Independence Bank of Chicago — General Fund	15,000.00*
Independence Bank of Chicago — General Fund	30,000.00*
Independence Bank of Chicago — General Fund	30,000.00*
Independence Bank of Chicago — PUSH EXPO '72	4,230.33
Stax Record Company, Memphis, Tenn. — General Fund	100,000.00
Total	$179,230.33

*The above loans are secured by certificates of deposits.

People United To Save Humanity
Audit Report
December 31, 1972

WASHINGTON, PITTMAN & McKEEVER
Certified Public Accountants
2400 South Michigan Ave.
Chicago, Illinois 60616

Telephone 326-2477

January 17, 1973

Members of the Board of Directors of
People United to Save Humanity
930 East 50th Street
Chicago, Illinois 60615

Gentlemen:

In accordance with your instructions, we have examined the statements of financial condition of the General Fund and PUSH

EXPO '72 as of December 31, 1972, and the related statements of income and fund balance for the period December 25, 1971, to December 31, 1972. Our examination was made in accordance with generally accepted auditing standards and accordingly included such tests of the accounting records and such other auditing procedures as we considered necessary in the circumstances.

PEOPLE UNITED TO SAVE HUMANITY is an Illinois not-for-profit corporation with headquarters at Chicago, Illinois. PUSH has been licensed to operate in five (5) other states, and have established branches or satellites in these states. *The actual operating expenses of these satellites have not been subject to our audit, but we have reviewed all transfers of funds from the national office to these satellites.*

In our opinion, the accompanying statements of financial condition and related statements of income and fund balance present fairly the financial position of General Fund and PUSH EXPO '72 at December 31, 1972, and the results of its operations for the period December 25, 1971, to December 31, 1972, in conformity with generally accepted accounting principles.

WASHINGTON, PITTMAN & McKEEVER

People United to Save Humanity

General Fund

STATEMENT OF FINANCIAL CONDITION

as of December 31, 1972

EXHIBIT A

ASSETS	GENERAL FUND	PUSH EXPO '72	TOTAL
CURRENT ASSETS			
Cash on Hand	400.00	10.00	410.00
Cash in Bank	103,083.97	4,082.77	107,166.74
Accounts Receivable — other	1,050.00	806.53	1,856.53
Accounts Receivable — Ticket Sales	—	19,529.05	19,529.05
Accounts Receivable — Booth Sales	—	33,483.30	33,483.30
Accounts Receivable — Special Events	3,300.78	—	3,300.78
Loans Receivable — Employees	2,317.21	75.00	2,392.21
Prepaid Insurance	4,516.00	—	4,516.00
Total Current Assets	$114,667.96	$57,986.65	$172,654.61

464

People United to Save Humanity

General Fund

STATEMENT OF FINANCIAL CONDITION
as of December 31, 1972

FIXED ASSETS

LAND	10,000.00		10,000.00
Building	198,437.80		198,437.80
Building Improvements	8,582.56		8,582.56
Equipment	7,931.39		7,931.39
Furniture & Fixtures	6,631.39		6,631.39
Total Depreciable Assets	221,583.14		231,583.14
Less: Accumulated Depreciation	4,585.38		4,585.38
Total Fixed Assets	226,997.76		226,997.76

OTHER ASSETS

Deposit — International Amphitheatre		1,000.00	1,000.00
Mortgage Insurance — Escrow	850.00		850.00
TOTAL ASSETS	$342,515.72	$58,986.65	$401,502.37

CURRENT LIABILITIES

Accounts Payable — Trade	$ 50,493.04	$45,023.17	$ 95,516.21
Accounts Payable — Employees	197.40		197.40
Installment Payable	1,947.24		1,947.24
Payroll Taxes Withheld	40,560.46		40,560.46
Accrued Payroll Taxes Payable	6,616.64		6,616.64
Notes Payable	175,000.00	4,230.33	179,230.33
Mortgage Payable — Current Portion	6,243.12		6,243.12
Total Current Liabilities	$281,057.90	$49,253.50	$330,311.40

LONG TERM LIABILITIES

8% Mortgage Payable — Independence			
Bank Maturity June 23, 1987	177,363.27		177,363.27
Less: Current Portion	6,243.12		6,243.12
	171,120.15		171,120.15
Installment Payable	5,517.18		5,517.18
Less: Current Portion	1,947.24		1,947.24
	3,569.94		3,569.94
Total Long-Term Liabilities	$174,690.09		$174,690.09
FUND BALANCE — DEFICIT*	113,232.27*	9,733.15	103,499.12*
TOTAL LIABILITIES AND FUND BALANCE	$342,515.72	$58,986.65	$401,502.37

People United to Save Humanity

General Fund

STATEMENT OF INCOME

From December 25, 1971, to December 31, 1972

INCOME

Saturday Morning Offering	$117,434.22	
General Contributions	126,133.39	
P.U.S.H. Cards	56,157.39	
P.U.S.H. Divisions	10,545.07	
Special Events	130,682.78	
Travel Reimbursement	15,901.69	
Salary Reimbursement	1,875.00	
P.U.S.H. Promotion	1,622.73	
Rental Income	2,866.00	
Piano Fund	800.00	
WVON Talkathon	26,001.23	
Building Fund	5,142.00	
Miscellaneous	22.04	
P.U.S.H. Reimbursement	16,288.27	
Interest Income	250.00	
Total Income		$511,721.81

OPERATING EXPENSES

Promotions	$ 2,419.97
Payroll	280,025.45
Supplies	10,823.77
Xerox	6,213.71
Travel	85,985.53
Entertainment	3,925.86
Telephone	38.092.10
Telegraph	6,602.02
Security Service	8,817.00
Equipment Rental	13,812.25
Employees Insurance Expense	3,785.68
Equipment Maintenance	453.07
Vehicle Expense	2,715.14
Rent	16,759.32
Building Maintenance	12,929.37
Heat	9,638.26
Utilities	5,026.57
Meetings and Retreats	2,443.27

P.U.S.H. Convention	2,335.37	
Postage	8,353.33	
Reproducing and Printing	15,260.28	
Decorating & Housekeeping	717.44	
Dues and Subscriptions	1,352.04	
Contributions and Donations	12,663.35	
Bad Checks	$ 1,571.80	
Bank Charges	461.82	
Professional Services	10,412.00	
Film Processing	2,853.57	
P.U.S.H. Choir	224.50	
Volunteer Expense	2,264.17	
City News Bureau	2,705.25	
P.U.S.H. Participation	7,441.83	
Insurance Expense	232.00	
Comparative Buying	20.00	
Freight	376.98	
National Expansion — New York	18,144.65	
National Expansion — Cincinnati	10,634.45	
National Expansion — Los Angeles	6,800.00	
National Expansion — Memphis	2,500.00	
National Expansion — Miami	500.00	
Social Security Tax Expenses	11,797.39	
Sales Taxes	269.48	
Moving Expenses	833.42	
Depreciation — Building	3,307.30	
Depreciation — Furniture and Fixtures	423.28	
Depreciation — Equipment	289.21	
Depreciation — Building Improvements	565.69	
Miscellaneous	3.50	
Burglary Losses	58.46	
Broadcasts	10,200.00	
Whitney Young Scholarship	1,000.00	
Payroll Taxes — Penalty	950.59	
Payroll Taxes — Interest	174.10	
Total Operating Expenses		648,165.59
NET LOSS FROM OPERATIONS*		136,443.78*
FINANCIAL EXPENSES		
Mortgage Interest	5,964.57	
Interest Expense — Notes	1,554.59	7,519.16
NET LOSS*		$143,962.94

People United to Save Humanity
General Fund

STATEMENT OF FUND BALANCE
December 31, 1972

EXHIBIT C

BALANCE — January 1, 1972		—
NET LOSS FROM OPERATIONS*		143,962.94*
Total		143,962.94*
ADD:		
Transfer from PUSH EXPO '72	$ 37,250.00	
LESS:		
Transfer to PUSH EXPO '72	6,519.33	30,730.67
BALANCE — December 31, 1972 — Deficit		$113,232.27*

People United to Save Humanity
Push Expo '72

STATEMENT OF INCOME
for the Year Ended December 31, 1972

EXHIBIT D

INCOME		
Booth Sales	$ 79,750.00	
Allied Booths	44,380.00	
Display Booths	67,753.30	
Government Agencies	11,900.00	
Community Organizations	5,300.00	
Educational Institutions	7,400.00	
Total Booth Sales		$216,483.30
Ticket Sales		312,750.35
Donations		8,894.30
P.U.S.H. Cards		2,189.65

OPERATING EXPENSES (Cont'd) **EXHIBIT D (cont'd)**

Total Income		
Less: Refunds		
Booths	300.00	
Tickets	3,192.00	3,492.00
Income After Refunds		
		536,825.60
OPERATING EXPENSES		
Publicity and Advertising	$ 61,845.31	
Show Production	103.070.91	
Facilities Rental	28,550.00	
Booth Set-up	58,857.65	
Floor Services	18,932.25	
Cultural Display	29,925.69	
Other Minorities	200.00	
Decorations	44,451.39	
Businessmen Breakfast	4,158.74	
Educational Expense	2,231.29	
Political Education Workshop	10,497.52	
Printing	22,398.15	
Travel and Transportation	4,933.47	
Telephone and Telegraph	14,049.27	
Tickets	7,547.52	
Equipment Rental	3,537.12	
Office Salaries	9,025.23	
Insurance	3,825.00	
General Office Expense	6,173.17	
Brinks, Inc.	1,876.00	
Booth Sales Promotion	3,476.69	
Administrative Meetings	487.48	
Security	36,665.00	
P.U.S.H. Card Program	506.00	
Communications	2,331.49	
Award Night	2,205.60	
Postage	934.90	
Returned Checks	9,130.00	
Bank Charges	12.78	
Commissions	4,273.25	
Total Operating Expenses		496,108.87
NET INCOME FROM OPERATIONS		40,716.73
FINANCIAL EXPENSES		
Interest Expense		252.91
NET INCOME		$ 40,463.82

People United to Save Humanity
Push Expo '72

STATEMENT OF FUND BALANCE

December 31, 1972

EXHIBIT E

BALANCE — January 1, 1972		$ —
ADD:		
Net Income from PUSH EXPO '72		40,463.82
Total		$ 40,463.82
DEDUCT:		
Transfer to OPERATION PUSH General Fund	$ 37,250.00	
Less: Transfer from OPERATION PUSH General Fund	6,519.33	30,730.67
BALANCE — December 31, 1972		$ 9,733.15

A Family Affair

STATEMENT OF INCOME

December 31, 1972

EXHIBIT F

SALES — TICKETS		$168,384.50
EXPENSES		
Food and Facilities	$ 64,551.48	
Publicity and Public Relations	36.90	
Entertainment	13,110.46	
Stage Erection and Draping	1,400.00	
Printing	716.85	
Interest Expense	269.48	
Returned Checks	193.90	
Total		80,279.07
TRANSFERRED TO GENERAL FUND		$ 88,105.43

In the following paragraphs, we submit comments on the principal items in the Statement of financial condition at December 31, 1972:

ASSETS

Cash in Banks The cash in banks was verified by certificates received direct from the depositories. The amounts in the respective depositories are as follows:

Independence Bank of Chicago, Chicago IL	$ 751.32
Independence Bank of Chicago, Chicago, IL	4,123.55
Independence Bank of Chicago, Chicago, IL	807.44
Seaway National Bank, Chicago, IL	3,273.40
Seaway National Bank, Chicago, IL	3,792.23
Freedom National Bank, New York, N.Y.	200.66
First National Bank of Cincinnati, Cincinnati, OH	135.37
Certificates of Deposits, Independence Bank of Chicago	90,000.00
Seaway National Bank, Chicago, IL	3,734.01
Seaway National Bank, Chicago, IL	347.45
Independence Bank of Chicago, Chicago, IL	1.31
Total	$107,166.74

LIABILITIES

Payroll Taxes Withheld Payroll taxes represent the amounts payable from the third quarter of 1972 to December 31, 1972. The payroll taxes are computed as follows:

Federal Withholding and FICA Taxes payable	$ 35,170.05
State Withholding Taxes payable	5,110.38
Local Withholding Taxes payable	280.03
Total	$ 40,560.46

Index